Co-Evolution of Symbolic Species in the Financial Market

Emil Dinga
Camelia Oprean-Stan
Cristina Roxana Tănăsescu
Vasile Brătian
Gabriela-Mariana Ionescu

Co-Evolution of Symbolic Species in the Financial Market

A Framework for Economic and Political Decision-Making

palgrave
macmillan

Emil Dinga
Romanian Academy
Bucharest, Romania

Camelia Oprean-Stan
Lucian Blaga University of Sibiu
Sibiu, Romania

Cristina Roxana Tănăsescu
Lucian Blaga University of Sibiu
Sibiu, Romania

Vasile Brătian
Lucian Blaga University of Sibiu
Sibiu, Romania

Gabriela-Mariana Ionescu
Romanian Academy
Bucharest, Romania

ISBN 978-3-031-31697-5 ISBN 978-3-031-31698-2 (eBook)
https://doi.org/10.1007/978-3-031-31698-2

This Palgrave Macmillan imprint is published by the registered company Springer Nature Switzerland AG.
The registered company address is: Gewerbestrasse 11, 6330 Cham, Switzerland

Paper in this product is recyclable.

Acknowledgement

This work has been supported by a Hasso Plattner Excellence Research Grant (LBUS-HPI-ERG-2020-XX), financed by the Knowledge Transfer Center of the Lucian Blaga University of Sibiu.

Contents

Abbreviations

Chapter 1

EPR	*Einstein-Podolsky-Rosen* experiment regarding the concept (and phenomenon) of entanglement in Quantum Mechanics.
FMAB-APH	*Financial Market Analysis and Behaviour. Adaptive Preference Hypothesis* (authors' book: Routledge Taylor & Francis Group, 2022)
nAIAG	*non-anthropic intelligence anthropically generated*

Chapter 2

AMH	Adaptive Market Hypothesis
APH	Adaptive Preference Hypothesis
BMH	Behavioural Market Hypothesis
CG	Cultural geodesic
DNA	Deoxyribonucleic acid
EMH	Efficient Market Hypothesis
FM	Financial market
IT	Individual transaction
RNA	Ribonucleic acid
TS	Trading strategy

Chapter 3

BIP	*Binomial Information-Price* (first co-evolutionary logical model proposed by authors in the present book)
DV	Decisional variable
EA	Economic agent
NOPAT	Net operating profit after tax
TCIP	*Trinomial Preference-Information-Price* (the second co-evolutionary model proposed by authors in the present book)
VNM	von Neumann-Morgenstern model of expected utility

Chapter 5

FEM	Phenomenological evolutionary model
KDF	K: hard component of preference; D: deliberative component of preference; F: functional component of preference

Chapter 6

CC	Intra-contingency contingency
CN	Intra-contingency necessity
NC	Intra-necessity contingency
NN	Intra-necessity necessity

Chapter 7

AI	Artificial intelligence
ASR	Abstractions, simplifications and reductionisms

List of Figures

List of Tables

CHAPTER 1

Introductory Concepts

Causality and Intelligibility

Causality

The concept of causality is a primary concept both in the theory of knowledge[1] and in praxiology. In most cases, this concept is found in the syntagm *the principle*[2] *of causality*[3] and expresses the belief in the idea that any event is an effect generated by another event that we call cause. Therefore, causality should not be confused with cause—while causality is a principle, cause is a hypostasis of that principle, that is, a contextual (spatial-temporal) manifestation of causality.[4] Causality is a kind of law—the law can be both causal and purely functional[5] or purely structural[6] (Hausman, 2009). A good criterion for distinguishing between genus (law) and species (causality) is the concept of time: where we have a physical time (or clock time), it is about causality, instead where we have a mathematical time (or ideal time), it is about the law. It follows, therefore, that from the perspective of time, mathematical time is the genus and physical time is the species.[7] Moreover, based on the distinction between causality and law, we can discuss about a confusion that is relatively common even in works with scientific claims: the confusion between determinism and causality—any event/phenomenon is causal, that is, it is subject to the principle of causality, but not any causal phenomenon is deterministic—the determinism means that a certain law conditions, in the same way, the behaviour of each individual

E. Dinga et al., *Co-Evolution of Symbolic Species in the Financial Market*, https://doi.org/10.1007/978-3-031-31698-2_1

in the population in question.[8] If a certain regularity applies to the average of a population, and not (in the same way) to each individual in that population, that regularity is called statistical law or, equivalently, stochastic law.[9] In line with the above, the famous model of economic theory, *homo œconomicus*, is, strictly speaking, a *homo... mathematicus*.[10]

From a logical point of view, causality is subject to modus tollens syllogism, that is:

$$\begin{gathered} A \to B \\ \bar{B} \\ \bar{A} \end{gathered} \tag{1.1}$$

Therefore, if we denote by C the principle of causality, with $C^e_{st(i)}$ the cause of the event e (or, equivalent, of the effect e) in the spatio-temporal context i, and with $O^e_{st(i+1)}$ the occurrence of the event e in the spatio-temporal context $(i + 1)$, then we have the following valid logical relations (with ' st ' is noted a state vector or, more generally, a spatio-temporal context):

$$\begin{gathered} C \to C^e_{st(i)} \\ C^e_{st(i)} \to O^e_{st(i+1)} \\ \left(\bar{O}^e_{st(i+1)} \to \bar{C}^e_{st(i)}\right) \vee \left(C^e_{st(i)} \to K^e_{st(i+1)}\right) \end{gathered} \tag{1.2}$$

which must be read as follows:

(1) the principle of causality necessarily (i.e., obligatory, inherent) generates the cause of the event e;
(2) the cause $C^e_{st(i)}$ necessarily generates $O^e_{st(i+1)}$;
(3) if, either $O^e_{st(i+1)}$ is not registered (observed) when $C^e_{st(i)}$ previously occurs, or another effect (K) is observed in that context, then it results that $C^e_{st(i)}$ is not the cause for $O^e_{st(i+1)}$.

Figure 1.1 suggests, synoptically, the functioning (logic) of the principle of causality.

Since causality[11] involves an arrow of time,[12] so that the cause is considered to be in the antecedent of the effect (or, equivalently, the effect is in

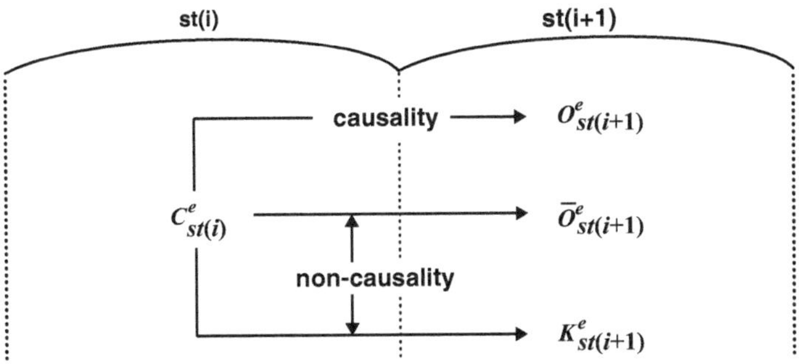

Fig. 1.1 Logical functioning of the principle of causality. *Source*: Authors

the consequent of the cause), we will make some considerations regarding the concept of spatio-temporal context.

- the spatio-temporal context (noted above with *st*, as a lower index) includes, as the name indicates, both a spatial and a temporal coordinate;
- as a result, causation can refer to the 'transfer' of the cause both between different spaces (at the same time[13]) and between different moments of time (in the same space) or the simultaneous transfer to different spaces and different times;
- the case of causal instantly transfer between different spaces will be ignored, so the other two cases mentioned remain in attention.[14]

The spatio-temporal context of the functioning of causality can be sketched (in a stylized way) as shown in Fig. 1.2.

Intelligibility

Causality assures us of the existence of a principle, in our Universe, which has a generative nature and purpose in terms of events, as spatio-temporal hypostases of processes. But how do we get from belief (which 'establishes' the principle of causality) to knowledge—be it scientific or a-scientific? Here comes another concept, more precisely a companion of the concept of causality, namely, the concept of intelligibility. While causality functions in the world regardless of the existence and presence of the cognitive subject, intelligibility is introduced or is 'claimed' by the subject. Therefore, to the objectivity of the principle of causality is opposed the subjectivity of the principle of intelligibility.

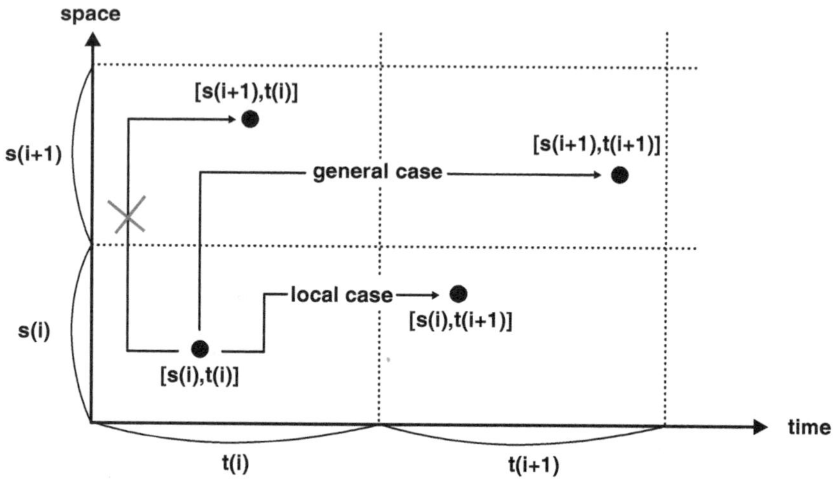

Fig. 1.2 The spatio-temporal context in the principle of causality working. *Source*: Authors

By intelligibility we mean a property of reality (objective, subjective or objectified) to have meaning. Needless to say, nothing in the world is perceived/observed if it has no meaning.[15] The meaning is given by a 'story'—by story is meant a narrative, regardless of the form in which it is developed (poetry, myth/religion, political ideology, philosophical theory, scientific theory, mathematical equation, drawing, music, etc.) that offers a specific justification for the existence or non-existence of an entity: Thing, property, relationship. In other words, causality comes from the world to the subject, while intelligibility comes from the subject to the world. The intelligibility of the world is a property that depends on the spatial-temporal 'cut'—for example, the intelligibility of the Universe as we, humans, experience it depends on the fact that we are in the Milky Way galaxy, that we are in the solar system, that we occupy the planet Earth, that we are endowed with consciousness, etc.

If, for the sake of discussion, we wish to carry on this examination, the following may be said:

- causality is the principle on which intelligibility is built (at least in the spatio-temporal 'cutting' in which we find ourselves);

- as presented above, causality could be considered by the nature of the noumenon, which is knowable only through the filter of intelligibility, which turns causality, for us, into a phenomenon;
- the intelligibility we generate (and 'throw' over the world) can be of different types, but in the present study, we are only interested in scientific intelligibility, that is, the intelligibility that can be subjected to interpersonal empirical testing (*Nota bene*: we separated the eutaxiological causality[16] from the teleological causality).

Figure 1.3 shows the essential relationship between causality and intelligibility.

In Fig. 1.3, intelligibility appears in two forms: (a) intelligibility *per se*—understood as the intelligibility allowed by the biological and psychological constitution of humans (especially the consciousness component of human psyche); (b) objectified intelligibility—understood as accessible (and shared) inter-subjective intelligibility.[17]

The most representative effect/impact of intelligibility is the generation of the concept of order. By order, in general, is meant a hypostasis of intelligibility, in specific fields: cosmic order, economic order, moral order and so on. Since the concept (not the term associated with it) of order will be 'absorbed' by the concept of theory/model (see below), here we only suggest, for those interested, to more analytical considerations regarding the concept of order in (Dinga, 2022).

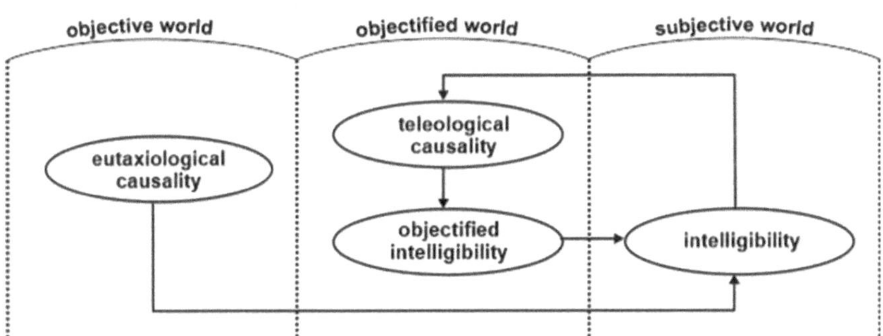

Fig. 1.3 The essential relationship between causality and intelligibility. *Source*: Authors

Theories

Starting from the last considerations above, it follows that intelligibility is manifested and usable only through scientific theories/models. Therefore, the world will be known exclusively through the meanings that such theories/models about the world offer or allow. Theories simply make the connection between causality (understood here exclusively as a eutaxiological causality) and intelligibility. The result of the creation of theories is, first of all, the emergence of an observable causality, that is, objectified one (e.g., the creation of an institution—let us say, the tax system—will generate causalities, e.g., *causa formalis*, which will in turn generate objectified intelligibility[18]). The most general (and representative) case of objectified intelligibility is that of scientific theories, so at the end of this paragraph, we will discuss some considerations from this perspective:

- any theory is sectoral,[19] so it generates causalities (or causal systems) only in that sector;
- however, there are inter-disciplinary (or, less frequently, transdisciplinary) attempts that integrate inter-sectoral domains of reality (e.g., systems theory or evolutionary theory);
- the generation of an objectified causality is essential for any type of human activity (either theoretical, praxiological or practical—see FMAB-APH, where the exhaustiveness of these three categories of human activity was shown);
- theories are *bright cones* that observe, interpret and 'recognize' only the phenomenology that enters these cones. The more general the theory, the less specific it is, obviously (a synoptic view of the relationships between causality, intelligibility and the categories of activity considered by theories is shown in Fig. 1.4).

Growth-Development-Evolution

The concepts presented in this paragraph were developed in the paper 'Growth, Development and Economic Sustainability in Romania (2007–2017)' (Dinga, 2018).

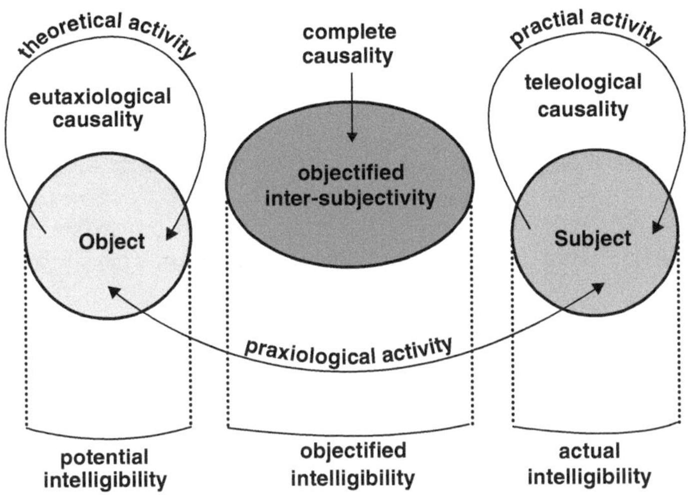

Fig. 1.4 Causality-intelligibility-theory. *Source*: Authors

Growth

Definition and Characteristics

Growth is, in general, that change which is manifested by a quantitative dimensional alteration of some system. In this sense, the quantitative alteration of the dimensional type does not have any preferential meaning, it can mean an increase of the dimension in question or, on the contrary, a decrease[20] of that dimension. Since growth represents a dimensional variation of the system, the registration and analysis of the growth require two essential methodological clarifications: (a) the parameters of the system in question, credited to express, by the variation of the associated numerical values, the dimensional variation of the given system; (b) the benchmark against which the dimensional variation of interest is evaluated. Although it seems that another aspect should be established, namely, the time (or periodicity, when the measurement and evaluation of growth is of a systematic and permanent nature) at which the measurement is made, we consider that, logically, it is under the benchmark parameter.[21]

Growth is a phenomenon that is actualized in geo-socio-historical circumstances, that is, in what we called above spatio-temporal context. In other words, its concrete manifestation is dependent on the context in which it occurs and in which, therefore, it is analysed. As the particular manifestation (at a given moment, in a certain context) of a phenomenon is called an event, it follows that, logically, the growth of a system is an event. As this event also interests us in terms of its variation over time (*Nota bene*: the difference in identity between two events of the same phenomenon is called process), we conclude that by growth we mean a *contextualized geo-socio-historical process whose defining parameter varies dimensionally*. Based on such a definition, we can now systematize the main characteristics (attributes, predicates) of growth. They are as follows:

- growth is a purely quantitative phenomenon;
- growth is of the nature of the mean, not of the nature of the purpose;
- growth refers to the variation (i.e., either to the increase or to the decrease) of the numerical value of the defining quantitative parameter established for a given system;
- growth has no structural or qualitative effects on the system in question, but only quantitative (dimensional) effects;[22]
- the increase is reversible (after a period of growth there may be one of stagnation—zero growth—or even decrease—negative growth[23]); this characteristic is closely related to the immediately preceding one because only what is structural is persistent; but growth is not a structural phenomenon, so it is only a functional one (at the limit, and with the necessary precautions, growth is a surface phenomenon, an epiphenomenon, not one of depth, that is, of a structural nature);
- growth will tend to produce those structural changes[24] in the system that are likely to increase growth resources in the next operating cycle of the system;[25] this tendency can be called the *self-catalytic* tendency of growth; this is an objective trend, independent of collective (political) decision-making;[26] it is an autopoietic effect of growth, which justifies the treatment of systems (especially economic or, more broadly, social) as living logical systems (Dinga, 2021);
- growth will use some of the results obtained to constitute buffers (redundancies) in case the growth conditions become unfavourable in the future; this trend, which reduces the ability of current growth to produce structural changes, can be called a *self-conservative* trend of the growth; this is a subjective tendency, dependent on the collective decision (which can be considered a political decision[27]).

Logic of Growth Modelling

The internal physiology of growth (which is generated, of course, by the reasons for behaviour) is, essentially, a permanent balance between the self-catalytic tendency and the self-conservative tendency. From a theoretical point of view, a theorizing could be developed here regarding a possible indifference curve between the two tendencies (opposite, without being contradictory[28]). Figure 1.5 suggests a graphical way to proceed in this matter (*Nota bene*: with R_{EG} the rate of economic growth was noted—to take as an example the case of the economic system).

If, from an algebraic point of view, we write the growth rate as a linear combination of the two trends of the growth phenomenon, we obtain:

$$R_{EG} = \alpha \cdot x + \beta \cdot y \tag{1.3}$$

where x is a function that describes the self-conservative tendency of growth and y is a function that describes the self-catalytic tendency of growth, then, putting the condition of constant growth rate and totally differentiating the above equality, it results:

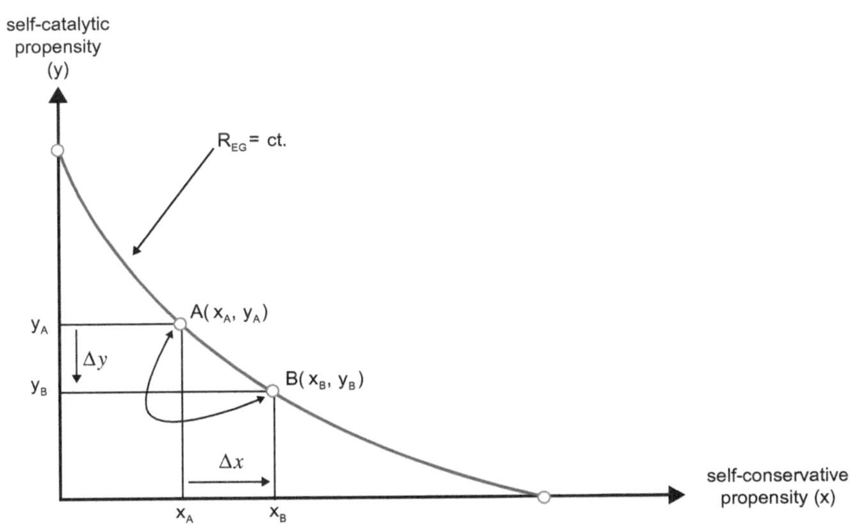

Fig. 1.5 The indifference curve of economic growth from the perspective of its two propensities. *Source*: (Dinga, 2018), p. 40

$$dR_{CE} = \alpha \cdot dx + \beta \cdot dy = 0 \tag{1.4}$$

$$RMS^{y/x} = \frac{dy}{dx} = -\frac{\alpha}{\beta} \tag{1.5}$$

where with $RMS^{y/x}$ the rate of marginal substitution between the two growth trends was noted.

Of course, the condition in Fig. 1.5 (stability of the growth rate) is an imbalance condition because the constant value of the growth rate leads to an exponential growth.[29] Under more realistic conditions, the growth rate can be considered zero (steady state of economic growth), which means that the numerical value of the defining parameter for the growth of that economic system (e.g., the value—nominal or real, as economic analysis needs—of GDP) remains constant. We will continue the analysis on the case of economic (positive) growth, which interests us in the rest of the study.

From a purely conceptual point of view, economic growth is a variation of the numerical value of the measurement parameter of the phenomenon called economic growth. Note this parameter[30] with φ_{EG}, considered in its absolute nominal value, is officially recorded by public statistical institutions, usually annually.[31] This means that the registration of an economic growth occurs when

$$\varphi_{EG}^{t} > \varphi_{EG}^{t-\varepsilon} \tag{1.6}$$

where with t, respectively $(t - \varepsilon)$ are noted the moments (years) in which the respective numerical values were recorded, with t and $(t - \varepsilon)$ natural numbers, and $t > \varepsilon$. Most of the time $\varepsilon = 1$, that is, the difference is calculated between two consecutive moments/years. As we said above, the calculated difference can be negative, that is, there is an economic decline (or negative economic growth). We do not go into more detail here regarding the evaluation of the parameter φ, we consider it as given. However, one more aspect needs to be considered. The parameter φ can only be expressed in monetary terms.

We recall that when φ refers to GDP, it is expressed in market prices. Therefore, the numerical value of the parameter φ also depends on the variation of prices. As economic growth means the dimensional variation of the parameter φ, it follows that this increase must express the variation of the quantities and not of the monetary values of goods and services realized in the national economy in the considered period (usually one financial year). As a result, the influence of the relative change in prices (i.e., inflation[32]) on the change in the monetary value of the parameter must be eliminated. By denoting inflation with i, then we can calculate a deflator[33] (an indicator that eliminates inflation from a nominal value, which we denote by d) as follows: $d = 1 + i$,[34] where with i is noted the general/average inflation in the economy, that is, that inflation that addresses the whole GDP. Then the two values of the parameter, measured in the two moments of time, must be made comparable in terms of quantities, so one of them will be adjusted with the deflator d. Because, as a rule, the prices increase, not decrease,[35] it is usual for the parameter at the time of calculation to be adjusted with the deflator that occurred between the two moments of time for the measurements, that is, the economic growth is calculated as follows:

$$\tilde{\varphi}_{EG}^{t} = \frac{\varphi_{EG}^{t}}{d_{t-\varepsilon}^{t}} \tag{1.7}$$

where the lower index of d indicates the reference time (year) $(t - \varepsilon)$ and the upper index indicates the calculation time (year) (t).[36] $\tilde{\varphi}_{EG}^{t}$ indicates the real growth, and φ_{EG}^{t} indicates the nominal one.

Therefore, the absolute economic growth[37] between $(t - \varepsilon)$ and (t) is rightly given by:

$$\tilde{\Delta}_{EG}^{t/(t-\varepsilon)} = \frac{\varphi_{EG}^{t}}{d_{t-\varepsilon}^{t}} - \frac{\varphi_{EG}^{t-\varepsilon}}{d_{t-\varepsilon}^{t-\varepsilon}} = \tilde{\varphi}_{EG}^{t} - \varphi_{EG}^{t-\varepsilon}, \text{ because } d_{t-\varepsilon}^{t-\varepsilon} = 1 \tag{1.8}$$

Of course, this absolute change of the parameter for measuring growth can be expressed (and usually is) in relative terms, that is, in rates of change in that parameter, but it does not introduce anything new from a conceptual point of view. The calculation of this growth rate (denoted $\tilde{R}_{CE}^{t/(t-\varepsilon)}$) is done as follows:

$$\tilde{R}_{EG}^{t/(t-\varepsilon)} = \frac{\tilde{\Delta}_{EG}^{t/(t-\varepsilon)}}{\varphi_{EG}^{t-\varepsilon}} = \frac{\tilde{\varphi}_{EG}^{t} - \varphi_{EG}^{t-\varepsilon}}{\varphi_{EG}^{t-\varepsilon}} = \frac{\tilde{\varphi}_{EG}^{t}}{\varphi_{EG}^{t-\varepsilon}} - 1 = I_{EG}^{t/(t-\varepsilon)} - 1 \tag{1.9}$$

where with $I_{CE}^{t/(t-\varepsilon)}$ was noted the index of economic growth.

Economic growth is a measurable effect of economic activity. Economic activity refers to the combination of the two standard factors of production, capital[38] and labour. The result of combining the two factors of production (*Nota bene*: that combination is made through technology and microeconomic management) is a level of monetary value of goods and services created in that economic system (as I said, usually at a national level) over a period of time (usually one year), which is measured by φ. So, if we denote by λ the labour factor[39] (or the labour force factor) and by k the capital factor, then we can write (denoting by ξ a production function, i.e., a function that transforms the production factors into a measurable production):

$$\varphi = \xi(\lambda, k) \tag{1.10}$$

Assuming, which is in accordance with rationality, that, within certain limits, the increase of the employed labour force, respectively the increase of the physical capital used, lead to the increase of the economic product, then we have to verify the mathematical conditions of the production function,[40] as follows:

$$\begin{aligned} \xi'_{\lambda} &\geq 0 \\ \xi'_{k} &\geq 0 \end{aligned} \tag{1.11}$$

Based on the production function, the logical concept of economic growth can be represented graphically, as shown in Fig. 1.6.

Development

The qualitative identity of a system is represented (and, in fact, ensured, maintained) by its structure. In other words, the more stable the structure, the less vulnerable to destabilization, and therefore to change, the more likely the quality of the system to remain unchanged. As, on the other hand, development means precisely the qualitative change of the system under the impact of growth, it follows that development involves variation in structure. So, *any variation in the structure of a system, under the impact of growth, is a phenomenon or process of development.*

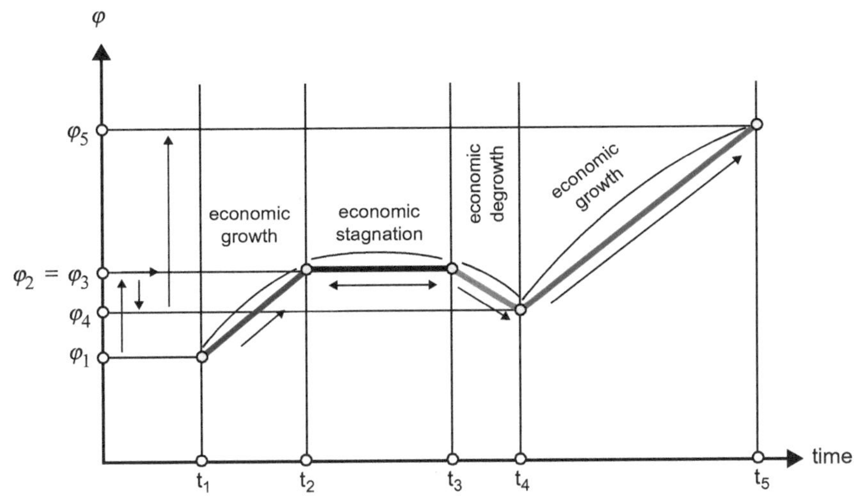

Fig. 1.6 The logical concept of economic growth. *Source*: (Dinga, 2018), p. 44

But how does this qualitative leap, which means changing the structure, occur under the empire of growth? We will set out some preliminary considerations in this regard.

- growth means, as we have seen, a dimensional variation of the system, more precisely the change of the numerical value of the parameter selected for measuring growth. This dimensional variation is the effect of both the internal connections of the system (its functionality) and its external connections (its behaviour). However, the dimensional variation of the system has no impact on the structure of the system; on the contrary, the more stable this structure is, the more undisturbed the growth and, in fact, the more predictable this growth is, so it is a necessary function of the structure;
- in order for the growth to generate a change in the structure, the variation of the dimensional parameter of the growth must exceed a certain threshold, which we can call the ***structural tilting threshold***. Of course, the numerical value of this tilting threshold depends on the nature of the system in question, its size and the number of features of its functionality and behaviour, but in principle, from a theoretical point of view, such a tilting threshold can be postulated;[41]

- in fact, at this point, we must appeal to the concept of system inertia (Dinga, 2001):
  - the evolution of a system goes through periods of structural stability (which we subsume to the concept of inertia[42]), followed by moments[43] of structural change (which we subsume to the concept of development triggering);
  - the inertial cycle of a system (in particular, an economic system) is the wrap-around period that includes inertia and structural tilting;
  - structural tilting occurs when a certain growth accumulation threshold is reached and is manifested by the variation of the structure (at this point in the discussion it does not matter the size, direction or speed with which the structure varies);
  - in general, therefore, thresholds are part of the inertial cycle. In this context, particularizing the analysis to the economic field, by economic threshold, we mean a certain value (quantity), measured in a specific way, of the independent variable of the economic process (that parameter noted, above, φ), at which the inertial breakthrough occurs in that process. This will be called the *main threshold*;[44]
  - there is an inertial tension (i.e., a tension to change) in the process of accumulating growth. This refers to the fact that the kinematic 'agglomeration' of the variation of growth ultimately determines, namely, when the tilting threshold is reached, an adjustment of the structure to the new dimensional state; this accommodation is manifested by the variation of the structure of the system in question[45] and has the significance, as previously shown, of the concept of development;
  - in fact, one can imagine a typology of economic thresholds that can be associated with the tipping threshold considered as a generic, an abstract threshold:

    according to the *reference* sphere, there are (a) *microeconomic* thresholds, which act at individual level (individual, household, company), (b) *macroeconomic* thresholds, which act on the whole national economy and (c) *world* economic thresholds, which act at the level of the world economy;

    according to the *effect* of reaching the threshold, we distinguish (a) *stabilization* thresholds and (b) *destabilization* thresholds;

    according to the *mode* of operation, we have (a) *singular* thresholds and (b) *binary* thresholds;

according to the *causal dependence*, we have (a) *independent* thresholds and (b) *linked* thresholds;
according to the *connection* with the economic cycle, there are (a) *ceiling*-threshold, for the destabilization produced in the contraction point, and (b) *floor*-threshold, for the destabilization produced in the relaunch (take-off) point.

Therefore, the accumulation of the change causes an accumulation of the change tension. That accumulation produces, at the moment of exceeding the tilting threshold, the variation of the structure of the system which, thus, loses its identity. Therefore, growth preserves the identity of the system, while development no longer does that. A system that bears a development impact is no longer the same system as it was before; it suffers an alteration of its identity. Let us highlight some of the defining characteristics of the concept of development, as they emerged from those presented above, particularizing them, of course, to the economic field, that is, talking about economic development:

- economic development can be defined as economic growth with structural effects;
- economic development is not purely quantitative, but involves the transfer of the quantitative variation of the economic process in the variation of economic structures;[46]
- economic development is, in principle, irreversible; the explanation for this irreversibility lies in the fact that, from the perspective of systems theory, structure is the parameter that ensures the identity (invariance) of a system; but economic development is 'poured' into the economic structure. The structure manifests that inertia (which can be called structural inertia or structural stability) to the point where the structural tilting threshold is reached, but once the new structure is installed, the inertia capacity of the system in question manifests similarly as in the anterior cycle. This self-feeding with inertial properties of any new structure makes the statement that development is an irreversible process (as opposed to growth, which is a reversible phenomenon) to have logical coverage. That is why in the problem of development we have inertial cycles, but these, unlike the quantitative economic cycles (specific to growth), are irreversible;[47]

- the transfer of economic growth into economic development (by changing the structure of the economic system involved[48]) generates, above a certain threshold of this transfer, a new paradigm of subsequent economic growth, generating a virtuous circle of the relationship between economic growth and economic development.

From the way the development process has been described, it follows that it can be represented graphically in a cycle-like way—the inertial cycle—by analogy with the graphical representation of the standard economic cycle, which refers to growth. Figure 1.7 shows the inertial cycle of the development concept.

Some comments may be helpful regarding the operation of the inertial development cycle, as shown in Fig. 1.7:

(a) as a system develops, the quantitative accumulation required to trigger the shift towards the next structural is greater. The explanation is as follows:
   - for a given system function (or for a limited set of given functions), there are a small number of permissible structural configurations for that system; if, in a first inertial cycle, some of

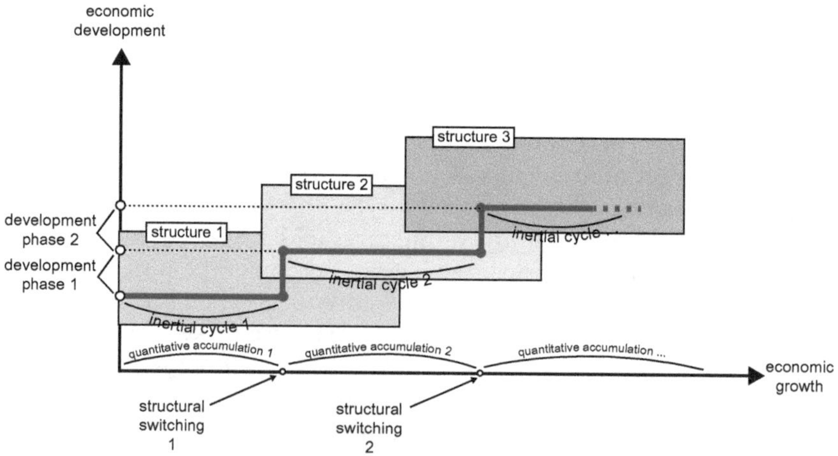

Fig. 1.7 Inertial cycle and the concept of development. *Source*: (Dinga, 2001), p. 93

these structural reconfigurations have been used (thus 'consumed'), there are fewer structural reconfigurations available in the system portfolio. In addition, each new restructuring strengthens the structural stability of the system, so for each of the following inertial cycles, quantitative accumulations of higher-than-previous growth will be needed in order to trigger new structural shifts. We believe that this increase in the quantitative accumulation required for new structural switches could have as a graphical representation an increasing, concave and asymptotic curve (Fig. 1.8).

Figure 1.8 shows that structural changes, that is, the emergence of new stages of systems development (e.g., in the case of economic systems) requires longer periods of quantitative accumulation of growth (as we argued above). On the other hand, it is empirically established that the emergence of new phases of economic development (i.e., the production of new structural changes) is becoming increasingly rapid. To eliminate

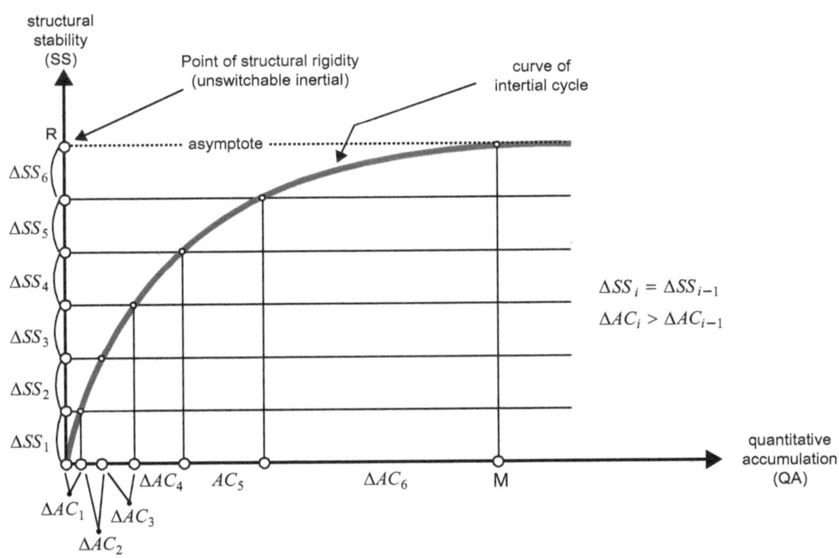

Fig. 1.8 Inertial cycles of the development are longer and longer. *Source*: (Dinga, 2018), p. 94

this apparent contradiction between theoretical precepts and empirical observations, we introduce two fundamental amendments:

- *equivalence of economic growth accumulations*: the increase in the time duration required for the next structural shift of the system is considered to be for the same quality of economic growth, that is, for the same quality of factors of production. In this case, for example, economic growth would, in turn, be asymptotically limited due to the quantitative depletion of both labour and usable capital goods. In reality, however, economic growth, although it remains purely dimensional in terms of effect, is undergoing qualitative improvements in terms of cause. Therefore, the labour force (through the increase of the professional qualification), the capital goods (through the technological innovation) and the microeconomic management acquire superior qualitative values, which increases the contribution of the qualitative input. It follows that equal economic growth occurs in ever smaller intervals, and the accumulation of growth necessary to reach the threshold of structural tilting also occurs in ever smaller intervals in time. Although the periods required for structural change are shortening, in fact, the accumulation of economic growth is the same in the shorter period. The explanation lies in the introduction of the concept of *equivalent accumulation of economic growth*. Let us make the following notations: λ_t: the amount of labour in year/time t; k_t: the amount of capital goods in year t; ω_t: the average productivity of the labour factor in year t; η_t: the average productivity of capital factor in year t; α: the share with which the labour factor participates in obtaining economic growth; β: the share with which the capital factor contributes to obtaining economic growth (obviously, $\alpha + \beta = 1$); r_t^λ : rate of change of the quantity of labour factor in year t; r_t^k : rate of change in the amount of capital factor in year t; r_t^ω : rate of change in average productivity of labour factor in year t; r_t^η : rate of change in average productivity of capital factor in year t. Then, we can write, for two periods signified by $(t - 1)$ and t the following relations:

$$\varphi_{t-1} = \alpha \cdot \lambda_{t-1} \cdot \omega_{t-1} + (1-\alpha) \cdot k_{t-1} \cdot \eta_{t-1} \tag{1.12}$$

analogously,

$$\varphi_t = \alpha \cdot \lambda_t \cdot \omega_t + (1-\alpha) \cdot k_t \cdot \eta_t \tag{1.13}$$

but

$$\varphi_t = \alpha \cdot \lambda_{t-1} \cdot \left(1 + r_t^{\lambda}\right) \cdot \omega_{t-1} \cdot \left(1 + r_t^{\omega}\right) + \left(1 - \alpha\right) \cdot k_{t-1} \cdot \left(1 + r_t^{k}\right) \cdot \\ \eta_{t-1} \cdot \left(1 + r_t^{\eta}\right) \tag{1.14}$$

Assuming the equivalence (equality) between the quantities of economic growth[49] in the two periods, it results:

$$\varphi_t = \varphi_{t-1} \tag{1.15}$$

that is,

$$\alpha \cdot \lambda_{t-1} \cdot \omega_{t-1} \cdot \left[\left(1 + r_t^{\lambda}\right) \cdot \left(1 + r_t^{\omega}\right) - 1\right] + \left(1 - \alpha\right) \cdot k_{t-1} \cdot \eta_{t-1} \cdot \\ \left[\left(1 + r_t^{k}\right) \cdot \left(1 + r_t^{\eta}\right) - 1\right] = 0 \tag{1.16}$$

We will consider the simplified case, which better expresses the variation of the qualitative input in the phenomenon of economic growth, in which the volume of the factors of production does not change.[50] Setting these conditions, $r_t^{\lambda} = 0$, $r_t^{k} = 0$, we have:

$$\alpha \cdot \lambda_{t-1} \cdot \omega_{t-1} \cdot \left[\left(1 + r_t^{\omega}\right) - 1\right] + \left(1 - \alpha\right) \cdot k_{t-1} \cdot \eta_{t-1} \cdot \left[\left(1 + r_t^{\eta}\right) - 1\right] = 0$$

$$\alpha \cdot \lambda_{t-1} \cdot \omega_{t-1} \cdot \left(1 + r_t^{\omega}\right) - \alpha \cdot \lambda_{t-1} \cdot \omega_{t-1} + k_{t-1} \cdot \eta_{t-1} \cdot \left(1 + r_t^{\eta}\right) - k_{t-1} \cdot \eta_{t-1} \\ - \alpha \cdot k_{t-1} \cdot \eta_{t-1} \cdot \left(1 + r_t^{\eta}\right) + \alpha \cdot k_{t-1} \cdot \eta_{t-1} = 0$$

$$\alpha \cdot \lambda_{t-1} \cdot \omega_{t-1} + \alpha \cdot \lambda_{t-1} \cdot \omega_{t-1} \cdot r_t^{\omega} - \alpha \cdot \lambda_{t-1} \cdot \omega_{t-1} + k_{t-1} \cdot \eta_{t-1} + k_{t-1} \cdot n_{t-1} \\ \cdot r_t^{n} - k_{t-1} \cdot \eta_{t-1} - \alpha \cdot k_{t-1} \cdot \eta_{t-1} \cdot r_t^{\eta} - \alpha \cdot k_{t-1} \cdot \eta_{t-1} + \alpha \cdot k_{t-1} \cdot \eta_{t-1}$$

$$\alpha \cdot \lambda_{t-1} \cdot \omega_{t-1} \cdot r_t^{\omega} + k_{t-1} \cdot \eta_{t-1} \cdot r_t^{\eta} - \alpha \cdot k_{t-1} \cdot \eta_{t-1} \cdot r_t^{\eta}$$

$$\alpha \cdot \lambda_{t-1} \cdot \omega_{t-1} \cdot r_t^{\omega} + k_{t-1} \cdot \eta_{t-1} \cdot r_t^{\eta} - \alpha \cdot k_{t-1} \cdot \eta_{t-1} \cdot r_t^{\eta} = 0$$

$$\alpha \cdot \lambda_{t-1} \cdot \omega_{t-1} \cdot r_t^{\omega} + \left(1 - \alpha\right) \cdot k_{t-1} \cdot \eta_{t-1} \cdot r_t^{\eta} = 0$$

$$\alpha \cdot \lambda_{t-1} \cdot \omega_{t-1} \cdot r_t^{\omega} = -\left(1 - \alpha\right) \cdot k_{t-1} \cdot \eta_{t-1} \cdot r_t^{\eta}$$

$$\frac{\alpha}{1 - \alpha} \cdot \frac{\lambda_{t-1}}{k_{t-1}} \cdot \frac{\omega_{t-1}}{\eta_{t-1}} \cdot \frac{r_t^{\omega}}{r_t^{\eta}} = -1 \tag{1.17}$$

By giving significations to ratios established, we have:

$$C_d^p \cdot C_d^{\lambda/k} \cdot C_d^{\omega/\eta} \cdot C_d^{r_t^\omega/r_t^\eta} = -1 \tag{1.18}$$

This is the mathematical condition of equivalence of the two quantitative variations of the economic growth between two successive moments of time,[51] where:

- $\frac{\alpha}{\alpha-1} = C_d^p$: the coefficient of exceeding the capital contribution by the labour contribution to the achievement of the economic growth parameter (both in the reference period and in the calculation period);
- $\frac{\lambda_{t-1}}{k_{t-1}} = C_d^{\lambda/k}$: the coefficient of exceeding the amount of capital used by the amount of labour used during the calculation period;[52]
- $\frac{\omega_{t-1}}{\eta_{t-1}} = C_d^{\omega/\eta}$: the coefficient of exceeding the average productivity of capital by the average productivity of labour in the reference period;
- $\frac{r_t^\omega}{r_t^\eta} = C_d^{r^\omega/r^\eta}$: the coefficient of exceeding the average productivity rate of capital by the average labour productivity rate during the calculation period.[53]
  - *relative autonomy of the economic structure in relation to the economic growth*: the economic structure can change without the causality necessary for the accumulation of economic growth. This autonomy of the variation of the structure in relation to the variation of the growth quantity is explained, especially by the internal logic of the institutional structure within the economic structure. Indeed, some incompleteness in the institutional structure, empirically found/observed, is eliminated precisely by the variation of this institutional structure. Likewise, any inconsistencies, redundancies or other functional dependencies between existing institutions will be adjusted/eliminated. This component of development is an autonomous component in relation to growth, so both components of the development process must be formally considered. If we note with D_C the development component that is dependent on growth (more precisely, on the accumulation of growth until the structural tilting point is reached), and with D_A the autonomous development component, as

explained above, then the development of a system (including its development economic) can be considered a linear combination of the two components (with D the phenomenon of development was noted): $D = \theta \cdot D_C + (1 - \theta) \cdot D_A$, with $0 \le \theta \le 1, \theta \in \mathbb{R}$ (Fig. 1.9 graphically illustrates this equation).

As component D_C decreases its contribution to development (i.e., the numerical value of the coefficient θ decreases), component D_A increases its contribution to development (the numerical value of the coefficient $(1 - \theta)$ increases). This kinematics of the coefficient $(1 - \theta)$ not only is the result of an algebraic functional relationship but expresses an empirically observable and logically provable social reality: institutional kinematics becomes, more and more, a cause rather than an effect of economic kinematics. However, the linearity of the combination of non-autonomous

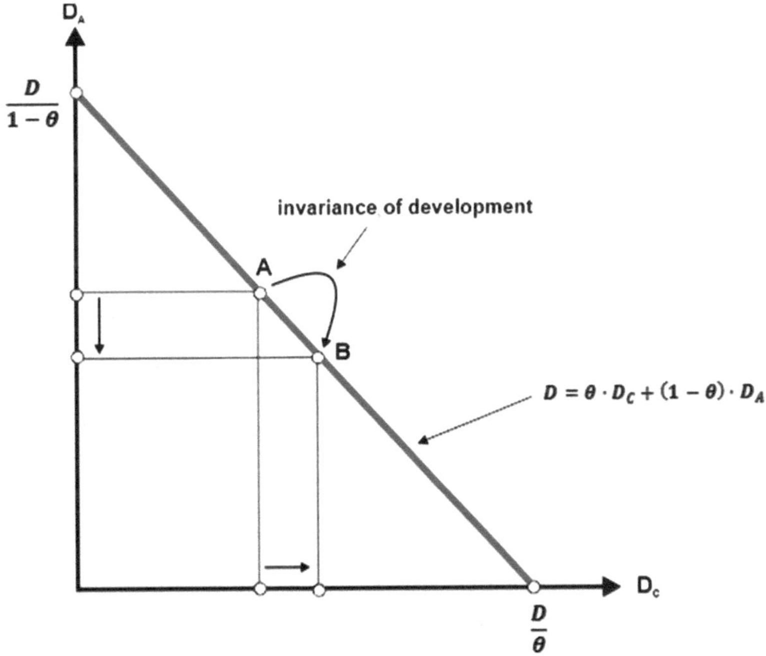

Fig. 1.9 Linear combination of the components of system development. *Source*: Authors

development (component D_C) and autonomous development (component D_A) is debatable. The empirical observation as well as the logical examination of the two components seem to indicate, rather, a decreasing contribution of the non-autonomous component, at the same time as an increasing contribution of the autonomous component. We can even hypothesize that the first component—the non-autonomous one—reduces its contribution with a decreasing rate of decrease (i.e., graphically, we have a decreasing and convex curve,[54]) while the second component—the autonomous one—increases the contribution with an increasing rate of growth (i.e., graphically, we have an increasing and convex curve[55]). Figure 1.10 illustrates this change in the phenomenology of the two components of development.

The composition of development, to which we referred above, is so important that it is one of the pillars on which the evolutionary (or evolutionist) economic theory is currently building up. The pillar we are referring to in this context is, of course, the institutional one.[56]

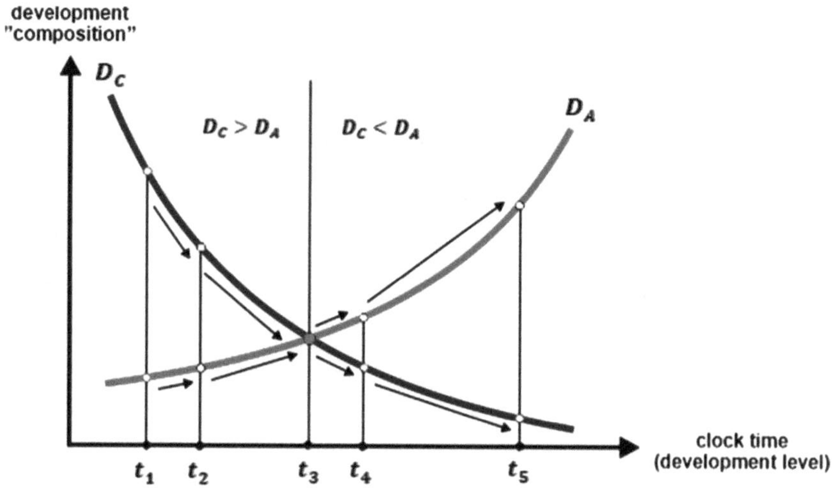

Fig. 1.10 Nonlinear combination of the components of system development. *Source*: (Dinga, 2018), p. 98

Evolution

The concepts of growth and development (exemplified on the economic case, as discussed above) referred to isolated systems that do not interact with the environment[57] or, more generally, where the interaction with the environment is considered an exogenous factor. In reality, however, the interaction of systems with the environment is internalized (endogenized) both in the case of the targeted systems and in the case of the interaction environment. This internalization is the logical channel through which, together with the concepts of growth and development, the concept of evolution enters the debate. The scheme of all the distinct categories of change in the Universe is shown in Fig. 1.11.

Thus, evolution is a category of change of matrix type, which takes different forms, depending on the context in which evolution takes place:

- if evolution is driven by growth, then it is called *development* (evolution of type A);
- both growth and development are part of the group of first-order changes—that is, changes that do not involve goals or values established by cultural subjects;

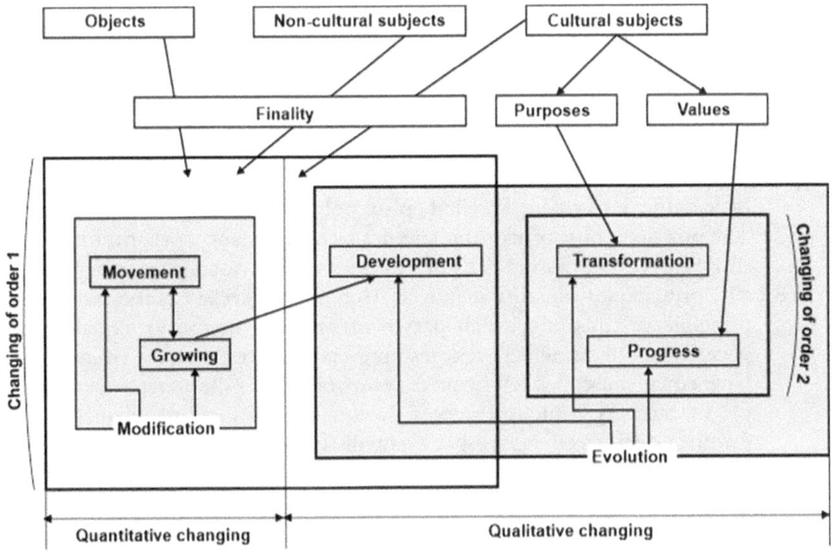

Fig. 1.11 Abstract typology of change in the Universe. *Source*: Authors

Table 1.1 Types of evolution

Type of evolution	*Name of evolution*	*Unity of evolution*	*The marker of evolution*	*Finality of evolution*
A	Development	Individual	Growth	Survival
B	Transformation[58]	Species	Purpose/goal	Adaptation[59]
C	Progress	Society	Value	Fulfilment

Source: Authors.

- if evolution is guided by the goals of cultural subjects, we call this type of change *transformation* (evolution of type B);
- if evolution is guided by the values of cultural subjects, we call this type of change *progress* (evolution of type C);
- it should be noted that both transformation and progress are part of the group of second-order changes—that is, which involve goals or values established by cultural subjects.

Consequently, we have three categories of evolution: (a) evolution as development; (b) evolution as transformation; and (c) evolution as progress. In terms of assigning to the individual, species or genus the different forms that evolution takes, our view is that the following systematization can be made (Table 1.1).

Notes

1. The theory of knowledge in general is called gnoseology, and the theory of scientific knowledge is called epistemology.
2. The principle must verify three predicates of sufficiency: (a) primitivity; (b) simplicity (even, tautology); and (c) universality (not simple generality).
3. The principle of causality manifests itself at two levels: (1) the *microscopic* principle of causality, which preserves *equality* (quantity): equal causes have equal effects, which denotes predictability; respectively, equal effects have equal causes, which denotes reversibility; (2) the *macroscopic* principle of causality, which preserves the quality/distinction: distinct causes produce distinct effects; respectively, distinct effects have distinct causes. One criterion for qualifying classical causality compared to causality in quantum mechanics is the following: classical causality is based on the microscopic principle of causality, while quantum causality is based on the macroscopic principle of causality.

4. From an epistemological point of view, the explanation is nothing else than a description of causation (more precisely of the cause involved in the factual interest).
5. For example, in algebraic mathematics, the concept of the function $y = f(x)$ implies that any x generates a y (more precisely, a unique y) but this does not mean that x is the cause of y.
6. Also in algebraic mathematics, the laws of the group (or of any other algebraic structure) are neither causal nor functional, but structural.
7. Note that the famous so-called Zeno paradoxes fraudulently (in fact, sophistically, i.e., on the basis of the interlocutor's intellectual inattention) replace mathematical time with physical time (*Nota bene*: mathematical time allows infinitesimals, e.g., analyticity to infinity), while physical time does not (here, as in terms of space or energy, there are atomic limits—in the original sense of the term atomic—it is about Planck quantities). Similar considerations can be formulated about the distinction between mathematical space (with n dimensions) and physical space (three dimensions—we ignore the allegations of string theory which, for now, is crystallizing and which 'decrees' more than three spatial dimensions).
8. More precisely, the law means dynamic law, that is, the law is applicable as such to every individual in the population. By abuse of language, laws are also called those regularities (established empirically) that apply to the average of a population, not to each individual: the so-called statistical laws.
9. We have referred elsewhere to another confusion that is made here, between the concept of *stochastic* (pattern of behaviour which is modellable from a statistical perspective) and the concept of *random* (non-existence of a pattern of behaviour). For example, many analysts use the expression random variable even though that variable refers to a stochastic process, that is, it is a stochastic variable. It should be mentioned as clearly and bluntly as possible that mathematics cannot model causality, but only legality, that is, the determinism. The fact that mathematical statistics (and its offspring, econometrics, cliometrics) claims to shape causality (which is always legal) is, of course, an uncovered claim.
10. In our opinion, economic theory is still due to the elaboration of a proper *homo œconomicus* model, in which both behaviourism and evolutionism (including the latter's species: institutionalism) are working today.
11. At least in the macroscopic field, since at the quantum level it seems that things are more complicated and counter-intuitive.
12. There is a universal arrow of time—provided by the increase in global entropy—but, of course, there may also be local (or subjective, as the case may be) arrows of time. An example of a subjective (i.e., subject-dependent) arrow of time is provided by the phenomenon of memory versus the phenomenon of anticipation: if a fact is part of the memory, it

means that that fact is situated in the past, and if it is part of the desirability/anticipation, it means that it is situated in the future.

13. Of course, this involves the difficult issue of instantaneous transmission of the action. The instantaneous transmission of action is forbidden by the theory of special relativity (the highest speed in the Universe is the speed of photons, and this speed is limited). However, entanglement theory offers a 'solution' in this regard. Although the aim of this study is co-evolution (hence the causality entangled) in the financial market, we will ignore this issue (for readers interested in the subject, we suggest a visit to the EPR—Einstein-Podolsky-Rosen—experiment and to the debates around this mental experiment).
14. However, the concept of entanglement not only allows this, but even establishes the 'obligation' of instantaneous transport of causal impact (of course, the explanation of entanglement is somewhat more subtle). Given the concept of cultural geodesic (operated in FMAB-APH (Dinga et al., 2022) but also in the present book), it seems that the entanglement is much more present (perhaps even inherent) in the social field and, in particular, in the functioning of the financial market. A logical (and quantitative) modelling of the economic/financial entanglement could be very useful both conceptually as well as methodologically and instrumentally in modelling the financial market, so having as a theoretical anchor exactly the mentioned concept of cultural geodesic. It is to be mentioned that our concept of *cultural geodesic* is somewhat analogous with Glen concept of metacontingency (Glenn, 2004). However, some new research show that the metacontingency seems to not address very well the concept of self-organizing (and, *a fortiori*, the concept of autopoieticity) of the cultural systems (Krispin, 2019).
15. Far beyond the modest ambitions of the present study, one could discuss the phenomenology (in Husserl's tradition) that considers that the task of philosophy as a science is to constitute meaning through what is called eidetic identification (i.e., identification of essence).
16. By eutaxiological causality we mean 'strictly objective' causality, consisting of *causa materialis*, *causa formalis* and *causa eficiens*, while by teleological causality we mean *causa finalis.*
17. It is obvious that all we have done here is to point out Popper's three worlds: (1) world 1—objective world; (2) world 2—subjective/psychological world; (3) world 3—world as the objectified effect of inter-subjective relationships.
18. Of course, there is not exactly an intelligence of institutions (or an institutional intelligence or, worse, an institutionalized intelligence), as some label-seekers are quick to proclaim (see a recent paper that holds this view, of the New Age type, by Enrico Gualini, *Planning and the Intelligence of Institutions*, (Gualini, 2019)), but an intelligence accepted in Popper's

third world (see note 17). Authors of the mentioned category can talk with some relaxation about mechanical intelligence (or, as it is also called, artificial intelligence; *Nota bene*: we consider that the correct phrase, here, is ***non-anthropic intelligence anthropically generated***: nAIAG).

19. The ambition of a theory about everything, that is present, for the time being, only in physics (and consisting in trying to unify in a coherent and consistent way the theory of gravity from general relativity with quantum theory) remains an ambition. However, in the a-scientific field, theories are predominantly theories about everything—see the Bible or the other great myths/religions of mankind. Perhaps, however, a theory of everything will not be able to completely go out of the metaphysical realm.
20. This possibility has already been intuited by economists who call economic decline as negative economic growth.
21. Indeed, the methodological obligation to establish the benchmark carries with it the methodological obligation to establish the moment against which the phenomenon of economic growth is assessed. However, it is often acceptable to consider, albeit redundantly, as a third methodological element of measuring growth, and benchmark moment too.
22. As we will see later, the amount of growth will have structural effects instead.
23. For example, the economic cycle refers only to the aspects of economic growth, thus measuring only the dimensional (quantitative) oscillations of the economic process in question. Like economic growth, the economic cycle can have (and, in general, has) qualitative effects but only under certain conditions, that is, its qualitative effects are not principled, but contextual, contingent.
24. We will see below that the structural impact of growth is the very content of the concept of development.
25. Of course, this does not happen by itself, objectively, but requires the intervention of the normative subject which, following *ex-post* and *ex-ante* analyses, will generate those rules that ensure structural changes be compatible and consistent with maintaining, accelerating or decelerating (as appropriate) of growth.
26. Probably one of the crucial issues today, when it comes to the sustainability of economic growth, is precisely the 'piloting' of this feature of the growth phenomenon. From another perspective, namely that of the network, the self-catalytic propensity to grow can be considered a *hub effect*: the exponential multiplication of network connections already made (Barabási, 2002).
27. For example, the Fiscal Compact (as well as other strategic documents of the European Union or other international financial organizations and institutions) requires that reserves/buffers (e.g., through budget surpluses) be set up in years of economic growth in order to be used in years when economic growth is weaker or there is economic decline.

28. Two predicates (in the logic of predicates) or two statements (in propositional logic) are in a contradictory relationship if the negation of one generates the other. Thus, the two entities cannot be simultaneously true or simultaneously false, that is, if one is true, then the other is false and vice versa (according to the principle of bivalent logic called the non-contradiction principle). Instead, two predicates (or two statements) are related of contrariety if they can be both either true or false.
29. Indeed, we can write: $\frac{dx}{x} = r$. Applying the integration operator to both members of the equation we obtain: $\int \frac{dx}{x} = \int r dr \to \ln(x) = r \to x = e^r$, considering that the primitive family of the right member of the equation contains only one primitive, that is, in the expression e^{r+C}, C is a real constant, $C = 0$.
30. The most common such parameter is GDP (gross domestic product). Although this macroeconomic indicator of the highest degree of aggregation admits a series of extremely strong and relevant theoretical, methodological and empirical critiques (relatively recently, three eminent macroeconomists joined these critiques—Joseph Stiglitz, Amartya Sen and Jean-Paul Fitoussi—through the study generically entitled *Beyond GDP*), so far no one has proposed, systematically and completely, a more appropriate indicator.
31. Sub-annual values (most often, quarter values), although used primarily by quantitative analysts such as econometricians, are of little relevance to the growth process because the most real or nominal economic behaviours are 'designed' for the annual significance interval (reporting, closing of financial flows, closing of payment of budgetary obligations, etc.).
32. Inflation is the rate of prices or, what is equivalent, the rate of the average price per economy (calculated either on the basis of Laspeyres or on the basis of Paasche or of Fisher).
33. Please note that inflation, as we know it at the common level, is a sectoral indicator (it refers only to a representative basket of goods and services that affects the average standard of living). At the most aggregated macroeconomic level, the deflator will refer to all goods and services in the economy, which is why it is also called the GDP deflator.
34. Indeed, we have, successively, $d_t = \frac{y_t}{\tilde{y}_t}$; $\frac{y_t - \tilde{y}_t}{\tilde{y}_t} = r_t^y$; $d_t - 1 = r_t^y \to d_t = 1 + r_t^y$, where d_t is GDP deflator, y_t is nominal GDP, $\tilde{y}_t$ is real GDP and r_t^y is the rhythm of nominal GDP with respect to real GDP (or the rhythm of inflation r elated to the nominal GDP).
35. Obviously, the expression 'usually' also ensures the reciprocal case of the decrease of the prices, more precisely, of the decrease of the average price.

36. It is immediately noticeable that the formula is general, that is, it works when we have no inflation (increase in average price), but deflation (decrease in average price). *Nota bene*: deflation should not be confused with disinflation, which denotes lowering inflation (not prices).
37. Usually, economic growth means real (i.e., deflated) changes in GDP value. Sometimes, it is helpful to calculate the nominal economic growth, when it must be specified that the values are nominal, that is, non-deflated.
38. Capital means capital goods, that is, capital as a physical asset (in the form of physical production technologies, no matter how digitized they may be) and not capital as a financial asset. Of course, physical capital will also be expressed in monetary form (in fact, for calculation reasons, labour is also expressed in monetary terms, e.g., as a level of wages, presumed to express in monetary terms the marginal productivity of the labour factor, as the monetary value of capital goods is presumed to express the marginal productivity of the capital factor).
39. Here labour force and work are considered conceptually substitutable, although, as is well known, some economic doctrines (such as Marxism) not only consider them different, but this difference is considered crucial in economic theory.
40. One of the most used production functions (by the way, with many criticisms, both from an economic and a mathematical perspective) is the Cobb-Douglas production function: $\varphi = \alpha \cdot \lambda^x \cdot k^y$, where α is a homogenization/calibration constant, x is the elasticity of φ with respect to λ ($x = \varphi'_\lambda \cdot \frac{\lambda}{\varphi}$) and y is the elasticity of φ with respect to k ($y = \varphi'_k \cdot \frac{k}{\varphi}$).
41. However, establishing its numerical value is an empirical issue, not a theoretical one.
42. Recall that in the case of the financial market, the inertial stability of some parameters—such as the price of a financial security—is called ***moment*** (not to be confused with the concept/term moment in time series analysis methodology) (Satchell & Grant, 2020).
43. The moment can be, in fact, a certain period but, as this period is considerably shorter than the period of inertia (and sometimes it can even be a moment from the concrete perspective of the measurement with the clock time), we will mention it, generically, as a moment and not a period.
44. There are also secondary thresholds, which are two, namely, (a) the threshold at which the economic system (more precisely, the system-environment interaction set) acquires the attribute of inertiality—we will call this threshold ***awareness threshold***; (b) the threshold from which the two interacting systems cease to communicate—we will call this threshold ***opaqueness threshold***.

45. It should be noted that the variation of the structure has no axiological relevance, so it cannot be said that 'the structure has worsened' or 'the structure has improved'. The situation is analogous to that of an evolutionary system in the biological world. This is one of the (main) reasons why the economic phenomenon is treatable from an institutionalist/evolutionary perspective.
46. Structure by branches and sub-branches, structure of foreign trade (import-export, tradable goods-non-tradable goods), structure by economic sectors (primary, secondary, tertiary, quaternary, quinary), structure of energy consumption, structure of employment and so on.
47. It should be noted that the standard economic cycles, associated with economic growth, are not perfectly ('punctually') reversible (i.e., there are some differences, but still quantitative, in this reversibility), but in contrast to the inertial cycle, the economic cycle is 'reversible'.
48. It seems not to be a perfect (mirrored) symmetry of the effect of economic decline on economic structure, but this supposed rigidity is not, to our knowledge, elucidated from a theoretical point of view, and blind empirical analyses (without a theoretical hypothesis) are, of course, sterile exercises (see, e.g., econometric analysis) designed only to help their authors gain access to academic positions.
49. We address the nominal value of the economic growth or, equivalently, the GDP deflator, equal to 1.
50. The treatment of the more general case, in which the volumes of the factors of production (whether they decrease or increase) vary, does not present difficulties compared to the simplified case, only, of course, it is more realistic.
51. In the case discussed, the moments of time are consecutive, but the relationship can be generalized for any case of successive moments.
52. This coefficient obviously means the inverse of the technical endowment of work.
53. From a conceptual point of view, this coefficient of outrunning is the very elasticity of the average labour productivity in relation to the average productivity of capital.
54. Mathematically, taking time as an independent variable, the equation of this component as a function of time has the first derivative negative, and the second derivative positive.
55. See note 51.
56. Named, by some authors (e.g., John Rawls), with the term *social structure* or, still, *basic structure*.
57. It is evident that the interaction of a system with the environment includes, as a species, the interactions among systems, since the other systems are, for a given one, components of the environment.

58. In the field of living things, the change that concerns the species is called evolution—in our opinion, keeping this term, when necessary, we will have to use either the term of transformation or the term of progress, as the case may be, for the evolution of the human species or symbolic species as language, routines, communication, norms (or normative systems), strategies, etc.
59. In the case of the human being, finality acquires either the 'look' of the goal (*Nota bene*: the goal is a consciously predetermined finality), as in the case of evolution as transformation, or the 'look' of value (axiological finality), as in the case of evolution as progress.

References

Barabási, A.-L. (2002). *Linked-the New Science of Networks* (1st Edition). Perseus Books Group.

Dinga, E. (2001). *The Inertial Phenomenon in the Economic Process.* Economică Publishing House.

Dinga, E. (2018). *Growth, Development, and Economic Sustainability in Romania (2007—2017).* Romanian Academy Publishing House.

Dinga, E. (2021). *Logically Living System: A Generative "Machine" for Autopoietic Systems* [Chapter 4]. Handbook of Research on Autopoiesis and Self-Sustaining Processes for Organizational Success; IGI Global.

Dinga, E. (2022). *Economy and Society. Theoretical, Methodological and Empirical Approaches.* Economică Publishing House.

Dinga, E., Oprean-Stan, C., Tănăsescu, C.-R., Brătian, V., Ionescu, G.-M., (2022) *Financial Market Analysis and Behaviour. The Adaptive Preference Hypothesis*, Routledge, Francis & Taylor Group.

Glenn, S. S. (2004). *Individual behavior, culture, and social change.* The Behavior Analyst, 27(2).

Gualini, E. (2019). *Planning and the Intelligence of Institutions: Interactive Approaches to Territorial Policy-Making Between Institutional Design and Institution-Building.* Routledge, Taylor & Francis Group.

Hausman, D. M. (2009). *Laws, Causation, and Economic Methodology.* Oxford University Press.

Krispin, J. (2019). *Culturo-behavioral Hypercycles and the Metacontingency: Incorporating Self-Organizing Dynamics into an Expanded Model of Cultural Change*, Perspectives on Behavior Science, 42(2).

Satchell, S., & Grant, A. (2020). *Market Momentum: Theory and Practice.* Wiley Publishing House.

CHAPTER 2

Co-evolution in the Financial Market

The Concept of Evolution—General Framework

Theoretical Basis of Evolution

From a logical point of view, as shown above, evolution can refer to three processes, both in the natural sphere and in the cultural sphere: development, transformation and progress. The concept of evolution (in its most general sense) came about life (living entities[1]), so in the field of biology. The credited researcher with the formulation of the theory of evolution, as we know it today, is Charles Darwin,[2] with his work *The Origin of Species by Natural Selection or Preserving Favoured Breeds in the Struggle for Existence* (Darwin, 1859/2009). Today's neo-Darwinism[3] contains, as a fundamental explanatory factor, the genetic theory (non-existent in Darwin's time), but, in principle, the initial theory is valid and has been continuously corroborated since its elaboration.[4]

Also, from a logical perspective, evolution is based on the following components: (a) mutation in the genetic 'program' (at the genotype level), (b) genetic recombination and (c) cumulative directional selection appearing at the level of the phenotype.

E. Dinga et al., *Co-Evolution of Symbolic Species in the Financial Market*, https://doi.org/10.1007/978-3-031-31698-2_2

Genotype
It represents the totality of the hereditary properties of an organism, manifested in the genetic composition (composition in alleles[5]) of that organism. The genotype is the 'site' of both the preservation and the change in the identity of the phenotype generated by the genotype in question. The genotype is a unit of replication (or replicator) at DNA level.[6]

Genetic Mutation
It refers to a change/modification of one gene (or several), more precisely a change in the structure of DNA or RNA. The mutation[7] can occur either before replication (as an effect of the action of viruses or physical environmental factors, such as radiation) or during the replication process (so-called translation error for protein synthesis), so the change/modification in question will be transmitted (or is liable to be transmitted) to the offspring during replication. The fundamental property of the genetic mutation is its random character (*Nota bene*: not stochastic one!). The genetic mutation occurs contingently (of course, based on the principle of causality) and its transmission, although necessary, is not completely accurate, both for reasons of DNA transcription into RNA (see Fig. 2.1) and as a result of genetic recombination.

We present, in Fig. 2.1, a scheme synthesized by us after the work of Richard Dawkins, *The Blind Watchmaker* regarding genetic replication (Dawkins, 2016).

Genetic Recombination
Like genetic mutation, it is random. It refers either to the rearrangement of genetic material from two different genetic units or to the repair of DNA that has already undergone mutations (*Nota bene*: so, the mutation that will eventually be passed on to offspring is the result of the initial mutation plus

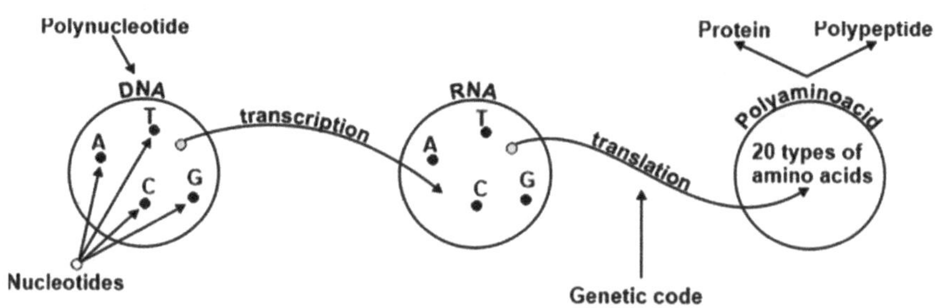

Fig. 2.1 Transcription, respectively, translation in genetic replication. *Source*: Authors

the result of repair—more exactly, of self-repair—of DNA). In eukaryotic[8] organisms (such as humans), recombination occurs during meiosis.[9]

Phenotype
If the genotype is the unit of replication, the phenotype is the unit of selection. By phenotype is meant the organism that has reached the stage of adulthood, that is, the stage in which the process of development has ended.[10] In other words, it means what we call the individual. In general, the developmental process is considered complete[11] when the individual is capable (physiologically) of reproduction, but depending on different contexts, there are other definitions (or predicates of sufficiency) in the matter (which, however, will not be addressed here).

Directional Selection
Unlike mutation and recombination, selection is directed, that is, it has a finality[12] (*Nota bene*: In the natural world, there is no purpose, but in the cultural world, the finality is, to a large extent, of the nature of purpose). The directionality of the selection is obtained by two properties: (a) by the cumulative character of the selection and (b) by operating the selection eligibility criterion—the best fitness in relation to the environment (in the largest sense).

(a) The cumulative character of the selection

Selection is exerted by the environment[13] on the individual, which leads to the evolution of the species (by increasing the share of individuals selected in the total population concerned), and has a cumulative character. This means that a selected mutation will still be able to undergo other mutations in the genes that were passed on to the offspring with the mutation in question, which are somehow consistent with or compatible with the previous mutation and so forth, so that, at some point, individuals living in a certain species are the result of these successive mutations,[14] that is, of the cumulative[15] character of the selection. The cumulative character of the selection generates what is called gradual evolution, and its punctuated (saltationist) character is also called catastrophic or explosive[16] evolution.

(b) The eligibility of the mutation

Eligibility of the mutation means the operation of a criterion that 'chooses', in fact, the mutation that will be maintained in the selected individual and thus will be perpetuated through his/her descendants. Eligibility is the effect of the criterion called *fitness*. In general, fitness means a property of the individual (phenotype) to adapt as well as possible to the environment (*Nota bene*: not necessarily at the optimal level, i.e., at that level of the *first-best* solution but at the level of sustainability or survival, i.e., at the level of the *second-best* solution or even, in some cases, *third-best solution*). This means that, of all the descendants of the individuals who have undergone mutations, this criterion will select, in order to survive, those individuals who have the best fitness.[17] As the list of fitness does not contain, as a rule (although it may contain by accident), optimal fitness, we are in the case of a *maximin* type of selection.

The Concept of Mechanism

The concept of mechanism is developed in the paper *Macroeconomic Adjustment Through Normative Mechanisms* (Dinga, 2020). Mechanism means a procedure[18] that connects in some way (mechanical, electrical, chemical, mental, social, institutional, etc.) a cause of an effect. Of course, there may be natural mechanisms (e.g., the rotation of the Earth around the Sun, which generates the effect of day-night succession), psychic mechanisms (e.g., the memory of an event, triggered by a smell associated, subconsciously, with that past event[19]) or social mechanisms (e.g., pandemic poverty generating social movements against rulers). Let us establish the predicates of sufficiency for a (generic) mechanism to exist and function.

- (**M1**) the existence of a *system*: as in the case of other concepts, the mechanism cannot function (more precisely, it cannot be observed, perceived, detected) unless it is 'affiliated' to a system, be it ontological or only gnoseological;[20]
- (**M2**) the existence of a number of *transformation operators*: the cause-effect relationship (or, more generally, the input-output relationship[21]). Transformation operators guarantee[22] that a certain cause will produce a certain effect based on a previously accepted theory—under the four important aspects that characterize an effect: quantitative, qualitative, structural and temporal (as rhythm). The number of processing operators depends, of course, on the complicatedness of the mechanism in question, being directly proportional to this degree of complicatedness.[23]

Since, in the literature, the confusion between complexity and complicatedness is relatively frequent, Fig. 2.2 shows the logical relation

Aggregate		System		Network	
SIMPLEX				COMPLEX	
simple	complicated	simple	complicated	simple	complicated

Fig. 2.2 Logical relationships simplicity-complicatedness-complexity. *Source*: (Dinga, 2020), p. 10

complicatedness versus simplicity, respectively, the logical relation complexity versus simplicity, as we consider them should be understood.

- (**M3**) existence of a *coordinating operator*: all the above-mentioned processing or transformation operators must be able to be coordinated in their action in such a way that the entity concerned, to which the mechanism is associated, has a different purpose from each transforming operator in part and to integrate these individual aims in a coherent and, above all, convergent way (*Nota bene*: frequently and synergistically). It can be seen that this predicate of sufficiency does not require a simple synergy (although synergy is involved in coordination) but requires more than that, namely, a *principle of order*. We require that this principle of order be 'under' a specific operator called the coordinating operator;
- (**M4**) the existence of a *replication operator*: the predicate of sufficiency called replication operator requires that the cycle of the mechanism described be not singular, in the sense that it requires that it does not work only once, that is, to have only one operating cycle, but its operation, regulated by the second and third predicates of sufficiency (specified above), may possibly be resumed indefinitely. Repeatability in operation is a *conditio sine qua non*, like other predicates of sufficiency, for the existence of a mechanism;
- (**M5**) existence of a *monitoring/control/adjustment operator*: this predicate of sufficiency refers to the changes that must occur in the mechanism for it to perform its functions without obsolescence and without reducing performance. Of course, adjustment is not possible without monitoring or controlling the operation of the mechanism concerned.

In order for a mechanism to generally exist, it is necessary for a particular object to simultaneously verify the five predicates of sufficiency mentioned above. The logical formalism of this definition is as follows:

$$M = \{M1, M2, M3, M4, M5\} \tag{2.1}$$

or equivalently:

$$M \leftarrow \left[(M1) \wedge (M2) \wedge (M3) \wedge (M4) \wedge (M5)\right] \tag{2.2}$$

It is easy to see, without the need for a dedicated qualitative analysis, that the system of five predicates of sufficiency for a generic mechanism verifies the three standard conditions of any definition based on predicates of sufficiency: (a) consistency (non-contradictoriness) of predicates taken two by two, (b) independence (non-redundancy) of predicates taken two by two and (c) completeness (aggregated sufficiency).[24]

Of the five predicates of sufficiency, the first two may be called *general predicates*, and the next three, special predicates. The justification for such a typology is that general sufficiency predicates are nominally present in any mechanism, while special sufficiency predicates are contextual (praxiological/empirical), that is, they are customized according to the specific mechanism in sight.

The Concept of Mechanism of Evolution

From the perspective of the objectives of this study, we are interested in a particular mechanism from the general mechanism presented above, namely, we are interested in the concept of mechanism of evolution.[25] In order to extract such a particular mechanism, we will have to examine the predicates of sufficiency of a general mechanism from the perspective of the concept/process of evolution.

- (**M1**) the existence of a *system*: in the case of the evolutionary process we have, obviously, systems—from the cell, in the nucleus of which is the replicator (gene)[26] to the phenotype (adult individual)—so, the predicate M1 is done;
- (**M2**) the existence of a number of *transformation operators*: the transformation operator is represented, in the evolutionary process, either by the DNA to RNA transcription operator or by the RNA translation operator in the synthesis of the protein in question[27]—so, the predicate M2 is done;

- (**M3**) the existence of a *coordination operator*: in the evolutionary process, there is a coordination both at the level of genotype—for example, between transcription and translation—and at the level of phenotype (where coordination is even more obvious), achieved by the filter that represents the maximin value of fitness in relation to the environment—so, the predicate M3 is done;
- (**M4**) the existence of a *replication operator*: as shown above, the gene is the replicator of the system itself. In a more general sense, we have a replication of the phenotype, but with the specification that it is about the replication of the phenotype associated with the best fitness (relatively) achieved in relation to the requirements of the environment—so, the predicate M4 is done;
- (**M5**) the existence of a *monitoring/control/adjustment operator*: regarding this predicate we will make the following slightly more analytical consideration: at the genotype level, there is no such operator—remember that the genetic mutation is random, not even stochastic—but at the phenotype level, such an operator is fully functional—directional or directed selection (whether it is cumulative or punctuated) ensures monitoring, control and adjustment, as appropriate, in the selection of those individuals who check the (relatively) best fitness in relation to the environment.

The Concept of Co-evolution

Theoretical Basis of Co-evolution

Species and Co-species

Regarding the (punctually) identification of the species, three definitions are proposed in the literature (Kratochwil & Schwabe, 2002):

a. *morphological* definition: individuals having the same structural features;
b. *genetic* definition: individuals who are reproductively isolated;[28]
c. *ecological* definition: symptomatic and synchronous species cannot form the same species.[29]

The process by which a species appears is called a speciation. There are two distinct categories of speciation:[30]

(i) *allopatric speciation* is due to the isolation of a species following the occurrence of an obstacle of physical (geographical) separation—a river, a mountain and so on. In allopathic speciation, two steps are required:
   - step 1: geographical separation;
   - step 2: development of isolation mechanisms (*Nota bene*: there are two types of isolation, namely, (a) metagametic isolation: incompatibility of mating and (b) progametic isolation: prevention of mating—the latter is also called cyclic or seasonal isolation);[31]

(ii) *sympatric speciation* is due to competition, or to arising of particular traits, between individuals (of a species) living in the same physical and temporal area.

The concept of co-species is quite controversial, both logically and epistemologically. *Logically*, a species is in connection (interaction) with any other species in the environment of the species in question, so for a given (fixed) species, a co-species should refer only to one species (chosen, in turn) from the environment, with which the fixed species is 'credited' to interact exclusively or predominantly. This is a rather pronounced abstraction, so logically speaking of co-species means operating a segmentation of the analysis space (of course, there may be cases where such segmentation is justified either theoretically or methodologically or instrumentally). From an *epistemological* point of view, the term co-species should separate between two entities that can only be defined in relation to each other—a co-species exists only in relation to (or associated with) a fixed species, so it is co-species not in general, but only in relation to the fixed species. This means that each species has (or, more generally, has only) one co-species, namely, from the perspective of a particular interest in knowledge or action.

Co-species: Ontological or Gnoseological Concept?

In principle, the co-species, regardless of how it is established, has an ontological status—it exists either as an objective or as a subjective reality, or (most often) as an objectified reality following the production of intersubjectivity. At the same time, the co-species is a target for knowledge (e.g., in the current study), so it has a gnoseological status in this regard. In the following, the concept of co-species will be considered to have, without doubt, an ontological status.

Co-species versus Environment
Given that any system exists and operates in an environment (where other systems are or may be, whether similar, different, complementary or competitive), the question of the relationship between system and environment arises from the perspective of the concept of species and co-species, respectively. The fact that not only the environment conditions or influences the immersed system in that environment but also the system in question conditions or influences the environment in which it is immersed is a known and recognized fact.[32] The question we want to examine here is whether the environment can play the role of species (more precisely, of co-species) for a given species that exists and functions in that environment.

- there are cases (well documented in the literature) of parasite-host systems, in which the parasite, as a system, exists and functions inside a host, the latter being, in turn, a system, cases in which obviously not only the host influences the parasite but also the parasite influences the host;
- in game theory (either cooperative, competitive or evolutionary), either player adapts to the other's strategy (more precisely, it has a reaction function—or reaction norm, as we have formulated the name of this interaction in our book entitled *Financial Market Analysis and Behaviour. The Adaptive Preference Hypothesis* (hence, FMAB-APH) (Dinga et al., 2022)—which is designed in relation to the partner's action). It is true that in the case of game theory, we no longer have the obvious case of immersing one system in another, but each player is, in fact, the environment for the other player;
- reality (in its three forms of objective, subjective and objectified) is organized and functions, from an ontological point of view, through systems, subsystems and supersystems. This means that any system is composed of subsystems, which are immersed in it, and this, in turn, is immersed in a supersystem. In other words, the interaction between systems can be done either horizontally—between systems that relate to the same degree of integration into the supersystem—or vertically—between systems that relate to different degrees of systemic integration. In the case of vertical interaction, we have exactly the problem of the relationship between the species (or, equivalently, co-species) and the environment.

In conclusion, we appreciate that the environment can be positioned either as pure adaptar[33] (does not undergo evolutionary processes or adaptation under the impact/influence of the species or co-species immersed) or as, in turn, species or co-species. Of course, the co-evolution process can only take place in the latter case. In what follows, we will customize and detail this conclusion in the case of the financial market.

The Concept of Co-evolution

Definitional Considerations

Generally, co-evolution means a process of two species that, in the process of their functioning, adapt to each other. In this sense, the distinction between adaptation and co-evolution is very clear: in the case of adaptation, only one of the species evolves, adapting to the other species which, in turn, is (considered) invariant. It can be said that in the case of co-evolution, a mutual selection, either successive or concomitantly, takes place between the two species involved.[34]

Co-evolution (as a process) is, in turn, logically, a species of the genus we can call interaction. Thus, the following types of interactions involving two species (i.e., involving co-evolution) can be identified (Futuyma, 1983):

- *competitive* interaction leads to divergence;
  - the fitness of each species is mitigated;
  - the acquisition of those features that limit the effectiveness or frequency of interactions;[35]
- *antagonistic* interaction leads to cycles or escalation of the interaction;
  - the victim's fitness (e.g., host, in the pair host-parasite) is mitigated by non-interaction;
  - the fitness of the operator (e.g., the parasite, in the pair host-parasite) is increased by interaction;
  - the victim develops traits that reduce the effectiveness or frequency of interactions, and the exploiter develops traits that have the opposite effect;
  - mutual selection is directional (regarding the phenotype);
- *mutualistic* interaction (*Nota bene*: cooperation) leads to convergence;
  - both fitnesses increase through interaction;
  - both species develop traits that favour the effectiveness and frequency of interactions;
  - selection is dependent on the frequency of interactions.

Co-evolutionary dynamics are governed by three main components: (a) the variation of inter-specific interactions within the population, (b) dependence of inter-specific interactions on local contexts (hotspots); (c) autonomous modification of genotypes.

The most significant co-evolutionary processes are (Kratochwil & Schwabe, 2002) (1) specific co-evolution: co-evolution between species; (2) diffuse[36] co-evolution: co-evolution between groups of species; (3) biocenoses[37] and ecosystems (e.g., phytocenoses, zoocenoses): (a kind of) general co-evolution.

The Mechanism of Co-evolution

Regarding the concept of evolution, there are two ontological levels, namely, (a) *microevolution*—refers to the evolution within a population and is manifested by changing the frequency of alleles; (b) *macroevolution*—refers to the formation of new species, families, orders and so on, that is, refers to speciation processes, in a very general sense.

As shown above, co-evolution is a species of evolution although, just as well, it can be shown that evolution is another name for the same concept, namely, the concept of co-evolution. However, overcoming the terminological differences, co-evolution can be manifested, from an observational point of view, in the two forms already mentioned above:

a. *pairwise* or reciprocal co-evolution—the two species that interact co-evolutionarily are punctually identified (Janzen, 1980);
b. *diffuse* or networked co-evolution—the two species that co-evolving interact cannot be identified precisely or can be identified only as groups of species (Gilbert, 1975).

There are authors who point out that in the co-evolutionary process, there must be at least one evolving species (of the two interacting species), otherwise we are dealing with a simple process of adaptation (including mutual adaptation[38]) (Kallis & Norgaard, 2010).[39] In any case, it seems that there is an (intrinsic) logic of the process of co-evolution, which, on the one hand, ensures the intelligibility (i.e., the possibility of describing in the form of a behavioural pattern) of this process, and, on the other hand, ensures the explanation (i.e., the causal description of the process) (Porter, 2006).

Six types of co-evolutionary mechanisms are discussed in the literature, named by putting together the terms that designate the two species (identified punctually) engaged in the co-evolutionary process (Kallis & Norgaard, 2010):

1. biological co-evolution;
2. social co-evolution;[40]
3. gene-culture co-evolution;
4. biological-social co-evolution;
5. social-ecological co-evolution.

Since, tangentially, co-evolution (and even the mechanism of co-evolution) has already been mentioned before, we choose to focus our attention, in what follows, on co-evolution in the financial market. This type of co-evolution falls, from the perspective of the typology presented above, into the category of social co-evolution, the sub-category of economic co-evolution, the type of financial co-evolution and the species co-evolution of the financial market (or, more precisely, of co-evolution *on* the financial market).

The Concept of Evolution in the Financial Market

Any evolutionary process involves a system, called ***adaptant***, and another system, called ***adaptar***, so that the adaptant-system bears the impact/influence of the adaptar-system and, as a result, acquires adaptation features that, by accumulation, become factors of evolution of the adaptant-system (*Nota bene*: if the adaptant-system and the adaptar-system pass successively in the 'role' of each other, we are obviously dealing with a process of co-evolution). In this paragraph, we will discuss the concept of evolution on the financial market, which means that we will have to indicate (define, characterize) the adaptant-system and the adaptar-system on the financial market, and, on this basis, we will later develop the concept of co-evolution on the financial market.

We look at the evolution of the financial market mainly from the perspective of economic preference, namely, from the perspective of adaptive economic preference (see, in this sense, the content of FMAB-APH). In this context, we will resume, for the continuity and consistency of the approach, the main options we have formulated so far (including in FMAB-APH), and we will complete them with the theoretical needs to model the price-information-behaviour relationship on the financial market.

Genotype and Mutation on the Financial Market

In our opinion, in the financial market, the genotype is represented by economic preference, regardless of considering it as given/fixed/immutable (as in the case of the neoclassical approach, for example in the EMH model of the financial market) or as a variable, as (partially) proceeds BMH or AMH and how (totally) we will consider in the whole economy of this research. In this context, we consider it is exaggerated (and unproductive, since it represents a mechanical analogy) to look for, in this genotype, genes or alleles, by similarity with the case of the biological organism. That is why we will build our own particular logical model of the financial market genotype based on the following basic considerations:

- the preference is not of a physiological nature (as is the gene or allele) although it is, of course, strongly biologically conditioned—the preference can exist only in the human individual;[41]
- consequently, the preference is of a psychological nature, which means that any 'genes' or 'alleles' of the preference must be sought at this psychological level (but, again, we do not encourage such a mechanically translation approach);
- mutations that may occur in preference are, therefore, caused by both psychological factors (of memetic[42] type, e.g., herd effect) and institutional factors (of semetic type, e.g., legal norms);
- in fact, we consider that there are three categories of mutagenic factors in the case of the financial market genotype, that is, of preference:
  - The *idiosyncratic* factor—generated by the physical constitution of the human individual as carrier of preference, by his level of education, instruction, by the family environment in which her developed, in a word, by the habit (or habitus[43]); we can also name this factor a *genetic* factor (*Nota bene*: here the term genetic does not have its meaning in biology, but rather expresses the basic, fundamental, structural aspect of preference generating).
  - the *normative* factor—generated by the social contract (objectified in the Constitution) or, more concretely, by the institutional-legal framework of the society in which the human individual lives and functions; we can also call this factor as a *semetic* factor;
  - the *memetic* factor—generated by the behaviour of other human individuals on the financial market, in the sense that some behaviours of some individuals are imitated, partially or totally, simultaneously or late, as such or adjusted/customized, by other individuals;

- of the three mutagenic factors, we consider that the idiosyncratic/genetic factor has a random impact, the normative/semetic factor has a non-random (and even non-stochastic) impact (in fact, to a considerable extent, having a directed impact, sometimes even programmatic[44] one), therefore, deliberative/discretionary, while the memetic factor can be described (with certain methodological precautions) as having a stochastic impact (at the limit, even random), undirected, although cumulative, in a certain sense.

Additional Discussion

(a) *What* seme *and* semetic *are meaning?*

It is obvious that the gene belongs to the natural world (and logic), while the meme belongs to the cultural world (and logic). The meme (in Dawkins's primary meaning and in the next added features, as well) are bearers of non-formal information, as derived, by idiosyncratic inferences, by the economic actors based on the observed behaviours in the market. The 'efficiency' of extracting the information needed to ground the financial decision from memes is low enough since it is depending on the own ability of the agents to interpret (correctly or, equally, wrongly) the potential content of the meme. Consequently, either by induction from memes or by deliberatively imposing according to a governmental programme of regulating the market, some (also cultural) supra-memes are formalized in the positive law—such formalized supra-memes we call *semes*. The reason for such a denomination (*Nota bene*: seme comes from the Greek *sēmeîon*—in English *mark*—which essentially refers to the meaning) consists of the fact that the seme is publicly decoded information, so it is liable to be uniformly interpreted by all the economic agents involved. So, we can say, the gene has a natural genesis, the meme has a cultural non-formalized genesis, and the seme has a culturally formalized (i.e., normatively, so mandatorily based) genesis. Consequently, *semetic* means based on semes, or caused by semes, or according to semes.

(b) *relationship between* memes *and* semes

The genesis of semes uses two channels: (a) the persistent and common memes which work in the financial market (*Nota bene*: this assessment is valid for any type of memes, no matter the field of interest) based on the 'principle'—an alley must be built exactly on the lane already used by people to cross a park; (b) the governmental programme regarding the normative framework to regulate the financial market functioning. So, the mechanism of the relationship between memes and semes can be described in the following way:

- some memes acquire a normative statute, by formalizing them into the positive law—this is the regulating phase;
- some semes lose their normative statute, by dis-formalizing them from the positive law—this is the de-regulating phase.

Nota bene: it is possible that the same memes which were previously formalized (so becoming semes) be, subsequently, dis-formalized (so cessing to be semes). In such a case, what happens with the dis-formalized semes? In our opinion, they equally could either re-become memes (maybe with quite different informational content than that of the initial memes) or lose any meaning for the behaviour in the financial market.

(c) *Why is it (conceptually) justified to introduce the* seme?

As we have said elsewhere, any economic (so, including financial one) activity/action is an artefact, that is, causally depending on the people's evaluation and decision. Since the myriad of actions at the financial market level has a synergic impact on society as a whole (e.g., by the negative externalities—spillovers, spin-offs, by-products, etc.), it is needed to both preserve society's 'safety' and pre-orient the economic/financial general activity to the societal desired end (*Nota bene*: such an end is liable and does not always and punctually match on the individual, independent, desired ends). So, the necessity that the whole prevails on the parts, the semes genesis seems totally justified.

We have previously discussed the concept of propensity and its conceptual, causal, conditional relationship with preference (including adaptive preference). We will briefly discuss the involvement of propensity in the issue of financial market genotype:

- as we have already shown, the differences between propensity and preference are relatively small. If we did not take into account the insistence of some researchers (such as Popper himself, who introduced the concept of propensity in relation to the objective probability of the singular case/event), to demand that the propensity be invariable,[45] we could equate, semantically, propensity with preference;

- whereas, in the following, we intend to operate such an equivalence, it is necessary to make the following clarifications in support of that equivalence:
  - propensity is the direct and almost exclusive cause of the idiosyncratic factor of preference. In other words, the idiosyncratic factor is the most conservative (but obviously not completely immutable) component of preference. This assertion is quite obvious, considering the way in which the idiosyncratic factor was described/defined above;
  - based on the previous consideration, we could advance the hypothesis that propensity, understood as an exclusive and inalienable cause of the idiosyncratic factor, is the hard component (hardcore) of preference. A fundamental consequence of such a conceptual positioning is the following: it is impossible to generate/design representative (average) agents based on propensity, although, as we will see, such representativeness can be achieved at the level of the other two components (or the other two factors) of preference—memetic, respectively, semetic;
  - based on the proposal made, we 'save' the (relative) invariance of the propensity,[46] allowing, at the same time, the variability of the preference from the perspective of its other two structural components.

Based on the above, Fig. 2.3 represents the positioning of the components of the mutagenic factors, regarding the genotype of the financial market (i.e., economic preference), from two perspectives: (a) conservability (or degree of invariance) and (b) objectivity (or degree of predictability).

Phenotype on the Financial Market

The Concept of Phenotype on the Financial Market

Regarding the concept of phenotype on the financial market, as suggested above, our proposal is in line with the suggestion made by Andrew Lo (Lo, 2019) that the phenotype of the financial market, that is, the 'adult' able of viable reproduction, is the *trading strategy*.[47]

Trading strategy (TS) means a hypostasis (actualization, objectifying, publicly observable manifestation) of the economic preference of an economic agent. That hypostasis is manifesting by performing an individual transaction (IT).[48] The attentive and reflective reader has already found

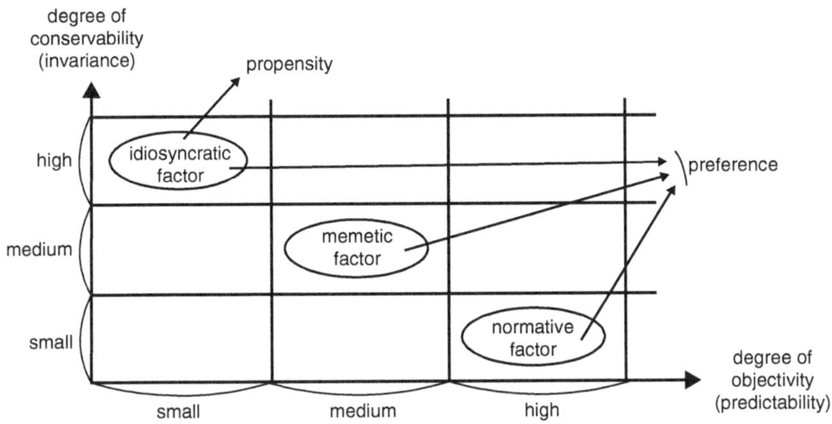

Fig. 2.3 Double positioning of mutagenic factors of genotype on the financial market. *Source*: Authors

that, by this definition, we have conceptually integrated the capability of the propensity (component of preference) to update itself according to and in the context provided by the environment, where, by the latter, we understand, in an aggregate way, the *cultural geodesic* of society (analogous to Popper's much more general concept—in fact, a universal one—of *situational availability*), discussed extensively earlier (FMAB-APH (Dinga et al., 2022)).

Therefore, the genotype (G) of the financial market is the preference (C), while its phenotype (F) is the trading strategy (TS). We will examine in a more analytical way the concept of financial phenotype.

- *first of all*, we need to establish that there is (or is not) the 'exercise capacity'[49] of the phenotype:
  - TS involves (from the human agent) a choice of a higher level of aggregation, more precisely, it involves the choice of a pattern, a master able to guide and 'deliver', in particular conditions, individual transactions that fall into that pattern;[50]
  - ignoring, for the moment, the fact that TS is chosen by a human agent,[51] we focus on the functioning, *per se*, of a TS:

    TS is able of choice, in turn, indeed, a TS works (or updates itself) only through individual transaction (IT); but ITs are simply (quasi-necessary) inferences from TS;[52]

- the fact that we are dealing with a pattern choice, obviously, indicates a high capacity of TS to function, on the financial market, as an 'adult' with 'full capacity to exercise';

- *second*, the logical relationship (causal, structural and functional) between TS and IT needs to be clarified:
  - since TS is the individual (phenotype) of the financial market, what kind of 'animal' is, then, IT? Our view on this issue is as follows:

    just as the biological individual (human agent) remains the same, although it has different manifestations on different occasions,[53] so IT represents a manifestation of TS in a given occasion, so that the TS concerned remains, however, within acceptable margins, the same;

    precisely the different occasions in which TS faces the environment (*Nota bene*: we will see that the environment of the financial market is the cultural geodesic), that is, the different ITs (which are exactly these occasions[54]) allow ITs to 'collect' the adaptations/mutations which will lead to the evolution of the species in question (we will see below that the species is, in our view, the financial market itself);[55]

    therefore, IT does not exist in itself[56] but is precisely the actualized hypostasis, in a spatio-temporal context, of TS;[57]

    based on the above, it follows, therefore, that IT is only the channel of interaction between TS and the environment (cultural geodesic),[58] not the very phenotype of the financial market;
  - the cause (formal and effective) of IT is TS; moreover, it can be said that TS is the model of rationality that allows the hypostasizing of TS in the form of IT;

- *third*, the following problem arises, at the same time logical, epistemological and methodological: whether preference (including its 'hard' component—propensity) is, as we agreed, responsible for choosing TS, and this choice is made by the human individual[59] (economic agent), what is the relationship between the human individual and the financial individual?[60] Our solution in this matter is as follows:
  - as in the case of Luhmann's theory, the human agent will be ignored throughout the procedural chain from the moment when TS was chosen until the moment when the mutagenic impact occurs; throughout this temporal and phenomenological course, the only entity that interests us is the financial individual, that is, TS;

- when, through IT, TS is confronted with refutations from the environment (in our case, this is, as we have shown, cultural geodesic, respectively, other TSs), then these refutations affect the preference (see the three mutagenic factors represented in Fig. 2.3);
- any of the three mutagenic factors can influence the preference;[61]
- the actually supported/integrated mutation by the preference[62] has as a direct effect the modification of the TS, that is, the phenotype, in the next cycle of use of the TS in question;[63]
- therefore, what the environment (cultural geodesic, respectively other TSs) selects, that is, TS, is constituted in stages of the evolution of the financial market; the explanation for this assertion is as follows:

  the financial market represents the set of all TSs that operate in a spatio-temporal context, that is, of all particular financial markets;[64]

  the fact that we consider the financial market to be made up of all the TSs, and not of all the ITs, is significant because ITs do not represent individuals but, as we have shown before, only hypostases of manifestation of the genuine financial individuals;

  thus, the relationship between propensity, preference, TS and IT can be formalized (illustrative rather than operational) as follows:

$$\begin{gathered}\mathbb{A}_{\mathbb{P}} \leftrightarrow \mathbb{P}_{\mathbb{A}} \\ \mathbb{P}_{\mathbb{A}} \leftarrow (\mathcal{P}_{\mathbb{A}}) \wedge (\mathcal{M}_{\mathbb{A}}) \wedge (\mathcal{N}_{\mathbb{A}}) \\ \mathbb{P}_{\mathbb{A}} \rightarrow \left\{TS_{\mathbb{A}}^{1}, TS_{\mathbb{A}}^{2}, \ldots, TS_{\mathbb{A}}^{n_{\mathbb{A}}}\right\} \\ TS_{\mathbb{A}}^{k} = \left\{IT_{TS_{\mathbb{A}}^{k}}^{1}, IT_{TS_{\mathbb{A}}^{k}}^{2}, \ldots, IT_{TS_{\mathbb{A}}^{k}}^{m_{k}}\right\}\end{gathered} \tag{2.3}$$

where

- $\mathbb{A}_{\mathbb{P}}$: human agent $\mathbb{A}$ who has the preference $\mathbb{P}$
- $\mathbb{P}_{\mathbb{A}}$: preference $\mathbb{P}$ assigned to human agent $\mathbb{A}$
- $\mathcal{P}_{\mathbb{A}}$: propensive factor (propensity) of preference $\mathbb{P}$ assigned to human agent $\mathbb{A}$
- $\mathcal{M}_{\mathbb{A}}$: memetic factor of preference $\mathbb{P}$ assigned to human agent $\mathbb{A}$
- $\mathcal{N}_{\mathbb{A}}$: semetic factor of preference $\mathbb{P}$ assigned to human agent $\mathbb{A}$
- $TS_{\mathbb{A}}^{k}$: trading strategy k generated by preference $\mathbb{P}$ assigned to human agent $\mathbb{A}$ ($k \in \mathbb{N}$, and $k = \overline{1, n_{\mathbb{A}}}$)

- $IT^{j}_{TS^{k}_{\mathbb{A}}}$: individual transaction j of the set of ITs allowed by trading strategy k assigned to human agent $\mathbb{A}$
  - *fourth*, there is the issue of the portfolio of TSs that a given preference can hold or allow or generate. Given the significance of the above notations, it would follow that a preference may be associated with a set (set) of TSs. This positioning is quite vulnerable, as it involves clarifying the way (or criteria) that allow the causal generation of that set of TSs; it seems much more natural, in our opinion, that:

    each preference should be associated with a single TS, so that the pressure of the environment on the TS (through IT) will lead (can lead) to causing mutations that will subsequently be subjected to the filter of validation or refutation by the environment. Therefore, the previous relationships will have to become:

$$\begin{gathered} \mathbb{A}_{\mathbb{P}} \leftrightarrow \mathbb{P}_{\mathbb{A}} \\ \mathbb{P}_{\mathbb{A}} \leftarrow (\mathcal{P}_{\mathbb{A}}) \wedge (\mathcal{M}_{\mathbb{A}}) \wedge (\mathcal{N}_{\mathbb{A}}) \\ \mathbb{P}_{\mathbb{A}} \rightarrow TS_{\mathbb{A}_{\mathbb{P}}} \\ TS_{\mathbb{A}_{\mathbb{P}}} = \left\{ IT^{1}_{TS_{\mathbb{A}_{\mathbb{P}}}}, IT^{2}_{TS_{\mathbb{A}_{\mathbb{P}}}}, \ldots, IT^{n_{\mathbb{A}_{\mathbb{P}}}}_{TS_{\mathbb{A}_{\mathbb{P}}}} \right\} \end{gathered} \tag{2.4}$$

Nota bene: This means that, from the perspective of the structure of preference (respectively, of proference), we will have another bijective correspondence, this time, between particular preferences and trading strategies (which, obviously, correspond to particular financial markets). However, compared to standard neoclassical approaches, there is no (and cannot exist) ordering or hierarchy of preferences, as they correspond to distinct trading strategies which, in turn, are incommensurable among them, precisely because the financial traded products/instruments to which those trading strategies are assigned are, also, incommensurable with each other. In other words, the particular preferences of the global proference[65] of an economic agent are positioned horizontally relative to each other. Let us examine the impact brought on the structure of proference by the changes in the set of trading strategies. In this regard, our opinion is as follows:

- there is no possibility to optimize[66] the portfolio of trading strategies (i.e., of traded financial products/instruments) because the particular preferences are not commensurable with each other;

- the impact of the changes suffered by a trading strategy on other trading strategies, if any (and which, of course, we cannot forbid by decree—in this case, it would mean proceeding in a similar way as the fundamentalist quantitativists of the neoclassical economic theory) is the result of its taking over by the free will of the economic agent, apart from any calculation of rationality;
  in this way, we accept the change of preference (on any of its particular components and through any of the three mutagenic factors) so as to allow the functioning of the concept of adaptive preference, which we have built under the name of *Adaptive Preference Hypothesis* (APH), as a theory/model of the financial market, in FMAB-APH.

Is There Phenotype Development in the Financial Market?

Our response is strongly negative in this regard, and this position implies an important and significant departure from the biological model and from the *tale quale* import of the mechanisms encountered in the biological evolutionary process. Once chosen by the preference of the human agent, a trading strategy (i.e., the financial market phenotype) is constituted (or is established) definitively and completely. So:

- although it represents the financial individual, TS is 'born' with full capacity to exercise, that is, directly in the adult stage; TS has no childhood, then reaching the adulthood. Therefore, TS does not go through a development process;
- being about the individual, obviously we cannot talk about evolution in the case of TS;
- therefore, TS, once generated (or allowed) by preference, manifests itself fully, immediately and to its full potential;
- the manifestation of TS takes place in the form of generating ITs that actually operate in the financial market environment, that is, within the cultural geodesic;[67]
- the mutations suffered by the TS (through the IT channel) modify it, according to the filter of the environment in which that TS operates, and the 'accepted' changes, by the environment, reconfigure the TS in the next episode of use (i.e., of generating the ITs). As mentioned above, this process represents, from a financial market perspective, the reproduction of the individual called TS.[68]

Selection in the Financial Market

First, the type of phenotype selection must be determined, as it operates in the financial market. From the above, it is quite obvious that there is a mixed selection: natural-cultural.[69] We argue this assertion as follows:

- the human agent is subject (primarily—both ontologically and chronologically—and, probably, predominantly) to natural selection.[70] If its propensity, and therefore, its economic preference, generates TSs which, objectified by ITs, are rejected by the environment (both the natural environment and the cultural geodesic), then the human agent in question disappears physically/biologically, as a result of natural selection;
- of course, the above-mentioned case is less and less manifested (and even possible) in contemporary reality (except, perhaps, the areas of the planet where human societies are still very little or not at all technological), but it remains a theoretical possibility;
- the dominant component of the selection on the contemporary financial market is the cultural one. This is manifested by the filter exerted by cultural geodesic (as well as other contemporary trading strategies) on the peculiarities of ITs, and the effect of this filtering is as a mutation in the propensity/preference that generates the TS selection;
- in turn, this mutation will be (or not) accepted/validated by the environment, first of all, by its cultural component, that is, by what we have called cultural geodesic, respectively, by the set of other contemporary trading strategies.

Second, the selection criterion in the financial market needs to be clarified. The problem to be solved here can be formulated as follows: what is the filtering basis of TS? We make the following considerations in this regard:

- we will have to introduce a selection criterion in the financial market, as we have one in the biological field (*Nota bene*: in the biological field, the selection criterion is, as it is known, the *fitness*, that is, the degree of adequacy of morphological/structural features, and physiological/functional characteristics of an individual of the species in question, to the environment);

- from a terminological point of view, we prefer to use, in the financial field, the term fitness as well, but we will establish its characteristics that make it intelligible (and operational) from the perspective of the financial market:
  - as in the biological case (but unlike the case of neoclassical economic theory, with its *homo œconomicus* model, i.e., unlike EMH, for example), TS fitness is (at most) a *second-best* level of performance;
  - however, from a relative (or comparative) point of view, the *second-best* (or, as the case may be, the *third-best*) degree is assessed from all TS updates (i.e., from all ITs) that take place in the market;
  - this means that every fitness that is selected by the environment will be a result of the *maxigiven* type.[71]

Third, the significance of the concept of fitness on the financial market, that is, regarding the fitness of TS, needs to be clarified. We find the following considerations to be helpful:

- as with the biological case, the fitness of a TS must ensure its survival. For a TS, to survive means to be maintained as the output (or operational function) of the preference with which it is associated and, of course, of the human agent who holds that preference;[72]
- an adequate fitness of TS means a positive net income from the financial transaction. The meaning of this assertion is as follows: a human agent (i.e., a financial agent—the latter being represented by the TS itself) does not compare his fitness with the fitness of other human agents (respectively, with the fitness of that of other TSs[73]), but with own expectations or with their own possibilities to trade on the financial market;[74]
- therefore, a good fitness has the meaning of that gain generated by IT (in fact, by all the ITs associated with a TS) which 'qualifies' the further use (i.e., the 'genetic' transmission) of TS involved in generating that fitness.

Fourth, the measure of TS fitness in the financial market needs to be clarified. Obviously, the measure of a TS fitness is the economic (monetary) measure of the net gain that TS brings to the human agent concerned. An issue that arises at this point of the discussion can be formulated through a set of questions: (a) During what period should this net gain be measured? (b) Does any negative net gain invalidate the involved TS? (c) Is there a significant threshold in the case of negative net gain? Our opinion on these questions is as follows:

(a) theoretically, there is obviously no standard time interval after which the human agent will perform the TS fitness assessment; for different agents, this interval will vary according to the idiosyncrasy of each, which involves both personal temperament and some personalized rationality calculations. Therefore, in our opinion, there are only empirical answers to this question;
(b) here, we have an issue which, partly and collaterally, we have discussed before. The problem is subsumed by the broader issue of testability. In a sense, a TS is, logically and epistemologically, a hypothesis or conjecture that, through IT (which can be assimilated to an experiment) is subjected to empirical testing. As is known from Popper's theory of falsifiability, the refutation of a hypothesis invalidates without appeal (i.e., it has the character of logical sufficiency) the theory from which that hypothesis was inferred.[75] If we were to do the same, an IT that is 'refuted' by the environment in which the financial market operates (i.e., refuted by the cultural geodesic or by a set of other TSs) would have to 'falsify', *eo ipso*, the TS to which it is associated, that is, to indicate an inadequate fitness of this TS. We consider, however, that in this case we are not dealing with the problem of truth (in which a single case of refutation has the character of decisional sufficiency, i.e., of *experimentum crucis*), so we do not think that a single refutation is sufficient for 'falsifying' the TS concerned. It is up to the human agent to assess whether or not the financial individual (i.e., precisely the TS in the case), which is disabled from the perspective of fitness, should be eliminated[76] or adjusted;
(c) the answer to this question is related to the answer we have given to the immediately preceding question—such a threshold of significance is contingent in nature and depends entirely on the assessment of the human agent who manages the TS concerned. Therefore, in our opinion, from a theoretical point of view, it is not possible to provide a general (theoretical) solution to this question.

The Mechanism of Evolution in the Financial Market

We will first discuss the question of whether the mechanism of evolution in the financial market is gradual (cumulative) or saltationist (explosive). We make the following considerations in this regard:

- in biology, the cumulative versus punctuated (catastrophic, explosive) character of evolution is always given by factors exogenous to the genotype (in the case of mutation) or phenotype (in the case of selection itself):

Nota bene: it should also be noted that there is a significant probability (or significant propensity) for a mutation character to 'choose' the same selection character; thus, if a mutation is itself punctuated and the environmental test is a corroboration of that mutation, then the selection will also be punctuated, and the same reasoning applies if the mutation is gradual (i.e., it is relatively small in terms of impact on the phenotype). However, although a 'from office' reasoning could lead to the acceptance of a possibility of gradual selection, we consider that the probability associated with such a possibility is negligible;

- in the case of the financial market (more generally, in the economic/social field), we consider that the rule is the punctuated mutation (and selection, as well), and the exception is the gradual mutation (and selection, respectively)—the reason for this positioning derives from the economic process itself (and the financial one especially): a fast process, with harsh sanctions for inadequate fitness, extremely sensitive to small differences in fitness;[77]
  - therefore, to the punctuated mutation corresponds the punctuated selection, and to the gradual/cumulative mutation corresponds the gradual/cumulative selection (with the strongly asymmetric probabilities mentioned above);
  - as the selection of TS is a process carried out by cultural geodesic (or other contemporary TSs), but only through the evaluation (int erpretation/hermeneutics) made by the human agent about the preference that generated the TS in question, it follows that a cumulative selection of TS requires models of hermeneutic rationality at the disposal of the human agent. Since the realism implied by the adaptive preference hypothesis excludes the hyper-rationality of the human agent (hence, the super-sophisticated and logically cognitively super-performing models of rationality), fully results in the conclusion, already mentioned above, regarding the exceptional nature of cumulative selection in the financial case.

From the above, the mechanism of evolution in the financial market can be represented, synoptically, as in Fig. 2.4. Notes: *P*: propensity; *M*: memetism; *S*: semetism.

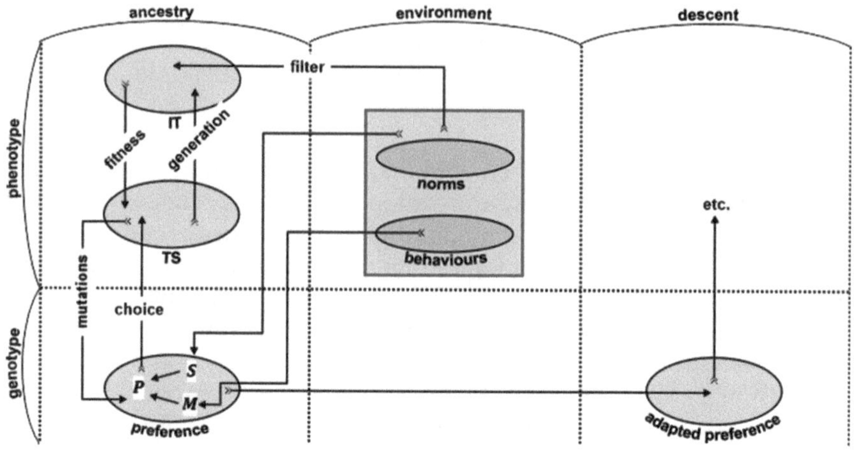

Fig. 2.4 A sketch of the mechanism of evolution in the financial market. *Source*: Authors

Additional Discussion
A laborious and very technical proposal regarding the evolutionary theory/model of the financial market is delivered by Bartholomew Frederick Dowling in his book entitled *Evolutionary Finance* (Dowling, 2005).[78] Below we provide a short look on the book.

(a) *some general considerations*
- the random (more exactly, in our opinion, the stochastic) is replaced by the deterministic, with the logical conceptual and methodological consequences—the type of distribution (which is not anymore Gaussian), the causality (which is not statistical anymore), the methodological approach (which is rather closed to chaos theory than to stochastic one);
- the driving purpose of the book is to elucidate the texture and the genesis of the information in the finance field (*Nota bene*: an issue ignored by the standard neoclassical models of the financial market, e.g., EMH);
- the basic conceptual anchor of the proposal is the analogy between the molecular replication and the information transmission in the financial field,[79] so the analogy with biology; in this context, the basic idea of the book is the way in which information emerges (and correlatively, what is the information's cost and how it influences the asset price);

- the general approach in the book is rather methodological than conceptual—for example, to get the financial phenotype (the asset price), the genotype (genome) of the financial market should be identified;
- Dowling proposes a behavioural chain in integrating the information into the final decision and action: *bytes/information-memes-themes-market sentiment-strategy-decision-action*,[80] in order to show how the information is evolutionarily generated in the financial market (and not stochastically);
- in our opinion, Dowling remains in the paradigm of optimality, which is contradictory to evolutionism (*Nota bene*: we think only sustainability is compatible with evolutionism);[81]
- the appeal to game theory of evolution is a bit artificial because they assume indefinite repeatability, but evolutionary mutations forbid pure repeatability—it's a repeatability of processes, not systems, in our view.

(b) *some analogies to our proposal*
- the variation of Dowling's strategy following information, by decoding it, is similar to extracting implicit information from observing behaviour (for us);
- both for Dowling and for us, information is constructed by the economic agent;
- as with us, informational contagion is accepted—memes, themes and trading strategies are so generated;
- as with us, the meme releases the latent information (called byte) into the behaviour.

(c) *some departures from our proposal*
- in our proposal the theme is overlapped on trading strategy;
- we think the themes (in our terms, trading strategies) must be formed not only based on memes but also on semes;
- what Dowling calls active investment, we call changing the trading strategy;
- with Dowling, the financial phenotype is the asset price, and with us, it is the trading strategy;
- with Dowling, there is a co-evolution between information and institutions, while with us, the co-evolution happens between information and behaviour;
- it is accepted that the market is driven by information (we believe by behaviour);

- for Dowling, the genes are exactly the involved players/actor/agents, while for us the genes are the preferences (more exactly, the proferences—see our previous book *Financial Market Analysis and Behaviour. The Adaptive Preference Hypothesis*, Routledge, Francis & Taylor Group, 2022);
- Dowling introduces the (positive) laws—that is, the normative framework—in the so-called element of culture, but this way the memes are mixed with the semes. In our opinion, the semes are 'different animals', with different functioning than the memes;
- based on the behavioural chain *bytes/information-memes-themes-market sentiment-strategy--decision-action*, information is placed at the initial link of the chain, while, in our proposal, information is at the end of that chain.

(d) *other mentions*

- (probably) the analogy/connection between the financial market functioning and the molecular replication in Biology is, however, maintained too close (e.g., the analogy with the four biological nucleotides seems to be simply artificial, and we think it was not required in the book's logic, at least not in that direct way);
- Dowling admits that the analogy between molecular evolution and the financial market one is metaphysical, not physical—but, we think that, in this context, the (factual) testability of the conjectures enacted under the theory of evolutionary finance acquires some vulnerabilities (*Nota bene*: according to Popper, the factual falsifiability still must remain in the positivism territory);
- even if the molecular evolution (primarily, replication) is considered as being of metaphysical or physical nature, a problem with the analogy between this evolution and the evolution in the financial field strongly arises: the molecules have no free will, their replication (and evolution) is of necessary type, while in the financial phenomenology, mostly such a replication (and evolution) is contingent. *Nota bene*: of course, two factors act, in the financial field, qua necessity, namely, (a) the norms provided by positive laws and (b) the rationality models agents use for decision-making, but both of them seem not to be of majority in the financial behaviour.

The Co-evolution in the Financial Market

Co-species in the Financial Market

Preamble

The fact that natural evolution is not exclusively genetic and that there is also an epigenetic evolution (i.e., an evolution that does not use the genetic mechanism) has long been known in the literature.[82] Thus, for example, Dawkins proposes an epigenetic channel that he calls a cultural channel[83] (Dawkins, 1976) which is very similar to the concept (and term) proposed by us—cultural geodesic. Epigenetic evolution takes place at the level of phenotype, not at the level of genotype, which brings us to the idea (which we have previously expressed) of the massive presence (some authors believe that it is even a predominant presence) of Lamarckism (to the detriment of Darwinism) in the social evolution, so also in the evolution that takes place in the economic field, respectively, in the field of the financial market. It follows that, with regard to the genesis of culture, the idea must be accepted that this is not a by-product of genetic evolution, but a *sui generis* mechanism of evolution which is complementary to genetic evolution (*Nota bene*: see above the type of gene-culture evolution). In this sense, for example, altruism cannot be satisfactorily explained through the genetic mechanism of evolution, but within the epigenetic mechanism, more precisely within the gene-culture mechanism of evolution. In fact, some authors consider altruism to be an emerging phenomenon within this last type of mechanism (Gintis, 2011).

The Concept of Co-species in the Financial Market

We have previously presented (and argued) our option to consider the financial market as a species, and TS as the (financial) individual of this species. We have also shown that the strong meaning of the concept of co-evolution is that in which there are two clearly delimited species (so we are in the case of pairwise co-evolution) that interact in a given environment, so that both species are able (that is, have the potential) to evolve, either genetically or epigenetically, or, obviously, through a combination of the two evolutionary channels. We recall that, in the case of the financial market, through a terminological translation, we accepted as genotype the preference, and as phenotype the TS; so in this conceptual framework, analogous to that of biology, there is no need to distinguish an epigenetic path, separate from the genetic one, in this mechanism of evolution—but, obviously, the concept of the genotype of the financial market has a purely metaphorical meaning (compared with the biological case).

So, the question is: if the financial market is the species (whose population is constituted by financial individuals called TSs), what is the (its) co-species? In accordance with one of the ways of forming the co-species, we propose the cultural geodesic be considered as the co-species of the financial market. Therefore, we have the co-evolutionary pair FM-CG, where, according to the previous notations, FM represents the financial market and CG represents the cultural geodesic.[84] Our arguments for this proposal are as follows:

- by considering CG as a co-species of FM, we eliminate the logical incompleteness from Andrew Lo's proposal on the adaptive market (AMH) (Lo, 2019). Of course, Lo's intention to propose to the scientific community AMH forced him to consider the FM as an 'adaptable' species. The problem is that, as we have shown several times in FMAB-APH, that adaptation does not exhaust evolution, so an adaptive market is not a logical condition of sufficiency for a market to function in an evolutionary way. For such a paradigm,[85] it is necessary for FM to evolve, not just to adapt. Lo's problem is further complicated when we understand that the author actually considers FM as an environment for TS, so he is considering an adaptation of the environment to the individuals of a financial population;
- FM, like any social artefact, is generated and conditioned (structurally and functionally) by the social environment, that is, by the basic structure[86] of society, manifested explicitly and permanently by its normative framework, which falls into a more general framework (which also includes tradition, values, customs, etc.) that we can call habit (like Peirce) or habitus (like Bourdieu) or, as we prefer, CG;
- CG not only requires the adaptation of FM to CG coordinates but, at origin, 'governs' the very constitution of FM, as Popper's third world ontological entity. Therefore, the FM that exists at a given time, that is, more precisely, in a fixed spatio-temporal context, is that FM that CG allows, validates and thereby perpetuates (as a *sui generis* mode of intergenerational FM, by analogy with the biological world);

- at the same time, CG suffers, in turn, the impact of the adaptation of FM: as we said, FM is constituted by the totality of TSs that function in that spatio-temporal context. Economic criteria (especially the criterion of profit, i.e., the net gain from financial transactions) ventilate these TSs—some are abandoned, others are perpetuated, others are imitated, etc.—which makes both the formal and informal regulatory framework (which together form the CG) to take into account these events/facts, and to adapt, in turn, to the financial market, which, in the next cycle, will lead to a new adaptation of FM and so on;
- in conclusion, CG is subject to the impact of FM, from the perspective of adaptation, as FM is subject to the impact of CG. It is obvious that, under these conditions, we are dealing with two distinct species,[87] so we are in the pair-type co-evolution model (co-evolution with two punctual co-species).

Circular Causality in the Financial Market

Co-evolution obviously implies reciprocity, both causally and structurally functionally. In this paragraph, this essential aspect will be discussed from the perspective of the co-evolution of FM--CG.

We have seen that the concept of co-evolution means an evolutionary tandem, in which each of the (two) co-species adapts and influences each other. Previously (see FMAB-APH), the concept of reaction norm, the reaction classes, as well as the (logical and algebraic) conditions that must be met for the reactions in question to be fetal, that is, to be accepted by the 'partner' (in the case discussed here, by the co-species), were discussed in relative details. We will resume, from the previous study, the notation part, adapting it accordingly to the objective of this paragraph:

- RN_t^a : reaction norm of adaptant at time t;[88]
- RN_t^A : reaction norm of adaptar at time t;
- AS_t^a : admissibility sphere[89] of reaction norm of adaptant at time t;
- AS_t^A : admissibility sphere of reaction norm of adaptar at time t;

The adaptation process is, in fact, the integration (endogenization) of the reciprocal reactions of the adaptant and the adaptar based on the following conditions of validity:

$$(\text{i})\ RN_t^a \subset AS_t^A, (\forall) t \in N \tag{2.5}$$

$$(\text{ii})\ RN_t^A \subset AS_t^a, (\forall) t \in N \tag{2.6}$$

(iii) sequence of reaction norms of the adaptant consists of even indices of *t*:

$$\mathbb{RN}^a = \left\{RN_0^a, RN_2^a, \ldots, RN_{2k}^a, \ldots\right\}, \text{ with } k \in N \tag{2.7}$$

(iv) sequence of reaction norms of adaptar consists of odd indices of *t*:

$$\mathbb{RN}^A = \left\{RN_1^A, RN_3^A, \ldots, RN_{2k+1}^A, \ldots\right\}, \text{ with } k \in N \tag{2.8}$$

(v) general sequence of adaptation by reaction norms is as follows:

$$\mathbb{RN} = \left\{RN_0^a, RN_1^A, RN_2^a, RN_3^A, \ldots, RN_{2k}^a, RN_{2k+1}^A, \ldots\right\}, \text{ with } k \in N \tag{2.9}$$

Please note that the adaptant (marked with *a*) is the co-species that adapts, and the adaptar (marked with *A*) is the co-species that causally (but sometimes purely functionally) generates an adaptation of the adaptant. We will customize the notations to the objective of this paragraph (we will start with FM on the position of species and with CG on the position of co-species[90]):

- RN_t^{FM} : reaction norm of financial market at time *t*;
- RN_t^{CG} : reaction norm of cultural geodesic at time *t*;
- AS_t^{FM} : admissibility sphere of reaction norm of FM at time *t*;
- AS_t^{CG} : admissibility sphere of reaction norm of CG at time *t*;

The conditions to be checked are therefore:

$$(\text{i})\ RN_t^{FM} \subset AS_t^{CG}, (\forall) t \in N \tag{2.10}$$

$$(\text{ii})\ RN_t^{CG} \subset AS_t^{FM}, (\forall) t \in N, \tag{2.11}$$

(iii) sequence of reaction norms of FM consists of its odd indices *t*:

$$\mathbb{RN}^{FM} = \left\{RN_1^{FM}, RN_3^{FM}, \ldots, RN_{2k+1}^{FM}, \ldots\right\}, \text{ with } k \in N \tag{2.12}$$

(iv) sequence of reaction norms of CG consists of its even indices *t*:

$$\mathbb{RN}^{CG} = \left\{ RN_0^{CG}, RN_2^{CG}, \ldots, RN_{2k}^{CG}, \ldots \right\}, \text{ with } k \in N \tag{2.13}$$

(v) general sequence of adaptation by reaction norms is as follows:

$$\mathbb{RN} = \left\{ RN_0^{CG}, RN_1^{FM}, RN_2^{CG}, RN_3^{FM}, \ldots, RN_{2k}^{CG}, RN_{2k+1}^{FM}, \ldots \right\} \tag{2.14}$$

The main logical characteristics of the co-evolution are, from the perspective of the circular causality between the two co-species, FM, respectively GC, the following:

- the primary action (*Nota bene*: i.e., the unprovoked action/reaction) is produced by CG. The explanation is obvious: FM cannot appear and (even more so)[91] can only function in the presence of a sufficient minimum of norms (either formal or informal, or—as a rule—of the formal-informal mix type) which, in essence, institutes FM. Therefore, at time '0', RN_0^{CG} occurs;
- the functioning of FM (once triggered) will produce actions/reactions on the CG, either with regard to the existing regulatory framework or with regard to new rules that prove necessary for the improvement of the functioning of the FM. Therefore, at time '1' occurs RN_1^{FM};
- as a result of the production of RN_1^{FM}, CG reacts, in turn, by adjusting the existing normative framework and/or by completing this normative framework, so RN_2^{CG} is produced, and the process continues indefinitely;
- of course, from a logical and institutional point of view, the first reaction norms (related to each of the two co-species) have a great impact, but over time, as mutual adjustment (i.e., co-adaptation) regulates the functioning of the co-special system, this impact (relatively) decreases.[92]

A synoptic image of the circular causality between the two co-species—FM and CG—is presented in Fig. 2.5.

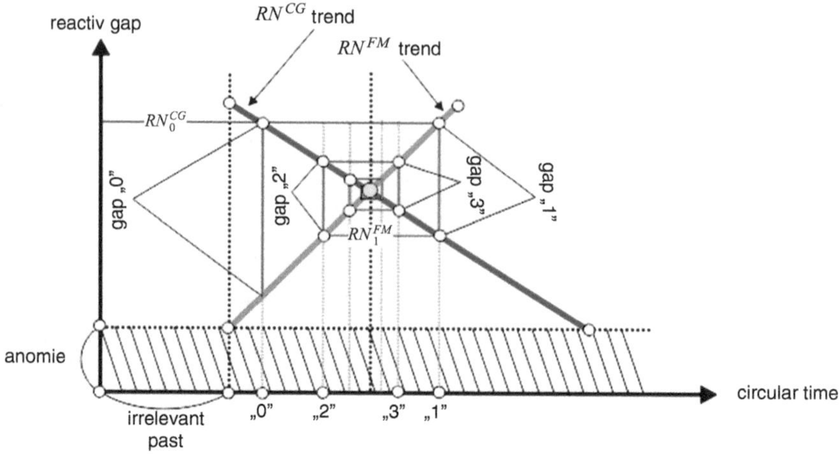

Fig. 2.5 Circular causality of FM and CG. *Source*: Authors

The Mechanism of Co-evolution in the Financial Market

Co-evolution in the financial market is, obviously, a co-evolution that takes place in the social field (more precisely, in the financial sub-sub-domain of the economic sub-domain of the social domain). Consequently, the co-evolutionary process takes place in all three directions mentioned above: (a) Genetic co-evolution (in the metaphorical sense of the term genetic, here), (b) memetic co-evolution and (c) semetic co-evolution. We will examine below the characteristics of the three channels of co-evolution on the financial market.

Genetic Co-evolution

The genetic co-evolution of FM-CG co-species refers to the mutations that the FM genotype, namely, the preference,[93] undergoes (including, to a certain extent, the propensity, which is the hardcore of the preference, as we said before) of the human agent. Analogously to the biological case of co-evolution, there are both endogenous and exogenous mutations of preference:

Endogenous Mutations

(d) On FM co-species

It refers to changes in preference (including propensity) as a result of psychological processes occurring in the human agent (*Nota bene*: which remains primarily a biological entity): development (biological, psychological and cultural) of the individual, the emergence of new beliefs, desires, patterns of life or of rationality, etc. Logically, endogenous changes in the financial genotype (i.e., the preference) are autopoietic processes.[94]

(e) on GC co-species

An important and difficult issue arises here: if CG is considered a species (more precisely, in the model we are discussing here, a co-species) we should develop the idea of the genotype and phenotype of this co-species. The following considerations crystallize our view on this issue:

- analogously to the way in which FM co-species was defined, CG co-species can be defined as the set of habits (or habituses), both codified and un-codified, in the formal normative framework and, therefore, included in the diffuse culture of the society;
- as a result, the genotype of CG would be nothing more than an essentialization of the genotypes (i.e., preferences) that exist and function in society (we are obviously considering only the financial sector, more precisely, only the financial market sector);
- if we consider only the preferences (with the assigned propensities) of financial type, then, of course, we obtain a financial co-species of CG;[95]
- therefore, to the question of what the genotype of the (financial) co-species is called CG, our answer is, the essentialization (either as a synergistic ensemble or as an intersection) of the preferences of human agents acting in the financial market or, more generally, in the financial field of social action;
- but how exactly does this essentialization arise? In our opinion, it already exists in the very basic structure of society, that is, in what is known as the social contract (which establishes this basic structure of society).[96] The codified normative expression of the basic structure of society is, of course, the Constitution.

In conclusion, endogenous genetic mutations concerning CG co-species are generated by the internal logic (causal, structural and functional) of the social habit (habitus) of the society in question. For example, if a tax rule refers to the compliance of the taxpayer with the payment of taxes to the public budget, then the internal logic of the CG requires the design and implementation of a correlative rule on the control (and sanction) of violation of the previous rule.[97]

Exogeneous Mutations

(a) on FM co-species

With regard to exogenous genetic mutations relative to the FM co-species, it is difficult, from a theoretical point of view, to delimitate this type of mutation from memetic or semetic mutations. In our opinion, exogenous genetic mutations on the financial market have an insignificant share, being completely marginal.

(b) on CG co-species

Regarding exogenous genetic mutations relative to CG co-species, we will say the following:

- any variation in the preference of human agents, manifested in variations in the selection of TS will affect the hardcore of the CG, that is, its genotype;
- as the CG genotype is an intersection/essentialization of the genotypes of the individuals in the population that form FM (i.e., of the preferences that generate TS), it results that an exogenous genetic mutation of CG refers to a mutation that comes from a TS;
- this is the qualitative sense in which we consider that the idea of exogenous genetic mutation related to the co-species called CG can (and should) be understood.

Memetic Co-evolution

Memetic co-evolution is, in terms of weight, intensity and frequency, the most relevant component of co-evolution on the financial market.[98] The concept of meme (Dawkins, 1976) refers to an evolutionary vehicle of selection by imitation of behaviour. Here, we have another strong confirmation of the conjecture (which we have made and which we maintain) regarding the evolutionary functioning of the financial market, namely, that there is a primacy—logical and often chronological—of behaviour over information.[99]

Logically, memetic co-evolution (*Nota bene*: as well as semetic co-evolution) is an epigenetic co-evolution, that is, it occurs outside the genetic channel/vehicle. The most important feature of memetic co-evolution is that it is exclusively endogenous, in the sense that it occurs only within the co-species in question but obviously not at the genotype level (as in the case of genetic co-evolution), but at the phenotype level.[100] We will discuss the main elements of memetic co-evolution for each of the two co-species of interest.

(a) on FM co-species

Within the FM co-species, memetism is manifested between the phenotypes of this population, that is, between trading strategies. A certain TS that gives favourable results will be observed (*Nota bene*: obviously, through the implicit type of information, discussed above, and which is derived, with the help of the resolutive competence of the human agent operating a certain TS, from the behaviour of other financial individuals which actually occurs on the financial market) and imitated by other TSs. Obviously, this implicit information is the prerogative of the human agent, not the TS *per se*, but, as Luhmann (Luhmann, 2012) does too, we will ignore the (indispensable) human agent and consider only the financial individual, that is, TS. Some specific considerations will bring further clarifications to the memetic co-evolution within the FM co-species:

- imitation of financial behaviour is the decisive result of a combination of rationality and emotion. This means that TS memetism is not purely a-rational, but partly rational—the human agent, who is emotionally anchored (at the level of belief) to his/her own preference/propensity, will examine, from the point of view of financial calculation, the opportunity to imitate a certain TS. Of course, as we have already mentioned (see, again, FMAB-APH (Dinga et al., 2022), which is focused on the adaptive preference hypothesis), the final decision will be a result between calculation and emotion;
- we think that a *sui-generis* filter of the observational competence of the human agent operating a certain TS must be accepted here as

well: the human agent observes only those TSs that have certain similarities with his/her own TS (or with his/her own TSs), that is, those TSs s/he can understand from the perspective of his/her own praxiology. Here, then, is another bright cone that affects observational competence, though not the other two competences of the human agent;

- from the ideatical perspective of the present book, this filter, which delimitates the observable TSs for the human agent concerned, is a kind of a pre-selection with a quasi-objective character that is operated by the human agent before s/he operates the actual selection on TS which will be imitated;[101]
- successful TS imitation will make that, over time, the 'alleles' of those TSs that are imitated by several human agents become dominant in the FM population, leading to the idea that, as with genetic selection and co-evolution, memetic selection and co-evolution at the FM level are of the population type as well.

One of the interesting problems in the case of memetic co-evolution at the level of FM co-species refers to *group selection*. We will make some additional considerations here:

- as we have shown on another occasion, the human agents operating on the financial market are not (of course, usually) natural individuals, but rather institutional individuals grouped in legal structures—firms, organizations, financial funds of various types and so on;
- in the sense described above, human agents act (i.e., have preferences) somewhat in a concerted manner, at the level of the aggregate structures of which they are part; in fact, we have groups of human agents;
- this means that the imitation (memetic takeover) of some TSs that prove to be (or are supposed to be) successful, is done at the group level;
- symmetrically, if the taking over (or not taking over) of a TS by the memetic mechanism results in the 'extinction' of a certain TS, this effect will affect not only a human agent but a group of such agents;
- we have the opinion, therefore, that, predominantly (more than in the case of genetic co-evolution in the financial market), the memetic co-evolution of the financial market is a co-evolution that involves group selection;

- the above conclusion leads to another (subsequent) conclusion, namely, to the fact that, within the group, phenomena of altruism, that is, of (economic) sacrifice of some human agents for the evolutionary benefit of the group can appear.

(b) on CG co-species

Regarding the CG co-species, the memetic co-evolution is also predominant, as in the case of the FM co-species. However, some important clarifications need to be made:

- the CG has, in general, two components: (1) a formal component (which will be discussed, in more detail, below) and (2) an informal component (which refers to values, traditions, history, education, family, etc.);[102]
- the memetic co-evolution of the CG co-species refers exclusively to the informal component;
- the way in which the memetic co-evolution at the CG level takes place can be described as follows:
  - *axiological imitation*: to some values that guide the behaviour in the financial market (i.e., directs the choice and realization of TS) can adhere other human agents who can thus adapt their preferences and, in many cases, even propensities, depending on these values and, as a result, they will select and apply other TSs than they have done before. In this way, there are changes in the CG—on the informal component, as we mentioned—which will change the share of some values in the CG of the economic/financial system in question, which means an evolutionary effect (in our case, of co-evolutionary type), obviously from a population perspective too;
  - *habuistic agglutination*:[103] some informal components of CG (e.g., traditions, rituals, etc.) may 'conquer' behaviours (and, as a result, may lead to TS selection) that would otherwise have been associated with other such elements. Thus, within a given CG, a memetic transfer is possible (mostly with a significant objective character) and, therefore, a memetic-type co-evolution of the CG, which self-catalyses.

A final issue of interest in the problematic of memetic co-evolution is the following: if memetic selection takes place within each of the two co-species involved (FM, respectively, CG), in what sense can we talk about co-evolution the two co-species (obviously, only from the perspective of the memetic channel)? We assume the following answer:

- any integration of a memetic impulse, by any co-species, represents a reaction (see the concept of reaction norm, discussed above) to the action of the other co-species, even if the process of adaptation/evolution occurs inside the population of each co-species;
- the validation of memetism within each co-species is done exclusively through the interaction with the other co-species. It can be said, with the necessary theoretical and methodological precautions, that each co-species acts as an environment for the other co-species, alternatively, so memetism actually functions as a process (channel) of co-evolution.[104]

Semetic Co-evolution

Semetic co-evolution[105] is the third channel of co-evolution on the financial market. From a conceptual point of view, semetic co-evolution represents the 'revenge' of Lamarckism on Darwinism, when discussing the evolutionary process in the social field (implicitly in the economic, respectively, financial one). Indeed, semetism involves, by definition, the intergenerational[106] or vertical/longitudinal transmission of characters acquired through the functioning of the phenotype—which is, as is easy to see, the exact content of Lamarck's theory of evolution.

(a) on FM co-species

As we have shown, the phenotype (adult individual) of FM co-species is the TS. A TS is a decision of a human agent on how (theoretically, operationally, organizationally, instrumentally, etc.) to conduct ITs on the financial market. IT is obviously carried out within the regulated framework (i.e., in the semetic framework) of the society in question. Therefore, the IT design will internalize this semetic framework, then, by validating/invalidating the IT, this effect will be reflected in the adjustments/adaptations that are made (or not, as the case may be) to the TS itself. The process of adjustment/adaptation of TS (i.e., the financial phenotype) as a result of the constraints exerted by the formal (codified) normative framework of the society represents the content of the semetic co-evolution of FM.

(a) on CG co-species

The semetic component of CG has increased in importance and impact (and, indeed, as share in CG) as human society has become more complicated, elaborate and deliberative. At the same time, the memetic component of CG is increasingly being monitored, controlled and adjusted by the semetic component.[107] In this procedural context, we make the following two considerations regarding the semetic co-evolution of the CG co-species:

- there are two channels of semetic co-evolution of CG:
  - *internal* (closed) channel refers to the internal logic of the formal regulatory framework on the functioning of the financial market. An institutional norm in the matter may require, from the perspective of internal functionality, another norm, of an administrative or corrective type. Thus appears a co-evolutionary process generated (causally, structurally and functionally) by CG itself;
  - *external* (open) channel refers to the pressure exerted by the actual behaviour of the FM as a result of the existing formal regulatory framework. Thus, if this normative framework is too restrictive, evasive behaviours of FM appear, and if it is too lax, incorrect (even illegal) behaviours of FM appear.[108] This way, the co-evolution of GG takes place under the rule of signals coming from FM (generally through memetic-type behaviours).
- CG co-evolution is not strictly sectoralized to FM co-evolution. As the CG covers the whole functioning of the society, the semetic part associated with the establishment and functioning of the FM is related to the rest of the CG, which refers to other compartments of life and social action. Thus, it can be said that there is an autonomous evolution (relative to FM) of CG, that is, an evolution that has an effect, directly or indirectly, on the functioning of FM. In other words, co-evolution itself can be said to have an internal component (co-evolution with FM co-species) and an external (or autonomous) component, which is associated with other sectors of society, except the financial sector (more precisely, except for the financial market).

A general overview of the co-evolutionary mechanism on the financial market can be represented as in Fig. 2.6.

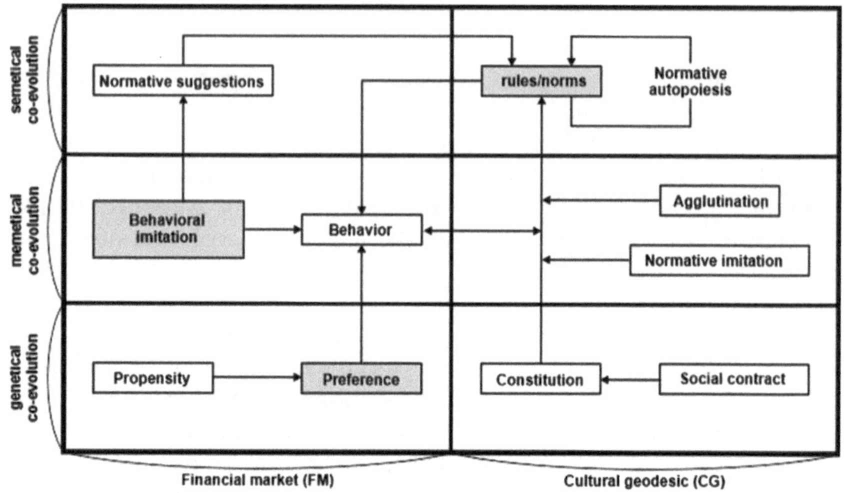

Fig. 2.6 Abstract scheme of the mechanism of evolution in the financial market. *Source*: Authors

Notes

1. The predicate of *living* is still controversial in the scientific community and even among philosophers, and the boundaries between living and non-living are becoming increasingly unclear and logically unconvincing.
2. It seems that Alfred Russel Wallace came to the same theory at the same time. As a result of his correspondence with Darwin on this subject, he persuaded Darwin to decide to speed up the completion of the elaboration and publication of his famous work, for fear of losing the priority of discovery.
3. It is accepted that neo-Darwinism appears after Ronald Fisher's contribution (not to be confused with Irving Fisher) regarding population dynamics (change in the relative frequency of genetic particles) (Dawkins, 2016).
4. There are, of course, alternatives to Darwinism: (a) Lamarckism; (b) neutralism; (c) mutationism; (d) molecular drift; (e) creationism, but they will not be examined in this study.
5. The allele is the shape that a gene can take (specific segment of the molecule DNA, i.e., deoxyribonucleic acid or RNA, i.e., ribonucleic acid, which determines the synthesis of a specific polypeptide chain and determines the phenotypic expression of a character), representing an alternative DNA sequence, with the same locus (physical position in the chromosome).
6. One important thing to note: genetic information is digital, not analogue, although, as it turns out, the brain function is analogue, not digital. (*Nota*

bene: that is why the assimilation of the human brain with a computer, which is digital, is a phantasmagoria of the writers of 'scientific' articles.)

7. Basically, there can be four categories of mutations: (1) genome mutations, (2) chromosome mutations, (3) gene mutations and (4) point mutations (mutation of a chemical base). In this sense, it is called polygenesis when a characteristic of the organism is generated by several genes, respectively, it is called polyphenia when a gene determines several characteristics of the organism.
8. Organisms endowed with cells.
9. Meiosis is the process of cell division that results in the generation of reproductive cells (gametes) in the case of sexual reproduction (there is also asexual reproduction in so-called prokaryotes, e.g., in bacteria). There are two types of recombination, namely, (a) intrachromosomal recombination (crossing over) and (b) interchromosomal recombination (chromosome dance). In addition, two other recombination processes may exist, namely, (1) genomic recombination and (2) recombination by transposition.
10. We remind you that, regarding the concept of development, it should be used only in relation to the individual (phenotype), while the concept of evolution should be used only in relation to the species.
11. The developmental process involves, as shown above, structural changes in the growth process of the individual (among other things, these structural changes ensure the reproductive function of the phenotype).
12. We remind you that the goal is a conscious and pursued purpose. It is not enough for the finality to be anticipated, not even predicted as such, it must be a conscious desirability.
13. The main role of the environment in the selection process of genetic mutations was not recognized from the beginning (neither by Carl Lineé, through his biological fixism, nor even by Lamarck, who was, however, an evolutionist). Only Darwin accepts that not only the environment shapes the species but also the species shapes the environment. In fact, as we will see below, the essence of the concept (and process) of co-evolution lies in this symmetry.
14. It is easy to see, in light of the above, that cumulative selection has the nature of a growth process.
15. I have mentioned, in previous studies (see FMAB-APH), the so-called punctuated equilibrium proposed by Gould and Eldredge (in their paper, *Punctuated equilibria: an alternative to phyletic gradualism*, in T.J.M. Schopf, ed., Models in Paleobiology. Freeman Cooper), (Gould & Eldredge, 1977). It seems, however, that punctuationists confuse gradual evolution with constant-velocity evolution (this is Dawkins's critique of Eldredge and Gould's position).

16. We will see that, in the social/economic/financial field, catastrophic developments are much more frequent than in the natural field (where, in fact, they are particularly rare).
17. We repeat that the word 'best' has a relative meaning to other contemporary and competing fitness, not an absolute one.
18. If the procedure is automatic, we call it an algorithm. Please note that this procedure (which usually has an anthropic significance) does not have to be applied by a cultural subject (human being), it can also be purely mechanical.
19. We all remember the anamnesis effect of the cake called madlen, in Proust (the character Marcel, from *In Search of Lost Time*).
20. For example, regarding the concept of world order, it can only be discussed in relation to a system on which the subject projects a gnoseologically generated principle of order, often *a priori* (i.e., without being inferred from the object on which it is to be applied).
21. As we have shown before, it is obvious that the input-output relationship can also mean non-causal transformation relationships, which transforms causal relationships into species for the genus called input-output relationships. Such non-causal transformation relations can be (a) nominal impulse transmission relations (which can also be called *functional* relations), for example, a trigonometric function; (b) coexistence relations (which can also be called *structural* relations), for example, an algebraic function, $y = f(x)$; (c) conservation relations (which can also be called *invariantive* relations), for example, a topological function.
22. The number of transformation operators depends on the nature of the system concerned and, generally, it is directly proportional to the degree of the complicatedness of that system.
23. By degree of complicatedness of an entity, we mean the degree of difficulty with which, in the context of the analysis (the state of science, the competence of the analyst, etc.), can be described its structure and functioning. Therefore, there is no link between the degree of complicatedness (of a system or process or mechanism) and the degree of complexity. Complexity is given only by unpredictability (as is the case, e.g., of the creation of the work of art), and unpredictability is given by the presence of freedom (with a more operational term for the concept of freedom, by the presence of free will).
24. The first two conditions can be easily demonstrated logically. As for the third (completeness), it must be assumed—in other words, it is the element of belief or arbitrariness in the logical construction of some mechanism.
25. Do not confuse the mechanism of evolution with the evolutionary mechanism—the latter applies the principles of evolution to itself, while the former applies itself to the principles of evolution.

26. In the case of mammals, erythrocytes (or haematite or red cells) do not have a nucleus, so they do not have DNA and cannot generate RNA.
27. In fact, there are two forms of reading information from DNA: (a) transcription into RNA and the formation of proteins which, in turn, influence the behaviour of the cell in question: horizontal or lateral transmission (to the phenotype), that is, we have development; (b) DNA copying/transcription: vertical transmission (to offspring): DNA-archive, that is, we have reproduction (*Nota bene*: reproduction + development + reproduction = evolution). Natural selection is essentially the result of competition in the vertical transmission of DNA.
28. Reproductive isolation refers to the fact that the individuals in question can only reproduce in a viable way (i.e., provided that the offspring can, in turn, reproduce) only among themselves (*Nota bene*: the most 'popular' case is that of the mule—mating between a horse and a donkey—the mule cannot have viable biological offspring).
29. Syntopic species: species that occupy the same physical area; synchronous species: species that occupy the same time 'area'.
30. Here only a general characterization is given, and later, namely, in connection with the financial individual and species, particular considerations will be developed.
31. If, after the first geographical separation, there is still the possibility that the two species resulting from allopatric speciation have areas of contact (including for reproductive relations), then we speak of *parapatric speciation*, that is, species resulting from sibling hybridization (Brener's Encyclopedia of Genetics, Second edition, 2013, pp. 222–224), (Maloy & Huges, 2013).
32. This mutual dependence/influence was mentioned by Charles Darwin in his famous and decisive work (already mentioned above), *The Origin of Species by Natural Selection or Preserving Favored Breeds in the Struggle for Existence*, published in 1861. The first Romanian edition of this work appeared in 1957, at the Publishing House of the Academy of the Romanian People's Republic, after the sixth edition of the original work, published (for the first time without updates) in 1902 at the John Murray Publishing House, London.
33. The concepts of adaptar (which refers to the environment) and adaptant (which refers to the system that adapts to the environment) were introduced in FMAB-APH (Dinga et al., 2022).
34. The most known case of co-evolution (intensely debated in the literature) is that of *prey-predator*. Regarding the mutual (reciprocal) selection, see also our conceptual proposals in FMAB-APH: adaptar and adaptant, respectively.

35. In fact, competitive co-evolution has several advantages (Simione & Nolfi, 2020) manifested through evolutionary innovations, with the following 'species': (1) escalation process, (2) directing the selection from the perspective of the competition, (3) identification/invention of new competitive methods and (4) solving, naturally, some difficult problems of competitive game theory. There are three types of progress of strategies in competitive co-evolution, namely, (i) local progress: against current competitors; (ii) historical progress: against past competitors; (iii) global progress: against future competitors. It seems that there is the possibility (not the probability!) of returning, cyclically, to previous strategies, so there is no linear progress of the strategies (Sinervo & Lively, 1996).
36. Diffuse co-evolution refers to the case where the two species that interact in the process of co-evolution cannot be punctually identified, so that the influences of all species on all species are taken into account. A particular case is the one in which one can identify (punctually) groups of species (a kind of mega-species) that enter the process of co-evolution (*Nota bene*: diffuse co-evolution could also be called co-evolution in the network; it should be noted that this diffuse co-evolution is predominant in the financial market).
37. The concept of biocenosis was introduced by Karl Möbius in 1877.
38. Please note that adaptation (including reciprocal adaptation) means changes that occur at the phenotype level but not at the genotype level, that is, as a consequence, those changes that are not transmitted intergenerationally through the process of reproduction (*Nota bene*: that is, in fact, the adaptation can be called, somewhat, barbaric, Lamarckian evolution).
39. The authors' assertion that co-evolution is not normative is curious. In our opinion, it is obvious that it is normative—genetic information is a norm, the reaction of the environment to the phenotype is also a norm (*Nota bene*: see the concept of reaction norm, discussed in FMAB-APH). Probably the authors in question have a narrow acceptance of the concept of norm—as the institutional norm or, even more restricted, the codified norm.
40. For example, in the form of supply-demand co-evolution (Lewin & Volberda, 1999), in which politics (or policy decision/policy norm) is considered an exogenous variable—that is, it is considered from the point of view of logical view, as an impulse or as a disturbance.
41. Similar to the consciousness that can exist only in the human individual body (*Nota bene*: the question of the possibility that the transhuman individual—but how transhuman?—or the fully cybernetized individual to have awareness or, more difficulty, consciousness, will, of course, be ignored in the economics of this study).
42. But, as we will see later, and directly, as the impact of the free will of the human agent.

43. As we will see, the idiosyncratic factor is a component of cultural geodesic that has been discussed in previous studies.
44. See, for example, where normative kinematics is influenced/determined by governance strategies or programmes.
45. Remember that the problem of inverse probability arises here.
46. We are obviously considering economic propensity (or, more precisely, the propensity of the human individual), not any propensity in objective reality.
47. We recall that, from the point of view of real economic production, the proposal put forward by Nelson and Winter in their 1985 paper: *An Evolutionary Theory of Economic Change*, published in Belknap Press, is analogous to ours (and Lo's, too) proposal, namely, routine can be defined as a productive strategy. In the same way, Niklas Luhmann proposed, in his work, *Introduction to Systems Theory*, published in 2012 by Polity Press, as a phenotype of the social system, the communication.
48. It is obvious here the suggestion of the connection with the concept of revealed preference, introduced in 1938 by Samuelson.
49. In civil law, by the individual's capacity to exercise is understood the (intellectual and mental) ability of that individual to exercise their rights and assume their obligations, in accordance with the regulatory framework of society. Similarly, by the 'exercise capacity' of the human economic agent will have understood his/her (intellectual and mental) capacity to exercise his/her rights and to assume the obligations in a free economy, in relation to his/her economic action (more specifically, with the action on the financial market). Further, by analogy, the concept of exercise capacity can be extended, as we do, in fact, to the financial individual, that is, to TS.
50. We do not forget that a TS always exists for trading a given (fixed) financial product/instrument that is traded on the financial market. In other words, between the set of traded products/financial instruments (more generally tradable) and the set of trading strategies there is a bijective (surjective and injective) relationship—it is very important to remember that this bijectivity is not limited to a certain economic agent, but refers to the integrated financial market (*Nota bene*: by integrated financial market, we mean the meeting of particular financial markets—each particular financial market corresponds to a certain trading strategy, i.e., a certain product/financial instrument).
51. As does Luhmann (see his paper, cited in footnote 48), when he ignores the human agent in the functioning of his phenotype in the social system: communication, although, obviously, communication is not possible without the human agent (a simple reception of a message—reception which can also be achieved by an automaton—does not transform the message, *eo ipso*, into communication, since the message needs interpretation, and the interpretation is only accessible to the human agent).

52. Thus, we avoided an accusation, presumably, of impersonalization of the IT choice by subordinating this choice to TS. Since TS is a choice of the human agent, IT is, *ipso facto*, a choice (of course, indirect, this time) of the human agent. Things are not different in the case of artificial intelligence: a machine, which learns, learns because the human agent has put in the program based on which the machine works learning instructions (or, in more subtle cases, self-learning instructions, e.g., for even modification of the learning program).
53. Here the term (and the concept) of occasion is that in praxiology, respectively, in modal logic with agents (see, e.g., the work of Romanian logician Cornel Popa, *Theory of description and language of mixed modal logics with agents*, Romanian Journal of Analytical Philosophy, 2009, or the work, translated into Romanian, in 1982, at the Scientific and Encyclopedic Publishing House, of the English logician Georg Henrik von Wright, *Norm and Action*), that is, it involves a chosen, fixed spatio-temporal context.
54. We suggest that the readers think of the term 'occasion' in its praxiological significance, as indicated by Tadeusz Kotarbiński.
55. We resume the observation, made in other places, that Andrew Lo proposes the individual/phenotype of the financial market as the trading strategy (as we do, by the way) and the financial market as the environment that makes the selection. But this way the species disappears: between the individual and the environment there is no evolving species. As Lo wants to say that the financial market is adaptive, we can assume that the market is evolving. Or, the market cannot be, at the same time, an evolving species and an environment that makes evolutionary selection! This problem is solved by us by introducing CG as the environment for FM.
56. Here the idea is that IT does not have an independent/autonomous existence (because it is inferred or inferable from TS, which is the model of rationality for IT) although, from a philosophical point of view (more precisely, from a nominalist perspective), only IT really exists, while TS is an abstraction, a general idea.
57. Let's adapt the famous example, from biology, that Lamarck uses: The giraffe is a phenotype/individual of the giraffe species (*Giraffa camelopardalis species*, from the *Giraffidae* family). At one point, a specimen of this phenotype is in a position to stretch its neck following high-altitude leaves to feed. If the nominal giraffe is the phenotype (equivalent here to TS), the specimen that extends towards the leaves, in a given space, at a given moment, represents a hypostasis of the nominal giraffe (equivalent here to IT). However, from an epistemological point of view, a delicate problem arises: the species is an ideal construct, it has no ontological status, instead the individual has an ontological status (see the old and subtle debate—

from logic, especially—called the dispute of universals, lat. *controversia universalium*). As we consider that TS is the financial individual, it follows, however, that it has an ontological status, and IT is the hypostasized manifestation of TS.

58. As we will show later, in the environment of the species called financial market, besides cultural geodesic, there are other ITs—the interaction between this given TS and this second component of the financial environment is also done at IT level—between ITs related to given/fixed TS data and ITs corresponding to these other TSs.
59. We remind you that once TS is chosen, the choice of IT is (necessarily) made by TS. The fact that, in reality, the decision, as a subjective fact, regarding IT, is also of the human agent is not relevant, because, as in any model of rationality (which can be assimilated to a system of axioms), theorems are logically necessary (i.e., mandatory), so the space of freedom for the decision of the human agent is very limited, at the limit, null, in the choice of IT.
60. Here and further, by financial individual, we will no longer understand the human individual acting on the financial market, but the phenotype of the financial market, that is, TS.
61. A more analytical development (and, especially from a more instrumentalist perspective) could establish a possible mix between the weights with which the three mutagenic factors act on the preference, as well as the thresholds or lags (or leads, after the case) involved in this process.
62. In our opinion, the preference behaves paradigmatically (more precisely, in the sense of the paradigm proposed by Thomas Kuhn—see his book, 1962/2012, 4th edition, *The Structure of Scientific Revolutions*, Chicago University Press).
63. The use of a TS in the next cycle is analogous to the 'production' of offspring in the biological model of evolution. In other words, TS evolves by integrating mutations that are accepted/validated by the environment of TS (i.e., by the cultural geodesic of the society or economic system in question).
64. Common sense would obviously indicate as financial individuals, exactly ITs, but in this case, TS should be the species. But then, what should be the status of the financial market? Of course, it should be the environment in which the species called TS evolves, but then what is the status of cultural geodesic? This should be a kind of supra-environment. Of course, it is not excluded that such a vision will be developed, but in our opinion, the proposal we have made is much more natural, except for the acceptance of the somewhat 'strange' status of IT.
65. See the Glossary for this term coined by authors. Also, see the logical and semantic very construction of this concept in the authors' book *Financial*

Market Analysis and Behaviour. The Adaptive Preference Hypothesis, Routledge, Taylor & Francis Group, 2022.

66. We ignore, of course, the well-known and much-awarded portfolio optimization models that lack the most important ingredient: logical, psychological and epistemological substantiation/justification—they 'jumped' directly to the mathematical formalization within *homo mathematicus*.
67. In the literature is already adjudicated the idea that, in the economic/social field, the fitness of the individual depends on the structure of social life (we call this structure with the syntagm cultural geodesic) (Gintis, 2011).
68. It should be noted that Andrew Lo, whose aspiration to revolutionize financial market theory is irrepressible, does not discuss such fundamental issues of a possible evolutionary theory of the financial market at all, as he (we have mentioned this several times) does not notice that, in the model it proposes (namely, the AMH model), it is missing the species that should evolve (perhaps, through adaptation).
69. The relationship between biology and the natural environment was initially discussed in the literature using the syntagm *nature-nurture* (*Nota bene*: the nature-nurture pair was introduced by Francis Galton, Charles Darwin's cousin). Subsequently, the syntagm *nature-culture* has been used, so that, lately (and under the influence of developments in anthropology, in particular), the triad *nature-nurture-culture* has been used. Obviously, the triad mentioned is the most realistic approach from an evolutionary perspective (*Nota bene*: here by the term nature is meant the biological component).
70. We ignore, here, without affecting the validity of the argument, the artificial (cultural) component of the selection of the human individual (e.g., through genetic engineering, sometimes under ideological impact—as is the case of eugenics).
71. The term *maxigiven* is obviously invented by us, based on the following reasoning: (a) the fitness associated with any mutation in the genotype is not maximum (it is not optimized) but, of course, it is not minimal (which would also mean an optimization) but it is simply what happens contingently in the spatio-temporal context in question. Therefore, the choice of the best fitness, which is a maximum, is made between variants/alternatives which, in turn, are neither maximized nor minimized, but actually given—so the concept just described should be called a *maxigiven*.
72. A collateral conclusion of this reasoning is this: there is a causal ascendant (or ontological primacy) of biological survival over financial survival. In other words, there is a causal ascendant (or ontological primacy) of the human agent over the financial agent (*Nota bene*: more generally, over the economic agent). If the human agent does not survive (among other things, and as a result of wrong TSs), the financial agent does not survive, either *ipso facto*. However, the opposite is not true: the financial agent (or

financial individual) may not survive (be refuted by the environment, i.e., by the cultural geodesic) but the human agent may survive in the form of another financial agent, that is, by changing his or her preference which, in turn, will select another TS.

73. We are not saying that this comparison/assessment does not happen or is not relevant (we remind, in this sense, that we have previously admitted a fitness that relates to the financial market champion), but that it is not the first criterion considered, at least psychologically.
74. We recall that, in the case of EMH, the reasoning is similar: the market is efficient (i.e., in the terminology used by us here, fitness is good, so acceptable from an environmental perspective) if the human agent in question (or, we can say, if TS, in our terminology here) makes a profit at the average level that the market allows (otherwise the market is inefficient—note the vulnerability of the terminology used by EMH followers here: the market is inefficient both when the agent makes a profit below market average and when it makes a profit above the market average; obviously the two meanings are viewed from diametrically opposite positions, but this is EMH).
75. We ignore here the objections that the Duhem-Quine thesis raises against the apodicticity of the Popperian criterion of factual testing (both for corroboration and for refutation).
76. It is clear that such elimination can only be done by adapting the preference (i.e., the propensity) that generated the TS refuted.
77. The informed reader immediately finds, at this point of the discussion, that the relevance of using chaos theory (or, equivalent, nonlinear systems theory) in modelling economic/financial events derives precisely from this high sensitivity of the economic process to initial conditions (in fact, this is the very definition of chaotic or nonlinear systems).
78. We transmit our gratitude to one of the reviewers (unknown for us) in the process of approving the publication of the book, who warned the authors about this book.
79. Strangely, however, Dowling does not provide any mention about the crucial concept of hypercycle, which is fundamental in the process of molecular replication as described by Manfred Eigen and Peter Schuster (1979) in their work *The Hypercycle. A principle of natural self-organization*, Springer-Verlag.
80. We could put the question: why does information lead to memes? This means the homogenization of behaviours—with us, behaviours produce information that does not necessarily lead to memes, but to own, often non-memetic, behaviours.
81. For example, optimality requires a first-best solution, while evolutionism (i.e., sustainability) always just requires a second-best solution.
82. See, among others, the work of George Price, especially his contribution to the formal modelling of natural selection through the famous Price equation (Price, 1970).

83. The concept of cultural geodesic has a broader meaning (and, at the same time, more applied) than that of cultural channel, because it implies an active role of this channel, analogous to gravitational attraction (*Nota bene*: see here the gravitational models developed both in economics as well as in sociology).
84. It is obvious to the attentive and reflective reader that we have here an overlap between the co-species called CG and the environment for the species called FM. But, as shown above, one of the ways to create co-species is to equate the environment of a species with a species, thus resulting in a pair of co-species.
85. In FMAB-APH, it is concluded that AMH is not a paradigm *per se* (more precisely, it is not a paradigm in the sense of Kuhn).
86. Here the syntagm 'basic structure' has the strong, powerful and foundational meaning of John Rawls's theory, as we mentioned before.
87. Needless to say, although we use the term species (respectively, co-species), we have in mind the acceptance of the social domain of these terms—it is, therefore, about symbolic species (respectively, co-species). (Deacon, 2007)
88. There is also the so-called problem of the first impulse (of the 'first bug'), so we will consider, by convention, that the first action is a kind of unprovoked reaction. Except for the first action—which can come either from the adaptant or from the adaptar—all the other interactions are actual reactions. Of course, just as the first action is not a reaction, neither is the last reaction an action (the reasoning is analogous to that used in networks or graphs for the first node and the last node in the network/graph).
89. The admissibility sphere is also called the sphere of fetality which means the property of a relationship (reactions) to be acceptable to the recipient (*Nota bene*: the meaning is perfectly similar to the content of the concept of fetality in the case of biological grafts).
90. It is obvious that, both logically and methodologically, it is of no importance which part we start with (here it is working, as it seems to us, a symmetrical functioning).
91. A pertinent and rather non-protocolary argument related to the standard positions, especially of neoclassical economists, on the primacy of the state (public factor) in the generation and maintenance of economic markets can be found in David Graeber's *Debt. The first 5000 years*, translated into Romanian by Art Publishing House, in 2020 (the work appeared in 2014, being published by Melville House Publishing).
92. It is probably not an exaggeration to consider, in this mutual adjustment process, the cobweb model used to describe the adjustment of the trading price to the equilibrium price (or, equivalent, to the natural price), as is the case in standard (i.e., neoclassical) microeconomics, as taught in universities.

93. Obviously, a preference that is not immutable, that is, one that is undergoing change, is nothing else than our adaptive preference (see FMAB-APH).
94. The autopoietic processes in the financial market will be examined in detail in the final part of this book when a hypothesis of the autopoietic (financial) market will be proposed.
95. Obviously, this is a purely methodological delimitation because, from an ontological point of view, the CG is a single one, so it acts on the different areas of social action from the perspective of a whole CG, not from that of some sectoral CGs.
96. According to the theory of social justice (see, e.g., John Rawls, *A Theory of Justice*, 'Al. I. Cuza' University Publishing House, Iași, 2012).
97. This is a typical case of correlating (based on the internal logic of coherence, consistency and completeness) the norm of designing public policies with the norm of administering the (norm) of public policy.
98. The freer a society is, the more extensive the memetic component of social (hence, also economic/financial) behaviour and vice versa, in the case of societies with a high degree of economic (and/or political) centralization, in which case the dominant component of this behaviour is the semetic one.
99. In this respect, our position is diametrically opposed to the one supported in EMH, where an irreducible primacy of information over behaviour is 'decreed' (remember that EMH refers to the informational efficiency of the market).
100. The phenomenon is analogous to that which occurs in the case of economic competition: they take place within the same 'species'—within producers/sellers, respectively, within consumers/buyers—never between producers/sellers, on the one hand, and consumers/buyers, on the other hand; between the two species happen negotiation (price, quantity, quality, temporality and other contractual clauses).
101. Elsewhere, the authors call this stage of selection as micro-selection.
102. The following aspect must also be specified: both the formal and the informal component of the CG are of an institutional type (they are, in the most general sense of the term, institutions or institutional norms). Therefore, it is not necessary to equate the formal character (which can also be called codified character) with the institutional character (which includes both formal and informal institutions).
103. The term *habuistical* is created by us starting from the concept of hub, more precisely, from the hub effect (Barabási, 2002). An interesting detail is that the hub effect was still intuited by Jesus Christ, who said, according to the evangelist Mark (Mark 4:25): 'for he that hath, to him shall be given; but from him that hath not, even that which he hath shall be taken away from him'. Although the canonical interpretation (which must obvi-

ously be politically correct)—see St. John Chrysostom's interpretation—is referring to spiritual 'goods' (such as faith in God), the assertion correctly expresses the effect of hub that is studied today in network theory. By a technical term, this is about the positive feedback or about networked positive feedback, called (by Eigen) *hypercycle*.

104. It should be noted that our paired concepts adaptant-adaptar suggest exactly this aspect: the adaptant and the adaptar alternatively play the role of selective environment for the other species.
105. Let us remember that, in our view, the seme is a codified meme, that is, a formalized meme. However, the semes have as their source not only memes, but also their own logic of formal cultural geodesic, for example, aspects of completeness of the formalized normative framework. From a praxiological point of view, however, the codifying of memes (as well as the symmetrical process—their decodifying) or, in other words, the regulation (as well as the symmetrical process—deregulation) is a very important source of variation of the formal (i.e., semetic) component of cultural geodesic.
106. But, obviously, also intra-generational, that is, horizontally/transversally.
107. In a (rather) approximate way and from a broader, political perspective, it can be said that the individual freedom of the human agent is transferred, to an increasing extent, from the memetic sphere to the semetic one.
108. For example, risky financial funds are less regulated than mutual funds, which makes financial transactions of the former be (or liable to be) illegal or incorrect.

References

Barabási, A.-L. (2002). *Linked-the new science of networks.* Perseus Books Group.

Darwin, C. (1859/2009). *Origin of Species by Natural Selection or Preserving Favored Breeds in the Struggle for Existence.* Romanian Academy Publishing House.

Dawkins, R. (2016). *The blind watchmaker: Why the evidence of evolution reveals a universe without design.* Penguin books.

Dawkins, R. (1976). *The Selfish Gene.* Oxford University Press.

Deacon, T. (2007). *The symbolic species: The co-evolution of language and the brain.* W. W. Norton & Company;

Dinga, E. (2020). *Macroeconomic Adjustment Through Normative Mechanisms.* Romanian Academy Publishing House.

Dinga, E., Oprean-Stan, C., Tănăsescu, C.-R., Brătian, V., Ionescu, G.-M., (2022) *Financial Market Analysis and Behaviour. The Adaptive Preference Hypothesis,* Routledge, Francis & Taylor Group.

Dowling, B. F. (2005). *Evolutionary Finance.* Palgrave Macmillan.

Eigen, M., & Schuster, P. (1979). *The Hypercycle. A principle of natural self-organization*. Springer-Verlag.
Futuyma, D. J. (1983). *Coevolution* (M. Slatkin, Ed.). Sinauer Associates Inc.
Gilbert, L. (1975). *Ecological consequences of a coevolved mutualism between butterflies and plants*. Coevolution of Animals and Plants, 210–241.
Gintis, H. (2011). *Gene–culture coevolution and the nature of human sociality*. Philosophical Transactions of the Royal Society B: Biological Sciences, *366*(1566), 878–888.
Gould, S. J., & Eldredge, N. (1977). *Punctuated equilibria: The tempo and mode of evolution reconsidered*. Paleobiology, 3(2), 115–151.
Janzen, D. H. (1980). *When is it Coevolution*? Evolution, 34(3), 611–612.
Kallis, G., & Norgaard, R. (2010). *Coevolutionary ecological economics*. Ecological Economics, 69, 690–699.
Kratochwil, A., & Schwabe, A. (2002). *Evolution, Coevolution, and Biodiversity*. In Frontiers of Life, Vol. Four: The Living World-Discovery and Spoliation of the Biosphere (Part Two), Editors: Elgene Box, Sandro Pignatti: Vol. IV (1st ed., p. 806). Academic Press, San Diego.
Lewin, A. Y., & Volberda, H. W. (1999). *Prolegomena on Coevolution: A Framework for Research on Strategy and New Organizational Forms*. Organization Science, 10(5), 519–534.
Lo, A. (2019). *Adaptive Markets: Financial Evolution at the Speed of Thought*. Princeton University Press.
Luhmann, N. (2012). *Introduction to Systems Theory*. Wiley.
Maloy, S., & Huges, K. (Eds.). (2013). *Brenner's Encyclopedia of Genetics*. Academic Press;
Porter, T. (2006). *Coevolution as a Research Framework for Organizations and the Natural Environment*. Organization & Environment - ORGAN ENVIRON, 19, 479–504.
Price, G. R. (1970). *Selection and Covariance*. Nature, 227(5257), 520–521.
Simione, L., & Nolfi, S. (2020). *Long-Term Progress and Behavior Complexification in Competitive Co-Evolution*. https://doi.org/10.48550/arXiv.1909.08303
Sinervo, B., & Lively, C. (1996). *The rock–paper–scissors game and the evolution of alternative male strategies*. Nature, 380.

CHAPTER 3

Binomial Co-evolution in the Financial Market—Preparing Issues

Introduction

This chapter will examine the general causal/correlation between information and price in the financial market and, on this basis, will provide an insight into the logical model of the process of co-evolution of information and price in this market (if and to what extent such a process exists or can be imagined with sufficient scientific credibility).

It will, of course, start with the acquisitions on the relationship between information and price in the financial market that have already been made (especially from the perspective of EMH, which builds its entire axiomatic, methodological and instrumental corpus around the concept of information), and from the results obtained in the field of co-evolution, examined in the previous chapter.

General Framework

In general, an observational variable (or an observable) is a variable that is (or can be) the subject of a record, either subjective or inter-subjective. For example, the finding of a change in the price of a particular asset by an individual (whether or not he is a participant in the phenomenology in question) is, of course, a highly idiosyncratic subjective record, but whether the change in that price is published by a public institution, it represents an inter-subjective registration (assimilated, according to those

E. Dinga et al., *Co-Evolution of Symbolic Species in the Financial Market*, https://doi.org/10.1007/978-3-031-31698-2_3

discussed several times before, to social objectivity—which is an objectification of inter-subjectivity). The recording in question can be of any kind: a perception, a psychological memorization, an external recording (written, sound, imaging, etc.).[1]

Based on the above, we can examine, from a more analytical logical perspective, the concept of observational variable in the financial market.

The Bright Cone

Earlier we have mentioned the gnoseological (and perceptional) restriction, called *bright cone* to which any observer/participant in the financial market is subjected—namely, that no one can observe/perceive/record only what his degree of instruction (general and specialized), and his expertise, experience or intuition allows him.[2] This is the main reason why, for example, in the financial market, there are (according to EMH, but also other models of economic systems) sophisticated actors and unsophisticated actors (the latter being also called 'noisy'—noisy traders—that is, actors who disrupt the 'rationality' of the functioning of the financial market or, equivalently, introduces noise into this market): sophisticated actors have a much wider and clearer bright cone than unsophisticated actors, because both experience and general training in the field of interest (including theoretical training) allows them to have access to a much larger field of view.[3]

Observational Competence

One can, of course, immediately make the connection here with the concept of observational competence, associated with the economic agent's ability to perceive the information mix available in the financial market. Therefore, the existence of the bright cone is manifested, from a praxiological point of view, in the sphere of observational competence of the economic agent in question. However, some important dissociations need to be carefully handled between the concept of bright cone and the concept of observational competence, which may have relevant consequences, especially methodological and instrumental, namely:

- the bright cone is always wider in scope than observational competence.[4] From a theoretical point of view, we could assimilate the 'bright cone' with a potential observational competence; respectively we could assimilate the observational competence with an actual bright cone. In any case, from the point of view of set theory, observational competence is a subset of the bright cone. If we denote the bright cone with $\mathcal{L}$ and the observational competence with $\mathcal{C}$, then we can retain the inclusion relation: $\mathcal{L} \supset \mathcal{C}$;

- in fact, a relationship of co-evolution (or, at least, of co-adaptation) can be retained between $\mathcal{L}$ and $\mathcal{C}$: $\mathcal{L}$ establishes (by action) a first determination (of quantitative type, but also of qualitative one) of $\mathcal{C}$, but the effective functioning of $\mathcal{C}$ will necessarily lead to the expansion of $\mathcal{L}$ (new experiences, learning, testing, etc. will expand the very sphere of $\mathcal{L}$—through a fetal reaction—which, in the next cycle, through the following reaction, will expand $\mathcal{C}$ etc.)[5]

Observational Variables in the Financial Market

Standard financial market models (EMH, BMH, AMH) recognize as observational variables (or simply as observable) only the informational observables.[6] As we have shown (and tried to prove) before, in the financial market, we must accept at least one binomial of information-behaviour and (at most, completely) a dominance of behaviour over information, but in no case a dominance of information over behaviour.[7] In this context, we have the opinion that, from an observational point of view, in the financial market we have a duality: (a) informational observables—to mark them with $\mathcal{I}$; (b) behavioural observables—note them with $\mathcal{B}$.

Informational Observables ($\mathcal{I}$)

These are the observables that the economic agent (interested, attentive and reflective—the condition of *IAR*) perceives/understands directly, without the need for interpretation.[8] In other words, the informational observable is recorded as such, primarily, it is perfectly intelligible, from the perspective of both the bright cone ($\mathcal{L}$) of the economic agent and that of the observational competence of that agent ($\mathcal{C}$).

As shown above, all known financial market models (notably the three so-called hypotheses in the financial market, mentioned above) focus on informational observables (EMH explicitly, BMH and AMH tacitly).

Behavioural Observables ($\mathcal{B}$)

These are the observables that the *IAR* economic agent records in two steps or in two phases:

(1) the *primary* phase—in which the economic agent registers a behaviour of the financial market;[9]
(2) the *secondary* phase—in which the agent transforms, by interpretation (based on his resolutive or hermeneutic competence), the observed/registered behaviour into information. We remind the reader that, in this phase, we are exactly in the case of acquiring implicit information, that is, in other words, in the obvious case of primacy (logical and, most often, also chronological ancestry behaviour over information).

In our opinion, at least from the perspective of variability, that is, the speed/intensity/quantity with which it changes in time and space, in the financial market, there is a massive domination of behaviour (i.e., of implicit information). Of course, it not necessarily results that this type of information (i.e., in other words, behaviour) is decisive in formulating the choice of trading strategy (perhaps not the most important, although the relative importance of the types of information is strongly contextually dependent), but it is, in any case, the most 'populated'.

Analytical Developments on Observables
On the basis of the above, we propose, in the following, a set of observables in the financial market, consisting of two sections: (iii.1) the section on informational observables ($\mathcal{I}$); (iii.2) the section of behavioural observables ($\mathcal{B}$).

Informational observables section ($\mathcal{I}$).

- *information-price* (p): price is the fundamental information of the financial market. This information essentially provides an exchange rate (in the broadest sense) between a monetary asset[10] (the currency legally circulating within the financial market in question) and a financial asset traded (or about to be traded) in the financial market, regardless of the degree of sophistication of that asset. Some important points are important in this regard:
  - the price is not to be confused with the value of the financial asset in relation to which it determines the 'exchange rate'. In this sense, when we use the term *price*, we always refer to the transaction price (past, current or anticipated), not the equilibrium price, that is, the value—to which the demand/supply tension of the financial asset in question leads it asymptotically;[11]

- however, it should be noted that any gain made (or expected, desired) by the trader in the financial market is based precisely on the difference between price and value: selling a financial asset at a price higher than the value, respectively buying a financial asset at a price lower than the value;
- for the time being, we will consider, as mentioned above, that the equilibrium price is identical to the value in the financial asset involved; the notation we will use for the equilibrium price is $\bar{p}$;
- the price, as an informational observable, is available, accessible and accessed[12] directly and as such, so, *qua* price. The economic operator finds this observable—in any possible way: public or private information, honest or illicitly obtained information, final information or information processed by himself[13]—always as such, that is, referring unambiguously to the price;
- therefore, the informational observable called price can be of two of the three categories of information discussed above: (a) *formal* (e.g., administratively set prices—it is not, generally, the case of the financial market, however, at least in the free economy case—as taxes rates on capital gain);[14] (b) *bound* (e.g., secret collusion protocols between large organizational players in the financial market regarding pricing,[15] and prices from confidential contracts or from strategies to be implemented);

- *information-non-price* (i): Information-non-price refers to any information that is not of a price nature (as explained above) but which (at least potentially) has the ability to influence the price kinematics;
  - like the observable price, the observable non-price can only be of formal type, respectively of bound type (it cannot be of implicit type);
  - in our opinion (summarizing, from an own perspective, some of the points of view expressed, in general, in the literature on this subject), there can be three categories of information-non-price:
    (a) information-non-price of *background*: It is the information-non-price that conditions, in general, permanently and imperatively, the entire functioning of the financial market: obviously, here is where all the formal information falls, so we will note this category of information-non-price with the same symbol with which the formal information was previously noted (i_x) (Dinga et al., 2022);
      - the information-non-price of background is *imperative* on the estimation that the economic agent makes regarding the price;[16]

(b) information-non-price of *event* (or occurrential information): This is information entered (into the financial market) by economic agents (individuals or organizations), either intentionally or unintentionally (communication errors, accidental leaks of information,[17] etc.), regarding aspects of one's activity—actions/abstentions (e.g., mergers, separations, bankruptcies and new financial instruments) expected/obtained results, trading strategies and so forth. In connection with the information-non-price of event, we also specify the following:
   - information-non-price of event can be personalized—a particular financial market player delivers this information (intentionally/tactically or accidentally)—or it can be impersonal—a certain event generates information (directly, as information, in order not to enter the area of behavioural observables);
   - information-non-price of event is ***decisive*** on the economic agent's estimation of the price;[18]
   - we note this category of non-price information with i_α;

(c) information-non-price of ***marketing*** (or, simply, marketing information): It refers to information (existing in itself, *qua* information) that is observed in the financial market in relation to a particular financial product, delivered by interested economic agents, with the purpose (either declared or—most often—hidden), to influence, in a 'white' way, the financial market:
   - 'white' influence on the market refers to the fact that this type of information-non-price is neither mandatory (such as information-non-price of background) nor decisive (information-non-price of event), but optional;[19]

Nota bene: A clarification must be made in relation to the imperative-decisive distinction (in the context in which the information-non-price of background was declared imperative and the information-non-price of event was declared decisive) (both from the perspective of the estimation that the economic agent makes on the price):

- from an economic perspective, the imperative character is weaker than the decisive character;[20]
- although it is imperative, the cost-benefit calculation can lead the economic agent to ignore the information-non-price of background, with the corresponding assuming of the sanction (visible hand) provided by the formal norm in question;[21]

- *a fortiori*, the information-non-price of event can be ignored, this time with the bearing of the economic consequences (regarding the profit) that the financial market (invisible hand) manages to the economic agent in question;
  - an interesting aspect of information-non-price of marketing relates to the self-reflective effect of the announcement in question:
    a 'self-fulfilment effect of prophecy' can occur, which is a kind of Oedipus effect.
    This effect can 'forget' its origin (especially if the act of producing information-non-price of marketing is not an honest one, trying, in fact, to mislead in the wrong and interested direction the trading strategies of competitors) and, thus, it can be exogenized in relation to its issuer, opposing it as an information-non-price of event.[22]
    the (possible) transformation of information-non-price of marketing into information-non-price of event, for the same economic agent, is a phenomenon that is not analysed at all in the literature, although it is a species of what, in the same literature, is known as the *law of the announcement effect*;
    a complete description of the mechanism for integrating the information into the price cannot ignore this phenomenon of self-transfer of information-non-price of marketing[23] towards information-non-price of event;
  - we note this category of information-non-price with i_β.

So, from a formal point of view, we can write:

$$\mathcal{J} = \{p, i\}$$
$$i = \{i_x, i_\alpha, i_\beta\} \tag{3.1}$$

Behavioural variables section ($\mathcal{B}$).

- *event* (e): is a change, occurring in the financial market or in connection with the financial market, located in the bright cone ($\mathcal{L}$) of the economic operator concerned, which is not a (commercial) transactional act or fact of another economic operator, identifiable as such (i.e., also being inside $\mathcal{L}$);

- the most important aspect of this behavioural observable is the risk of being confused with information-non-price of event (i_a). We also specify that the event information refers (also) to an event, but appears to the agent (i.e., it is perceived by the agent) as such, *qua* information—in any form, written, oral and so forth—while the event is, so to speak, an-informational,[24] meaning that it does not present itself to the agent *qua* (in the pure quality of) information;
- the location of the event in $\mathcal{L}$ is mandatory, as in the case of informational observables, because, in fact, the event that is not in $\mathcal{L}$ does not exist (it does not occur, it cannot exist) for the economic agent in question;[25]
- the following question can be asked: if the event can only exist in $\mathcal{L}$, will it have any effect (and by what mechanism) on the economic operator concerned? The following considerations express our views in this regard:
  by virtue of the network of connections operating in the financial market (in fact, in general, in the economy), an 'opaque' event for one economic operator will be (more precisely, may be) 'visible' for another economic operator;
  the economic operator who 'sees' the event in question, will update[26] his action in the financial market (through the implicit information thus obtained);
  if this updating of the action falls within the $\mathcal{L}$ of the economic agent who initially did not have access to that event, then, for the latter agent, we are no longer talking about the event, as behaviourally observable but about action (the second behavioural observable species—see below);

- *action* (a): is a change, produced within the financial market or in connection with the financial market, located in the bright cone ($\mathcal{L}$) of the economic operator concerned, which represents a (commercial) transactional act or fact of another economic agent, identifiable as such (i.e., also being inside $\mathcal{L}$);
  - from a terminological point of view, the observable so-called action refers directly to behaviour (just as the observable so-called event indirectly refers to behaviour);
  - the action is that (behavioural) observable which produces most of the information which the economic operator concerned will use of his own choosing;[27] the relationship (as a mix) between the three types of information (along the three informational mixes) is subject, of course, to the conjectures proposed in FMAB-APH;

- in principle, there is no filtering regarding the actions of the other agents participating in the financial market,[28] so that any action (which can only be indirectly related to the functioning or state of the financial market) is of interest to the economic operator concerned.

So, from a formal point of view, we can write:

$$\mathcal{B} = \{e, a\} \tag{3.2}$$

Figure 3.1 illustrates the relative incommensurability of the bright cones of the economic agents in the financial market, which leads to differences in 'visibility' between the agents, regarding the events produced on this market (with *EA/k* was noted the economic agent *k*, with e_i^k was noted the event e_i 'visible' from the perspective of the economic agent *k*).

Event e_1^1 is visible to EA/1 (because $e_1^1 \in \mathcal{L}^1$) but it is invisible to EA/2. In contrast, event e_1^2 is visible to EA/2 (because $e_1^2 \in \mathcal{L}^2$), but it is invisible to EA/1. The event $e_1^{1,2} \in \left(\mathcal{L}^1 \cap \mathcal{L}^2\right)$, so it is visible to both economic agents.[29]

Regarding the event-action relationship, discussed above, Fig. 3.2 gives a graphical picture of this important specification regarding the real functioning of the financial market.

A synoptic picture of the observables in the financial market (as analysed above) can be presented as in Fig. 3.3.

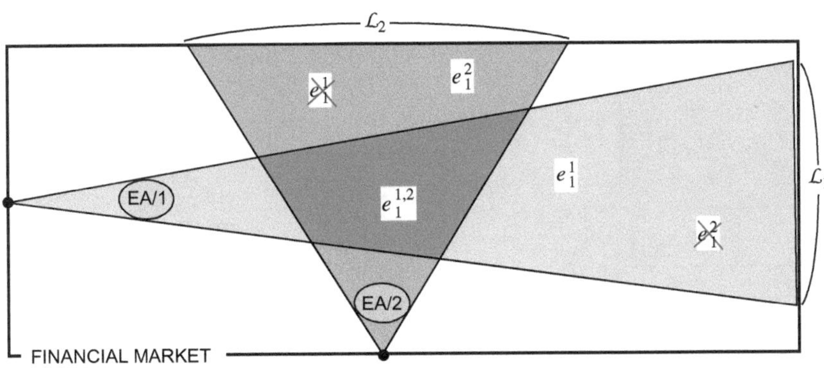

Fig. 3.1 Bright cones and the visibility/observability of events in the financial market. *Source*: Authors

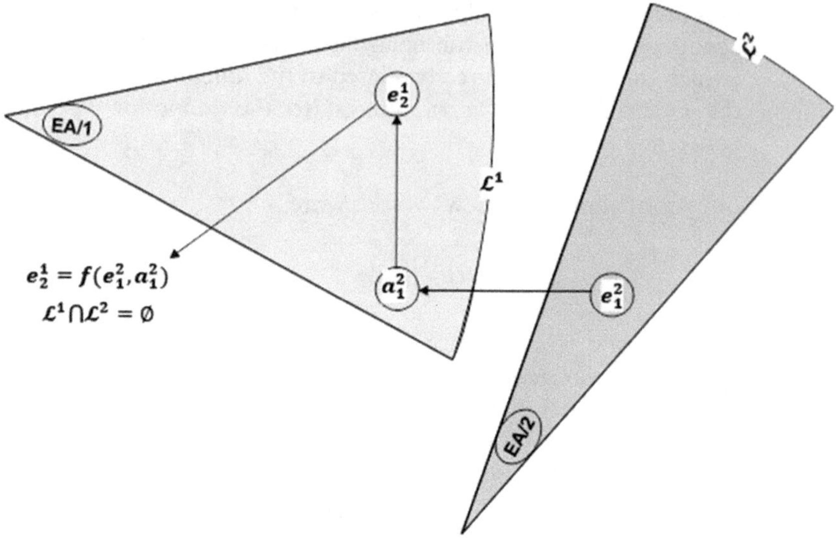

Fig. 3.2 Event-action relationship in the financial market. *Source*: Authors

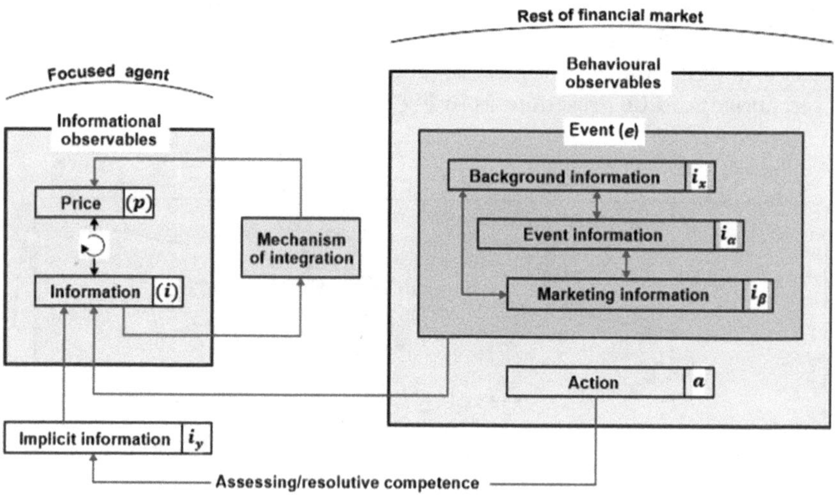

Fig. 3.3 Logical relationship between financial market observables. *Source*: Authors

Short Discussion

- both categories of observables (informational and behavioural, respectively) require treatment before being integrated into the decision/action (behaviour) of the economic agent concerned. This means that the economic agent, considered interested, attentive and reflective (IAR condition), will carry out a *sui generis* hermeneutics on both informational and behavioural observable;
- the hermeneutics applied to the informational observable ($\mathcal{I}$) is different (both in nature and in degree/intensity) from the hermeneutics applied to the behavioural observable ($\mathcal{B}$);
  - in case $\mathcal{I}$, only is needed to integrate the new information into the existing information base of the economic operator concerned,[30] while in case $\mathcal{B}$, two more phases/stages are needed (which we will refer in what follows);
  - the hermeneutic phase is quasi-automatic,[31] so the informational observable has, as a rule, an immediate effect, both from the perspective of time (without significant delays) and from the perspective of mechanism (without intermediaries, unmediated);
  - instead, the hermeneutics applied to behavioural observable is a reflective[32] one, being based on resolutive competence (which is under the 'aegis' of the active hypothesis—see FMAB-APH);
- it is necessary to describe, explain and (as far as possible) demonstrate three mechanisms that work in the perspective of the binomial information—price:
  - ($\mathbb{A}$) the mechanism for transforming[33] the behavioural observable called *event* into information-non-price;
  - ($\mathbb{B}$) the mechanism for transforming the behaviour observable called ***action*** into information-non-price for the economic operator concerned, respectively into an *event* for another interested, attentive and reflective economic agent (IAR condition) in the financial market (see Fig. 3.1);
  - ($\mathbb{C}$) the mechanism for transforming the information-non-price into price.[34]

Decisional Variables in the Financial Market

Observables are only a means to the economic operator's purpose—the purpose being, of course, to carry out the financial transaction intended to bring the agent concerned a profit (net income). Since, in this study, we are only interested in the price—information binomial (the crucial binomial of EMH,[35] as we know), we will not develop causal, structural or functional descriptions up to preference/propensity (this issue will be approached in Chap. 5, within the trinomial preference-information-price).

Therefore, the observables, both informational and behavioural, will have to be integrated into a decision (choice). The logical chain of this choice goes (as shown in previously) to the choice of trading strategy, which will generate, on an inferential basis, the set of individual transactions in the financial market, but we will here restrict the analysis to the mentioned binomial. In this context, preference (including its hardcore—propensity) is considered given/fixed. This working hypothesis is not different from the one used by EMH, but in the case of the present study, this is a hypothesis that will be eliminated when examining the preference—information—price trinomial. Also, the preference is not examined here, also from the perspective of the impact it may suffer from observables (observational variables), although, of course, later, exactly this impact will be the added value of our research—in contrast to the approach in AMH.

The Concept of Decisional Variable—Visiting the Rational Expectations Issue

The problem of the decision (at least from the perspective of neoclassical economic theory) is simply baroque, in terms of the multitude of studies and approaches. In this field, of course, the financial market is a 'leader', the financial decision benefiting from an irrepressible plethora of analyses, proposals, modelling and so forth. There is, however, a common denominator of all these approaches, a common denominator which obviously results from the conceptual basis of the approaches in question (*homo œconomicus* model), namely the *rational expectation*. Although we do not intend to develop the issue of rational expectations here (since they are not the subject of research), as it is a benchmark against which we will come up with our own proposal,[36] it is useful to outline the decision-making mechanism based on rational expectations.[37]

- as we have shown in Chap. 1 of FMAB-APH, the theory of rational expectations has its origins in the works of John Muth (Muth, 1961), resumed (without mentioning, of course, Muth—a not so rare practice in the community of economists!) by Robert Lucas Jr, in his macroeconomic work (Lucas & Sargent, 1981);[38]
- contextualizing the discussion in the financial market, the rational expectation will have to be seen from a price perspective (the main informational observable, as we have already shown);
- if we denote by p the market transaction price,[39] by $\tilde{p}$ the expected price (desired, hoped, etc.), and by ε a random variable that can deviate the transaction price from the expected price,[40] then we can write:

$$p = \tilde{p} + \varepsilon \tag{3.3}$$

respectively, E denotes the mean or the mathematical expectation:

$$E[p] = \tilde{p}, \text{as } E[\varepsilon] = 0 \tag{3.4}$$

- the theory of expected utility does not work in the personalized[41] exchange, but only in the impersonal one (i.e., under the rule of the 'invisible hand');
- the best-known model of rational expectations or expected utility is that provided by John von Neumann and Oskar Morgenstern, called the von Neumann-Morgenstern (VNM) model. We briefly present the fundamental elements of this model (which is considered a decision model, i.e., it is developed within the decision theory) (Chateauneuf et al., 2009):
  - utility is considered an axiomatic measure of preference;
  - the behaviour of the individual is considered to be a rational behaviour;
  - the decision is made on the basis of axioms concerning its preference and its mathematical properties;
  - the axioms (as well as the decision taken on their basis) take into account the consequences of the choices. If we denote by V_i the version of choice i, with $\succ$ the case of strict preference: $V_i \succ V_j$, as $V_i \succ V_j \leftrightarrow (V_i \succeq V_j) \wedge (\overline{V_j \succeq V_i})$, with $\succcurlyeq$ the case of non-strict preference and with $\sim$ the case of indifference: $V_i \sim V_j$, as $V_i \sim V_j \leftrightarrow (V_i \succcurlyeq V_j) \wedge (V_j \succcurlyeq V_i)$, then the VNM model works on the basis of seven axioms:

$$\begin{aligned} &V_i \succ V_j \\ &V_j \succ V_i \\ &V_i \sim V_j \end{aligned} \tag{3.5}$$

A2.
the relation of preference is transitive

$$\left(V_i \succ V_j\right) \wedge \left(V_j \succ V_k\right) \rightarrow \left(V_i \succ V_k\right) \tag{3.6}$$

the relation of indifference is transitive

$$\left(V_i \sim V_j\right) \wedge \left(V_j \sim V_k\right) \rightarrow \left(V_i \sim V_k\right) \tag{3.7}$$

the relation of indifference is symmetrical

$$\left(V_i \sim V_j\right) \rightarrow \left(V_j \sim V_i\right) \tag{3.8}$$

A3. the individual can also consider probabilistic mixes of versions: let be V_i and V_j; if we denote by p_i the probability of realizing the version V_i and by p_j the probability of realizing the version V_j, then we can construct a mixed version, denoted V_{ij}, so that:
$V_{ij} \equiv [V_i \cdot p_i; V_j \cdot p_j]$, with the conditions (Kolmogorov) $p_i \geq 0$, $p_j \geq 0$, $p_i + p_j = 1$. Then for $(\forall)p_i$:

$$\begin{aligned} &V_i \succ V_j \rightarrow V_i \succ V_{ij} \\ &V_j \succ V_i \rightarrow V_{ij} \succ V_i \end{aligned} \tag{3.9}$$

A4. be three versions, in the next global relation of preference: $V_i \succ V_j \succ V_k$; be the mixes: $V_{ik}^{\alpha} = \left[V_i \cdot \alpha_i; V_k \cdot \alpha_k\right]$, where $\alpha_i \geq 0$, $\alpha_k \geq 0$, $\alpha_i + \alpha_k = 1$, so that $V_{ik} \succ V_j$ and the mix $V_{ik}^{\beta} = \left[V_i \cdot \beta_i; V_k \cdot \beta_k\right]$, where $\beta_i \geq 0$, $\beta_k \geq 0$, $\beta_i + \beta_k = 1$, so that $V_j \succ V_{ik}^{\beta}$

Nota bene: This axiom is the equivalent of the axiom of continuity in the economic theory of general equilibrium.

A5. be three versions: V_i, V_j, and V_k, in the following relation of preference:

$$V_i \succ V_j \succ V_k : \text{then,} \left(V_i \succ V_j\right) \rightarrow \left(V_{ik}^{\alpha} \succ V_{jk}^{\alpha}\right) \tag{3.10}$$

A6. $\left(V_i \sim V_j\right) \rightarrow \left(V_{ik}^{\alpha} \sim V_{jk}^{\alpha}\right);$ (3.11)

A7.$V_{ij}^{\beta} \rightarrow \left[\lambda \cdot V_{ij}^{\beta};\left(1-\lambda \cdot V_j\right)\right] \sim \left[\lambda \cdot \beta \cdot V_i;\left(1-\lambda \cdot \beta\right) \cdot V_j\right];$ (3.12)

- based on the seven axioms, the ***utility function*** U associated with V_i is defined: the utility function associates to the version in question a real number having the following properties:
  (a) $\left(V_i \succ V_j\right) \rightarrow \left[U\left(V_i\right) > U\left(V_j\right)\right]$(the function U is monotonically increasing in relation to preference); (3.13)

  (b) $\left(V_i \sim V_j\right) \rightarrow \left[U\left(V_i\right) = U\left(V_j\right)\right];$ (3.14)

  (c) be $V_{ij} = \left[p \cdot V_i; \left(1-p\right) \cdot V_j\right]$ a probabilistic mix;
  of V_i and V_j; be V a version so that $V \sim V_{ij}$;
  then: $U\left(V\right) = p \cdot U(V_i) + \left(1-p\right) \cdot U\left(V_j\right);$ (3.15)

  (d) based on (a), (b), (c), then U is preserving itself related to the linear transformation operator : $\widehat{U}\left(V_i\right) = a \cdot U\left(V_i\right) + b$, with $a > 0, a, b \in \mathbb{R}$ (3.16)

- be V_j and V_k, so that $U(V_j) = 1$, $U(V_k) = 0$, then:
  (i) if $V_j \succ V_i \succ V_k$, then the probability p is determined, for which:

$$U\left(V_i\right) = p \cdot U\left(V_j\right) + \left(1-p\right) \cdot U\left(V_k\right) = p \cdot U\left(V_j\right) = p, \quad \text{where } p \in \left[0,1\right]; \tag{3.17}$$

  (ii) if $V_i \succ V_j \succ V_k$, then the probability q is determined, for which:

$$V_j \sim \left[q \cdot V_i;(1-q) \cdot V_k\right], \text{ that is:}$$
$$U(V_j) = q \cdot U(V_i) + (1-q) \cdot U(V_k) \rightarrow 1 = q \cdot U(V_i) \rightarrow U(V_i) = \frac{1}{q} \geq 1; \tag{3.18}$$

(iii) if $V_j \succ V_k \succ V_i$, then the probability γ is determined, for which:

$$V_k \sim \left[\gamma \cdot V_j;(1-\gamma) \cdot V_i\right] \text{ that is: } U(V_k) = \gamma \cdot U(V_j)$$
$$+(1-\gamma) \cdot U(V_i) \rightarrow 0 = \gamma + (1-\gamma) \cdot U(V_i) \rightarrow U(V_i) = -\frac{\gamma}{1-\gamma} \leq 0 \tag{3.19}$$

The Concept of Decisional Variable—Visiting the Adaptive Expectations Issue

Adaptive expectations are a more modest[42] theory in terms of the ambition to identify the 'correct' or at least favourable transaction price for the economic operator. The first use of this concept belongs to Irving Fisher (his 1911 work, *The Power of Money*). In 1956, Paul Sagan used adaptive expectations to examine hyperinflation. Milton Friedman uses this concept for both the consumption function[43] and the function that describes the long-term Philips curve.[44]

In essence, given a variable in relation to which a prediction value is sought for year, v_t^p, and whose value realized in year $(t-\tau)$ is known ($v_{t-\tau}^a$), then we can write the following algebraic relation regarding the prediction value:

$$v_t^p = v_{t-\tau}^a + \lambda \cdot \left(v_{t-\tau}^p - v_{t-\tau}^a\right) = v_{t-\tau}^a + \lambda \cdot \Delta v_{t-\tau} \tag{3.20}$$

where was noted with λ a prediction adjustment coefficient based on the error found in the previous prediction—the difference between the predicted value and the actual value achieved in the year $(t - \tau)$. Usually, $\tau = 1$, so the relation of the adaptive expectation is written:

$$v_t^p = v_{t-1}^a + \lambda \cdot \left(v_{t-1}^p - v_{t-1}^a\right) = v_{t-1}^a + \lambda \cdot \Delta v_{t-1} \tag{3.21}$$

As for the numerical value of the coefficient λ ($\lambda \geq 0$ and $\lambda \in R$), it depends on the hypothesis considered:

(a) $\lambda < 1$: prediction adjustment is prudent (under-confident): only a fraction of the gap between the previous prediction and the value at the time the previous prediction was made is taken into account to correct the new prediction.
(b) $\lambda = 1$: the adjustment of the prediction is confident: the whole value of the mentioned gap is taken into account in the correction of the new prediction.
(c) $\lambda > 1$: the adjustment of the prediction is contrarian[45] (or over-confident): the economic agent adjusts his new prediction 'over-bidding' on the previous error in the formulation of the prediction, so that the new prediction passes to the 'opposite' side.

For $\tau = 1$, the operation of the various values for λ is synoptically suggested in Fig. 3.4.

It should be noted that the issue of adaptive expectations is inconsistent (contradictory) with EMH, which states the irrelevance of any judgement

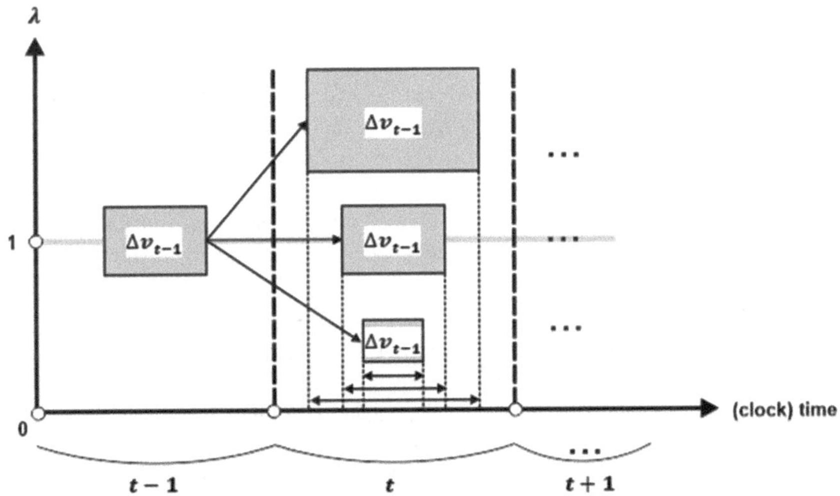

Fig. 3.4 Adjusting correction of the new prediction as a function on λ. *Source*: Authors

made on past values of variables (in this case, price) for the future value of those variables. Of course, *per a contrario*, EMH is perfectly compatible with the standard model of rational expectation (see the stylized VNM model above). Instead, AMH is consistent (or, at least, compatible) with the concept of adaptive expectations. Our own vision will integrate the results obtained in terms of adaptive expectations in the modelling (logical and quantitative) of adaptive preference, respectively of the trinomial preference-information-price (which will be examined later).

The Predicates of Decisional Variables

Analogously to the concept of observational variable (or observable), in this section, we will fix the concept of decisional variable.

In general, we will only discuss the issue of sufficiency predicates of the decisional variable (DV), not those of necessity.[46] In our opinion, the predicates that, through their simultaneity, generate a decisional variable in the financial market (i.e., they are predicates of sufficiency for that decisional variable) are the following:

- SP_{DV}^{1} : it is of a ***discriminatory*** type, that is, it is of the nature of a selection criterion. This predicate ensures that the variable in question (which aspires to the qualification of decisional variable) has the property (potential, capacity, vocation) to distinguish between opportunities.[47] However, the distinction can only operate if the criterion, once applied, has as certain effect, exactly this distinction/discrimination. There is no need to say more about this predicate, because, as shown above, once there is a selection criterion, preference distributes the probabilities that ensure the choice made be 'correct' for the agent in question. As can be seen immediately, none of the four informational observables discussed above is of the nature of a selection criterion;
- SP_{DV}^{2} : it is of the '***or-or***' type, that is, it makes dichotomous[48] 'cuts' in the set of opportunities (or in the set of accessible alternatives). This predicate assures that the application of the decisional variable establishes unambiguously (crispy) what is favourable (or indicated as such) by what is unfavourable. This choice 'without rest' leads to a high degree of operationality of the decisional-making variable in question, on the one hand, and to the cascading applicability of the decisional-making variable, to the point of isolating a single alternative/opportunity on which the final choice of economic operator establishes;[49]

- SP_{DV}^{3} : allows a ***cardinal*** (numerical) expression,[50] that is, ensures a direct commensurability (by quantitative comparison) between the dichotomous alternatives examined by the economic agent in order to make the final (operational) decision.

From a logical point of view, therefore, we can write:

$$DV = \left(SP_{DV}^{1}\right) \wedge \left(SP_{DV}^{2}\right) \wedge \left(SP_{DV}^{3}\right) \tag{3.22}$$

Defining of the Decisional Variable

For theoretical needs, based on the sufficiency predicates identified above, it is now possible to formulate the definition of the decisional variable in the financial market. We propose the following definition: ***a decisional variable is a discriminatory, dichotomous and quantitative variable, having the potential to, based on informational observables, choose the behavioural alternative with the best contextual value.***

In connection with the proposed definition, a few additional clarifications may be useful:

- the decisional variable operates on the basis of informational variables, as identified and described above;
- although preference (including propensity, as the hardcore of preference) has a driver role in the choice, from the perspective of the present research, we will consider that preference is given/fixed/immutable; therefore, the only variable on which the choice depends, through the decisional variable, is then the set of informational observables:

$$DV = DV\left(\mathcal{I}\right) \tag{3.23}$$

A Typology of Decisional Variable

The problem of the typology of the decisional variable in the financial market is now posed, in a similar way to the problem of the typology of the observational variable. Obviously, a typology requires, in advance, criteria for typology (classification). We propose the following two criteria: (a) the target of choice; (b) the method of choice.

(a) choice target (T)

It refers to the outcome/finality of the choice. According to this criterion, we consider that the following decisional variables can exist:

- (DV_T^1): decisional variable of result aiming the *trading strategy* (TS). As shown previously, the economic agent needs, to operate individual transactions,[51] a master-transaction, or a pattern-transaction, which generates, analogously to a model of rationality, individual transactions. Therefore, this decisional variable positions the economic operator in question in a sui generis model of rationality, which is both a constraint grid and a centre of inspiration for its actions in the financial market;
- (DV_T^2): decisional variable for ***individual transaction*** (IT). The individual transaction is a concrete-historical (spatio-temporal) manifestation of TS. Since, in our opinion, from an evolutionary perspective, TS represents the (financial) individual of the financial market (which, in turn, is constituted as an objectification of this financial individual), we conclude that IT represents a hypostasis of TS. More specifically, IT is the way in which TS manifests itself in relation to the environment of the species called financial market, that is, with cultural geodesic and other contemporary TSs—manifestation, in turn, of the situational context of the society (economic system, more precisely) in question, respectively of the population of trading strategies in operation.

It should be noted that, from a decisional variable point of view, the economic agent does not need anything else, his action in the financial market being exhausted by the taking of the two categories of decisions. The idea that the retained outcome decisional variables are not independent of each other should be repeated, since $DV_T^2 = h\left(DV_T^1\right)$.

A problem arises here, namely: is there a portfolio of TSs, respectively, is there a portfolio of ITs?[52] Our opinion, ***prima facie***, is that the TS must be unique for an 'episode' of the economic agent's action in the financial market (which, from an operational point of view, is always a particular financial market, that is, targeting a fixed product/financial instrument), namely that TS derived from preference. Instead, IT is usually a list (a portfolio), formed either on the basis of the past, that is, on the basis of an archive, or on a logical basis, that is, by derivation (or derivability) of IT from the assumed TS.

Short Additional Discussion

As it is known, in the standard models of the financial market (or the models already accepted in the scientific and praxiological community around the financial market—EMH, BMH, AMH), it is considered that the decisional variable, at least in the choice of IT, is the price.[53] We, on the other hand, consider that the price is not a decisional variable, but an observational variable of informational type. In defence of our option we make the following statements:

- the price itself (*qua* price) has no relevance in the choice, unless it is compared to a pre-accepted benchmark—for example, a price limit, either minimum or maximum[54]). But accepting a benchmark logically involves a comparison operation. So, in this process, we have an informational basis (price observable) and a selection criterion based on this informational observable—but this is the very definition of the decisional variable, as can be easily seen from those already stated above. Therefore, it is not necessary (nor possible, by the way) for the price to be, in itself, a decisional variable. Its acceptance as a decisional variable (i.e., of the target type) in the established financial market models logically ignores at least one implicit assumption (namely, the benchmark mentioned above);
- in the case (most often, it seems, even in the case of EMH which, *prima facie*, does not concern this case) in which the aim is not to obtain a price higher than the average market price, but a positive net profit (i.e., a price which, without necessarily exceeding the average market price, at least covers the costs of setting the price—search/information costs, risk-taking/hedging costs, etc.), we still have a benchmark that acts as an anchor[55] in the decision/choice: the mentioned gap between the price and the cost of setting the price;
- therefore, in principle, the observational variables are only the 'raw material' on the basis of which the decision/the choice is made in the financial market;

(b) choice way (*W*)

It refers to the way in which, technically (often even instrumentally), the choice is made (either for TS or for IT), that is, the decision is made in the financial market. In our opinion, from this perspective, the following decisional variables can exist:

- (DV_W^1): *better than market*—is the decisional variable that (usually by calculation[56]) integrates the information to determine whether, in that IT (assigned, of course, to the corresponding TS) the information concerned, 'promises' a price which will lead to a return in the financial transaction above the market average;[57]
- (DV_W^2): *better than relevant challenger*—is the decisional variable that (usually also by calculation) integrates the information to determine if, in the respective IT (assigned, of course, to the corresponding TS) the information concerned 'promises' a price that leads to a return in the financial transaction that exceeds the return obtainable (or already obtained) by the best performing competitor (namely, the champion of that market) in that financial market. Some clarifications need to be made about this decisional variable:
  - *first of all*, what is meant by a relevant competitor?

    the relevant competitor is a competitor competing with the given (fixed) economic operator for the same potential 'prize' of the financial market. Specifically, it is that economic agent who, if s/he would successful with his own financial transaction (his/her own IT), could (i.e., there is a probability or an expectation—sometimes even a quantitative calculation in this regard) reduce from the profit obtainable by the given (fixed) economic operator;

    of course, there are many competitors in the same market (here the term market does not refer to the financial market as a whole, but to the particular market of a fixed financial object) but, of all, the economic agent concerned (fixed) focuses on the best one, that is, to the one with the greatest potential to reduce its expected profit;

    therefore, a definition of the relevant competitor for a given (fixed) economic operator could be the following: *that competitor that competes in the same particular market and has the best chance to win;*[58]

- *secondly*, why is not the trading strategy *beating the market* equivalent to that of *being better than any competitor* in the market, and therefore better than the relevant one?
  as it is known (since EMH) to beat the market means to get a return above the average return that the market offers/allows; the problem is that an average, by definition, includes both higher than average yields and lower than average yields;[59]
  as defined above, the relevant competitor will certainly be (at least in the relevant target market) above the average of that particular market, so s/he may not be beaten even if the market is beaten;

Nota bene: we obtain, thus, a sui generis ordering of the modal (i.e., by modality) decisional variables, which means that, in the ascending order of the 'strength' of the decisional variable of choice we can write: DV_W^1, DV_W^2.

Functioning of the Decisional Variable

The functioning of the decisional variable refers to the (logical) mechanism by which the observational variables are used by the decisional variables in the choice. The synopsis in Figure 3.5 provides the main suggestions we want to make in this regard (*Nota bene*: according to the background of the research, the preference will be 'ignored' in the description of the mechanism—since we are, for the moment, within the binomial information-price, not in the trinomial preference-information-price, which is coming later).

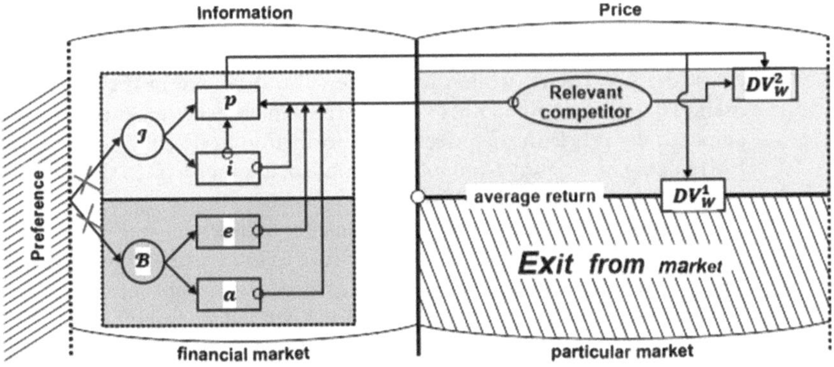

Fig. 3.5 Logical mechanism of the binomial information-price. *Source*: Authors

Notes

1. The concept of *observational* differs, of course, from one field of interest to another—so, for example, in quantum mechanics, an observable (i.e., an observational variable) is not an ontological entity—thing, property, or relation—but a mathematical operator that 'notices' that entity.
2. Obviously, the concept of bright cone can be extended to all human activities, including those of a practical nature—religious, moral, political, etc.
3. In fact, many studies have shown that one of the most influential causes of the financial crisis that began in August 2007 in the United States was the opacity (for many economic players in the financial market) of financial derivatives and other 'esoteric' instruments, such as packing high-performing loans together with non-performing loans, insuring and re-insuring loans so packaged, etc. However, this interpretation can easily be reduced, from a theoretical point of view, to differences in bright cones between participants in financial transactions.
4. From a semiotic point of view (but also from an evolutionary perspective), the referential of the bright cone is the genus for the referential of observational competence, considered a species.
5. The fact that the impact of $\mathcal{C}$ on $\mathcal{L}$ is uni-directed, only extends the referential of $\mathcal{L}$, never restricts (contracts) it, seems self-evident and, in fact, indisputable, because the praxiological action (combined with the practical action) of the economic agent acts only in the sense of its operational 'enrichment'—see the impact of the learning process. Here is a place for a para-phrasing or adaptation of Ronald Fisher's fundamental theorem on evolution (especially under the clarification of this theorem by Robert Price, who is the 'father' of the famous Price's equation of evolution).
6. Despite its name, BMH infers from behaviour the contents of the 'black box' also in an informational way. Although, as we have previously shown, information is the vehicle of *last* resort of the kinematics/dynamics of the economic phenomenon (including the financial market), it is not the vehicle of the *first* resort, while the last seems to originate in the behaviour itself. Therefore, neither BMH nor AMH (which does not explicitly and emphatically proclaim the priority of information in decision-making—as EMH does) move away from information, so, in other words, they remain informational (information-based).
7. We mention, here, the strongest argument: preference—the propensive cause of any behaviour—is too little sensitive to information, it is predominantly based on belief (namely, on what has been called propensity).
8. Although, of course, there is a need for a secondary interpretation: for example, the fact that the price of a financial asset has risen is perceived primarily, but whether or not that increase falls at some momentum is sec-

ondary information, which must be extracted from the agent concerned in a reflective way and often on the basis of a pre-existing model of rationality.

9. In fact, obviously, the economic agent records the behaviours of other economic agents that act *in* the financial market, but on the whole of the recorded behaviours, it can be said, with a little abuse of language, that it records the behaviour *of* the financial market. What, in this case, we have called as language abuse, in the case of AMH is a genuine expression, because this model of the financial market considers that the financial market adapts to the behaviours (more precisely, to the operation of trading strategies) that occur indeed (we have discussed elsewhere some logical inaccuracies of Lo's point of view in this regard).
10. As mentioned above with regard to the categories of economic flows in the economy (in general), the monetary asset expressed by price is, from a conceptual point of view, a financial economic flow, while what we usually call financial assets is, conceptually, a nominal economic flow. However, it is useless to introduce (and use) these unusual distinctions here in the terminology that is currently used in financial market issues, so we will use the names already mentioned in the main text.
11. Recall that the gravitational mechanism of the transaction price around the equilibrium price, with the tendency to the coincidence between the transaction price and the equilibrium price is called, in microeconomics, the cobweb model.
12. Here we evoke, of course, the three informational mixes established and examined towards this issue—see FMAB-APH (Dinga et al., 2022).
13. Here the term *processing* does not mean the finding of the price from non-price information (as we will see, that happens in the case of behavioural observables) but instead to the processing of some also primary price information, to determine other information (secondary, tertiary, etc.) that consists of (useful) varieties of the transaction price: for example, the average price, the current price, etc.
14. Although this observable does not represent a price itself, it is the basis for calculating the (acceptable) transaction price, because the latter must be judged (from the perspective of profit) after the taxation of profit (NOPAT: net operating profit after tax).
15. It is understood that the observable in question refers to the price agreed in the collusion, not to the very fact of the collusion—in the latter case, we would not be dealing with an informational observable, but obviously a behavioural observable one (more precisely, we are dealing with implicit information).
16. Non-price information of background falls into the category of public information that Fama is talking about in EMH, that is, information which, in this case, is fully, immediately and cost-freely integrated into the price that operates in an efficient market.

17. We do not confuse the accidental leakage of information with the tactical (intentional 'leakage' of such information, the latter case being part of a misinformation strategy—misleading competitors in the financial market—see the imported expression of *fake news*).
18. Like non-price information of background, the non-price information of event falls into the category of public information that Fama talks about in EMH, that is, information that, in this case, is fully, immediately and cost-freely integrated into price working in an efficient.
19. The predicate 'white' has a meaning analogous to the predicate 'white' in the phrase 'white lie', but—beware!—it may be exactly of the nature of the 'white noise' in the financial market, identified by precise means of spectral analysis of time series (previously discussed in several places).
20. From a legal point of view, it is, of course, the opposite.
21. Sanction which, as Gary Becker points out in many of his works, is simply taken into account (in his monetary terms—e.g., a penalty) when calculating the expected utility (obviously in the mathematical model of *homo œconomicus*). See Gary S. Becker's *The Economic Approach to Human Behavior* (University of Chicago Press, 1976), for details.
22. This reflective effect of the non-price information of marketing (which could also be called a boomerang effect) could be the subject of a more analytical examination of the operator (psychological, memetic or otherwise) that transforms non-price information of marketing into non-price information of event.
23. As is well known, one of the 'accusations' brought against EMH (both by direct critics and by indirect ones—the later as in the case of Andrew Lo) is exactly the absence of a description of a mechanism by which information is integrated (completely, immediately and without transaction cost) into the price.
24. This an-informationality of the event is a *prima facie* property, because, through the resolutive competence, the economic agent extracts from the event what we called implicit information.
25. Since the bright cones are different for different economic agents (for obvious reasons), it results, also from this perspective, that the economic agents are not (cannot be) homogeneous in the financial market.
26. We mention the three 'species' of the genus called updating: (a) eliminating; (b) introducing; (c) adjusting/modifying.
27. From the perspective, also, of its inclusion in the price, along the lines suggested by EMH—the theory which, as mentioned several times before, does not present, however, a mechanism by which information is integrated into the price, this integration/inclusion being, simply, decreed.
28. The state itself is considered, firstly and foremostly, a regulatory agent, not a player one. However, given that, for the needs of financing the budget

deficit, the state (through the Ministry of Finance) issues financial governmental securities (bonds) it will be considered among the 'other economic agents'.

29. Each of the economic agents in Fig. 3.2 is represented inside its own bright cone in such a way that they have a past and a future within the bright cone concerned. Obviously, in the past, the bright cone narrows to a point (i.e., the point, more precisely, the moment when the biological individual in question became an economic agent).
30. The problem of transforming information into cognizance or knowledge, although important (and subtle), goes beyond the objectives of this study, but the transformation phase in question will be retained (nominally) when it will be built the (quantitative) binomial information-price mechanism in the co-evolutionary process in the financial market.
31. As (the behaviourist) Kahneman would say, it is up to the system 1 of thinking.
32. In Kahneman's terminology, s/he will use the system 2 of thinking/decision, which is, of course, also the seat of (our) resolutive competence.
33. We will see below that this stage/phase of the information-price binomial is analogous (though not similar, having a different nature) to the stage/phase of translating information from m-RNA into protein synthesis, in the case of biological evolution.
34. The problem is the integration of the price (of the informational observable called price) in the price, more precisely, of the adjustment of the estimate of the transaction price (targeted for the envisaged transaction) when receiving a price type information. The following is a very important point: a price observable that does not refer to the target price (i.e., the price of the target financial object to be the subject of a financial market transaction) is a non-price information. However, if the informational observable of price type refers exactly to the price considered by the economic agent, then there is no need for an integration mechanism, because the price is automatically adjusted with its new received value.
35. It should be noted that neither BMH nor AMH goes beyond this binomial, although BMH is more firmly anchored in preference (examined, however, predominantly from an empirical perspective), and AMH is more firmly anchored in adaptation (*Nota bene*: the adaptation of the financial market, not of preference, as we did in FMAB-APH).
36. We recall that the EMH model is entirely built on the theory of rational expectations.
37. To remember that the theory of rational expectations is a reaction to the theory of adaptive expectations. From the perspective of our research objectives, the theory of adaptive expectations is more appropriate than that of rational expectations (see the concept of adaptive preference discussed in FMAB-APH). We appreciate that the 'return' from the theory of

adaptive expectations to that of rational expectations is an example of mathematization for the sake of mathematization, an effect of a pan-mathematical attitude which, apart from awarding Nobel prizes, did not contribute much to the advance in scientific (i.e., factually testable) knowledge.

38. Although both Muth and other analysts (e.g., Deirdre McCloskey) with whom we have 'met' before, point out that rational expectations are not to be confused with (and do not even imply) the rationality of the economic agent, in the present study we will not make this (subtle) distinction, although later, for reasons that will be mentioned at the right place and time, the distinction will be reconsidered.
39. p can be considered (at the limit) to be the equilibrium price ($\bar{p}$), generated by the relations between supply and demand in the market of a fixed/given financial object.
40. ε is considered independent of $\tilde{p}$. In our opinion, this is an oversimplification—because the random factors could be considered to be related (at least correlatively) to the expected price.
41. Personalized exchange is a 'complication' that will be examined later when the issue of price discrimination (discrimination of space, time, quality, gender, ability to pay, etc.) is discussed.
42. However, even with regard to rational expectations (seen as distinct and somewhat independent from rationality), the idea is accepted that they represent a modest positioning, from an intellectual point of view, of the economic agent in question (McCloskey, 1998).
43. It is about the consumption function based on permanent income (income considered throughout the working life—an aspect treated by Milton Friedman, for example, but also by Modigliani), not about the consumption function based on current income (the latter being known as the Keynesian consumption function).
44. The Philips curve refers to the causal (or correlational) relationship between inflation and unemployment rate. The short-term Philips curve is declining (with the unemployment rate on the abscissa and inflation on the ordinate), while the long-term Philips curve (precisely as a result of adaptive expectations) becomes rigid relative to inflation.
45. See the concept of the contrarian trading strategy, discussed in previous studies (for example, associated with the moments recorded in the time series of interest).
46. For the time being, we will consider that the predicates of necessity (predicates that 'appear' subsequently to the generative action of the predicates of sufficiency) coincide exclusively and exhaustively with those of sufficiency.
47. In the most general (and abstract) sense, an opportunity (not only economic) is a possibility that is in the area selected by the preference of the (actional/praxiological) agent concerned.
48. Exactly in the sense of the concept of distinction used by Spencer-Brown.

49. The informed reader immediately notices the analogy of this sufficiency predicate with the way decision trees are constructed (including the financial market). We remind you that by assigning probabilities (either frequential-objective or subjective) to the various 'branches' of the decision tree, the expected utilities can be calculated, as mathematical averages/hopes.
50. As it is known, a generic economic object can be associated with/assigned to two categories of measurements: (a) cardinal measurements—usually numerical values—which allow the quantitative comparison between alternatives; (b) ordinal measurements, which allow the qualitative comparison between alternatives—the most used method of qualitative comparison is the ordering (hence the name as *the measurement*), that is, establishing a hierarchy, usually just the hierarchies of preferences. We mention, in passing, the problem of the incommeasurability of preferences (or, more precisely, of hierarchies), discussed, from a logical perspective, by Kenneth Arrow, under the name of theorem of impossibility.
51. The term *individual transaction* means a one-time transaction (even if it is obviously repeatable—although, in principle, in economics no event is perfectly repeatable, but this methodological problem will be ignored for the time being), not a transaction that belongs to a given individual (biological/physical or organizational).
52. Please note that the meaning of the term *portfolio* here is 'civil'—a list known and accepted of positions for both TSs and ITs—having no the scientific significance held in the portfolio theory (see, for latter, for example, Markowitz, Sharpe and others in this regard).
53. The yield, which is sometimes also considered a decision-making variable in these models, can be reduced, both logically and economically, to price. Therefore, according to Occam's razor, we should not accept anything other than price as a decisional variable in the financial market. In fact, as we show in the main text, even the price *qua* price is not a genuine decisional variable.
54. The most common case of such a price-benchmark is where the latter (the reference) is the average financial market price for the financial object concerned. This reference is a floor-price: in order to 'beat' the market, the actual (or anticipated, as the case may be) transaction-price must be above the average market price. It should be noted that in the 'classic' case, the floor-price is, in fact, the cost of production.
55. Here, exactly in the sense in which Kahneman's researches in the behavioural economics use the concept of *anchoring*.
56. The calculation does not logically imply the exclusivity of the rational—there may be a rationality/emotion mix, different, of course, from individual to individual, in this calculation—see the triplet proposed by us in previous studies: E^1E^2P.

57. In the language of EMH (but also of AMH), this is to say that the decision that beats the market is made.
58. The problem of establishing these chances is obviously a problem that remains within the topic of choice—so, as we have already shown, the informational observable is not enough for the choice, but it needs a 'specialized' variable, that is, what we have called the decisional variable.
59. The trivial case where the average is equal to all the values involved in its calculation is out of the question (although it should be noted that this is exactly what EMH 'prophesies' when it addresses the topic of the informationally efficient market). Obviously, one can see here the justification for the analysis that Grossman and Stiglitz make of the fundamental axiom of EMH—in the so-called GS paradox—which we referred to in FMAB-APH. (Grossman & Stiglitz, 1980).

References

Chateauneuf, A., Cohen, M., & Tallon, J.-M. (2009). Decision Under Risk: The Classical Expected Utility Model. *Decision-Making Process: Concepts and Methods.*

Dinga, E., Oprean-Stan, C., Tănăsescu, C.-R., Brătian, V., Ionescu, G.-M. (2022). *Financial Market Analysis and Behaviour. The Adaptive Preference Hypothesis*, Routledge, Francis & Taylor Group.

Grossman, S.J., Stiglitz, J.E. (1980). *On the Impossibility of Informationally Efficient Markets*, The American Economic Review, vol. 70, no. 3.

Lucas, R.E., Sargent, T.J. (1981). *Rational Expectations and Econometric Practice*, Volume 1, University of Minnesota Press.

McCloskey, D.N. (1998). *The Rhetoric of Economics. Rhetoric of the Human Sciences*, University of Wisconsin Press.

Muth, J. F. (1961). *Rational Expectations and the Theory of Price Movements.* Econometrica, 29(3), 315–335.

CHAPTER 4

Binomial Co-evolution in the Financial Market—Mechanisms

Information and Price as Symbolic Species

So far, the examination of the information-price binomial has been done, from the perspective of current financial market models, in a standard way.

In the following, we will deal with the context in which both information and price are considered symbolic species in the financial market, in preparing the hypothesis: the co-evolution of information-price pair (or binomial information-price, or BIP) in the financial market.

Symbolic Species

Previously, both the concept of species and the concept of co-species have been characterized to a sufficient extent and from a general perspective. Obviously, the most well-known hypostases of the two concepts are those in the field of biology, that is, in the field of life (of living beings). Even in the case of the human being, as so much immersed in sociality and culture, it is, as a species, 'claimed', to a large extent,[1] from his/her biological status and natural origin.

Information and price are products of human action, more precisely, of the action of individuals (as such or as organizations, respectively) in the economic market (from the perspective of our research interest, the economic market will be restricted to the financial market).[2] It is obvious, therefore, that information and price are institutional (or, more precisely,

E. Dinga et al., *Co-Evolution of Symbolic Species in the Financial Market*, https://doi.org/10.1007/978-3-031-31698-2_4

conceptual-institutional) 'animals', being part, as we have shown many times before, of Popper's third world—objectifications of inter-subjectivity.

The Concept of Symbolic Species

Terence Deacon (Deacon, 2007) spoke systematically about symbolic species (with conceptual roots in biological species). Deacon treated, from a co-evolutionary perspective, but based on the results of research in neuroscience, evolutionism, linguistics, semiotics, the relationship between language and the brain.[3] Language and the brain have been treated as two species that co-evolve—overcoming the famous egg-hen paradox—by proposing a mechanism by which not only language is considered a function/result of the brain (standard case) but also the brain, in turn, is considered a function/result of the language. However, in fact, in our opinion, Deacon sees the co-evolution between the two symbolic species mentioned rather as a co-adaptation, not as a co-evolution properly, because it does not offer/propose an evolutionary or co-evolutionary mechanism as such, with the three fundamental moments known: random mutation, random recombination, cumulative (or, as the case may be, punctuated) selection. Although the three moments are evoked in the mentioned work (including the punctuated speciation), they are not put, in a cohesive theory, under the sign of genotype, respectively of the phenotype—that is, in a symbolic mirror related to those found in biology.

In order to extract (and define) the concept of symbolic species, we will have to identify the predicates of sufficiency that, once verified, will necessarily 'deliver' that concept. We consider that the predicates of sufficiency of a symbolic species could/should be the following:

- to have a genotype, susceptible to mutations (random or deliberate, as appropriate);[4]
- to have a phenotype, subject to selection (cumulative or punctuated, as appropriate);
- there is an environment in which the phenotype is immersed;
- to belong to culture (more precisely, to be a cultural product).

Note that the first three predicates of sufficiency are common predicates with those of any species (including biological species), while the last predicate assures that the species concerned is symbolic—that is, it is a creation, deliberate or emerging,[5] of the cultural interaction between human individuals involved.

Based on the proposed sufficiency predicates, we can now formulate a general definition (below, we will also provide an operational definition) of the concept of symbolic species: *that species, of conceptual/institutional type, which is generated as an effect, deliberative or emerging, of cultural interaction*.

Short Discussion

From the way the symbolic species has been defined above, the possibility of identifying an endless set of such species in human society is extremely high. This baroque (epistemologically suffocating) must somehow be limited. In other words, we need to find a filter that selects, from all the effects of cultural interaction, those that 'qualify'—from what point of view, according to which criterion?—as symbolic species. In fact, even in the general definition of the symbolic species, since it has to check the predicates of sufficiency of a species, this verification is, in itself, a very frequent filter of selection. Thus, no result of cultural interaction that does not present genotype, phenotype and a corresponding environment will be allowed to pass in the category of symbolic species.

Since our intention is to obtain an evolutionary (respectively co-evolutionary, where appropriate), both logical and quantitative model for the financial market, more particularly for the adaptive preference, the sufficiency predicates assumed above will be useful not to populate too much the world of symbolic species.[6]

Before examining information and price (elements of the binomial of interest as symbolic species), three questions need to be elucidated, at least in part: (a) Why is there a need (what is the added value provided) for an evolutionary (or evolutionist) approach of the information-price relationship? (b) How accurate should the analogy of the concept of symbolic species with the concept of biological species (the most scientifically concept of species known by now)? (c) What is (or should be) the relationship between an emerging co-evolution with a deliberative (possibly programmed) one in the information-price binomial?

(a) the more and more evolving stream in economic theory in general, and especially in financial theory, will gradually[7] lead to larger and larger non-neoclassical approaches to economic and financial phenomenology. Financial theory (including its logical and quantitative models) must remain at the forefront of conceptual-theoretical and methodological innovations in economic knowledge, as has been the case in the past. Therefore, our proposal and analysis on a co-evolutionary model of the information-price binomial in the financial market, based on the assumption of symbolic species of these two categories, can be a contribution (which, of course, can be assessed in terms of associated added value only by the scientific community) exactly in this direction of research and practice (more precisely, praxiology);

(b) we believe that, as in any analogy, caution must go beyond fascination. In this sense, the analogy of the symbolic species information, respectively price, must preserve their character of institutional/cultural creations, and the evolutionary or co-evolutionary mechanism of this binomial must be developed regarding, especially, the financial market itself. We are therefore in favour of a prudent approach and, above all, to avoid any *tale quale*-ism[8] that would import, from biological evolutionism, at the superficial level (thus carrying the risk of conceptual or operational non-fetality), concepts and mechanisms that are specific to living organisms;[9]

(c) the question is neither rhetorical nor superfluous, because symbolic species, being effects (results) of cultural interaction in human society, are full of teleological 'ingredients'—goals, expectations, anticipations and so on—which increases the likelihood that their evolution will be intellectually designed (e.g., at the level of the regulatory framework). In our opinion, the mixed (emergent-deliberative) character of information-price co-evolution cannot be disputed: the emergent character is imprinted by the free play of supply and demand generated by the invisible hand in the financial market,[10] while the deliberate character is imprinted, on the one hand, by the inherent teleology in the human individual and, on the other hand, by the normative and institutional framework within which the financial market operates. Based on the categories of information, respectively, of informational mixes (both concepts were previously developed), in the following will be evaluated/estimated the relationship between emergent and deliberative character in the process of co-evolution of the information-price binomial.

Some Analytical Developments

Preamble

We recall that previously (see especially Chap. 1), we proposed that, at the level of the financial market, the financial individual should be considered the trading strategy (TS), and the species should be considered the financial market itself. In this sense, the financial market is immersed in what we have called cultural geodesic (component of the institutional/situational context of the society concerned), which is, thus, its environment. Therefore, regardless of whether we consider the financial market as a species and cultural geodesic as the environment in which this species evolves or, alternatively, we will consider both the financial market and cultural geodesic as co-species (both symbolic, of course), so as generating a process of co-evolution, the main co-evolutionary process of research will target this symbolic pair.

In this context, we will describe, in fact, another co-evolutionary pair (the information-price binomial), which does not replace the previous pair, but is complementary to it. In a way, we have, in the case of the information-price binomial, a micro co-evolution, while the co-evolution of the financial financial-geodesic market could be qualified as a macro co-evolution.[11]

From a conceptual point of view, one can, of course, conceive of a concentric (more precisely, multicentric) vision in which co-evolutionary processes occur in each 'circle', so that these micro effects influence the macro effects which are visible/observable as co-evolutionary process just at the 'last circle'. This suggestion (or intuition) will obviously not be further developed in this study, but it remains in our attention for the possibility of further generalizations in the field of co-evolution in the financial field or in the financial market.

(1) Symbolic species: information.

In order to describe the information *qua* symbolic species, it is necessary to establish the component elements of any species in general:[12] (a) phenotype; (b) genotype;[13] (c) mutation;[14] (d) informational synthesis; (e) epigenetic (or para-genetic) evolution; (f) selection.

(a) informational phenotype (f_i): based on previous discussions on informational mixes in the financial market, we believe that the informational phenotype (i.e., the individual) should be the accessed information, or the accessed informational mix (m_u). Therefore, neither the available informational mix (m_d) nor the accessible informational mix (m_a) are informational individuals, but only the accessed informational mix. The main argument for this choice is that the real human individual[15] (not the ideal neoclassical economic theory—like in the proposals of Samuelson or Fama—that is, the mathematical model of *homo œconomicus*) is not aware of the available or accessible informational mix but only of the accessed informational mix.[16] Practically/praxiologically, for the human individual, the information exists only in the form of the accessed informational mix (m_u).

(b) informational genotype (g_i): if the informational individual is m_u, what is the genotype of the information? In order to elucidate this issue, we will discuss the other typology of information, which we proposed earlier (in addition to informational mixes typology), namely the typology of categories of information that operate in the financial market: (i) formal information; (ii) implicit information; (iii) bound information. In this context, let us consider the issue of informational genotype (g_i):

- as previously shown, any informational mix of the three such mixes identified, consists of all three categories of information, with the weights and kinematics discussed at the time (see *Financial Market Analysis and Behaviour. Adaptive Preference Hypothesis*, or FMAB-APH). Therefore, the informational mix accessed (i.e., the informational individual) also consists of the three categories of information;
- we will exclude from the potential to be mutated the category of bound information; indeed, this category of information does not enter into programmatic deliberations (as in the case of formal information) or contingent changes (as in the case of implicit information). In fact, bound information expresses most accurately (and in the most appropriate way) the idea that, for the human individual, only the informational mix accessed matters—the bound information is generated if and only if it is accessed;[17]

- a question now arises: which of the remaining categories of information—formal and implicit, respectively—is (functions as) the informational genotype? In other words, which of the two categories of information is liable to undergo changes/mutations that are subsequently transmitted to the phenotype (i.e., to the informational mix accessed)? In this context, we develop the following qualitative reasoning:
  - formal information is information that is deliberately modified (possibly programmatically—for example, on the basis of governance strategies or programmes and, of course, starting from the basic structure of society, approved in the Constitution). The problem is that this deliberativeness is not 'hosted' at the level of the human individual associated with the informational individual, but at the level of the normative structure (situational context, respectively cultural geodesic). But this structure is not completely outside the phenomenological sphere of the information-price binomial, so outside the information from the perspective of this binomial;
  - based on the above considerations, we propose that formal information should not be part of the informational genotype, for example, as a source of deliberate or discretionary mutations (see point (c) below) and even less, of course, as a source of random mutations; indeed, from the perspective of the human agent (who operates transactions in the financial market), the change in formal information (deliberate at the level of the situational context) is not random (e.g., the economic agent may stay him/herself at the origin of changes in formal information—either directly or indirectly, such as through lobbying);
  - what can be said, now, about the implicit information? As already shown, the implicit information is that information produced by the human agent concerned him/herself, by observing the behaviours in the financial market.[18] It is clear that the production of implicit information[19] is a hybrid of deliberation (the ability of the economic operator to 'translate'—the economic agent produces the implicit information consciously, deliberately, and even, to a large extent, rationally, using models and, as has been shown, on the basis of its resolutive competence) and randomness (*Nota bene*: randomness

derives from the unpredictability[20] of other economic agents behaviour, on the one hand, and from the given economic agents accidents regarding his/her interest, attention and reflectivity—the condition of the interested, attentive and reflective (IAR)—with which s/he observes or does not observe the respective behaviours).

Figure 4.1 visualizes, in a synoptic way, the issue of informational genotype, by combining the two types of information-informational mixes, respectively, categories of information.

Therefore, in summary, the informational genotype can be described as follows:

- only the implicit component between the three categories of information constitutes the informational genotype (g_i);
- in Fig. 4.1, therefore, the informational genotype is represented by the information category denoted i_y, and the informational phenotype is represented by the accessed informational mix, denoted m_u;

therefore, the informational phenotype is characterized by a high level of deliberativeness and a mix character (it is located in the N-E corner in the

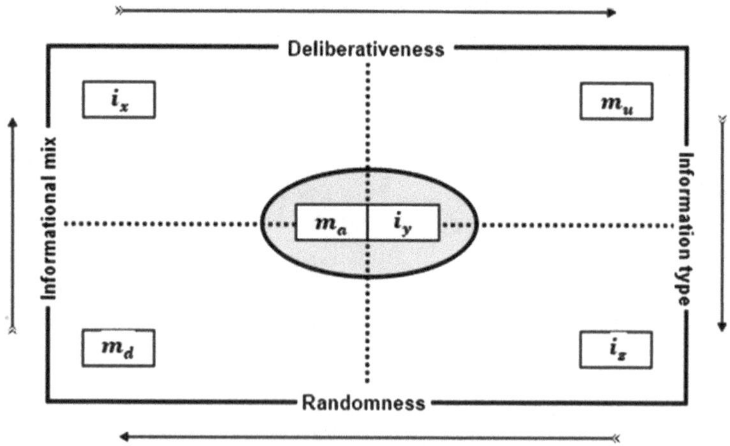

Fig. 4.1 Topological positioning of the informational genotype. *Source*: Authors

rectangle in Fig. 4.1), while the informational genotype is characterized by a medium level from the mix perspective and also by level medium of deliberativeness, located in the middle of the rectangle in Fig. 4.1 (it contains, as shown above, both a deliberative determination and a random determination);

Figure 4.2 shows a structural relationship between the informational phenotype and the informational genotype.

(c) mutation in information (m_i)
- as shown above, three categories of mutations can occur:[21] (i) random mutations; (ii) deliberate (scheduled, intentional, premeditated) changes; (iii) hybrid mutations.
  (i) *random* informational mutations (note them with m_i^a), from the perspective of the economic agent targeted in the analysis, can occur only with respect to some of the implicit information contained in the accessed informational mix (i.e., in the informational phenotype: m_u). Let us note a very important fact here: there may be random informational changes in the available informational mix as well as in the accessible informational mix, but they are not 'visible' to the economic operator,[22] whose IAR condition is: supposed to focus on the accessed informational mix (obviously by definition); in this way, the only random informational mutation occurs at the level of the implicit information;

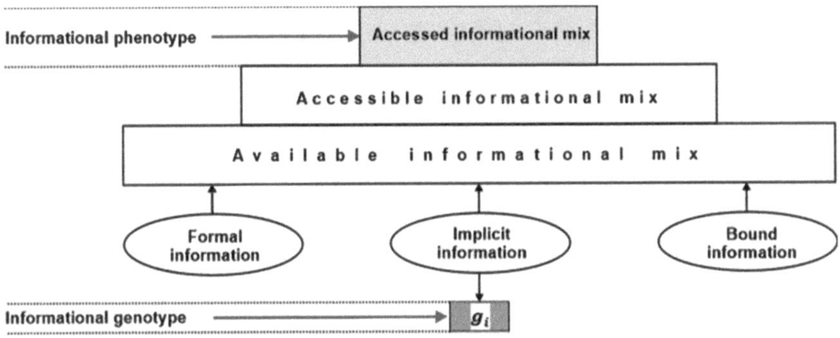

Fig. 4.2 Structural relationship phenotype-genotype within information. *Source*: Authors

(ii) *deliberate* informational mutations (note them with m_i^{db}), from the perspective of the economic agent targeted in the analysis, may occur in the case of bound information contained in the accessed informational mix (i.e., in the informational phenotype: m_u). Indeed, bound information is the category of information whose accession is decided exclusively and completely by the economic operator concerned. In this case, the informational mutation must be understood as follows: the economic operator already[23] has a 'stock' of bound information; some components of this stock have expired (no longer provide a competitive advantage) and others have been adjusted; the economic operator, if s/he uses this type of information again, will face the update of that information. Alteration of bound information, as described above, can be formalized as follows: denote by Si_z^t the stock of bound information held by the economic agent at time t, with $\Delta i_{z-}^{t,t+\tau}$ the bound information invalidated (for various reasons) in the interval $[t, t+\tau]$, with $\Delta i_{z+}^{t+\tau}$ newly entered information in stock at the time of a new 'request' for bound information. Then, the stock of bound information to the moment $(t+\tau)$ is:

(iii) $$Si_z^{t+\tau} = Si_z^t \ominus \Delta i_{z-}^{t,t+\tau} \oplus \Delta i_{z+}^{t+\tau} \quad (4.1)$$

So,

$$m_i^{db} = Si_z^{t+\tau} \ominus Si_z^t = \Delta i_{z+}^{t+\tau} \ominus \Delta i_{z-}^{t,t+\tau} \quad (4.2)$$

Nota bene: $\ominus$ is an operational constant (an operator) that has the meaning of a logical difference, that is, it is not a simple algebraic difference, but one that can mean, for example, the elimination of some characteristics or significations from the previous information; symmetrically, $\oplus$ is an operational constant (an operator) that has the meaning of a logical sum (additivity), that is, it is not a simple algebraic sum, but one that can mean, for example, the addition of features or meanings to the previous information. The way in which the two operational constants operate is, of course, to be specified at the right time.

(i) hybrid information mutations (note them with m_i^h), from the perspective of the economic agent targeted in the analysis, can occur in the case of total implicit information contained in the accessed informational mix (i.e., in the informational phenotype: m_u). The hybrid character results from the combination of the partial rationality with which the economic agent 'translates' the behaviours observed in the financial market into implicit information and the accidentality (contingency, randomness) with which these behaviours are observed (*Nota bene*: see note 74 in this matter). The relationship between the deliberate and the random character is, of course, an empirical, local and contextual problem, not being able to receive a theoretical elucidation, which, by definition, is general or even, at the limit, universal. Obviously, $m_i^a \subset m_i^h$. A very important clarification must be made here, however: in addition to m_i^a, the mutation at the level of implicit information is also of the deliberative type, which we note with m_i^d (let us remember, however, the following non-identity:[24] $m_i^d \not\equiv m_i^{db}$).

Therefore, the informational mutation, that is, the mutation that occurs at the level of the genotype of the symbolic species called information, is the following, provided that the 'target' of the informational mutation (i.e., the informational genotype) is exclusively the implicit information:

$$m_i = \left\{ m_i^a, m_i^d, m_i^h \right\} \tag{4.3}$$

A graphical description of the phenomenology of informational mutation can be made as in Fig. 4.3.

(d) informational synthesis (or synthesis of information) (s_i)
- by analogy with the processes of transcription, respectively translation,[25] which occur in the standard mutation in the field of biology, here we will give the debate some considerations on the process by which the informational mutation leads, in the end, to obtaining information which, in turn, will stay on the basis of the price estimation in the financial market trading decision. In this context, we present our opinion in the matter:

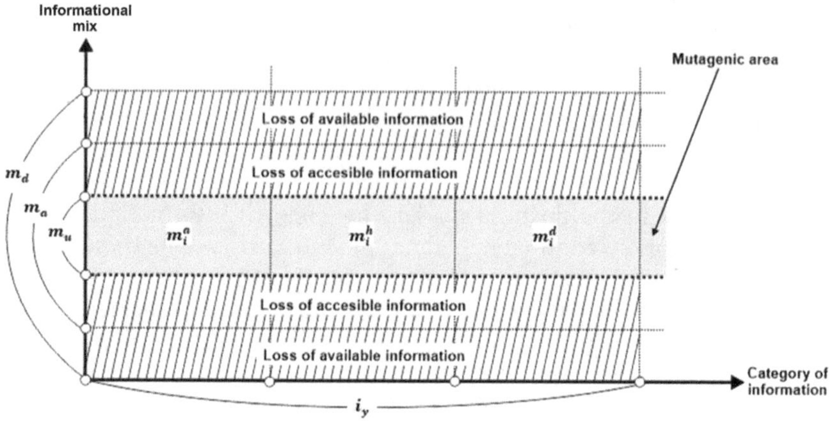

Fig. 4.3 Phenomenology of informational mutation. *Source*: Authors

note the structure of current information held by an economic operator who intends to operate in the financial market at time *t* with S^t. For example, this structure can be represented by a three-component vector:

$$S^t = \begin{pmatrix} i_{x,t} \\ i_{y,t} \\ i_{z,t} \end{pmatrix} \tag{4.4}$$

where, somehow, the three components can be associated with numerical values;[26]

- note a mutation, at the level of the informational genotype, that is, at the level of the implicit information, which takes place at the moment $(t + \tau)$[27] with m^τ;
- obvious, $m^\tau = f\left(m_{i,\tau}\right) = f\left(m_{i,\tau}^a, m_{i,\tau}^d, m_{i,\tau}^h\right)$;[28]
- to simplify the discussion, suppose that the synthesis operator (function) f is linear, that is: $f\left(m_{i,\tau}\right) = \rho_a \cdot m_{i,\tau}^a + \rho_d \cdot m_{i,\tau}^d + \rho_h \cdot m_{i,\tau}^h$, under the condition of unit closure of weights, that is: $\rho_a + \rho_d + \rho_h = 1$, and $\rho_a \geq 0$, $\rho_d \geq 0$ and $\rho_h \geq 0$;

- an alternative to the additive linearity hypothesis of the function $\mathfrak{f}$ is that this function be of vector type, that is, to be written as:

$$\mathfrak{f}\left(m_{i,\tau}^{a}, m_{i,\tau}^{d}, m_{i,\tau}^{h}\right) = \begin{pmatrix} \rho_a \cdot m_{i,\tau}^{a} \\ \rho_d \cdot m_{i,\tau}^{d} \\ \rho_h \cdot m_{i,\tau}^{h} \end{pmatrix} \tag{4.5}$$

- then (continuing with the vector version) the structure of the information[29] at time $(t + \tau)$ will be:

$$\mathcal{S}^{t+\tau} = \begin{pmatrix} i_{x,t} \oplus \rho_a \cdot m_{i,\tau}^{a} \\ i_{y,t} \oplus \rho_h \cdot m_{i,\tau}^{h} \\ i_{z,t} \oplus \rho_d \cdot m_{i,\tau}^{d} \end{pmatrix} \tag{4.6}$$

- of course, there is the problem of numerical values for the weighting coefficients $\rho_{(\bullet)}$, where $(\cdot) \in \{a, d, h\}$; in this regard, we make the following qualitative considerations on the behaviour of an economic agent, in the financial market, in relation to the information:

  if we consider the vector form of the function $\mathfrak{f}$, we no longer need the algebraic condition of closure $\rho_a + \rho_d + \rho_h = 1$, so, with the condition of non-negativity, each of the coefficients of taking over the mutations appeared at the level of the three categories information can have any real subunit value, so $\rho_{(\bullet)} \in [-1.1]$;[30]

  the (quantitative) takeover of the informational mutation is, in general (but with specificities that will have to be examined later), inversely proportional to the quantity actually produced from that mutation; the assumption is acceptable if we take into account the limited capacity of the real economic agent (not the ideal one, as in EMH or, more generally, in the mathematical model of *homo œconomicus*) to process information;

  in relation to the category of bound information (i_z), which is actually produced by the economic operator concerned, the takeover coefficient is obviously equal to 1;

- in relation to the category of formal information (i_x), the mutation coefficient is inversely proportional to the amount of mutation actually produced;
- in relation to the implicit information category (i_y), the mutation takeover coefficient is also inversely proportional to the amount of mutation actually produced. Here are some things to keep in mind: if implicit information is also produced by the economic operator concerned, then why (as in the case of bound information) the mutation found in this category of information is not taken up entirely in the new information structure? The answer is easy: the implicit information is not taken over entirely by the economic operator either, so it can be assumed, without seriously deviating from the real mechanism of the financial market, that the takeover of the mutation in the implicit information will follow 'the fate' of the implicit information acquired themselves—is not taken over in its entirety. As for the inverse proportionality of this takeover, it is also quite reasonable, based on the same argument used in the case of formal information (see above).

A graphical presentation of the behaviour of an economic agent regarding the taking over of the information mutations is provided in Fig. 4.4.

- another issue to be discussed is, of course, that of the lag with which a mutation, once produced, enters the new structure of information. In the formalization proposed above, the lag is considered null: a mutation produced, in any of the categories of information, in the interval $[t, t + \tau]$, let's say, at moment $t \leq \delta \leq \tau$, enters the structure of the information at the moment δ. One might consider lags (possibly different for the three categories of information), so if we denote by $\theta_{(\cdot)}$, where $(\cdot) \in \{a, d, h\}$, the lag related to the manifestation of the mutation that appeared at the level of each category of information in the new structure of the information from the moment $(t + \tau)$, then it can be written:

$$\mathcal{S}^{t+\tau} = \begin{pmatrix} i_{x,t} \oplus \rho_a \cdot m^a_{i,(\tau-\theta_a)} \\ i_{y,t} \oplus \rho_h \cdot m^h_{i,(\tau-\theta_h)} \\ i_{z,t} \oplus \rho_d \cdot m^d_{i,(\tau-\theta_d)} \end{pmatrix} \tag{4.7}$$

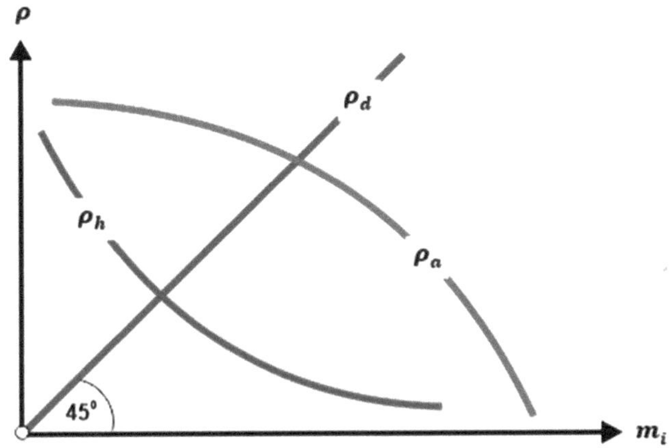

Fig. 4.4 Takeover of informational mutation in the new structure of information. *Source*: Authors

If $\theta_a = \theta_d = \theta_h = \theta$, which can be accepted, in a reasonable approximation, obviously:

$$S^{t+\tau} = \begin{pmatrix} i_{x,t} \oplus \rho_a \cdot m^a_{i,(\tau-\theta)} \\ i_{y,t} \oplus \rho_h \cdot m^h_{i,(\tau-\theta)} \\ i_{z,t} \oplus \rho_d \cdot m^d_{i,(\tau-\theta)} \end{pmatrix} \tag{4.8}$$

In the most common case, $\tau = 1$, respectively $\theta = 0$, so:

$$S^{t+1} = \begin{pmatrix} i_{x,t} \oplus \rho_a \cdot m^a_{i,1} \\ i_{y,t} \oplus \rho_h \cdot m^h_{i,1} \\ i_{z,t} \oplus \rho_d \cdot m^d_{i,1} \end{pmatrix} \tag{4.9}$$

- we conclude the discussion of the problem of informational synthesis (or synthesis of information) with the following aspect: the analytical form of the coefficients ρ (according to the graph in Fig. 4.4):

- ρ_d is a linear function[31] with a slope equal to 1, which ensures that the mutation found deliberately, by accessing the bound information, is taken over in its entirety;
  the relaxation of this hypothesis (of slope equal to 1) is not unnatural: the economic operator may decide that some mutations found in the case of bound information do not operate in the new structure of information (e.g., that mutation is not credible or is suspected is false, illegal or manipulative, etc.), in which case $0 < b < 1$. Such a pattern of behaviour can therefore be maintained in the 'portfolio';
- ρ_a is a nonlinear, decreasing and concave function;[32] the interpretation of these characteristics is as follows:
  as the quantity of mutations (random, from the economic perspective, as we have already shown) of implicit information increases, there is a reduction in the takeover of these mutations in the new information structure—at first the decrease is moderate, but then it accelerates;
  the explanation for such a behaviour (possible, and which we even presume) is that the increase in the amount of changes in the implicit information usually expresses the increase/accentuation of behavioural constraints in the financial market; as a result, the economic operator is becoming increasingly reluctant to update its implicit information as it faces a narrowing of opportunities sphere;[33]
  however, changes in the implicit information may refer not only to increasing constraints but also to reducing them. We consider, however, that the general (aggregate) allure of the curve of the function ρ_a is the one suggested in Fig. 4.4: decreasing and concave;
- ρ_b is a decreasing and convex function;[34] the interpretation of these characteristics is as follows:
  as the quantity of mutations (hybrid, from an economic perspective, as we have already shown) in the implicit information increases, there is a reduction in the uptaking of these mutations in the new information structure—at first, the decline is accelerated, but later it moderates;

the explanation for such a behaviour (possible, and which we even presume) is that the increase in the amount of mutations in the implicit information has smaller and smaller marginal values, because the new observed mutation[35] adds to the previous implicit information that has a certain stability generated by the relative stability of behaviour, including at the aggregate level of the financial market (which in turn can be presumed, without introducing too many artificial elements, as an *ex cathedra* stability);

the decrease in the marginal value of the hybrid mutation is explained precisely by the fact that the higher the amount of mutations in the implicit information, the more of these mutations 'fit' with the previous patterns of behaviour, so the less hybrid mutations are relevant to the economic operator concerned;[36]

(e) translation (t_i) and transcription (c_i)

- the problem of transcription, respectively of translating the informational mutation into the new structure of information (see point (d) above) is of the greatest relevance for modelling the co-evolution of the information-price binomial. Together with the similar issue that will be discussed at the symbolic species *price* of the binomial, this issue is the skeleton on which the co-evolutionary mechanism of the mentioned binomial will be built. In the following, we develop some ideas that we consider essential for identifying a solution:
  - the issue of transcription will be discussed below, after discussing the issue of translation, because, as we will see, the transcription of the informational mutation depends on the translation of this mutation and follows the latter, both in logical and chronological order;
  - the mutation in formal information as well as the mutation in the bound information are integrated as such in the new information structure, according to the 'algorithms' mentioned above (by the way, as you will see below, the mutation in the formal information, respectively the mutation in the related information belong to the epigenetic domain, not to the genetic one);

Here are some previously used notations:

- $P^{(1)}$: price;
- $C^{(1)}$: context (contextualization);
- $C^{(2)}$: calculus;
- A: action;
- $P^{(2)}$: probability assigned to a choice;
- $P^{(3)}$: preference;
- R: rationality (motivation, justification);
- $E^{(1)}$: experience of economic agent;
- $E^{(2)}$: emotion;
- B: behaviour;
- D: decision (choice);
- N: observation (registration) of behaviour;
- i_y: implicit information.

Based on the above, the following four behavioural 'devices' can be constructed that describe the phenomenology of information in the binomial information-price (but they are useful, of course, for the general behaviour in the financial market):

- $E^{(2)}P^{(3)} \equiv \mathfrak{A}$: propensive (affective, a-rational) device;
- $E^{(1)}C^{(1)}P^{(2)} \equiv \mathfrak{G}$: geodesic device (path dependence);
- $RC^{(2)} \equiv \mathfrak{R}$: rational device;
- $P^{(1)}A \equiv \mathfrak{P}$: praxiological device.

- information of the mutation in the observed behaviour is placed only on the mutation in the implicit information (Fig. 4.5 shows the general lines of argument in the issue of translating the behaviour into information);
- based on Fig. 4.5, we consider that the following suggestions are (largely) likely to provide an idea of the process/mechanism of translating behavioural mutation into informational mutation (again, we are only considering the generation/production of implicit information):
  - *moment (1)*: on the basis of its propensity device ($\mathfrak{A}$), the economic operator forms its bright cone relative to the visibility of the behaviours exhibited in the financial market; Within this bright cone, the economic operator observes (records) the behaviour of the financial market (in the broadest sense, i.e., the set of behaviours that are exhibited by other economic agents in the financial market);

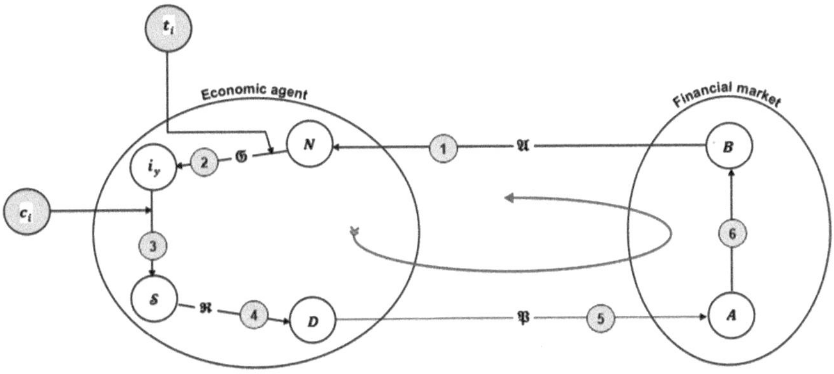

Fig. 4.5 Mechanism of translating the behaviour into information. *Source*: Authors

- *moment (2)*: based on the geodesic device (𝔊), the economic agent translates[37] the observed behaviour (B) into implicit information (i_y); more specifically, the economic operator translates the mutation occurred in the observed behaviour into the mutation of the implicit information s/he already holds;
- *moment (3)*: the change found in the implicit information is transcribed in the existing structure of the information held by the respective economic agent, thus resulting in the new structure of the information (or new informational structure) now available to the economic agent concerned;
- *moment (4)*: based on the rational device (ℜ), the economic agent makes the choice of the trading strategy[38] to be followed in the new informational conditions (i.e., in the new informational structure); indeed, the decision to take action is at this point;
- *moment (5)*: based on the praxiological device (𝔓), the economic agent implements (operationalizes) the chosen trading strategy (A); in fact, the economic operator simply exhibits a certain behaviour in the financial market, consistent with the new informational structure acquired;[39] this display is, of course, in the form of the individual transaction (IT) (or set of individual transactions);
- *moment (6)*: the action taken by the economic operator enters the 'stock' of financial market behaviour (B), the cycle in question being repeated on the basis of the same logical algorithm;

(f) epigenetic evolution of information (e_i)
- firstly, we must say that the three categories of information in the financial market (formal, implicit, bound) are distinct from each other;[40] that is, information belonging to one category cannot belong to one of the other two categories[41] at the same time;[42]
- an epigenetic evolution (which obviously involves a mutation and a selection, like any evolution) would therefore imply an evolution that does not use the genetic vehicle of information (i.e., the genome or the genotype of information);
- as stated above, this means that the informational mutation must take place either at the level of formal information or at the level of bound information, which are categories of information that do not 'fit' into the informational genotype;
- as bound information cannot be mutated,[43] it turns out that, in the field of information, we have an epigenetic evolution at the level of formal information. From a typological point of view, the evolution of epigenetic information is of mixed type: partly the modification of the formal information appears to the economic agent as random, partly even the economic agent concerned can initiate or support the respective modification. Since we have denoted the hybrid genetic informational mutation (which occurs at the implicit information level) with m^h, we will denote the hybrid epigenetic informational mutation (which occurs at the level of formal information) with m^{hf}.

The systematization of informational mutation (genetic and epigenetic) is represented in Fig. 4.6.

(g) selection of information (s_i)
- as it is known from the evolutionary theory developed for the biological domain (i.e., for biological, non-symbolic species), the selection is made at the phenotype level. Therefore, the environment (in the general case), through the constraints and opportunities it applies to the phenotype (i.e., the adult individual of the species) retains or marginalizes those individuals whose mutations provide a 'comparative advantage'[44] over individuals in that species who do not hold those mutations;
- we said earlier that the phenotype (individual) in the case of information is the accessed informational mix: m_u (which is part of the accessible informational mix: m_a, which, in its turn, is part of the available informational mix: m_d);

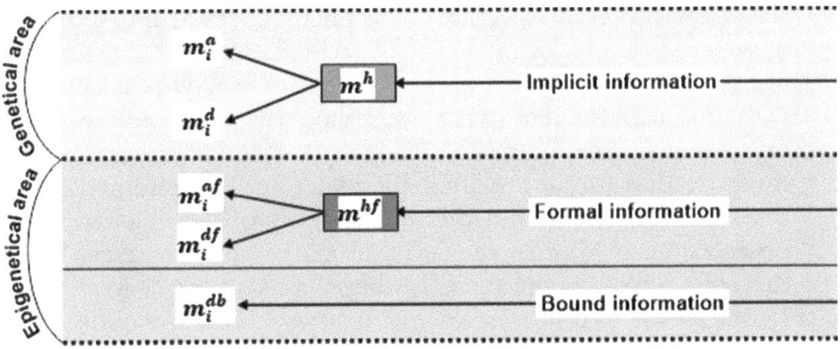

Fig. 4.6 Genetic area and epigenetic area in informational mutation (evolution). *Source*: Authors

- given that in a binomial mechanism, such as the price-information pair, one of the co-species functions as a selective medium for the other co-species (and, of course, reciprocally), we will postpone discussing the selection stage until after examination of the co-species price (in fact, both selections—of information and of price—will be discussed further together).

(2) Symbolic Species: Price

(α) On the Structure of Price

We have seen above what the structure of the information is—we remind you that neither EMH nor AMH discusses such a topic, although, in our opinion, it is crucial in understanding and explaining the functioning of the financial market, including the decision-making process in financial market. The question is: is there an analogous (with the information) price structure? In this regard, we discuss the following assumptions and opinions:

- in the financial market, the price appears to the economic agent, *prima facie*, as a monolith—more precisely, as a numerical value, having as unit of measure the currency of interest (usually the currency of the economic system concerned, although sometimes it can be also expressed in the reference currency). Even if this numerical value can be organized in time series (which happens in almost all cases of financial decision that need to seem as scientific as possible), each record in those time series is monolithic. From the external examination of a price—that is, of the numerical value which we call price—no internal structure of this variable can be inferred;

- the possible internal structure of the price[45] could be useful from the perspective of identifying sufficient components for the price to be, like the information, considered a co-species in evolutionary relation with the information (what we called the co-evolution of the information-price binomial);
- the extraction (or, at the limit, the 'decreeing') of an internal price structure is therefore not the responsibility of the financial market observer/agent, but of the financial market analyst/researcher. In this regard, we propose the following scheme of discussion:
  - one of the well-known price structures[46] (in any economic market, therefore also in the financial market) is the following:

$$p = c + \pi \tag{4.10}$$

where p means the price,[47] c means the total unit cost,[48] π means the unit profit;

  - we also need to introduce the concept of ***value*** here: the value associated with a good, that is, product or financial instrument[49] means the price intuited by the economic agent in relation to that financial good that will work (will be exhibited by that financial good) at some moment in the future;[50]
  - since the value is, in turn, a price too (since it is also expressed in monetary terms), we will change the previous notations to make room also for the value: thus, we will denote the current price (observed, i.e., the price noted above with p) with p_t^o, which means the price observed at time t, respectively we will denote the value of the same financial good, at the moment $(t + \tau)$ with $p_{t+\tau}^e$, which means, therefore, the price, estimated by the economic agent involved, for the targeted financial good, at the moment $(t + \tau)$, with $t, \tau > 0$ and $t, \tau \in N$;
  - thus, from the perspective of the economic agent who trades (or intends to trade) a financial good in the financial market, the expected profit will be:[51]

$$\pi_{t,\tau} = p_{t+\tau}^e - p_t^o = \Delta_{t,\tau}^p \tag{4.11}$$

- in principle (but, of course, nuances may appear), the trading decision[52] is made on the condition:

$$\Delta^{p}_{t,\tau} > 0 \tag{4.12}$$

To this condition, as we will explain later, can be associated to a probability (most probably, a subjective one) extracted from the propensity that characterizes (as a hardcore, persistent or even invariant, over a period of time) the preference—which we have previously called *proference*;

- therefore, from the perspective of the economic agent (and as, in fact, the analyst believes), the price has two components: (a) a certain component: p^{o}_{t}; (b) an uncertain component: $\Delta^{p}_{t,\tau}$;
- now, we will have to determine what means *price* for the economic agent; in our opinion, the economic agent is interested in the variable price in its form noted above with $p^{e}_{t+\tau}$. So, regarding the price structure in the financial market, we think that the following option is required:[53]

$$p^{e}_{t+\tau} = p^{o}_{t} \oplus \Delta^{p}_{t,\tau} \tag{4.13}$$

(β) Price as Symbolic Species

To describe the price *qua* symbolic species, we will proceed in a similar way to how we examined this issue in the case of information.[54]

(a) price phenotype (f_p)

After establishing the price structure from the perspective of the economic agent, identifying the phenotype associated with the symbolic species called price is not too difficult: the individual of price is the price of interest for the economic agent, that is: $p^{e}_{t+\tau}$, or value. The consequences of such a 'choice', from the perspective of the evolutionary model of price, are the following:

- the selection of the price, made by its environment (which is considered, in fact, as being exactly the information, within the information-price binomial) is made exactly with respect to $p^{e}_{t+\tau}$, even if the selector information refers or not to the moment $(t + \tau)$; the reference of the information to the moment of interest is inferred by the economic agent him/herself, especially regarding the implicit information (because the formal information, respectively the bound information explicitly refers to the moment of interest, even if by epigenetic way);

- being an information-price co-evolution, this co-evolution will occur, for the most part, through co-adaptation;[55]

(b) price genotype (g_p)
- regarding the price genotype, we are of the opinion that it can only be $\Delta^p_{t,\tau}$. We provide the following arguments:
  - the p^o_t component is the definite (or fixed) component of the price, so it can no longer undergo mutations;[56]
  - the only component that can be mutated is the uncertain component of price, which is exactly $\Delta^p_{t,\tau}$;

Nota bene: we will see below that the co-adaptation relationship (obviously based on the fetality of the reaction norms between information and price) occurs between m_u and $\Delta^p_{t,\tau}$;

(c) price mutation (m_p)
- firstly, we will note that, acting on the genotype, in the case of price, the mutation will manifest itself at the level of $\Delta^p_{t,\tau}$;
- secondly, it must be said that the main cause of the change in price is the change in information;
- thirdly, it is important to point out that, massively, the informational mutation that acts on the price (more precisely, on $\Delta^p_{t,\tau}$) is the one that appeared within the implicit information, that is, at the level of the observed behaviour in the financial market;[57]
- as the most relevant behaviour on the market is the price mutation itself, it immediately follows that we have, here, a peremptory example of the mutuality (reciprocity) of exercising the (fetal) reaction norms between information (especially under the category of implicit information) and price;[58]

(d) price synthesis (s_p)
- we will first discuss the price synthesis in the standard case of EMH.[59] As already mentioned, Fama does not present the mechanism by which the information available on the market is integrated into the price, presenting the situation as a natural,

automatic and necessary result, possibly dictated by the ubiquitous and omnipotent invisible hand;
- be the current price at time *t*: p_t^a, and the information available on the market[60] at that time, $i_t^{\to t}$ (*Nota bene*: the sign ' → ' in the upper index, placed before '*t*', indicates the accumulation of information from the past till the moment *t*);
- be the future price: $p_t^{t\to}$ (*Nota bene*: the sign '→' in the upper index, placed after '*t*', indicates the idea that it is a predicted price and the prediction is made at the moment *t*);
- then: $p_t^{t\to} = p_t^a$. Of course, this is the prediction of sophisticated (rational) economic agents, because i-rational (unsophisticated) economic agents will consider $p_t^{t\to} \neq p_t^a$, thus introducing the so-called noise on the market (which will eventually be exploited by sophisticated economic agents);

- regarding the price synthesis in the AMH model, a mechanism based on information structure and price structure is not presented here either, although the suggestion is that the price is predictable, because not all past information is integrated automatically, completely and without cost in price, so there remains a margin of use for the information omitted for the purpose of making price predictions;[61]
- now we will propose a mechanism (from a perspective, for the time being, logical, abstract) to take over the information mutation into the price mutation, within the conceptual framework adopted by us in this study:
  - note with $var(m_u)$ the variance of the accessed informational mix m_u (*Nota bene*: remember that m_u is the phenotype of information); based on the variance, we can determine the coefficient of variation of the accessed informational mix: $\upsilon_{m_u} = \frac{\sigma_{m_u}}{\overline{m}_u}$, where $\sigma_{m_u} = \sqrt{var(m_{m_u})}$ is the standard deviation of the accessed informational mix, and $\overline{m}_u = \frac{\sum_{j=1}^{n} m_u^j}{n}$ is the average of the accessed informational mix (*n* is the number of records in the time series, indicating the period/interval over which the statistical analysis in question is performed);
  - note with $var(m_p)$ the variance of the price; based on the variance, we can also determine the coefficient of variation of the price: $\upsilon_p = \frac{\sigma_p}{\overline{p}}$, where $\sigma_p = \sqrt{var(m_p)}$ is the standard deviation of the price, and $\overline{p} = \frac{\sum_{j=1}^{n} p^j}{n}$ is the average price;[62]

- we can have the following alternative, exclusive and exhaustive situations of behaviour of the economic agent:
  $\upsilon_{m_u} > \upsilon_p$: conservatorism
  $\upsilon_{m_u} = \upsilon_p$: neutralism
  $\upsilon_{m_u} < \upsilon_p$: innovationism
- the relative ratio between the two coefficients of variation must be correlated/combined with the moments of information, respectively the price; note the moment of the accessed informational mix with $m(m_u)$, and the moment of the price with $m(p)$. We propose to calculate the two moments[63] as follows:

primary moment $m^{[0]}$: is the moment characterized by the invariance of the absolute values of the two variables (*Nota bene*: the primary moment has the meaning of a zero speed of variation):

$$m_{m_u}^{[0]} = {}_{m_u}^{[0]}\Delta_{t+\tau,t} = m_u^{[t+\tau]} - m_u^{[t]}, \text{ unde } t, \tau \in \mathbb{N} \tag{4.14}$$

respectively,

$$m_p^{[0]} = {}_p^{[0]}\Delta_{t+\tau,t} = p^{[t+\tau]} - p^{[t]} \tag{4.15}$$

usually, $\tau = 1$, so:

$$m_{m_u}^{[0]} = {}_{m_u}^{[0]}\Delta_{(t+1),t} = m_u^{[t+1]} - m_u^{[t]} \tag{4.16}$$

respectively,

$$m_p^{[0]} = {}_p^{[0]}\Delta_{(t+1),t} = p^{[t+1]} - p^{[t]} \tag{4.17}$$

Nota bene: it is not necessary to calculate this moment for a certain period, because the result is trivial: if each additional moment is zero, the amount will be zero. This is because, by definition, the moment ceases at the first situation in which ${}_{(\cdot)}^{[0]}\Delta_{(t+\tau),t} \neq 0$.

secondary moment ($m^{[1]}$): is the moment characterized by the invariance of the two speeds of variation (*Nota bene*: the secondary moment has the meaning of a zero acceleration of variation):

$$m^{1}_{m_u} = {}^{[1]}_{m_u}\Delta_{(t+2\tau),t} = {}^{[0]}_{m_u}\Delta_{(t+2\tau),(t+\tau)} - {}^{[0]}_{m_u}\Delta_{(t+\tau),t} \tag{4.18}$$

respectively,

$$m^{[1]}_{p} = {}^{[1]}_{p}\Delta_{(t+2\tau),t} = {}^{[0]}_{p}\Delta_{(t+2\tau),(t+\tau)} - {}^{[0]}_{p}\Delta_{(t+\tau),t} \tag{4.19}$$

usually, $\tau = 1$, so:

$$m^{[1]}_{m_u} = {}^{[1]}_{m_u}\Delta_{(t+2),(t+1)} = {}^{[0]}_{m_u}\Delta_{(t+2),(t+1)} - {}^{[0]}_{m_u}\Delta_{(t+1),t} \tag{4.20}$$

respectively,

$$m^{[1]}_{p} = {}^{[1]}_{p}\Delta_{(t+2),(t+1)} = {}^{[0]}_{p}\Delta_{(t+2),(t+1)} - {}^{[0]}_{p}\Delta_{(t+1),t} \tag{4.21}$$

tertiary moment ($m^{[2]}$): is the moment characterized by the invariance of the two accelerations of variation (*Nota bene*: the tertiary moment has the meaning of a zero speed of the acceleration of variation or, equivalent, of a zero acceleration of the speed of variation):[64]

$$m^{[2]}_{m_u} = {}^{[2]}_{m_u}\Delta_{(t+4\tau),t} = {}^{[1]}_{m_u}\Delta_{(t+4\tau),(t+2\tau)} - {}^{[1]}_{m_u}\Delta_{(t+2\tau),t} \tag{4.22}$$

respectively,

$$m^{[2]}_{p} = {}^{[2]}_{p}\Delta_{(t+4\tau),t} = {}^{[1]}_{p}\Delta_{(t+4\tau),(t+2\tau)} - {}^{[1]}_{p}\Delta_{(t+2\tau),t} \tag{4.23}$$

usually, $\tau = 1$, so:

$$m^{[2]}_{m_u} = {}^{[2]}_{m_u}\Delta_{(t+4),t} = {}^{[1]}_{m_u}\Delta_{(t+4),(t+2)} - {}^{[1]}_{m_u}\Delta_{(t+2),t} \tag{4.24}$$

respectively,

$$m_p^{[2]} = {}_p^{[2]}\Delta_{(t+4),t} = {}_p^{[1]}\Delta_{(t+4),(t+2)} - {}_p^{[1]}\Delta_{(t+2),t} \tag{4.25}$$

By combining the relative values of the moments with the relative values of the coefficients of variation, we can draw up the following table of the behaviour of the information-price binomial in the financial market based on the first two moments (Table 4.1, in Annex).

Nota bene 1: in Annex (Table 4.2) we also give a suggestive picture (incomplete, leaving this supplement to the discretion of the interested reader) which contains all three moments, with meanings, of course, finer than in the case of two moments.

Nota bene 2: the order relation '>' refers to the time interval over which a certain value is kept (of the level either of the first difference or of the second difference, etc., as the case may be), so $x > y$ means that the interval in which x is valid is longer than the interval in which y is valid.

(e) transcription (c_p) and translation (t_p)
  - transcription and translation problems in the case of price[65] are less difficult than similar problems in the case of information. In addition, in the matter of price, there is no anymore a question of translation, t_p (by obvious reasons), but only that of transcription,[66] c_p;
  - transcription (c_p)
    - the transcription of the mutation in the price genotype must be operated in the price phenotype: with the notations adopted above, it follows that $\Delta_{t,\tau}^{p}$ must be transcribed into $p_{t+\tau}^{e}$ (technically, as already shown, is simply added to p_t^{o});[67]

(f) epigenetic evolution of price (e_p)
  - we have seen that, at the level of the co-species called information, there is an epigenetic evolution, namely the one anchored in the (non-genetic) vehicles, formal information, respectively bound information (the mutations in question can be both of random and deliberative nature). In our opinion, an epigenetic evolution cannot exist in the case of the co-species called price. We support this position with the following arguments:

- in order for there to be an epigenetic evolution, it is necessary to identify a vehicle which, apart from the price genotype (which is, as shown above, $\Delta^{p}_{t,\tau}$), can generate or induce, in attention of the economic agent, variations in the expected price;
- being within the co-species called price, we are not 'allowed' to use information (of any category or in any informational mix) to say that there is a non-price vehicle that leads to price changes;
- therefore, it follows that the only vehicle valid for the occurrence of mutations in the expected price level is the price (more precisely, $\Delta^{p}_{t,\tau}$), the obvious conclusion being that in the case of the co-species called price there is no mutation, selection or epigenetic evolution;

(g) cumulative price selection (s_p)
- as in the case of information selection, we will discuss price selection in the next section.

Co-evolutive Mechanism of the Binomial Information-Price

Preamble

We have seen, in the previous sections, the analytical details of the information and price co-species, which are symbolic species that 'live' in the financial market. As we mentioned before, the evolutionary model that the research project proposes is that of adaptive preference but, as a result of the stage (and, to a certain extent, even as conceptual exercise), two other processes are evolutionary treated: the information-price binomial, respectively the trinomial preference-information-price (TCIP).

This section should provide an approach from two perspectives (which are, obviously, complementary): (a) a logical perspective of the information-price binomial; (b) a quantitative perspective of this binomial. Since from the quantitative point of view, the binomial cannot be separated from the trinomial, the discussion of the quantitative part will be postponed, so, for the moment, it will be examined only from the qualitative/logical perspective of the binomial. The results obtained will be useful, as we said, to achieve the ultimate goal pursued in carrying out the research project: a hypothesis of adaptive preference in the financial market—opposable to both the invariant preference hypothesis (proposed by EMH) and the adaptive market hypothesis (proposed by AMH).

Logical Description

Objectives

In designing the logical mechanism of the information-price binomial (hereinafter referred to as BIP) we will pursue the following four specific objectives: (a) the description of each symbolic co-species as a selector environment for the other symbolic co-species; (b) co-adaptation and co-selection of the two symbolic co-species; (c) cyclicity and cycles in the BIP mechanism; (d) graduality and punctuatedness[68] in the logical mechanism of BIP.

(a) co-species and selector environment in BIP

The selection of a trait generated by the mutation produced in the genotype is an operation that manifests itself on the unit of selection, that is, on the phenotype. The operation in question is performed by the environment in which the species is immersed, and the selection criterion is the fitness provided by the mutation concerned. If the mutation is (usually) random,[69] instead, the selection is directional. This directionality is provided by the fitness criterion, that is, the degree of comparative (or competitive) advantage brought by the mutation at the phenotype level. This advantage can be manifested in two directions: (i) an advantage opposable to other individuals of the species or to other species that are immersed in the same environment; (ii) advantage opposable to the environment as such. Although the first type of advantage is also highlighted through the environment, it is useful, from a methodological point of view, for it to be highlighted separately. In fact, the first type of advantage operates structural changes at the species level—by increasing the share of individuals who possess the trait that confers the advantage, here operating the concept of population selection (and evolution), while the second type of advantage operates changes in the population immersed into environment.

Assuming that information and price are examined as co-species in the BIP, logically, each co-species will have to be considered as a selector environment for the other. In other words, we have to consider that the information is immersed in the environment called price and, conversely, the price is immersed in the environment called information. In this hypothesis (a bit autarchic, for methodological reasons) the two symbolic co-species change each other's roles: the one that was *adaptar*, becomes *adaptant*, and the adaptant, in turn, becomes adaptar. Some clarifications are needed here:

- co-species, at a given time, can have only one of the two positions: either adaptant (co-species that adapts or is selected) or adaptar (co-species that selects);
- it is not necessary (i.e., mandatory) that, in a given cycle (see below for a more detailed discussion of cyclicity), after being in a certain co-evolutionary position, a co-species to immediately place oneself on the alternative co-evolutionary position—it can replicate the position held a number of times, depending on the co-evolutionary context;
- there is no accuracy in applying the so-called fitness criterion (more specifically, the fitness improvement criterion) in the selection process:
  - *first of all*, fitness is not (neither in nature nor in society) an optimal and, therefore, even less a de-contextualized maximum. It is, as we said before in several places, a *second-best* solution that, in this context, provides a *modus vivendi*[70] between species and environment, a situation from which both the species and the environment gain. In essence, therefore, it can be said that achieving fitness in the selection process is a *win-win* an-extremizing process;
  - *secondly*, although it directs the selection, fitness has no axiological significance—it expresses neither progress nor regress at the phenotype level (and, of course, even less at the environmental level), it is simply an adequacy, always local and always temporary (i.e., in other words, always there is just a contextual adequacy) between the individual/phenotype and the environment: this relative character is particularly important from an epistemological point of view.[71]

Returning to the two symbolic co-species in question, we consider that the problem of the relationship between the co-species and its selector environment can be described synoptically as in Fig. 4.7.

(b) co-adaptation and selection in BIP

In this paragraph we need to discuss how selection (in fact, co-selection) occurs in the case of BIP. Specifically, it is about clarifying the mechanism by which the mutation in the informational genotype (remember that it is the implicit information) is transmitted/transcribed onto the price and,

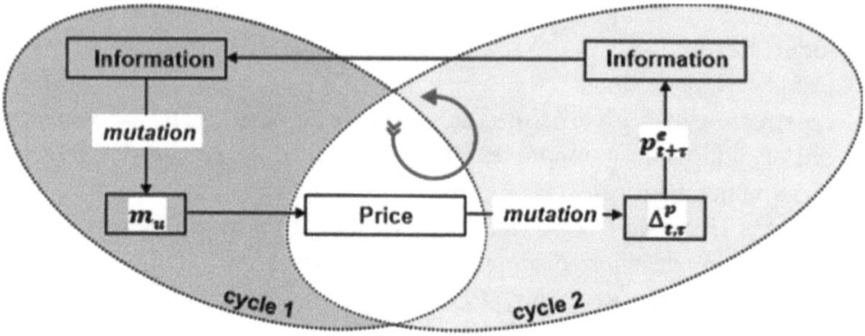

Fig. 4.7 Co-species and selector environment. *Source*: Authors

then, the clarification of the mechanism by which the mutation in the price genotype (remember that this is $\Delta^p_{t,\tau}$—see Fig. 4.7) is transmitted onto the information.

Obviously, these mechanisms need to be based on the action/reaction functions that work in the case of BIP. The operating logic of the two paired mechanisms can be described as follows:

(i) the impact of information on the price follows the following path: from the informational phenotype to the price genotype, so we have the impact 'arrow': $f_i \rightarrow g_p$;
(ii) the impact of price on information follows the following path: from the price phenotype to the informational genotype, so we have the impact 'arrow': $f_p \rightarrow g_i$;
(iii) the production of the impact $f_i \rightarrow g_p$ is logically equivalent to the selection that the environment of information (i.e., the co-species price) makes regarding the informational individual (f_i); the non-production of the mentioned impact is logically equivalent to the non-selection (or negative selection of) the informational phenotype by its environment (price co-species);
(iv) the production of the impact $f_p \rightarrow g_i$ is logically equivalent to the selection that the environment of price (i.e., the co-species information) makes regarding the price individual (f_p); the non-production of the mentioned impact is equivalent, from a logical point of view, to the non-selection (or negative selection) of the price phenotype by its environment (co-species information);

(c) cyclicity and cycles in BIP

Partly, we referred to the issue of cyclicity, respectively of cycles in BIP operation, when we discussed the issue of co-adaptation and selection in this binomial. Consequently, we will only add some details here:

- there is, of course, micro-cyclicity (e.g., as shown in Fig. 4.8 or in the description of the co-adaptation and co-selection mechanisms at point (b) above), which concerns a single 'race':

$$f_i \rightarrow g_p \rightarrow f_p \rightarrow g_i \rightarrow f_i \quad (4.26)$$

if it starts with the informational phenotype, respectively:

$$f_p \rightarrow g_i \rightarrow f_i \rightarrow g_p \rightarrow f_p \quad (4.27)$$

if it starts with the price phenotype;

- but one can conceive, at the level of environment and long-term functioning of the financial market, also a macro-cyclicality, which aims at a trajectory comprising several micro-cycles but which 'returns' to the starting point. A synoptic representation of a macro-cycle in the BIP is proposed in Fig. 4.8 (with $f_i(k)$ the informational phenotype existing at time k was noted and, analogously, for the other variables in the figure).

Therefore, a formalization of a micro-cycle with a starting point in information is as follows:

$$f_i(k) \rightarrow g_p(k) \rightarrow f_p(k) \rightarrow g_i(k) \rightarrow f_i(k+1), \text{ with } k = 0,1,2,\ldots \quad (4.28)$$

A formalization of a micro-cycle with a starting point in price is as follows:

$$f_p(k) \rightarrow g_i(k) \rightarrow f_i(k) \rightarrow g_p(k) \rightarrow f_p(k+1,), \text{ with } k = 0,1,2,\ldots \quad (4.29)$$

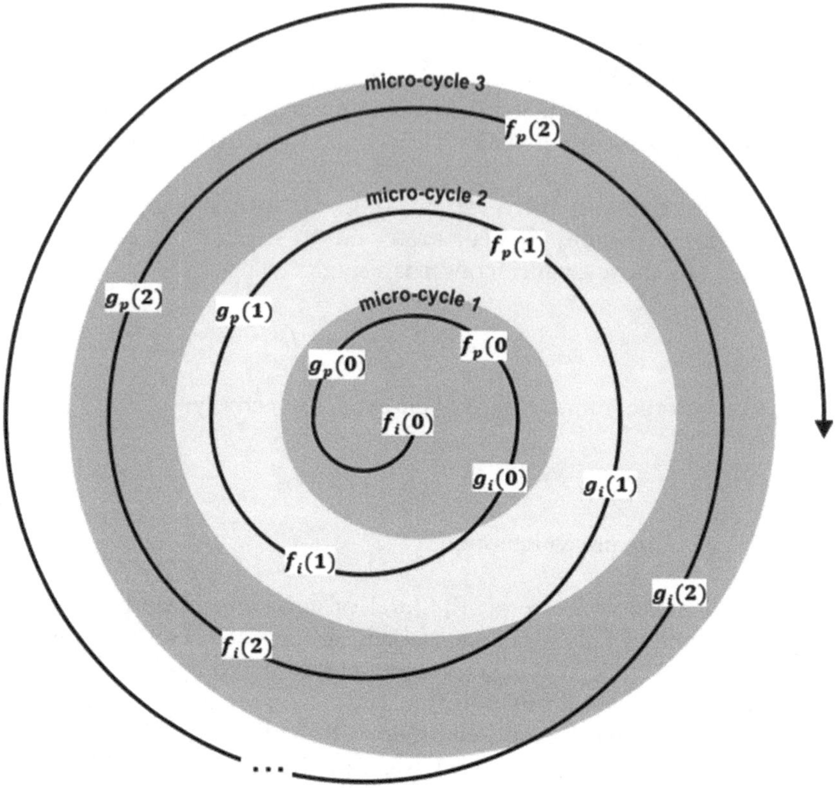

Fig. 4.8 A BIP macro-cycle containing three micro-cycles. *Source*: Authors

Additional discussion

- the 'counter'[72] of the micro-cycles advances one step, from state k to state $(k + 1)$ exactly when a variable reappears in the co-evolutionary chain (variable f_i, if the co-evolutionary chain starts with the information, respectively the variable f_p, in case the co-evolutionary chain starts with the price);
- the problem is: there is a criterion[73] based on which to choose between the two co-species (information, respectively price) as the necessary point (here, obviously, in the logical sense of the term 'necessary') of departure in the development of the co-evolutionary

chain or co-evolutive chain? We present our opinion in this matter: the starting point (the variable) in the co-evolutionary process BIP is the price (more precisely, the phenotype of the price, i.e., in the notation used in this study, f_p). We argue this position in principle as follows:

- the *first argument*: based on the primacy of behaviour over information (assumption assumed, both on the basis of belief and on the basis of logical reasoning, in the whole research project), the economic agent observes, firstly, the behaviour. But behaviour is, *prima facie*, a price-bearer, and only secondly does it deliver information (namely, as has been shown several times before, as 'translation'—made by the economic agent him/herself—of behaviour into implicit information);
- the *second argument*: the purpose of the entire hermeneutical work (from observation, to translation, calculation and decision) of the economic agent, is to arrive to the price, that is, more precisely (and from an operational perspective), to choose a trading strategy (or/and an individual transaction) in the financial market that would allow it to 'beat' the market (or the relevant competitor, as the case may be); therefore, it is seen that, metaphorically speaking, the alpha and omega of the whole behaviour of the economic agent is to infer the price from price. In other words (which was evident from our entire presentation above, as well as from previous studies), information is a means—more precisely, the main means, because, as we will see later, this quality of information will be, partially, 'usurped' by the very preference—to achieve the purpose, that is, the convenient price. So, our choice is that, in the financial market, from the perspective of BIP (*Nota bene*: in the perspective of TCIP, things will change), the abstract logical form of the co-evolutionary chain is:

$$f_p(k) \rightarrow g_i(k) \rightarrow f_i(k) \rightarrow g_p(k) \rightarrow f_p(k+1), \quad \text{with } k = 0, 1, 2, \ldots \tag{4.30}$$

Figure 4.8 illustrates synoptically the relationship between micro-cycle and macro-cycle in BIP.

(d) graduality and selective punctuatedness in BIP

The issue of graduality, respectively punctuatedness (which is clarified, at least at the level of hypothesis, in the evolution of biological 'objects') requires a brief discussion in the context of BIP. We offer the following opinions for debate:

- graduality *qua* graduality (i.e., as it is understood in biological evolution) is a rare exception in the selection that works within the BIP. The economic operator will ignore the mutations (either genetic or epigenetic) occurring in either the informational genotype or the price genotype, as long as the variations involved in the mutations concerned do not reach the (completely idiosyncratic,[74] of course) significance threshold of the economic operator concerned;
- the question can (however) be asked whether mutations that do not reach the threshold of significance, accumulate, somehow, although they are not operated/taken over/capitalized in the choices, so that there is a point of 'drop that filled the glass', in which the decision of the economic operator does not consider infinitesimal variations (*Nota bene*: we agree to call infinitesimal variations, although somewhat inappropriate, those variations which, each taken separately, do not reach the threshold of significance) but their accumulated amount over a period of time does that reaching.[75] Our answer to such a presumptive question is *affirmative*: the economic agent, from a psychological point of view, will 'remember', at each infinitesimal variation of the mutations, the previous infinitesimal variations—obviously, s/he will not keep a strict accounting of them, and the evaluation that 'the glass is filled' is not of a rational nature, but of a psychological nature; in addition, a mathematical algebra does not work here, but a psychological algebra does;[76]
- in the case discussed immediately above, really is the decision to take into account this accumulation of infinitesimals of the nature of a co-evolutionary leap (i.e., in the already established terminology, of a punctuated equilibrium)? Our answer to this (new) presumptive question is, this time, *negative*:

- the moment in which the awareness of the mutation (therefore the affectation of the decision) occurs, is not relevant; as a result, it does not matter how long it takes to accumulate the tension created by infinitesimal variations until the (quantitative) threshold of significance of the economic agent is reached—from a qualitative point of view, we still have a mutation, a selection (more precisely, co-selection) and a gradual evolution (more precisely, co-evolution);
- from a logical point of view, we will simply consider that reaching the threshold of significance of the mutation is a single mutation (mutational singularity, we could call it), and not a synthetic (aggregative) mutation of several analytical mutations;

- and yet, what about punctuatedness (or punctuated equilibrium) in the case of BIP? We offer the following considerations in this matter:
  - first of all, we will take into account our position from the point of view of graduality, as it was formulated and argued above—namely, we will stipulate that, on a regular basis (i.e., in the vast majority of cases), the financial market, in particular, within BIP, there is no gradual change in the occurring of mutations, neither in the realization of selections and, consequently, nor in the evolutionary process (more precisely, of the co-evolutionary process);
  - in this context, the logical conclusion is that (almost) all mutations, selections and, therefore, co-evolution in BIP, occur in a punctuated manner:

    the punctuated character, asserted above, is obvious in the epigenetic case: both the variation of the formal information and the variation of the bound information occur in a punctuated way, not gradually; one of the most obvious explanations[77] (in the case of formal information) is that the probability of complying with the new norm is directly proportional to the gap contained in the new norm with respect to the previous corresponding norm.[78] Similarly, in the case of bound information, the economic operator uses large, singular variations in the acquisition of this type of information, because the shock caused in the market by a decision based on such large gaps is more likely to bring profit than one based on small gaps in this type of information;

let us now discuss the plausibility of the punctuatedness of mutation, selection and co-evolution in the genetic case of BIP:

- it is, we believe, obvious that, in the case of implicit information (which constitutes the informational genotype ($i_y \rightarrow g_i$)), the economic agent (IAR condition) will decide for him/herself whether a certain variation observed in the behaviours of the financial market can (or should) be translated into implicit information, so if the decision to 'translate' (or not) a behavioural variation into implicit informational variation is dimensionally conditioned (also psychological conditioning, of course, although in this case, subjectivism may be accompanied by a good dose of rationalism, however): a behavioural observation error is possible,[79] a deliberate misleading by competitors in the financial market (which may simulate some behaviours) is possible as well, or there is a simple financial noise;[80]
- if the economic operator will proceed as in the case of the epigenetic mutation, that is, it will 'accumulate' the small gaps observed in the behaviours of the financial market, until reaching a certain degree/threshold of significance—including from the perspective of the possibility of translating into the implicit type of information—we think that we still have a punctuated type of genetic mutation (with the same arguments, *mutatis mutandis*, as those offered when discussing the epigenetic mutation).

Logical Model of BIP

At the end of this section, we propose a logical (abstract) model of how BIP works. *Nota bene*: as the binomial information-price (BIP) is structurally and, of course, functionally included in the trinomial preference-information-price (TCIP), the *quantitative* aspects of the information-price co-evolution will be examined, as we have already announced, in the next two chapters of the research.

The graphical representation of this logical model is given in Fig. 4.9. The red, dotted trajectory indicates the co-evolution within the BIP of the two co-species (at the level of phenotypes, of course), the blue trajectory, continuous, indicates co-the evolution of the co-species (at the phenotype

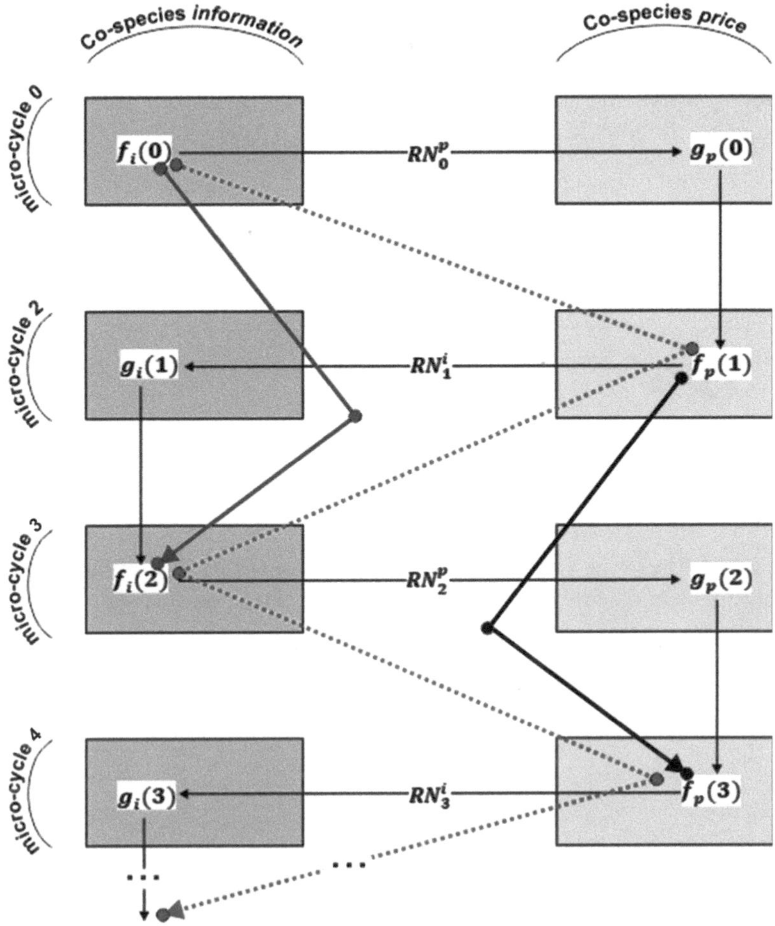

Fig. 4.9 Co-evolutive logical mechanism of BIP. *Source*: Authors

level) called information, and the green trajectory, continuous, indicates the co-evolution of the co-species (at the phenotype level) called price. RN_k^p indicates the fetal reaction norm for the co-species price, in the micro-cycle *k* and RN_k^i indicates the fetal reaction norm for the information co-species, in the micro-cycle *k*. Only four causally linked micro-cycles were taken as an illustration.

Annex: Systematics of the Binomial Information-Price

Table 4.1 presents a matrix of the information-price binomial behaviour related to the first two moments of the two co-species.

Table 4.1 Behaviour of the binomial information-price: the cases $m^{(0)}$ and $m^{(1)}$

m_{m_u} \ m_p		1. $m^{(0)} < m^{(1)}$	2. $m^{(0)} = m^{(1)}$	3. $m^{(0)} > m^{(1)}$
1.	$m^{(0)} < m^{(1)}$	...	...	...
2.	$m^{(0)} = m^{(1)}$	...	...	...
3.	$m^{(0)} > m^{(1)}$	...	...	...

Source: Authors

Table 4.2 presents a matrix of the information-price binomial behaviour related to the first three moments of the two co-species.

Table 4.2 Behaviour of the binomial information-price: the cases $m^{(0)}$, $m^{(1)}$ and $m^{(2)}$

m_{m_u}	m_p	1.	2.	3.	4.	5.	6.	7.	8.	9.	10.	11.	12.	13.	14.	15.	16.	17.	18.	19.	20.	21.	22.	23.	24.	25.	26.	27.
1.	$m^{(0)} < m^{(1)} < m^{(2)}$	...	...	...	...	...	...	...	...	...	...	...	...	...	...	...	...	...	...	...	...	...	...	...	...	...	...	...
2.	$m^{(0)} < m^{(1)} = m^{(2)}$	...	...	...	...	...	...	...	...	...	...	...	...	...	...	...	...	...	...	...	...	...	...	...	...	...	...	...
3.	$m^{(0)} < m^{(1)} > m^{(2)}$	...	...	...	...	...	...	...	...	...	...	...	...	...	...	...	...	...	...	...	...	...	...	...	...	...	...	...
4.	$m^{(1)} < m^{(2)} < m^{(0)}$	...	...	...	...	...	...	...	...	...	...	...	...	...	...	...	...	...	...	...	...	...	...	...	...	...	...	...
5.	$m^{(1)} < m^{(2)} = m^{(0)}$	...	...	...	...	...	...	...	...	...	...	...	...	...	...	...	...	...	...	...	...	...	...	...	...	...	...	...
6.	$m^{(1)} < m^{(2)} > m^{(0)}$	...	...	...	...	...	...	...	...	...	...	...	...	...	...	...	...	...	...	...	...	...	...	...	...	...	...	...
7.	$m^{(2)} < m^{(0)} < m^{(1)}$	...	...	...	...	...	...	...	...	...	...	...	...	...	...	...	...	...	...	...	...	...	...	...	...	...	...	...
8.	$m^{(2)} < m^{(0)} = m^{(1)}$	...	...	...	...	...	...	...	...	...	...	...	...	...	...	...	...	...	...	...	...	...	...	...	...	...	...	...
9.	$m^{(2)} < m^{(0)} > m^{(1)}$	...	...	...	...	...	...	...	...	...	...	...	...	...	...	...	...	...	...	...	...	...	...	...	...	...	...	...
10.	$m^{(0)} = m^{(1)} < m^{(2)}$	...	...	...	...	...	...	...	...	...	...	...	...	...	...	...	...	...	...	...	...	...	...	...	...	...	...	...
11.	$m^{(0)} = m^{(1)} = m^{(2)}$	...	...	...	...	...	...	...	...	...	...	...	...	...	...	...	...	...	...	...	...	...	...	...	...	...	...	...
12.	$m^{(0)} = m^{(1)} > m^{(2)}$	...	...	...	...	...	...	...	...	...	...	...	...	...	...	...	...	...	...	...	...	...	...	...	...	...	...	...
13.	$m^{(1)} = m^{(2)} < m^{(0)}$	...	...	...	...	...	...	...	...	...	...	...	...	...	...	...	...	...	...	...	...	...	...	...	...	...	...	...
14.	$m^{(1)} = m^{(2)} = m^{(0)}$	...	...	...	...	...	...	...	...	...	...	...	...	...	...	...	...	...	...	...	...	...	...	...	...	...	...	...
15.	$m^{(1)} = m^{(2)} > m^{(0)}$	...	...	...	...	...	...	...	...	...	...	...	...	...	...	...	...	...	...	...	...	...	...	...	...	...	...	...
16.	$m^{(2)} = m^{(0)} < m^{(1)}$	...	...	...	...	...	...	...	...	...	...	...	...	...	...	...	...	...	...	...	...	...	...	...	...	...	...	...
17.	$m^{(2)} = m^{(0)} = m^{(1)}$	...	...	...	...	...	...	...	...	...	...	...	...	...	...	...	...	...	...	...	...	...	...	...	...	...	...	...
18.	$m^{(2)} = m^{(0)} > m^{(1)}$	...	...	...	...	...	...	...	...	...	...	...	...	...	...	...	...	...	...	...	...	...	...	...	...	...	...	...
19.	$m^{(0)} > m^{(1)} < m^{(2)}$	...	...	...	...	...	...	...	...	...	...	...	...	...	...	...	...	...	...	...	...	...	...	...	...	...	...	...
20.	$m^{(0)} > m^{(1)} = m^{(2)}$	...	...	...	...	...	...	...	...	...	...	...	...	...	...	...	...	...	...	...	...	...	...	...	...	...	...	...
21.	$m^{(0)} > m^{(1)} > m^{(2)}$	...	...	...	...	...	...	...	...	...	...	...	...	...	...	...	...	...	...	...	...	...	...	...	...	...	...	...
22.	$m^{(1)} > m^{(2)} < m^{(0)}$	...	...	...	...	...	...	...	...	...	...	...	...	...	...	...	...	...	...	...	...	...	...	...	...	...	...	...
23.	$m^{(1)} > m^{(2)} = m^{(0)}$	...	...	...	...	...	...	...	...	...	...	...	...	...	...	...	...	...	...	...	...	...	...	...	...	...	...	...
24.	$m^{(1)} > m^{(2)} > m^{(0)}$	...	...	...	...	...	...	...	...	...	...	...	...	...	...	...	...	...	...	...	...	...	...	...	...	...	...	...
25.	$m^{(2)} > m^{(0)} < m^{(1)}$	...	...	...	...	...	...	...	...	...	...	...	...	...	...	...	...	...	...	...	...	...	...	...	...	...	...	...
26.	$m^{(2)} > m^{(0)} = m^{(1)}$	...	...	...	...	...	...	...	...	...	...	...	...	...	...	...	...	...	...	...	...	...	...	...	...	...	...	...
27.	$m^{(2)} > m^{(0)} > m^{(1)}$	...	...	...	...	...	...	...	...	...	...	...	...	...	...	...	...	...	...	...	...	...	...	...	...	...	...	...

Source: Authors

Notes

1. As we have noted on other occasions, transhumanism is increasingly reducing the significance of the phrase *to a large extent*.
2. The definitional specificity of the financial market in relation to the (general) economic market is that the financial market operates only in the nominal economy, while the economic market generally operates in any of the three types of economic activity: real, financial, nominal. It can be said, of course, that the financial market is a species of the genus called economic market. *Nota bene*: to the presumptive question whether the expression 'economic market' is not pleonastic, our answer is negative: there are many other markets—that is, exchange mechanisms—in society: for example, the political market; it also seems that language or, more precisely, conversation, is a market, because ideas are exchanged.
3. Following this work, a compilation (*The Symbolic Species Evolved*, with Theresa Schilhab, Frederik Stjernfelt, Terrence Deacon, editors) was published in 2012 by Springer Netherlands, which discusses the main consequences of the symbolic co-species hypothesis.
4. The issue of non-random mutations (namely, discretionary, deliberate) will be a topic of discussion in both this chapter and the following chapters. Here we mention that the mutations produced at the level of the biological species can be, to a certain extent (of course, indirect), of cultural origin as, in fact, the specialized literature shows, quite convincingly.
5. The non-restriction of the genesis of the symbolic species to the deliberate case (or to the deliberate cause) is crucial: for example, resuming the subject of Deacon's work, language (*Nota bene*: we are talking about articulate language, because language, from a general semiotic perspective, is also possessed by non-human animals) is a cultural product, not simply a social one. One can mention here a causal distinction between deliberate vs. emergent character of the genesis of a species: deliberate genesis is associated with the teleological cause, while the emerging genesis is associated with the effective/efficient cause.
6. The tendency, quite common of some authors, to avoid reductionism (*Nota bene*: which remains, of course, a formidable research tool, despite the hasty and superficial labels that apply to it) makes many conceptual typologies to remain inflationary, and in fact, for this reason, it should not be of much use.
7. According to both the paradigm model (Kuhn) and the research program model (Lakatos), more and more researchers will leave (explicitly but especially implicitly) the neoclassical mainstream and enter the evolutionary territory. We are, in fact, dealing with a speciation of a new mainstream in economic theory (and praxiology).

8. The paraphrasing of *black-box-ism* is obvious here. Mario Bunge spoke for the first time about black box-ism (Philosophy of Science. Vol. 2, *From Explanation to Justification*, Transaction Publishing, 1998).
9. Both the information and the price (respectively the binomial in question) must be treated as living species in a logical sense (see, in this context, Emil Dinga, Chap. 4, *Logically Living System—A Generative Machine for Auto-Poietic Systems*, published in Handbook of Research on Autopoiesis and Self-Sustaining Processes for Organizational Success, in 2020, at IGI Global Publishing House) (Dinga, 2021).
10. We recall that Adam Smith, credited with the wording 'invisible hand', did not use the phrase 'invisible hand' as such in his book on economics (Wealth of Nations), but in two other non-economics papers: *History of astronomy*, respectively *Theory of moral feelings*.
11. Of course, the micro-macro separation we are talking about here does not refer to the sphere aspects—because both the information-price binomial and the financial market-cultural geodesic market binomial cover the same extensive sphere, namely the financial market—but to the structural aspects: the binomial information-price belongs mainly to the microstructure of the financial market.
12. The symbolic nature of the information has already been established above. We strongly state that by symbolic nature of information we mean that information is culturally generated (by the functioning of the financial market under the impact of the action of participants in transactions) and we do not make any connection with the semiotic aspects associated with the term *symbol*. Such latter view of the term symbol is completely outside the scope of the research.
13. It usually begins with a description of the genotype, then the phenotype. However, given that the (logically) treatment of information as a (symbolic) species is not found in the literature, it is necessary, first, to establish/clarify the *informational individual*, so to speak, that is, the phenotype.
14. Of course, here we will have to discuss, in a more applied way than we did before regarding the symbolic species, the relationship between emergent and deliberative in the mutation that occurs at the level of information.
15. It should be noted that the 'population' of concepts regarding the *individual* in our research has increased: we have a *human individual* (the economic agent who trades), a *financial individual* (trading strategy), an *informational individual* (the accessed informational mix).
16. That is, the information experienced by the individual him/herself.
17. To make a comparison with real economic flows, while formal information is of the nature of the good (the time of its use differs from the time of its production), the implicit information is of the nature of durable goods

(experience and expertise of 'decoding' behaviours and thus, the generation of implicit information has a certain duration and repeatability in time), the bound information is of the nature of the services (the moment of its production coincides with the moment of its use or the moment of its consumption).

18. Not only regarding the behaviour of other economic operators (either cooperative or competitive) but, also, of course, the behaviour of the normative authority in the financial market, if and to the extent that this behaviour is transparent. But, even in this case, we have to operate the required dichotomy: the formal information is random (not totally but for the most part) for the economic agent, while the information acquired by that agent by observing the behaviour of changing formal information is by the nature of the implicit information.
19. It should be noted, here, an aspect that deserves to be developed, from an analytical point of view (both conceptually and methodologically), namely the fact that, since the implicit information is acquired by a given economic agent through the 'translation' of the behaviours of other economic agents which, however, in turn, substantiated their behaviours including by acquiring implicit information obtained from observing the behaviour of the economic agent concerned, there is a mutual catalysis of the production of implicit information from implicit information. A quantitative modelling of this process would be interesting and, perhaps, useful (*Nota bene*: the use of Eigen's concept of hypercycle may be of a great usefulness here as well).
20. Once again, it results the fundamental distinction between random (unpredictable), stochastic (statistically predictable, i.e., at the average of the population concerned) and deterministic (necessarily predictable).
21. Unlike the biological case, where only random mutations can exist (*Nota bene*: however, the transhumanist direction of research—and practice—could, of course, introduce deliberate mutations as well; in fact, genetic engineering addresses exactly this aspect; probably a biological evolution 'contaminated' with deliberate genetic mutations should be renamed as *prevolution*, where the *pre* particle, which fuses its final 'e' with the initial 'e' of *evolution*, signifies the character (also) premeditated of the biological evolution).
22. Recent concerns about the *economics of attention* examine exactly these aspects of the 'visibility' of the economic (financial) world for a given economic agent (concerns link, as we understand things, economic theory and, especially, economic behaviour, to what phenomenology—especially the Husserlian one—examined long before: the intentional creation of reality (Hendricks & Vestergaard, 2019). See also in the same area of concern the work *Human Capacity in the Attention Economy*, (Lane &

Atchley, 2020). Also the chapter *Behavioural Inattention*, prepared by Xavier Gabaix for Handbook of Behavioral Economics (Bernheim et al., 2018), which develops, from an accentuated psychological and anthropological perspective, the open issue of behaviourism in economics. In the same area of research, we also recommend Chap. 4, *Fallacies as Cognitive Virtues*, by Dov M. Gabbal and John Woods, from Games: Unifying Logic, Language, and Philosophy (Gabbay & Woods, 2009). It should be noted that in the terminology used in this study, this 'ingredient' was called the *IAR* status (or condition) of the economic agent (namely, interest, attention, reflectivity).

23. Obviously, the obsolete aspect of the bound information must be taken into account here, but if we assume that the 'stock' of bound information is invariant during the analysis period, then we do not have 'wear' (or inadequacy or inconsistency) regarding the previous bound information. We will, however, deal with the general case, in which we have such obsolescence.
24. In other words, we have, somehow, two types of deliberativeness: choice deliberativeness (m^{db}), respectively a rationalization deliberativeness (m^{d}).
25. Recall that transcription/transcribing refers to the transition of genetic information from DNA to m-RNA (messenger RNA), and translation refers to the formulation of the 'command' from m-RNA for protein synthesis.
26. For example, these numerical values may refer to informational entropy—such as Shannon informational entropy—or to measurements associated with another technical/calculating modality.
27. Specifically, which occurs in the interval $[t, t + \tau]$.
28. A question might be asked: why is the m^{h} component of the informational mutation vector maintained, since m^{a} and m^{d} deplete the entire mutation, that is, $(m^{a}) \bigcup (m^{d}) = m^{h}$? In our opinion, the distinction between m^{a} and m^{d} is not unvague, because the two categories (sets) are not totally independent of each other (i.e., formally, $(m^{a}) \bigcap (m^{d}) \neq \emptyset$ is not true). In other words, there is (or may be) a third category of mutations that is neither of m^{a} type nor of m^{d} type, and which we cautiously denote by m^{h}. So, m^{h} denotes the synergic effect of interactions between m^{a} and m^{d}.
29. Please note (again) that neither EMH nor, for the time being, AMH discusses or examines the issue of information structure when asserting their price integration. In fact, as we have mentioned elsewhere, EMH does not even propose a hypothesis or theory of this integration of information into price, merely declaring it as a matter of course. In our research, we propose both a structure of information in the financial market and a mechanism for taking over information in the price (more precisely in the decision to choose the price, the trading strategy or the individual transaction in the financial market).

30. The suggestion that $\rho_{(\bullet)}$ is of the nature of subjective probabilities is becoming increasingly clear. In fact, in what follows, we will consider them in this very position, even more specifically—as 'emanations' of preference which, in turn (as we have stated before) is an 'emanation' of propensity. Here there are two problems: (a) the problem of negative values of probability—this problem does not raise problems, because the concept of negative probability in economics is common; (b) the problem of the supraunit values of the probability, respectively of the sum of the probabilities from an exclusive and exhaustive distribution—this problem is active because we gave up the (Kolmogorov) condition $\rho_a + \rho_d + \rho_h = 1$. But already, at least in the behavioural economics, the supraunit probabilities, respectively the supraunit sum of the probabilities from an exclusive and exhaustive distribution, are commonplaces and are considered values that real economic agents 'access' in a common way, especially from a psychological perspective.
31. Not to be confused with the affine function: $y = a + b \cdot x$. A linear function is an affine function where $a = 0$ (the linear function passes through the origin of the Cartesian coordinates system). In our case, $b = 1$, so $\rho\_ \rho_d = m_i^d$.
32. So: $\rho_a = f\left(m_i^a\right)$, with $\frac{\partial f}{\partial\left(m_i^a\right)} < 0$; $\frac{\partial^2 f}{\partial\left(m_i^a\right)^2} < 0$.
33. Of course, the economic agent who has such a reluctant behaviour in taking over the changes from the formal information assumes the associated risk (but an adequate cost-benefit analysis can ensure that, from the perspective of net gain, such reluctance is 'rational').
34. So: $\rho_h = g\left(m_i^h\right)$, with $\frac{\partial g}{\partial\left(m_i^h\right)} < 0$; $\frac{\partial^2 g}{\partial\left(m_i^h\right)^2} > 0$.
35. This is, obviously, about the mutation observed in behaviour (*Nota bene*: the behaviour of other economic agents, that is, the aggregate behaviour of the financial market) which is then translated into implicit information.
36. A more analytical explanation could be as follows: (regarding ρ_α): a concave curve registers smaller variations than the variations of the independent variable when the last increases from a small size (or equivalently, the dependent variable already has high values), and that curve registers larger variations than those of the independent variable when the last increases from high values (or, equivalently, the dependent variable has already small values); (regarding ρ_h): the explanation is 'in the mirror' with the previous one, because of the convex allure of this curve, that is, larger variations than the independent variations (at the beginning) and smaller variations than the independent variations (later).
37. The attentive reader has already noticed (this being in its bright cone if read all the previous!) that the logical order (and, of course, the chrono-

logical one) between the production of the transcription and the production of the translation is reversed, in our proposal, compared with biological case: in the biological case, first the information is transcribed (from DNA into m-RNA), then the information from m-RNA is translated into the synthesis of the protein concerned, while in the case of the financial market (more precisely, in the case of generating implicit information), first is performed the translation (mutation) of the behaviour into (mutation regarding) the implicit information, then is performed the transcription (of the mutation) of the implicit information into the new informational structure of the economic agent.

38. In some cases, it is just a matter of choosing an individual transaction within a previously chosen trading strategy.
39. In principle, this behaviour appears to other participants in the functioning of the financial market as an 'outcome' of a black-box. In turn, by replicating the behaviour of the economic agent in question, the other economic agents will infer (translate) from the new behaviour of our economic agent, mutations at the level of their own implicit information.
40. From an algebraic point of view, this means that $(i_x) \bigcap (i_y) = (i_y) \bigcap (i_z) = (i_x) \bigcap (i_z) = \varnothing$, so $(i_x) \bigcup (i_y) \bigcup (i_y) = I$. From a topological point of view, the three sets, corresponding to the three categories of information, provide a topological covering the set of information (I).
41. For example, as we will see below, bound information passes, almost as soon as it is acquired, into implicit information, but it becomes implicit information as it loses its membership of the bound information category.
42. Maybe we should 'claim': *at the same time and in the same respect*, as the principle of non-contradiction in bivalent (Aristotelian) epistemic logic is defined.
43. A brief additional discussion will shed some light on this issue: the mutation exists in connection with changing information. So, the problem can be formulated, in an equivalent way, as follows: is there, at the level of the economic agent, a stock of bound information? Our answer is negative: bound information, once acquired (in any way), enters the stock of implicit information, as if it had been acquired through a translation process. This means that, at any given time, the structure of the information contains, with respect to the component element called bound information, the null value. The (genetically) formation of the new informational structure will take into account the bound information acquired at that time. But, in the very next moment, the bound information component regains the null value, and so on.
44. It seems that there is no need to accept (or introduce) degrees in this marginal competitive advantage, which means that any such marginal advantage can have the effect of selecting the individual who holds it. But,

of course, the discussion in this matter should not be considered closed in any way, because the thresholds of significance are ubiquitous in both kinematics and deliberation.

45. It is understood that we are talking about a generic, abstract price (i.e., about any possible price), obviously associated with objects traded in the financial market.
46. It is important to note that we are talking about the concept of transaction price, not the equilibrium price (the latter being assimilable, as we will see in later studies, with the natural price).
47. Remember that the price is always a unitary measurement (it refers to a unit of good/service).
48. It is not interesting, in the economy of the present study, to describe more analytically the total unit cost. One of these structures refers to the composition of the total unit cost of the unit cost of labour, the unit cost with depreciation of fixed capital, the unit cost of raw materials and energy from third parties. Another structure refers to the composition of the total unit cost of the fixed unit cost and the variable unit cost.
49. Obviously, by financial good we mean something (usually a financial security) traded or tradable in the financial market).
50. Needless to say, the value does not really overlap with the equilibrium price, although this (approximate) overlapping is generally possible, because of the overestimation or underestimation of the equilibrium price which the trader may do (as behaviourism claims).
51. Please note that this algebraic condition (whether it is estimated by calculation or is simply intuitive—in both cases there is obviously the possibility of error) is valid for both purchase and sale, respectively for both exploitable positions (short or long).
52. This is about the decision to choose an individual transaction (IT, in the previous notations), which is part of a pre-existing trading strategy (TS in the previous notations), not about the choice of the trading strategy itself—the latter decision is more complicated and it will be treated within the trinomial preference-information-price.
53. The uncertain component of the price structure is, of course, determined, at the level of the efficient cause, by the demand-supply rapport for the targeted financial good/title, the rapport in case being manifested at the moment $(t + \tau)$. In this sense, the position expressed by Farmer (Farmer & Lo, 1999) remains valid, which we also agree on, although we will develop another analytical path (but not another conceptual path) for this purpose.
54. In the case of price, there is an additional element of discussion: the analogous of recombination in biological evolution. This issue will be taken up in detail when the quantitative aspects of co-evolution for both BIP and TCIP will be studied.

55. This consequence, which we will extract and will further operationalize, does not weaken the concept of co-evolution, because co-evolution does not imply the existence of a standard selector environment but assimilates the co-species involved with the selector environment. It should be noted, however, that both co-species operate in an embedding environment (in our case, as mentioned in previous studies, this is cultural geodesic), so ultimately both co-species are subject to a higher order selection (the one operated by cultural geodesic). However, in the first instance, the acceptance of a mutually exercised selection of the two co-species—information, respectively price—understood, however, as mentioned above, as an 'extended' co-adaptation, is scientifically acceptable.
56. We remind that EMH assumes that the current price may change (essentially, also through the variation of the supply-demand rapport for the targeted good/title) but that these changes cannot be inferred by anyone based on the information held (usually from the past). The explanation given by this model of the financial market is a bit metaphysical: all the information available on the market (*Nota bene*: we have reduced the scope of the available information mix to the accessible information mix, then a further reduction of the scope of accessible information mix to the accessed information mix—what has been called the informational phenotype above) have already been integrated into the price.
57. Which obviously preserves our assumption of the primacy of behaviour over information
58. In the following, we will detail this idea more analytically.
59. Obviously, Fama did not discuss the issue in these evolutionary terms, because he remained confined to the neoclassical project of economic theory (and, therefore, also of financial theory). Fame simply 'decrees' that any available information is integrated automatically, instantly, completely, and at no cost, into the price (*Nota bene*: someone more scrupulous could introduce a kind of demon here—perhaps, to be called Fama's demon, by analogy with Maxwell's demon, in the field of statistical thermodynamics—which ensures that available information is entered into the price under the conditions just specified—needless to say that, in this context, informational entropy would greatly complicate the discussion, if taken into account). We have seen that, moreover, Lo (who wants to be an evolutionist) does not detail these aspects either, although here he would have had a much wider margin of conceptual manoeuvre than in the narrow framework of the neoclassical model.
60. We remind that Fama does not provide a price structure. Moreover, logically, the description of the mechanism for integrating information into price implies the existence of a price structure (as well as an information structure). *Nota bene*: however, a certain structure of information, but not

from a qualitative point of view, but from the perspective of origin, is also presented by Fama, when it accepts—because he did not propose from the begin—the three degrees of informationally efficiency of the market). In the absence of a price (and information) structure, Fama could not present any such integration mechanism. In our study, we tried to fill these two fundamental vulnerabilities of EMH.

61. In addition, as we have shown elsewhere, the Grossman-Stiglitz paradox forbids the irrelevance of the past to the predicted price.
62. The calculation of the coefficient of variation has the role of making comparable (at a-dimensional level) the variability of the information and the variability of the price, because, as it is known, neither the variance nor the standard deviation is comparable in two different time series, because the unit of measurement (hence the numerical dimension) introduces a dimensional incommensurability.
63. We recall that by the concept of moment we do not mean the moments calculated by statistics (mean, variance, kurtosis, skewness), but a property of the records from a time series to be invariant (either a level invariance—zero order moment, an invariance of the first difference—moment of order 1, or an invariance of the second difference—moment of order 2). Of course, moments of order greater than 2 can also be calculated, but the significance of such moments/invariants must firstly be clearly determined. The calculation method is identical to that used by econometricians when trying to determine the stationarity of a time series (if the series is not stationary for level values, then the 1st order differences are calculated and the stationarity test is applied, for example, the unit root test; the same about the cointegration of the two non-stationary series must be checked—*Nota bene*: in the cointegration operation the non-stationary must be of the same order). A work that develops the idea of the moment in the time series through more sophisticated technical means is *Momentum: Theory and Practice* written by Stephen Satchell and Andrew Grant (Satchell & Grant, 2020).
64. From a mathematical point of view, in the continuous case, the primary moment is calculated as a derivative of the first order; the secondary moment, as a derivative of the second order; and the tertiary moment, as a derivative of the third order. The derivation variable is obviously the time variable.
65. Please note that it is not a question of translating (or transcribing) of information into the price or vice versa, of translating (or transcribing) of price into the information but, in the same way as the information case, about translating (or transcribing) the mutation in the price genotype into the price phenotype.

66. The explanation for the lack of a translation step is that the mutation in the price genotype appears directly as a price variation ($\Delta^{p}_{t,\tau}$), while in the case of information, the mutation appeared as a variation of behaviour, not of information.
67. We remind that this addition is done logically (through the operator ⊕), not algebraically (through the operator +).
68. The 'barbarism' of ***punctuatedness*** is obviously generated by the mechanism of ***punctuated equilibrium*** proposed by Eldredge and Gould in 1971, as an alternative to gradual selection or, as the latter is also called, to phyletic gradualism.
69. We specify again that, in the social (economic) field, we also have a discretionary, programmatic mutation, so that the 'final' mutation represents a mix of random (emergent) and discretionary (deliberative).
70. *Modus vivendi* which is based on a *modus operandi* consisting of fetal (reciprocal) norms of action/reaction.
71. However, in the case of mutation and selection in human society, where the two processes acquire (more and more accentuated) deliberative characteristics, an 'axiological arrow' appears in evolution, respectively in co-evolution. In the case of BIP, obviously, the fitness has an axiological character or, at least, a rationalizable or rationalized one.
72. This counter is, of course, not exactly a chronological counter (that is, a clock-type counter), but rather a logical counter, that is, one that measures state changes. For example, in the case discussed here, the counter in question moves to the next 'moment' when a certain variable reappears in the logical chain of co-evolutionary concatenations: thus, when f_i reappears, it is 'dated' by one-step increment, and so on. Very interesting (and this aspect will, of course, be developed in the later stages of the research) is that we can judge the moments of a series of times—moments in the sense specified above)—from this co-evolutive perspective, which could lead to a reconsideration of predictability and even models of rationality for the functioning of the financial market.
73. Here we are interested in the existence of an objective/ontological criterion, not a subjective/epistemological one, that would 'force' the co-evolutionary process in the case of BIP to start from one of the two co-species in question rather than to the other co-species.
74. The idiosyncratic nature of the significance threshold of the mutations in the two genotypes is indisputable, in our opinion (otherwise, the whole behaviourism would be a bad joke, as well as the Nobel Prizes awarded for behaviourist and psychological work in economics).
75. Obviously, we do not ignore the problem of additivity here: variations may not be additive—either algebraically or logically—or some variations may

neutralize previous variations, so the aggregate result of infinitesimals that individually do not reach the threshold of significance is, in itself, a distinct issue which, however, will not be discussed in the present study but will be resumed in subsequent studies.

76. We remind the reader of the concept of *mental accounting* in behavioural studies (see, e.g., Richard Thaler and Cass Sunstein, *Nudge: Improving Decisions About Health, Wealth, and Happiness*) (Thaler & Sunstein, 2009).
77. We must recognize that here we pay (with pleasure) tribute to the behaviourist 'paradigm' of financial behaviour.
78. Here we bring, again, into question the bizarre behaviour (but obviously not so, although it is not anchored in psychology, as in the case of humans, but in physiology) of frogs that can stay to be boiled alive if the water temperature gradually rises and not punctuated.
79. We guide the reader to the two types of mistakes that can be made (discussed elsewhere in previous studies), with very different consequences for the 'fate' (as a player in the financial market of) the economic agent concerned.
80. However, it should not be understood, from here, that the real/concrete economic agent (not the one in the *homo mathematicus* model) is able to detect all these eventualities that can make him prudent in making some decisions.

References

Bernheim, B. D., Della Vigna, S., & Laibson, D. I. (Eds.). (2018). *Handbook of behavioral economics: Foundations and applications.* North Holland.

Deacon, T. (2007). *The symbolic species: The co-evolution of language and the brain* (1st ed.). W. W. Norton & Company;

Dinga, E. (2021). *Logically Living System: A Generative "Machine" for Autopoietic Systems—Chapter 4.* In Handbook of Research on Autopoiesis and Self-Sustaining Processes for Organizational Success—Chapter 4—Logically Living System – A Generative Machine for Auto-Poietic Systems. IGI Global.

Farmer, D. J., & Lo, A. W. (1999). Frontiers of Finance: Evolution and Efficient Markets. *Proceedings of the National Academy of Sciences of the United States of America, 96*(18), 9991–9992.

Gabbay, D. M., & Woods, J. (2009). Chapter 4. Fallacies as Cognitive Virtues. In O. Majer, A.-V. Pietarinen, & T. Tulenheimo (Eds.), *Games: Unifying Logic, Language, and Philosophy* (pp. 57–98). Springer Verlag.

Hendricks, V., & Vestergaard, M. (2019). *The Attention Economy: Markets of Attention, Misinformation and Manipulation* (pp. 1–17).

Lane, S., & Atchley, P. (Eds.). (2020). *Human Capacity in the Attention Economy.*

Satchell, S., & Grant, A. (2020). *Market Momentum: Theory and Practice | Wiley*. Wiley.

Thaler, R. H., & Sunstein, C. R. (2009). *Nudge: Improving decisions about health, wealth, and happiness.* Penguin Books.

CHAPTER 5

Preference as Symbolic Species

Preamble

This chapter extends the co-evolutionary binomial information-price (BIP), discussed in Chap. 3, to the trinomial preference-information-price trinomial (TCIP) *Nota bene*: to not cause confusion between the abbreviation of preference (P) and the abbreviation of price (P), we decided to abbreviate the preference with C (from credence, which is logically equivalent to preference). The reason is obviously the inclusion of preference into the (co-)evolutionary mechanism of the functioning of the financial market, because preference (adaptive, as will emerge from the following analysis, and as asserted and examined in FMAB-APH, (Dinga et al., 2022)), is a conceptual and methodological axis of the authors' scientific work.

From a methodological point of view, we will proceed in a similar way to the one in which we proceeded with the other two symbolic species (information, respectively price), so that there is a symmetry and a unit of treatment of the symbolic species in question. In this way, both the similarities and the differences between the new co-species, namely, preference, and the co-species already examined can be identified more easily.

The reader will be noticed, of course, that by introducing preference into our discussion, we have moved from the 'two-body problem' to the 'three-body problem'.[1] The analogy between the problem of Newtonian mechanics and the problem that concerns us here is not only metaphorical: indeed, as we shall see, the formalization of the rules of reaction

E. Dinga et al., *Co-Evolution of Symbolic Species in the Financial Market*, https://doi.org/10.1007/978-3-031-31698-2_5

between three 'targets' implies some difficulties (logical and of mechanism) that did not occur in the case of BIP and for which it must be found acceptable and realistic solutions. This means that we will have to proceed in a similar way to that dealing with the problem of the three bodies (and, of course, the problem of the two bodies): identifying a 'fixed point'[2] around which the three co-species 'gravitate'—we anticipate that this should be exactly the return of the individual transaction (IT) in the trading strategy (TS), either to the market average or to the relevant competitor, but the exact way in which this 'fixed point' is identified and formalized will be revealed only by the conduct of the research.[3]

As only the conceptual-logical aspects of information and price have been examined in the previous chapter, the quantitative formalization part of the (co-)evolutionary mechanism of the BIP in financial market will be treated within the formalism that will be developed in this study on to TCIP because, as shown above, BIP is a subspecies of TCIP.

Preference as a Symbolic Species in the Financial Market

Forming of TCIP requires that all three of its components—information, price and preference—be, first and foremost, symbolic species of the financial market and, second, co-species in relation to each other. Of course, one of the ways to deal with this issue is to study the three pairs of co-species that can be formed:[4] (a) information-price; (b) information-preference; (c) price-preference. As the first pair of co-species was dealt with in Chap. 4, it remains to examine the remaining two pairs. However, based on the methodological pattern acquired in the information-price co-species analysis, we will 'jump' directly to TCIP, so what remains to be done before the very design of TCIP is to examine the preference as a species and, respectively, symbolic co-species in the financial market.

Both the concept of economic preference and that of adaptive preference have been discussed *per se*, as we have already mentioned in detail in FMAB-APH (Dinga et al., 2022), so here we will not resume the theoretical, definitional or typological aspects in question. In the following, we will summarize the key features that 'qualify' the (adaptive) preference as a candidate for the status of a symbolic species in the financial market.[5]

The Logical Structure of Preference

The analytical examination of the preference from the perspective of the quality of a symbolic species in the financial market is conditioned (as in the case of information, respectively of the price) by its structure. In this paragraph we will therefore try to identify the logical structure of the (adaptive) preference.

Proference.
FMAB-APH (Dinga et al., 2022) introduced the concept of *proference* (from *pro*pensity and pre*ference*) to suggest the strong (though relatively inextricable) link between propensity and preference. Although the concept of proference is, perhaps applicable, in any field where preference (i.e., pre-existing belief) works, we will restrict the discussion to the economic field and, in fact, to the functioning of the financial market.

Propensity has been defined as a predisposition of the last substratum (i.e., a predisposition which, in turn, needs no other logical basis or justification), an inclination[6] of the generic individual to act, i.e., to and externalize the will, under certain given conditions (context). We recall that this concept (though not the term itself) was still proposed by Aristotle in his Physics but, in a relatively unambiguous way, it was introduced into the scientific debate by Karl Popper (1959) as expressing a kind of intrinsic objective probability, of non-frequential type, specific to the singular event. The intrinsic nature of propensity is the crucial element here, meaning that a phenomenon or process, under certain conditions (i.e., in a specified context), has a natural, somehow esoteric, inclination towards a certain development, a certain target, or a certain behaviour. The debate over the suggestion that this propensity be considered as a kind of probability (objective non-frequential probability of the singular event[7]) is vast and still unfinished, and we have referred to it extensively before.

But another suggestion about propensity was that it could be considered a *cause of the cause*.[8] In fact, in the following, we will exploit exactly this suggestion. For this we can use a graphical representation (Fig. 5.1).

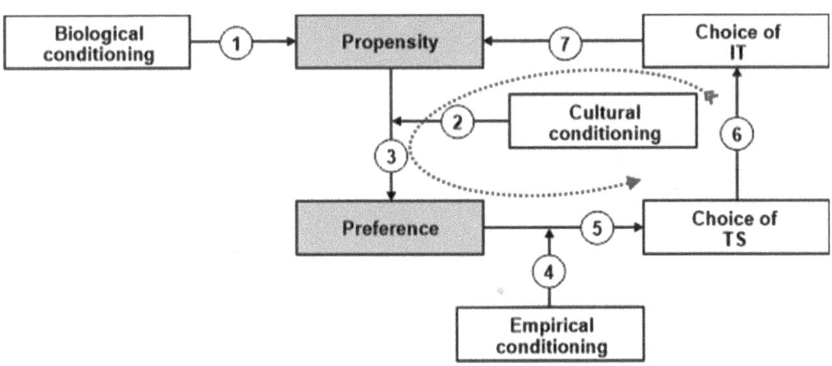

Fig. 5.1 Logical relationship between propensity and preference. *Source*: Authors

where, keeping the previous notations, TS means trading strategy and IT means individual transaction.

Short Discussion.

- proference functions as a relationship of determination (in the causal sense[9]) from propensity to preference (phase '3'). This means, in our opinion, that the preference has a large stability[10] because, as we believe, the propensity, in turn, is very elastic, in the sense that it has strong properties both robustness (resistance to disturbances) and resilience (ability to return to the state or trajectory—or (very) near the state or trajectory—from which it was dislocated/disturbed[11]);
- the shift from propensity to preference, or the manifestation of propensity as a cause of preference,[12] is not unconditional—this shift is made in specific, concrete cultural contexts (phase '2');
- except for phase '1' (biological propensity conditioning), all other phases are repeatable (possibly cyclically, but this cyclicity must be justified separately) as the human economic operator acts (trades) in the market;
- the manifestation of the preference in the financial market is made, of course, through the empirical filter (we have an empirical conditioning—phase '4'—of the manifestation of the preference in choosing the trading strategy—phase '5');
- instead, the choice of the individual transaction no longer depends on the preference (not directly, more exactly), but (almost) exclusively on the chosen trading strategy—phase '6'; somehow, the trading strategy acts as a model of *sui generis* rationality—the individual transaction is no longer the subject of a choice, it is necessarily analogous to how a lemma results from a theorem or a theorem results from a set of axioms;[13]
- however, the individual transaction is the test of the transaction strategy—depending on its return, there is the possibility of influencing the propensity (phase '7'), and the cycle resumes.

A Proposal for the Structure of Preference.
Based on the above, we can now move on to identifying the possible (or a possible) logical structure of the preference. Before submitting a proposal to attention, a few things are worth mentioning:

(i) we do not consider that there is a pure preference, that is, a preference which is the exclusive result of culture and experience, but that, in reality, preference is what we have called, in this paper, proference;
(ii) in this sense, preference also has an important (and relevant) biological component and, through biology, an important (and relevant) psychological component. We use the term psychological here especially from the perspective of the subconscious;[14]
(iii) although, in most cases, we will continue to talk about preference (more precisely, adaptive preference), we will always keep in mind the concept of proference;
(iv) on the basis of the previous mention, we will also make our proposal regarding the logical structure of preference, which is, more precisely, a logical structure of proference.

Our proposal for the logical structure of the preference is as follows: a ternary structure (*KDF* model) that allows the functioning of the mechanism described in Fig. 4.1. *Nota bene*: for methodological reasons, the *KDF* model will be presented in the order *K* - *F* - *D*.

- (*K*) *hard component* (hardcore): the hard component of preference (i.e., proference) is propensity itself. The qualification of this component as 'hard' is justified by the following:
  - it is the most *elastic* component of preference—robustness, respectively resilience is manifested in the highest degree in this component of preference/proference;
  - propensity (as a dispositional inclination of the human individual) has a predominantly biological determination, a determination that is quasi-invariant, which gives it a very high stability (although, as we will show, not even immutability or invariance);
  - the propensity must be considered, in our opinion, as generative, institutive (therefore, as a genuine cause), for the manifest preference (i.e., that preference that chooses the trading strategy—see Fig. 5.1), hence its qualification as *core*;

- the hard component establishes the axiological matrix (A) on the basis of which the trading strategy (TS) will be chosen;
- (*F*) *functional component*: the component that 'faces' the financial market strategically, namely the component that makes the effective choice of the trading strategy to be followed by the economic (human) operator. The characteristics of this component are as follows:
  - is the most *plastic* component of the preference—the impulses coming from the individual transaction (depending on the return it provides for the economic agent, by confronting the environment—both cultural geodesic and other contemporary trading strategies) have the greatest potential impact to change of preference;
  - at the level of this component, there is a first accumulation of the preference change tension, an accumulation subject, however, to an inertia that we will talk about later, and which requires a critical mass of this change tension accumulation,[15] to transmit the 'message' to the deliberative component of preference (see below);
  - the functional component of preference behaves like a *sui generis* tester, it directly (i.e., operationally) confronts the environment of the financial market, that is, the factuals;[16]
  - the functional component chooses the individual transaction (IT), as a logical inference from the trading strategy already chosen;
- (*D*) *deliberative component*: is an intermediate component into which the impulses for change enter from the transactional environment of the financial market, i.e., from the functional component (*Nota bene*: these impulses are inherently associated with individual transactions) and from which, under certain conditions to be specified, the impulses of change go towards hard component of preference/proference. The characteristics of this component are as follows:
  - the deliberative component of preference is logically situated between the hard component and the functional component[17] of preference, being a decision-making filter as to what (and even when) impulses for change will reach the hard component (propensity) of preference;
  - somehow, if we are to accept a model of rationality in the internal mechanism of preference functioning, it will be (should be) placed within the deliberative component of preference;

- from a structural point of view, the deliberative component has an osmotic character—it performs tests and choices both in the direction of the hard component and in the direction of the functional component of preference;
- it combines the properties of plasticity with those of elasticity, in idiosyncratic proportions, although not completely immutable—it can be said that there is a relative balance, at the level of this component, between plasticity and elasticity[18] face to change tension;
- at this component occurs a second accumulation of the preference change tension, which is also subject, as in the case of the functional component, to inertia, that is, to the formation of a critical mass of the change tension in question, before the message is transmitted to the hard component of preference;
- the deliberative component chooses the trading strategy (TS), based on the axiological matrix 'established' by the hard component.

Nota bene: The informed reader will immediately notice the parallel that can be drawn between our proposal on the logical structure of preference/proference and the logical structure proposed by Imre Lakatos—in his *research programme* concept, as a description of the generic scientific research methodology—for the 'reconciliation' of the concept of paradigm proposed by Kuhn with the concept of factual refutability (falsifiability) proposed by Popper.[19] This analogy (see Annex 1 on the concept and typology of analogy, presented in FMAB-APH (Dinga et al., 2022)) can give a model of (adaptive) preference in the financial market some paradigmatic characteristics, i.e., the theory of paradigm (in Kuhn's sense) can be applied to the functioning and evolution of preference in the financial market, precisely through the critical masses required of both the functional and the deliberative component to pass on the accumulated momentum for change (i.e., the equivalent, in Kuhn's paradigm concept, of discarding the anomalies found in 'normal'[20] functioning of the preference in question). This analogy seems all the more potentially productive as, like Kuhn's condition for the existence of a paradigm, we have suggested that the preference of an economic agent is unique at some given point, because it is generated/caused by the propensity of the agent, which is, obviously, unique at some point. The suggestion we are referring to here may, moreover, be a direction for further research.

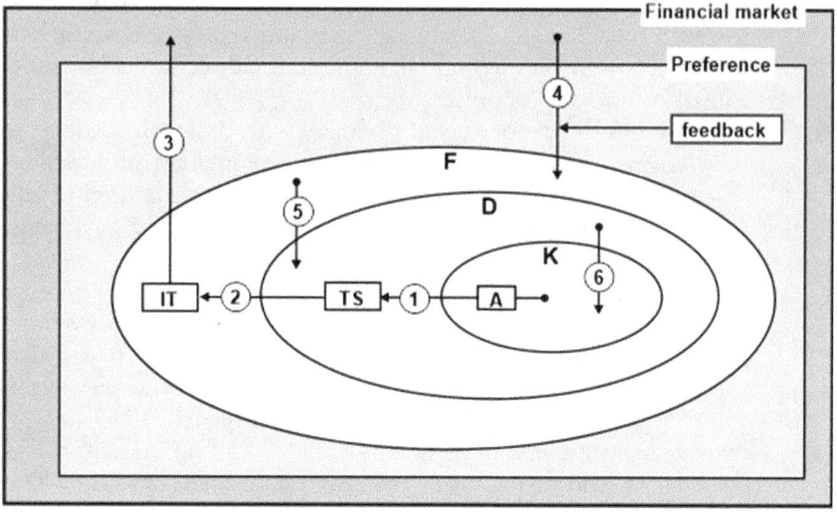

Fig. 5.2 Structure of preference/proference. *Source*: Authors

Figure 5.2 shows, in a synoptic way, the mechanism of adaptive preference, from the perspective of its logical structure, as the latter was proposed above.

Short Discussion.

(a) regarding the logic of Fig. 5.2:

- *phase '1'* refers to the decisive conditioning exerted by the hard component (more precisely, the propensity that characterizes the economic agent) on the preference, namely, through the axiological matrix (A)—values, traditions, beliefs[21] –, on the deliberative component (*Nota bene*: as seen in Fig. 5.2, the hard component is not directly related to the functional component); the effect of this determination is, in fact, the choice of trading strategy (TS). Please note that the choice of trading strategy is not a mechanical (or quasi-mechanical) inference from propensity, for the following reasons:
  - propensity itself is not clearly defined, as unambiguous or as having the ability to provide certainty;[22]

- propensity does not work completely in a rational way (as we said before, it is largely—if not decisively—of subconscious origin) but it is, as the name suggests, an inclination,[23] a predisposition, a potential orientation, an impulse;[24]

- *phase '2'* generates the individual transaction (IT) by inference from the trading strategy (also quasi-mechanical, but with a more accentuated deliberative character, however, than in the case of inferring the trading strategy from propensity):
  - the trading strategy represents a greater constraint than the one imposed by the propensity. In fact, to a large extent (therefore, not entirely), the trading strategy is a model of rationality of the second order (if we accept to consider the propensity as a model of rationality of the first order) for the choice of the individual transaction;
  - we suggest that the trading strategy, once chosen on the basis of propensity, provides, like any model of rationality, a 'short list' of individual transactions consistent and coherent with the trading strategy in question, of which, to a certain extent (with a certain, very low, degree of freedom, as we suggested earlier) the economic operator can choose or design, as the case may be, the individual transaction that s/he will actually operate in the financial market;
  - we mention that the choice of the individual transaction from the 'short list' is not made by rational calculation (master rational calculation has already been done by the trading strategy) but on quasi-mechanical inferential bases, that is, based on local, temporary or, as the behaviourists say, based on contextual intuitions (the anchoring effect, e.g.—see an examination of a comprehensive list of such effects, of a psychological[25] nature); (Kahneman, 2012)
- *phase '3'* represents the effective operationalization of the individual transaction in the financial market. This individual transaction will transmit the resulting outcome (e.g., the net return obtained by the economic operator) to the functional component of the preference (see phase '4');
- in turn, the functional component forwards to the deliberative component a kind of assessment of the impact that the individual transaction had on the expectations of the economic operator concerned (see phase '5'), in an attempt to establish the correc-

tions to be applied to the latter component. The way this feedback operates refers to the adjustment of those contextual psychological imponderables, mentioned above, at phase '2', so that the inference of the individual transaction from the trading strategy, in the next transactional cycle, will be made within these adjustments;

- adjustments made to deliberative components are (or may be) passed on from this component to the hard component of the preference (phase '6') which is therefore also subject to adjustments. Essentially, the latter feedback holds the possibility and the mechanism of the adaptive preference functioning.

(b) on the logic of adjusting preference components:

- all three feedbacks (from the financial market—more precisely, from the financial market environment, in fact—to the functional component, from this to the deliberative component and from the latter to the hard component) occur only if a threshold of significance of the result obtained, in each case separately, is reached. Thus, in order for the feedback from the financial market to the functional component of the preference, which refers to the (net) return generated by the individual transaction in question, to be 'communicated' to the deliberative component, that return needs to be placed outside the expectations of the economic agent,[26] both in the favourable and in the unfavourable sense. Thus, if we denote by $\theta_{(x)}$ (where $x \in \{F, D, K\}$), the acceptable margin of acceptance for the economic agent with respect to the gap of the actual result compared to its expectation (i.e., exactly the limits of the significance threshold), with g the gap in question, with R the actual result of the individual transaction, with $\overline{R}$ the expected/anticipated result, then we can write:

$$g = \left|R - \overline{R}\right| \tag{5.1}$$

Therefore, the generation of feedback occurs only when is verified the condition:

$$g > \theta \tag{5.2}$$

- the significance thresholds for the three feedbacks are different. We believe that their descending order of magnitude is as follows:

$$\begin{aligned} &\theta_K : \theta_D : \theta_F, \text{ or} \\ &\theta_F < \theta_D < \theta_K \end{aligned} \tag{5.3}$$

- that is: the rigidity to change (i.e., robustness) of the three components of preference/proference decreases from the centre to the periphery—the functional component is the most sensitive to exceeding the significance threshold (formalizable by $\theta_F < \theta_D$, respectively $\theta_F < \theta_K$,[27] respectively $\theta_D < \theta_K$).[28] In other words, the peripheral (i.e., functional) component is the most sensitive to the gap, followed by the deliberative component and, finally, the hard component, which has the lowest sensitivity to the gap.
- a brief remark should be made about resilience (or the ability to return from the state or trajectory generated by the application of feedback). Rigidity (robustness) is a property with symmetrical action in relation to the state/trajectory of the system to which it is associated: the higher it is in the face of the disturbance, the greater it is when it returns from the disturbance. It turns out that rigidity behaves conservatively in both directions, which means that, from the perspective of symmetry over time, robustness and resilience are inversely proportional. The conclusion is that resilience will act all the later as the duration of the system's resistance to disruption has been longer.[29] If this seems to be the conclusion of the manifestation of resilience in time, what can be said about the behaviour of resilience in space?[30] We believe that, in terms of restoring the disturbed system (bringing it to the state or on the trajectory as before the disturbance), resilience is affected by the phenomenon of hysteresis—*grosso modo*, hysteresis captures some of the 'intensional' effect of the disturbance, which means that resilience will restore the state of the system not exactly in the one it had before the disturbance, but in its proximity (neighbourhood). In fact, the idea must be accepted that, due to perturbation, despite the space resilience (as we called it for reasons of symmetrical terminology with time resilience) the disturbed system learns, which means that a perturbation will always leave a mark on the target system. Given the 'order' of rigidity of the three components of preference, the issues of robustness, resilience, and learning can be represented graphically as in Fig. 5.3.

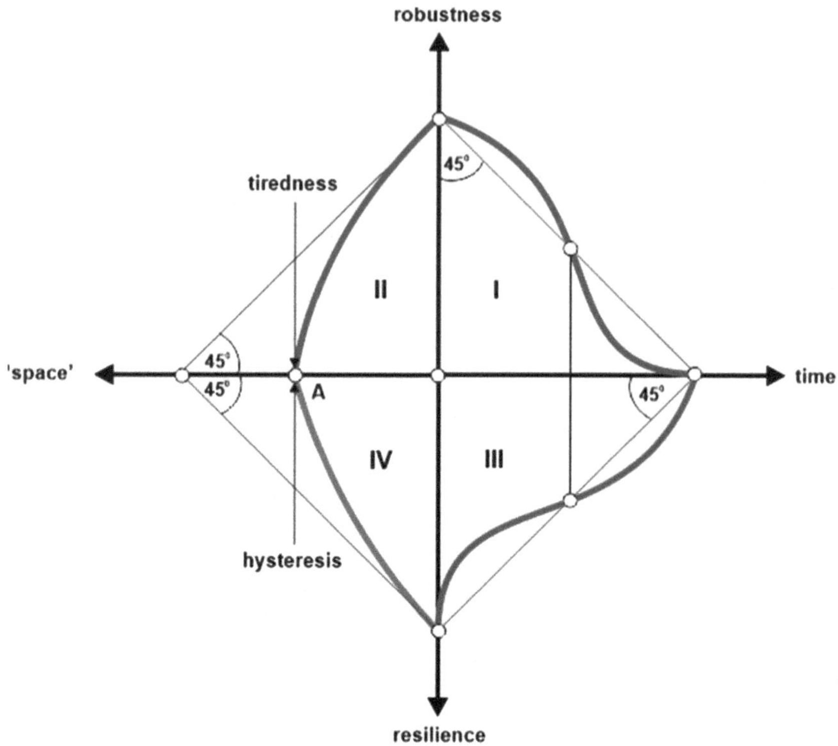

Fig. 5.3 Behaviour in 'space' and time of robustness and resilience. *Source*: Authors

Comment.
The graph exhibits four areas:

- **I**: *robustness as function on time*: this resistance property of any system decrease decelerated (the curve is concave) as the duration to face a generic perturbation increase; however, at a given time, depending on the idiosyncrasy of that system, an inflection point occurs and the decreasing of the robustness becomes accelerated (the curve becomes convex), until the robustness is definitively infringed. The (conjectured) explanation consists in the fact that the 'attack' of the perturbation meets a fresh capacity to resist but, after a while, the resources of such resistance begin to exhaust and the robustness decreases more rapidly than until then;

- **II**: *robustness as function of 'space'*: the robustness is permanently and decelerated decreasing (the curve is only concave). But this case has an important feature, namely the robustness has a horizon of action narrower than the expected one. Such a phenomenon is the result of some (conjectured) tiredness which the robustness manifests in its action in 'space'. The tiredness is objectified by stopping the robustness action in some zones/issues falling under the perturbation. So, if, relative to time, the robustness decreases accelerated after a while, relative to 'space' the robustness simply does not act everywhere;
- **III**: *resilience as function of time*: by contrast with the robustness, the resilience decrease, in the beginning, in an accelerated mode (the curve is convex), then, after an inflection point, its decreasing becomes decelerated (the curve becomes concave). The (conjectured) explanation is as follows: the 'attack' of the perturbation meets a relatively inactive device of resilience, so the capacity of recovering the state (or the kinematic position) of the perturbed system decreases accelerated. Then, the resilience device is activated and, although its potential continues to decrease, such decrease is decelerated;
- **IV**: *resilience as function of 'space'*: like the robustness, the resilience decreases accelerated as the 'space' expands (the curve is only concave). The (conjectured) explanation is one quite well-known in the literature: the resilience is characterized by hysteresis (a lack of memory of the previous path of the system in the case), so the recovery is narrower than the previous perturbation (either as dis-location or dis-positioning, after the case).

As for the mechanism for adjusting the preference/proference components under the impact of the disruption (i.e., the production of a financial market return above the significance/meaning threshold given by the economic operator involved), it can be represented as in Fig. 5.4.

- another problem is that (which has been mentioned before) of accumulability. That is, the question may be asked: does the economic operator react to the first exceeding (or reaching) of the significance threshold? Our opinion on this matter is as follows:
  - there is, as in any human behaviour, a logistic curve for the accumulation of the cause for triggering the effect (Fig. 5.4 showed such a logistic curve regarding the passage between the significance thresholds of the preference components);

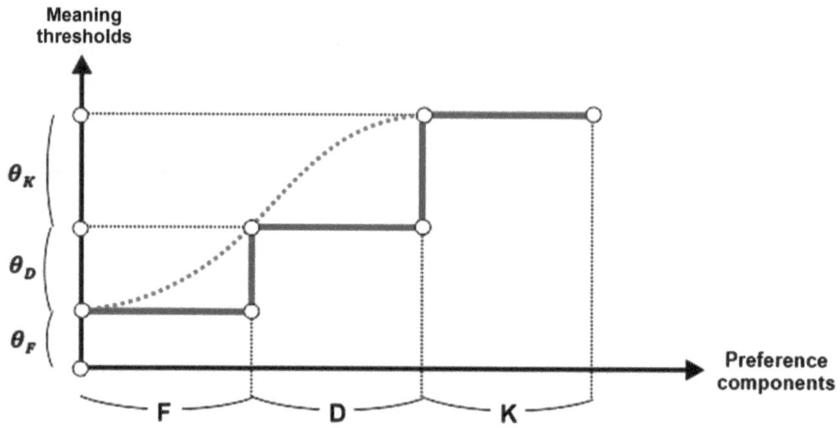

Fig. 5.4 Significance thresholds for adjusting the preference components. *Source*: Authors

- as a result, the economic operator tries to ascertain whether the achievement of the significance threshold is conjunctural or systematic, whether it is reversible or not in the short term, etc., which means that there is an accumulation of change tension regarding the adjustment of the component in question of the preference;[31]
- behaviourism also brought into debate some purely heuristic behaviours that influence both evaluation and decision-making in the context of the accumulation of change tension, generated by results that go beyond the threshold of significance (either favourably or unfavourably): this is about the memory effect (so to speak) and which, in essence, refers to the fact that the last event has a comparatively greater impact (even on substantially equal quantifications) than events of the same class, but which are more distant in the past; as we will see below, this will influence the decision to change the affected component of the preference (or, as the case may be, to change the very significance threshold);

Nota bene: so, a complication (even more important) of the problem of adjusting the components of the preference refers to the possibility (and the related conditions) to change the very significance thresholds. We will present some opinions (without extensive development) in this matter:

- the change in significance thresholds is equivalent, to a relevant extent, to the (potential) change in the components of the preference. Indeed, a narrowing of the margin of acceptance of the gap between the expected effect and the effect actually achieved means a decrease in the significance threshold, i.e., an increase in the sensitivity (plasticity) of the component to which the change in that significance threshold refers, so a greater potential than that component to undergo changes in response to that gap;
- the economic operator can substitute the modification of the preference component (when the associated significance threshold is exceeded) with the modification of the significance threshold itself, for the future. This can happen when the economic operator is particularly 'attached'[32] to the existing profile of the preference component in question;[33]
- an issue that is both logical and psychological at the same time should also be discussed here:
  - the inclination of the economic agent towards second-order preferences (see the note immediately above) makes the change of significance thresholds have a decreasing 'probability' going from the periphery to the centre of the preference/proference structure: thus, the first change reaction occurs at the functional component level of preference, then (if raising the threshold of significance is no longer useful—a gap that is too large, so that no longer triggers any response is as if, physiologically, we lose our ability to feel physical small pains, so we can die if we no longer have the sensation of pain to degrees that are not lethal—we move to change the threshold of significance of the deliberative component and, based on the same reasoning, to change the threshold of significance of the hard component);
  - it is obvious that the (quantitative) change of a significance threshold is a function of two factors: (a) the secondary preference specific to the component in question; (b) the value by which the significance threshold of the component from the periphery has already been modified;[34]
- the debate on preference is largely centred around the dilemma *given preferences—adaptive preferences*, but in the case of adaptive preference, no more analytical examinations such as the one above developed on the thresholds of significance and, especially, regarding the possibility of substituting the change of preference (more precisely,

of the components of preference) with the modification of the significance thresholds associated with the components of preference will be done. Accordingly, we will set out some additional considerations here:

- *first of all*, being about the possibility of a substitution, we can discuss the existence of an indifference curve between the change of the significance threshold and the change of the affected component of the preference. The issue of the indifference curve is controversial—the vast majority of approaches draw it in a two-dimensional plane (with the two substitutable variables on the coordinate axes, respectively) as a decreasing and convex curve, often (roughly) symmetrical with respect to coordinate axes;[35]
- *secondly*, if we introduce the second-order preference (preference for preference), different for different components of preference/proference, then the stylized shape of the indifference curve, mentioned above, must undergo adjustments;
- *thirdly*, the structure of preference, as assumed in the present study, is a *centre-periphery*[36] structure generated by logical and psychological considerations. However, the subjective probabilities assigned by the economic agent to the second-order preference (*Nota bene*: the second order of preference can only be 'quantified' by these probabilities) can change the order 'decreed' theoretically, so that in real life there to be a resultant of to this order, which, obviously, is not immutable either;
- *fourthly*, all these considerations (which can be realistic and justified) introduce so many imponderables, intersecting causalities, conditionalities that are difficult to detect and, above all, to measure, that it becomes obvious that invariants need to be found, although relatively, to allow reasoning with an acceptable degree of certainty or, at the limit, probability. Fig. 5.5 shows an image of the problem of the indifference curve between the change of the preference component and the change of the significance threshold associated with the component concerned;

Taking into account the actual return (R), more exactly, the gap $g = \left| R - \overline{R} \right|$, and putting on abscissa the gap (g), and on ordinate the ratio $\frac{\theta}{x}$ (so, $\frac{\theta}{x} = h(g)$) we can draw a kinematics as in Fig. 5.6. The notations have the following mathematical significations:

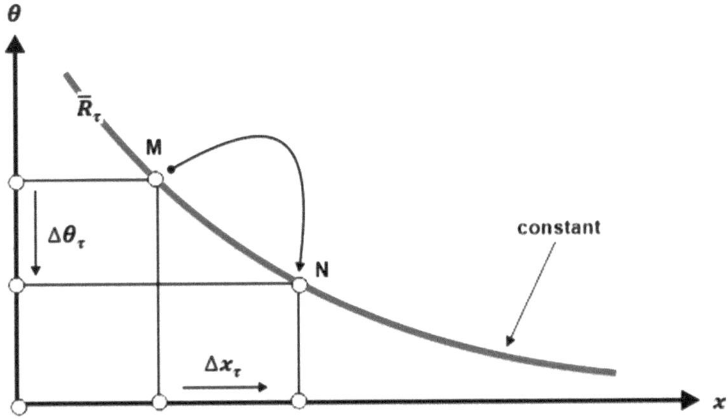

Fig. 5.5 Indifference curve signification threshold-preference component. *Source*: Authors

$$\begin{aligned}
&1: \left[\frac{\partial(h)}{\partial g} > 0\right] \wedge \left[\frac{\partial^2(h)}{\partial g^2} > 0\right] \\
&2: \left[\frac{\partial(h)}{\partial g} > 0\right] \wedge \left[\frac{\partial^2(h)}{\partial g^2} < 0\right] \\
&3: \left[\frac{\partial(h)}{\partial g} < 0\right] \wedge \left[\frac{\partial^2(h)}{\partial g^2} < 0\right] \\
&4: \left[\frac{\partial(h)}{\partial g} < 0\right] \wedge \left[\frac{\partial^2(h)}{\partial g^2} > 0\right]
\end{aligned} \tag{5.4}$$

A stylized interpretation of Fig. 5.6 is done below (by each of the four remarkable cases):

- (**1**) if $g = 0$, i.e., $R = \bar{R}$, the preference for preference is totally inactive[37] ($\theta = 0$). As g increases (either if $R > \bar{R}$ or $R < \bar{R}$, because the module of g), the ratio h increases decelerated (the curve is convex). Such an increasing is done by the increasing of θ in the mentioned ratio.[38]

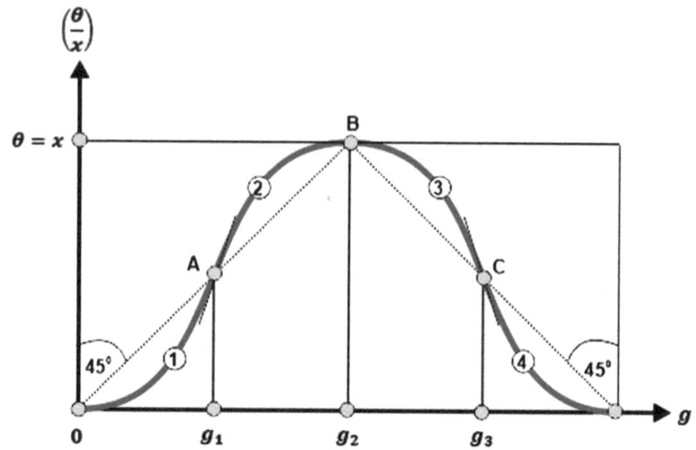

Fig. 5.6 Relationship between *h* and *g*. *Source*: Authors

- (**2**) after an inflection point (A, namely in the point g_1 on abscissa) the increasing of *g* will generate a decelerated increase of θ (so, of *h*, given *x*= constant). This time *h* is concave. The explanation for the change of the allure of *h* is the following: after matching a 'quantity' of change in the preference for preference (i.e., of θ), the conservative property of the propensity is activated and the individual becomes stingier with the modification of θ;
- (**3**) at point B, θ equals *x* (so, *h* = 1), in the point g_1 on abscissa. This point should be considered as a (relatively immutable) ceiling of change in θ, because, as said before, of the conservative characteristics of the propensity of the individual. Next, to the extent that as *g* continues to increase, the ratio *h* decreases in a decelerated way. The (conjectured) explanation is: never the preference for preference (components) can be higher than the preference for the significance thresholds, because changing the limits of those thresholds is not only easier to do but, especially, does not change the propensity. Again, the conservativeness of the propensity works—it manifests until point C, which is a new inflection point;
- (**4**) from point C (which has as abscissa g_3) forward, to the extent that as *g* increases further, the decreasing of ratio *h*, that is, of θ, becomes accelerated. The reason is the following: individual will

interpret such (high) gap of actual return related to the expected one as something un-natural, so s/he could believe that a non-orthodox phenomenon is a cause for such a size of g—as consequence, the individual becomes much more caution regarding the changing of his/her preference for preference.

Additional Comment.

- As, psychologically, rather θ is (relatively) constant/rigid, Fig. 5.6 can be replicated by measuring on ordinate, ratio $\frac{x}{\theta}$, but such an analysis, based on the above one, mutatis mutandis, is left, as an exercise, for the interested reader;
- What about the case in which x is not constant? We can think that θ and x verify the algebraic invariance $\theta + x = 1$,[39] where $\theta, x \in [0,1]$. This means that the higher θ is, the lower x is, and vice versa. However, in our opinion, such a hypothesis is unrealistic, because a so high elasticity of the two variables, to each other, cannot be accepted, again for psychological reasons.

A More Analytical Discussion.

(i) *first of all*, it is necessary to clarify what is meant by $\Delta\theta$ and Δx, respectively:
  - the variation/modification of the significance threshold ($\Delta\theta$) refers to the widening, respectively narrowing of the interval in which the change of the return is (still) acceptable for the economic agent concerned. Thus, a return in the financial market that is unsuitable for the agent (e.g., it is too low compared to expectations[40]) will urge the agent to become less 'pretentious' and selective, thus reducing his sensitivity to the signals transmitted by kinematics of return;
  - the variation/modification of the component (in question a) of the preference (Δx) refers to the following:
    for $x \equiv F$: an 'enlargement' of the functional component of the preference means that a wider typology of individual transactions becomes accessible to the economic operator, within the same trading strategy; things happen conversely when there is a 'narrowing' of the functional component of preference;[41]

for $x \equiv D$: similar to the previous case, a 'widening' of the deliberative component of preference means that several alternative trading strategies become accessible to the economic operator (compared to the previous state), within the same propensity; things happen conversely when there is a 'narrowing' of the deliberative component of preference;

for $x \equiv K$: 'widening' the hard component of preference refers, of course, to extending the economic operator's propensity. But what exactly does 'extending propensity' mean? In our view, an increase in the propensity means an increase in the economic agent's psychological readiness to engage in financial market operations, a 'deepening' of its operational determination or, in other words, an increase in the likelihood that the economic operator in question will carry out commercial operations in the financial market;[42]

(ii) *secondly*, the direct (or inverse) proportionality between the variation of the significance threshold and the variation of the component (in question a) of the preference must be established:

– Figure 5.5 shows an inverse proportionality of this kinematic relationship, but how can it be justified? We present the following reasoning:

the value of the indifference curve is given by the (net) return expected by the economic agent following the individual transaction that it operationalized in the financial market (noted $\overline{R}_\tau$: return at time τ);

when the significance threshold is reduced/narrowed, a smaller deviation from the actual return than expected will signal to the economic agent that something is wrong with the performance of his/her transaction (in other words, the economic agent becomes more sensitive to disturbances);

increasing the economic operator's sensitivity to disruption causes more individual transactions to 'acquire' the likelihood of being abandoned as underperforming, thus narrowing the scope of the economic operator in pursuit of the expected return;

in order to counteract this narrowing of the operational sphere, generated by the narrowing of the significance threshold,[43] the component (in question a) of the preference should be extended;[44]

(iii) *thirdly*, if the measurement in the case of $\Delta\theta$ is quite obvious, what can be said about the measurement in the case of Δx ? We present the following point of view:

- for $x \equiv F$: the functional component of the preference can be measured by the number of types[45] of individual transactions that the economic agent operates in the market. Therefore, the extension of this component simply aims to increase the number of such types of individual transactions, and to reduce the component means to reduce the number of types of individual transactions acceptable[46] to that agent;
- for $x \equiv D$: the deliberative component of the preference can be measured by the number of trading strategies within which the economic agent operates in the market the types of individual transactions discussed above. In FMAB-APH (Dinga et al., 2022), we opined that, at some point, in a certain financial market,[47] the generic economic agent has (or accepts or is accessible to) a single trading strategy that represents a master strategy (a quasi-model of rationality) to infer the types of individual transactions. We consider, however, that it is useful a relaxation at this point of discussion, so we assume that there may be several trading strategies, possibly competing with each other, in the deliberative component of the economic agent.[48] Therefore, as in the case of the functional component of the preference, the deliberative component can also be measured quantitatively by the number of trading strategies available to the economic agent (therefore, also with a potential character);
- for $x \equiv K$: the problem of measuring the hard component (hence, implicitly, its variation) of preference is more difficult, because this component has a different nature compared to the two previously discussed. Accordingly, we will first set out some helpful considerations:

  essentially, the hard component is the very propensity that characterizes the economic agent (in the most direct sense, more precisely, his/her belief—largely subconscious—about the action in the financial market). This belief is, of course, an *a priori* property of the agent, hence a strong resistance to change, the resistance (robustness) being induced by experience too;[49]

as a result, a change/adjustment in the hard component of the preference can no longer be described in dimensional/extensional aspect (i.e., extension vs narrowing) but, possibly, in intensional aspect or, as the case may be, in qualitative aspect.[50]

the intensional description of the hard component measure refers to the degree of belief (propensity), namely the strength of the economic agent's belief that the belief held is 'correct'.[51] Therefore, the change/adjustment of the intensional side of the propensity refers to the change/adjustment (either increase or decrease) of the degree of conviction in one's belief, a change/adjustment that occurs almost unconsciously, being revealed to the economic agent him/herself only through subsequent actions (in this sense, the actions following the intensional modification/adjustment of the propensity constitutes, for the agent him/herself, revealed preferences);

the qualitative description of the measure of the hard component refers to the replacement of the existing belief with another one.[52] Although this change is not so 'observable from inside'[53] for the economic agent in question—we believe that the economic agent suffers a real axiological shock at a change of belief—this change is rather unaware/non-reflective;

consequently, unlike the first two components of preference/proference (functional component, respectively deliberative component), in the case of the hard component we have a certain weightlessness from the point of view of observing, so also from the perspective of measurement. In this sense, the hard component must be considered a black-box and its condition can only be deduced from the exhibited outputs—more precisely, from the behaviour of the economic agent concerned[54] (we are coming, again, to Samuelson's revealed preference);

(iv) *fourthly*, the question is how the change in a significance threshold is influenced by the change in the previous significance threshold in the set of the three structural components of preference?[55]

– the fact that there are three thresholds of significance[56] indicates the existence of a *sui generis* redundancy in the structure of preference, which is likely to counteract the disturbances coming from the financial market;

- in this regard, we propose the operation of the following 'rules' in changing the significance thresholds:

  the chronological order of change of the significance thresholds is from the periphery to the centre, that is, firstly the significance threshold of the functional component is changed, then that of the deliberative component and, finally, the significance threshold of the hard component;

  regarding the quantitative relationship between the change of a significance threshold and the change of the subsequent significance threshold in chronological order (and, of course, also in logical order), we think that there must be a significance threshold of the subsequent component related to the variation of the significance threshold to the antecedent component;

  this (secondary) threshold of significance can only exist in the deliberative component, respectively in the hard component—it does not exist in the functional component of preference. Figure 5.7 shows an explanatory logic diagram for these last considerations (we make the following additional notations: φ—the change coefficient of the significance threshold subsequent to the already modified significance threshold; θ^s—the significance threshold subsequent to the already modified significance threshold; $\tilde{\theta}$ —the maximum value (admissible, acceptable, desirable) change of the significance threshold; Δ^s—the magnitude with which the subsequent significance threshold changes: $\Delta^s = \varphi \cdot \Delta\theta$).

(v) *fifthly*, what can be said about a possible 'order of priority' of changes made by the economic operator/agent? Is the change in the significance threshold a priority over the change in the (concerned) component of the preference, or is it the other way around? Our opinion is as follows:

- the threshold of significance is the first 'line of defence' (subjective, of course) of the economic agent against the disturbances coming from the financial market (more precisely, obviously, from the environment of the financial market); therefore, the agent's first reaction to market action is to change the significance threshold (in the chronological order mentioned above);

Fig. 5.7 Logical scheme of modifying the subsequent significance threshold.
Source: Authors

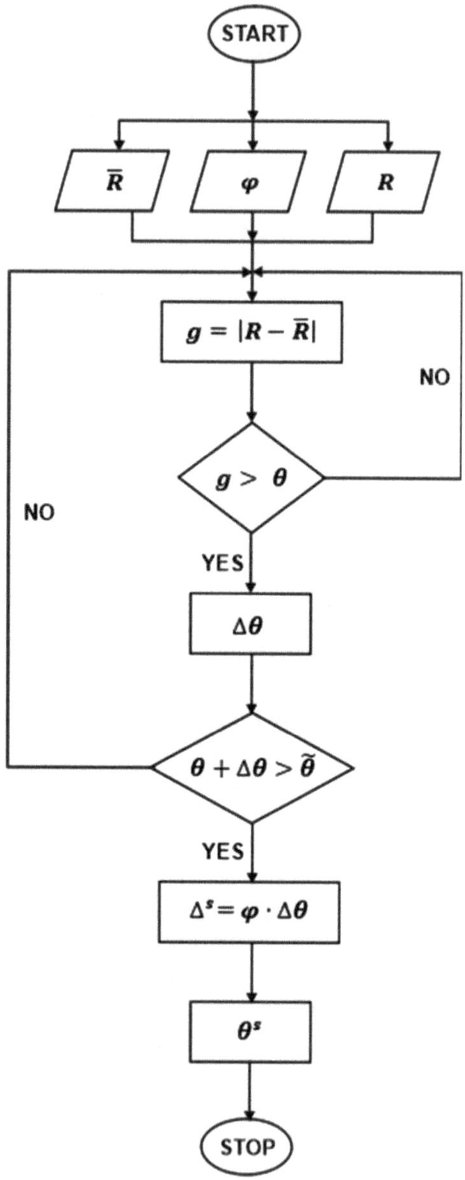

- the problem is, in fact, the following: after the economic operator has exhausted the robustness valences of the first significance threshold, his/her next 'move' is to change the preference component of the significance threshold whose valences have been exhausted or s/he proceeds for changing the next significance threshold (belonging to the next preference component, observed from the periphery to the centre)? Although, of course, the behaviour of the economic agent is idiosyncratic in this matter, a logical analysis (with a presumed character of generality or probability) can be given—our opinion is, on this subject, the following:

  the economic operator will prefer to change the interface with the financial market in relation to the change of preference itself, that is, s/he will prefer to change the significance threshold rather than the related preference component, because the change of significance threshold is reversible and controllable, while the change of preference component (in fact, of preference) is usually ('sufficiently') irreversible;

  however, when the economic operator finds that the financial market shows no signs of reversibility, that is, the probability that the change in the significance threshold is reversed becomes uncertain, s/he will proceed to change the related component of the preference;

  a new problem arises here: suppose an economic agent has changed the significance threshold of the functional component of his preference until additional changes in the significance threshold no longer bring (more precisely, they no longer seem to bring) positive marginal value in terms of (net) return from financial transactions. Obviously, in this case, s/he will proceed to change the very functional component of the preference. The question that arises at this point is: for the new functional component of preference (e.g., we could admit that a new category of individual transactions has been introduced as acceptable in this functional component), what significance threshold will work? the current one (i.e., the one modified up to the zero or negative marginal value of the return), the one immediately preceding, the one existing before the first or, as the case may be, the last change in the significance threshold? In our opinion, when changing the preference component (functional, in the case discussed here, but of course the conclusion is valid and applicable to any preference component), the significance threshold must be reset to the value before its first change. In this way, the process of changing the significance threshold, respectively the components of the preference, is repeated in the same way, but under the conditions of the new component of the preference, as it has been modified;

(vi) further, we will make/take over some notations:

- θ_F: the significance threshold of the functional component of the preference; θ_D: the significance threshold of the deliberative component of the preference; θ_K: the significance threshold of the hard component of the preference
- the 'decreed' order (of the dimensional type) between the three significance thresholds is: $\theta_F < \theta_D < \theta_K$
- $b_{(x)}$: Bayes *a priori* probability[57] for component (x) of preference/proference (where: $x \in \{F, D, K\}$);
- $g_\tau = |R_\tau - \overline{R}_\tau|$, where: R_τ is the actual result of the individual transaction, at time τ, and $\overline{R}_\tau$ is its expected/anticipated (more generally, normed) result;
- $\Delta\theta_{(x)}$: the size by which the significance threshold of the 'x' component of the preference changes;
- $\varphi_{(y)}$: the coefficient of change of the significance threshold subsequent to the significance threshold already modified, where $y \in \{D, K\}$; the possible values (in the set of real numbers) for this coefficient are: $\varphi_{(y)} \in [0, 1]$—the value '0' is taken when no change is made in the existing significance threshold and the value '1' when, simply, the significance threshold is abolished. The abolition of the significance threshold can have two alternative consequences which are diametrically opposed, namely:
  a. the economic agent becomes hyper-sensitive to any return that is not punctually equal to the expected one and then goes directly to the modification of the component of the preference concerned—this alternative implies an extremely high volatility of the economic agent's behaviour;[58]
  b. the economic agent accepts any actual return, without making any comparisons with the expected return—this situation of apathy is possible but, obviously, in the short or very short term, because it involves the financial 'death' of the agent

concerned if the actual return is systematically (and possibly largely) below of the expected one;

- $\theta^{s}_{(y)}$: significance threshold subsequent to the already modified significance threshold;
- $\tilde{\theta}_{(x)}$: the maximum value (admissible, acceptable, desirable) change of significance threshold;
- $\Delta^{s}_{(y)}$: the size by which the subsequent significance threshold changes;
- $d^{(2)}_{(x)}$: second-order preference (between changing the significance threshold of component (*x*) of preference and changing that component itself (*x*)) (*Nota bene*: we believe that the second-order preference can be quantified by a propensive-type probability, that it already exists in the decision-making structure of the economic agent, i.e., it has an *a priori* character); obviously, it is a Bayes a priori-type propensive probability, and the way in which such a second-order preference operates is typical for Bayes probability operation, that is (for the 'average' case, as for a Gaussian distribution of economic agents' propensities): if $d^{(2)}_{(x)} < 0.5$, then the economic agent will prefer to change the significance threshold of the (*x*) component of the preference, and if $d^{(2)}_{(x)} \geq 0.5$, then the economic operator will prefer to modify the (*x*) component of the preference itself; that the following order relation works with respect to the three structural components of preference, from the perspective of second-order preference:[59]

$$d^{(2)}_{(F)} > d^{(2)}_{(D)} > d^{(2)}_{(K)} \tag{5.5}$$

or, equivalently:

$$\left(1 - d^{(2)}_{(F)}\right) < \left(1 - d^{(2)}_{(D)}\right) < \left(1 - d^{(2)}_{(K)}\right) \tag{5.6}$$

Nota bene 1: we will enounce the following conjecture: if $g_{\tau_i} = g_{\tau_j}$, then $\left(\tau_i < \tau_j\right) \rightarrow \left(b_{(x)}\left[\tau_i\right] > b_{(x)}\left[\tau_j\right]\right)$, where with $b_{(x)}\left[\tau_k\right]$ we noted the *a priori* Bayes probability as allocated to the change of component (*x*) of the preference as a result of the gap found at time *k*.

Nota bene 2: in terms of the accumulability of change tension (i.e., of the gap g), there is obviously a temporal accumulative (depending on after how many occurrences of g the decision is made to change the component concerned of the preference) and a spatial, more precisely, quantitative[60] accumulability; of course, each economic agent has his or her own 'preference' for this pair of phenomena: some will prefer that, after an episode or a small number of unfavourable (or too favourable[61]) episodes, make a change in preference component, others will expect such episodes to be repeated long enough to make a decision;[62] the same goes for spatial/dimensional/quantitative accumulability: some will wait for a large amount of anomalies to accumulate, others for a smaller amount;[63]

Nota bene 3: the issue of the moment (Satchell & Grant, 2020) is also related to accumulability (either temporal or spatial), in the sense discussed above. In other words, does the accumulability have to be formed continuously (i.e., within the moment) or can it also be formed 'in pieces',[64] so in interrupted sequences of moments?[65] A separate research topic remains here, related to what we might call the 'echo' or 'obsolescence' of the accumulation of the tension of change (for the time being we ignore this development, which requires and allows, of course, analytical formalizations of interest, at least theoretically and psychologically);

- in examining the indifference curve between the variation of the significance threshold and the adjustment of the (concerned) component of the preference, the criterion of indifference (or invariance) must, of course, be established. In principle, such a criterion must aim at a utility/ophelimity for the economic operator who is trading in the financial market;[66] this utility must have the property of additivity or, more generally, a property of equivalence between the utilities/ophelimities provided by the significance threshold or the (concerned) component of the preference, respectively;
  - our proposal in this regard is as follows: when choosing between a change in the significance threshold and an adjustment of the preference component associated with that threshold, the trader is interested in the return which his/her individual transaction (operationalized by the functional component of preference) brings it to him/her;[67]
  - consequently, the choice is made between varying (i.e., widening or narrowing) the significance threshold[68] or adjusting the com-

ponent of the preference so that, theoretically (i.e., at the level of expectation), the market return does not change;[69]

- based on the above notations, we can develop the following formalizations regarding the behaviour of the economic agent, in connection with the relationship between the variation of the significance thresholds and the variation of the preference components:
  - *portability/transition* relations: $\Delta_D^s = \varphi_D \cdot \Delta\theta_F$, respectively, $\Delta_K^s = \varphi_K \cdot \Delta\theta_D$ (*Nota bene*: we assume that $\varphi_K < \varphi_D$);
  - *trigger/initiation* relations: $\Delta_D^s = \varphi_D \cdot \tilde{\theta}_F$, respectively, $\Delta_K^s = \varphi_K \cdot \tilde{\theta}_D$ (*Nota bene*: we assume that $\tilde{\theta}_D < \tilde{\theta}_F$);

Additional Comments.

The question arises as to whether the same correction coefficients (φ) can be used for the variation of significance thresholds (in the case of portability relationships) and for the variation of preference components (in the case of trigger relationships), as given above. Of course, in the case of a 'normal' real economic agent, i.e., without hyper-intellectual abilities of calculation and analysis, as they are assumed by the *homo œconomicus mathematical model*, it seems reasonable to accept that the economic agent will show the same dimensional predisposition to change both for the significance threshold and for the components of preference. On the other hand, however, admitting the second-order preference introduced earlier, it is equally reasonable to differentiate between the two categories of 'quantities' of change. For the needs of this study, we assume to consider the two coefficients (applied to the significance threshold, respectively the components of preference) as the same—that is, as having the same numerical value.

- *choice/operation* relations: even if the numerical values of the correction coefficients for the significance thresholds, respectively for the preference components are the same, the economic agent will still have to choose between targeting one or another of the 'targets' regarding the preference components. Regarding this choice, the relations of choice/operation work as described below:

$$\left(\Delta_{(i)}\theta_F \rightarrow \tilde{\theta}_F\right) \wedge \left(\Delta_{(i+1)}\theta_F < \Delta_{(i)}\theta_F\right) \rightarrow d_{(x)}^{(2)} = D \tag{5.7}$$

where: $\Delta_{(i)}$ means the variation recorded at the time (i);

- since the variation of the component F of the preference reached its ceiling, but the next variation of that component falls again under the ceiling, this means that the economic agent (the individual), 'gains' a new manoeuvre room to decide, so s/he will use the D component of preference

$$\left(\Delta_{(i)}\theta_F \rightarrow \tilde{\theta}_F\right) \wedge \left(\Delta_{(i+1)}\theta_F > \Delta_{(i)}\theta_F\right) \rightarrow d_{(x)}^{(2)} = K \qquad (5.8)$$

- since the variation of the component F of the preference reached its ceiling, and the next variation maintains over that ceiling, this means that the economic agent registers a trend (or moment) which non-ambiguously signalizes a change in the physiology of the (financial) market, so it is needed to appeal directly to the K component of preference

$$\left(\Delta_{(i)}\theta_F \rightarrow \tilde{\theta}_F\right) \wedge \left(\Delta_{(i+1)}\theta_F = \Delta_{(i)}\theta_F\right) \rightarrow d_{(x)}^{(2)} = F \qquad (5.9)$$

- since the variation of the component F of the preference reached its ceiling, and the next variation punctually maintains that reaching, this means that the economic agent should operate (some) changes only on the F component of preference. In other words, the situation keeps around the 'equilibrium', so the most appropriate lever to handle that situation is based on the F component of preference.

Preference as Symbolic Species

As in the case of the information, respectively the price, for the description of the preference *qua* species (more precisely, *qua* symbolic species) we will have to examine the following components: (a) symbolic character of the preference; (b) phenotype of the preference; (c) genotype of preference; (d) mutation in case of preference;[70] (e) synthesis of preference; (f) transcription in case of preference; (g) translation in case of preference; (h) the epigenetic (or para-genetic) evolution of preference; (i) preference selection.

(a) the symbolic nature of the preference

In the previous discussions, we used as a criterion for establishing the symbolic nature of the information, respectively the price, the social nature, the social and cultural artefact of the two mentioned concepts. Indeed, both information and price are not natural entities, but social constructs[71] or, in other words, objectifications of inter-subjectivity. Does this criterion remain valid in the case of preference as well?[72] We present a brief discussion of this issue in the following:

- preference is fundamentally a belief, regardless of the nature of that belief (rational, religious, metaphysical, mystical, or, as the case may be, an inextricable mix of all of these) and how it was acquired (by reflection, by education, by imitation, by experience);[73]
- being a belief, it would seem, *prima facie*, that the preference should be considered as belonging to the natural world, respectively to the psychology of the individual or, with a less usual terminology in positive approaches (such as the one here), as belonging to the transcendental. In this sense, therefore, preference could not constitute a symbolic species, but an inalienable feature of a biological species (the human individual), thus departing from the sphere of interest of the subject stated here. This first appearance (to remain within the phenomenological terminology) is, however, false, because:
  - belief is by no means innate—it is formed in the social and cultural framework of society, through social action/cooperation. Individual takes over (whatever his/her own filters it uses for this and whatever s/he adds or modifies) the value matrix of the society in which s/he is immersed, so to consider that belief is autonomous in relation to culture is both an ontological and epistemological error;
  - individual's psychology (idiosyncratic and inalienable) is 'altered' in social cooperation, by acquiring a social component (at least, as a way of manifestation), induced by the inevitable sociality of the individual;[74]
- based on the above, we consider that belief (i.e., preference[75]), although located in the psychology of the human individual, is, in turn (and to a large extent), an artefact, a social construct. Therefore, logically, the preference should be considered to be symbolic. However, there are some differences between preference as a symbolic species, and the other two symbolic species discussed in the

paper (information, respectively, price) and they should be mentioned, as they will have an important role and significance in the following analytical developments:

- although all three symbolic species function through the individual (either by his/her action or by the interpretation/valuation of the individuals of the symbolic species in question—in the latter case it is, in fact, about assigning meaning to those symbolic individuals), the preference constitutes (and, at the same time, establishes) itself as a hermeneutic (interpretative/evaluative) and decisional (choice, selection) court. Both the information and the price gain significance exclusively within and through preference. It is no exaggeration to say that information (or price, as the case may be) has as many different meanings as human individuals, so how many distinct preferences make their assessment. In this sense, it can be said that the information (respectively the price) is marked, in terms of significance, by preference. This is an important and relevant methodological and instrumental ascendant of the preference in relation to the other two symbolic species, an ascendant that will count in the further modelling/formalization;
- even the models of rationality used by human individuals in evaluating information or price are affected by preference: firstly, the very choice/acceptance of a certain model of rationality is conditioned by preference—we can hardly believe that an individual who shares a belief based on empathy, solidarity and sociality, for example, will share the (mathematical) model of rationality proposed by *homo œconomicus* paradigm;
- the 'held by preference' in Popper's third world is different from that held by information or price: while the last two are completely determined by culture, preference also has an important biological ingredient, through its psychological conditioning;
- the reciprocal impact of preference, on the one hand, and of information or price, on the other hand, is asymmetric: the change of preference under the impact of information or price is a 'material' one—the preference itself undergoes changes (we will show this in the right time)—while the change in information or price under the impact of preference is a 'formal' one—meanings are associated with the two symbolic species which, however, do not transform them as such, but they continue to remain identical with themselves even if, for different human being individuals, they have different meanings.

(b) preference phenotype (f_c)

- we propose to consider, as a phenotype (adult individual) of the symbolic species called preference, the trading strategy; the reasons for this proposal are as follows:
  - previously (see FMAB-APH) the trading strategy has already been considered as the ***financial individual***, i.e., in the terminology used in this paragraph, the phenotype itself;
  - correlating this proposal with the preference structure already discussed above, it results that the phenotype of preference is generated by its deliberative component—that is, by that component which, as we have shown, 'delivers'/chooses the trading strategy;
  - it follows, therefore, that the selection which the financial market (to be read as: financial market environment) makes on preference is exercised at the level of its deliberative component, an aspect that the evolutionary literature also accepts (Lo, 2019; Nelson & Winter, 1985) although, obviously, unrelated to the structure of preference which, as far as we know, is not addressed;
  - as shown in FMAB-APH (Dinga et al., 2022), although the selection is made at the level of the deliberative component of the preference, the 'trigger' of the selection refers to the individual transaction (within the functional component of the preference) and which represents a concrete, contextual (almost 'automatic') hypostatization of the trading strategy;
  - it follows, therefore, that the economic agent, as a human individual, is, symbolically, the 'bearer' of the financial individual; as we have already shown, a human individual can be the bearer of several financial individuals, as a result of the adjustment of the deliberative component under the impact of the return received from the financial market, so that an adjustment can result in more than one accepted trading strategy;
- regarding the preference phenotype, we add the following considerations:
  - the phenotype of the preference coincides (not from a nominal point of view, but only from a generative point of view) with the phenotype, so to speak, of the financial market[76] (remember that, in our opinion, it is not the financial market that selects the trading strategy, as Lo suggests, e.g., but this selec-

tion is made by the environment in which the financial market, as a species, operates—by environment we mean cultural geodesic, part of the situational context, on the one hand, and other contemporary trading strategies, on the other part);

- there is, of course, a particular aspect in the concept of financial market phenotype,[77] namely that the individual/phenotype is generated/caused even by the preference. We insist on this aspect because, in fact, it constitutes the ontological support, so to speak, of our concept of adaptive preference, as it has already been examined, in its general determinations, in FMAB-APH (Dinga et al., 2022), and how it will be developed, in this chapter, in the trinomial preference-information-price;
- as in the case of any symbolic species (see the information, respectively the price, discussed in Chap. 4), the phenotype of preference is 'born' directly as adult; consequently, the trading strategy does not undergo development processes, as it happens with the biological phenotype, but only (of course, through the species that incorporates it—namely, the financial market) evolution processes. This immutability of the trading strategy (the financial individual) is, in part,[78] the effect of the deliberative[79] nature of its generation (such generation that will be discussed in detail below, on the issue of genotype);

(c) preference genotype ($\mathcal{g}_c$)

- the most natural 'candidate' for the preference genotype is, of course, its hard component—propensity. From a macroscopic point of view, so to speak, in the previous, enough emphasis has been placed on the generative character of the propensity over preference (see, in particular, our concept of *proference*, which makes the two entities—propensity and preference—relatively indistinguishable; this section will discuss also the microscopic perspective of this determination);
- in addition, the logical structuring of the preference on the three components, one of which is the propensity (the hard, 'deep', substrate[80] component of the preference) reinforces the idea that, from a financial market perspective, we are dealing with a proference, that is, with a self-generating mechanism of preference;[81]

- although, at a basic level, the generative relationship from genotype to phenotype, in the case of preference, is illustrated in Fig. 5.7, we can develop here more about this essential process of the symbolic species nature of preference. In this regard, Fig. 5.8 provides the main coordinates and suggestions in this regard:

Short Discussion.

(i) the genotype is the most conservative component of preference/proference, claiming itself from its hard component, that is, from what we call propensity. As unlikely as it may seem, economic agents are not as innovative as some financial market theories/models claim,[82] maintaining an (of course, strongly idiosyncratic) relationship between security (conservatism) and flexibility (innovationism), and this 'equilibrium' is obviously not entirely of rational extraction;

(ii) the terminological distinction made (see Fig. 5.8) between generation and causation is not accidental: causation is stronger and has a more pronounced imperative character (though not an absolute one, of course) than generation; thus, the hard component *generates* the deliberative component, but the concrete expression of the hard component (namely, genotype) *causes* the concrete expression of the deliberative component (namely, phenotype);

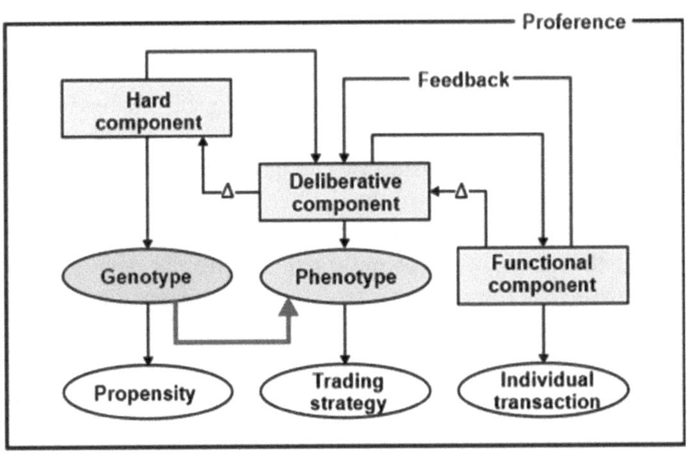

Fig. 5.8 Relational mechanism genotype-phenotype in the case of preference. *Source*: Authors

(d) genetic mutation in case of preference (m_c)

- a first issue with the genotype addresses the autonomy or non-autonomy of its modification in relation to the 'rest' of the preference, that is, in relation to the deliberative and functional components of the preference, respectively:
  - as we have already shown, the propensity is influenced by the changes made, on the one hand, to the significance threshold of the deliberative component and, on the other hand, by the change in that deliberative component itself;[83] it is, therefore, the deliberative (i.e., non-emergent) channel of variation/mutation in the preference genotype. This channel is indisputable and, in our opinion, has the main share in the genetic mutation of the preference, precisely as a result of the symbolic quality of the species preference;
  - we also point out that the functional component of preference does not have direct 'access' to the hard component, that is, genotype/propensity—its influence occurs only indirectly through the deliberative component (either as a result of the modification of the latter component or as a result of the change in its significance threshold);
  - let us now examine the possibility of random mutations in genotype (i.e., propensity):

  by random mutations at the level of propensity we mean those changes in propensity which are neither made of nor aware for the (human) economic agent in question. This definition is supported by the following considerations:
- the fact that they are not carried out by the economic agent results, in turn, from the fact that the economic agent's activism/agency is exhausted by the deliberate change (which is generated by the change of the deliberative component or the change of the significance threshold of the latter component), and the fact that they are not aware for the economic operator is required precisely by the randomness invoked here—a change in the propensity (even if not caused by the economic agent) that the economic agent is aware of, leaves 'traces' regarding the new propensity (e.g., it may exacerbate or, conversely, resorb that change, in both cases moving to the area of deliberative change

or, which is almost the same in this matter, to the area of quasi-deliberative change);

- there are a multitude of factors (in most cases the random change of propensity being the effect of a competition among such factors, i.e., of a causal complex[84]) that can generate such random changes: variations in the educational base (more precisely, in the level and quality of instruction) of the economic agent, variations in the cultural baggage (and in its quality), variations in the religious faith, variations in the ethical edifice (i.e., in the principles of behaviour committed towards the community), unnecessary influences of the behaviour of other economic agents in the financial market (i.e., the memetic impact), etc.[85]

(e) preference synthesis (s_c)

- here we must discuss the mechanism by which the mutation produced at the level of genotype (i.e., at the level of propensity), regardless of the nature (deliberative or emergent) of that mutation and regardless of the channel through which it affects the genotype is taken in the structure of preference. We will first make some methodological clarifications (but which also have conceptual values):
  - we saw that, in its generic sense, preference (more precisely, proference) has three components arranged concentrically, from the periphery to the centre: the functional component, the deliberative component, the hard component;
  - however, we will have to determine what is ultimately the preference that the economic agent exhibits in the financial market (perhaps the preference that may be the subject of Samuelson's so-called revealed preference). This clarification is needed to discuss not only the issue of preference synthesis, but also the other issues that are examined below;
  - in this context, we propose that the 'actual' preference be considered the deliberative component of the proference—that is, what we have called the phenotype of preference above. This proposal has at least the following justifications:

    in the financial market, it is exhibited the trading strategy (even if through the concrete, particular and repeatable intermediation of the individual transaction)—*à propos* of the revealed preference;

the environment in which the trading strategy is operated (cultural geodesic, respectively the other contemporary trading strategies) performs the selection process (in the evolutionary sense, obviously) precisely on the phenotype (i.e., on the trading strategy);

the trading strategy is both rigid[86] and plastic, that is, it has both conservative/elastic properties and innovative/plastic (evolutionary) properties. Moreover, the literature devoted to this issue generally goes towards that bi-directions: (i) EMH considers the preference to have the property to be objectified in the financial market (in our terminology, to produce individual transactions, i.e., to have a generative role, just like the trading strategy); (ii) AMH explicitly proposes that the object of selection (made, in the latter model, by the financial market!) be also the trading strategy (Lo, 2019); (iii) other (evolutionary) models of the economic process propose solutions which are similar to our proposal: for example, the concept of routine as an objectification of a 'hidden' preference, so the selection process being carried out on this routine (Nelson & Winter, 1985);[87]

- if we accept that the 'true' preference of the economic agent is the one exhibited by the deliberative component of the proference, then the synthesis of the preference can be described as follows:
  - preliminary remarks:

    note that we are dealing with an inverted phenomenon in relation to the phenomenon by which the impulse to change came from the deliberative component to the hard component, either aimed at to change the significance threshold of this the latter component or aimed at to change the component in question itself—so, this time, the impulse for change comes from the hard component of the proference to its deliberative component, or, equivalently, from genotype to phenotype;

    should we also accept significance thresholds regarding the transmission of the impulse to change from genotype to phenotype? Our answer is negative in this respect, based on the following reasons: (i) the preference phenotype shows neither robustness, nor resilience, nor inertia in relation to taking over the impulse of change coming from the genotype;[88] (ii) the genotype change is transmitted without any filtering to the phenotype (i.e., to the configuration or profile of the trading strategy), namely, it is transmitted in a ratio, so to speak, of 1: 1; (iii) although the transmission of the genotype change to the phenotype is not of the nature of objectifying a genetic code/program (as in the biological case[89]), nevertheless the phenotype is, in its overwhelming part, logically necessary, once a change in genotype is recorded;

- a functional spiral must be accepted in the case of the synthesis of preference; this spiral is the result of the way in which the influence of changes in the opposite direction occurs—that is, from the deliberative component to the hard component. We develop, to some extent, this idea in the following:

the kinematics of the financial market return and, in particular, the kinematics of the gap between the actual return and the expected one, transmits, as shown above, impulses to change either the significance threshold of the hard component or the hard component itself, and these impulses are coming directly from the deliberative component but indirectly, of course, from the functional component of preference;

if we take into account only the modification of the hard component, as an effect of the input from the deliberative component, then we have, in fact, a deliberative (non-emergent) modification (mutation) of the preference genotype;

but, as shown in this paragraph, this mutation changes the phenotype (which has as its source the deliberative component, in this case the trading strategy);

the new trading strategy will generate changes in the individual transactions that will again face the return of the financial market, and so on;

it is obvious, therefore, that there is an interdependence between the deliberative component (phenotype) and the hard component (genotype) from the perspective of both formation of genotype mutations and, respectively, their impact on the phenotype;

from a 'technological' point of view, this interdependence can be dominated by positive feedback (in which case it can be represented as a spiral) or it can be dominated by negative feedback (in which case it can be represented as a sinusoid);

in a more general case, we can have sinusoids wrapped by a spiral or vice versa, spirals wrapped by a sinusoid. Figure 5.9 attempts to provide a visual representation of the two possible cases of the necessary interdependence between the deliberative component (phenotype) and the hard component (genotype) in terms of the impact of genetic mutations.

(f) transcription of preference (c_c)

- as in the case of the symbolic species discussed above, transcription (and translation, if any) is of the utmost importance and relevance in the design and justification of the trinomial preference-information-price, representing the 'key' to the whole proposal. At this point, therefore, it is necessary to discuss how the mutation in the genotype (genetic mutation, therefore) is transmitted in the phenotype, within the next 'generation'.[90] We first make some specific considerations:
  - the hard coordinate (propensity) does not have the property of *dimensionality*, as it has both the deliberative component and the functional component of preference (proference),[91] in other words, the hard component does not 'increase' or 'decrease', does not 'expand' or 'shrinks';
  - not having the property of dimensionality, the hard component has, instead, that of *plasticity*. By the property of plasticity we mean the following:

  the hard component may undergo changes of the following two types (mainly):
- changes in *degree*: intensifications/dis-intensifications of the force with which it requires the configuration of the deliberative component (i.e., the world of trading strategies) at a certain 'arrow' of propensity (*Nota bene*: by 'arrow' of propensity we mean the direction in which the human economic agent is placed from the perspective of operating transactions in the financial market—e.g., risk aversion vs risk appetite,[92] aligned strategies vs contrarian strategies, and other similar dichotomous positions);

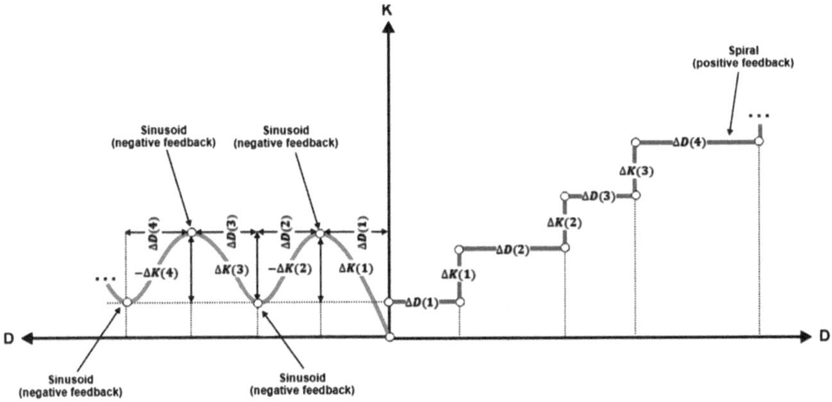

Fig. 5.9 The two types of interdependencies genotype-phenotype in the preference case. *Source*: Authors

- changes in ***meaning***: changes in the economic agent's propensive 'arrow', at the same intensity of the configuration force of the deliberative component (or, of course, as the case may be, at different intensities);[93]

  the changes suffered are irreversible (or, if reversible, have a hysteresis—i.e., a residual memory of the disturbed state—so great that such reversibility is equivalent, at least functionally, to an irreversibility or a quasi-irreversibility); this means that the propensity (hard component of the proference) is inelastic, has no resilience or this is insignificant;[94]

  - the question is obviously whether plasticity (or rather, its variation) can be measured and, if so, how such a measurement can be made. We propose the following solution to this problem:

  with regard to 'quantitative' changes, that is, changes in the propensity intensity of the hard component, these can be measured using the Bayes a *posteriori* probability.[95] We consider that Bayesian probabilities (*a priori*, respectively *a posteriori*) can be assigned to the propensity intensity, that is, to the 'quantity' of belief/propensity because, being of the nature of belief, the propensity is subjective and, to a large extent, subconscious. Consequently, it has the same nature as the Bayesian probability which is, in fact, a belief;[96]

be $b_K^{\to t_0}$: Bayes *a priori* probability assigned to the propensity intensity of the hard component of preference/proference; it therefore expresses the degree/strength of the belief at that time (t_0);

be a genetic mutation produced (in the ways already discussed above) at the level of propensity. This genetic mutation is 'quantified' by the change in the Bayes *a priori* probability of the propensive intensity and, therefore, by its transformation into Bayes *a posteriori* probability of this intensity; from a qualitative point of view, there is, therefore, a variation (either increase or decrease—as *a posteriori* Bayes probability is higher, respectively lower than *a priori* Bayes probability) of the economic agent's belief in the preference/proference phenotype;

note *a posteriori* Bayes probability with $b_K^{t_1 \to}$, at the moment (t_1);

a posteriori Bayes probability (more precisely, the difference between *a priori* Bayes probability and *a posteriori* Bayes probability), which we denote by $\Delta b_k = b_K^{\to t_0} - b_K^{t_1 \to}$, will generate, in phenotype (i.e., in the existing trading strategy at the level of the deliberative component of the preference) a change;

it must be determined, of course, what kind of change occurs in the phenotype. We have seen that, when the impulse to change the phenotype comes from the functional component (i.e., through the individual transaction), the change is purely dimensional—some trading strategies are abandoned or, as the case may be, new trading strategies are included in the deliberative component of the preference. This change, as the name of the preference component in question says, is deliberate (at the limit, rational, based on calculation, even in its simplest form—e.g., cost-benefit analysis, weighted with either the risk or mathematical expectation). This time, therefore, in the case of an impulse coming from the hard component to the deliberative one, we consider that the impact is no longer dimensional, but of a qualitative nature;[97]

based on the above, we are of the opinion that the impact of the genetic mutation on the trading strategy (or trading strategies, as the case may be) will be manifested in the variation of his/their fitness. By the variation of the fitness of the trading strategy (i.e., of the preference phenotype) we mean the variation of the number of compatible individual transactions inferable from the affected trading strategy. In other words, the variation of the economic agent's belief (propensity) is manifested in the variation of the 'capacity'[98] of the trading strategy to operate individual transactions in the market;

if we denote by $C_{TS_i}^{t_0}$ the capacity of the trading strategy *i* (i.e., the number of individual transaction classes allowed by that trading strategy at time t_0) and by ϕ a coefficient/parameter[99] that takeover the change of Bayes probability assigned to the hard component, then we propose the following formalization (by transforming the parameter ϕ into a function of the gap between the *a priori* Bayes probability and the *a posteriori* Bayes probability):[100]

$$\phi = \log_2\left[1 - \Delta b_k\right]$$

$$\Delta C_{TS_i}^{t_1} = (-1)^{\varepsilon} \cdot \phi \cdot \Delta b_k \cdot C_{TS_i}^{t_0} = (-1)^{\varepsilon} \cdot \Delta b_k \cdot \log_2\left[\Delta b_k\right] \cdot C_{TS_i}^{t_0} = \qquad (5.10)$$

$$= \log_2\left[\Delta b_k\right]^{(-1)^{\varepsilon} \cdot \Delta b_k} \cdot C_{TS_i}^{t_0}$$

putting, to simplify writing: $\Delta b_k = g$, we have:

$$\Delta C_{TS_i}^{t_1} = \log_2[g]^{(-1)^{\varepsilon} \cdot g} \cdot C_{TS_i}^{t_0}$$

$$C_{TS_i}^{t_1} = C_{TS_i}^{t_0} + \Delta C_{TS_i}^{t_1} = C_{TS_i}^{t_0} \cdot \left(1 + \log_2[g]^{(-1)^{\varepsilon} \cdot g}\right)$$

$$\varepsilon = \begin{cases} 0, for\ g < 0 \\ 1, for\ g \geq 0 \end{cases} \qquad \text{(where)}$$

- some clarifications on the function ϕ:
  in general, the higher Δb_k, the higher ϕ [101]
  the value of ϕ is also subject to the significance threshold—this time the significance threshold refers to Δb_k: below a certain value of Δb_k, for example $\underline{\Delta} b_k = 0$, $\phi = 0$;

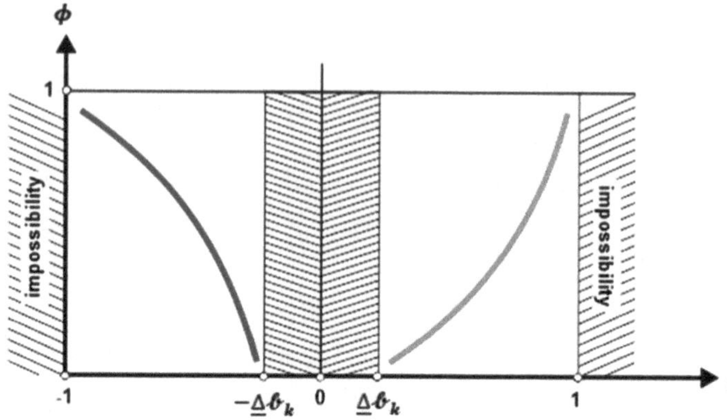

Fig. 5.10 Variable ϕ (the conceptual form), with assigned signification thresholds (I). *Source*: Authors

Figure 5.10 visually exemplifies the shape of the variable ϕ as a function of g.

By way of illustration, for $|\underline{\Delta} b_k| = 0.1$, the Matlab representation[102] of the variable ϕ is given in Fig. 5.11.

Comment.
For the case of increasing of *a posteriori* Bayes probability compared with the corresponding *a priori* value, the acceleration of ϕ is very high (e.g., for $g = 0.9$, $\phi = 3.32$). In behaviourist language, it could be said that the economic agent is very reluctant to reduce the scope of operationalization of the trading strategy (i.e., to reduce the deliberative component of preference), while showing a (seemingly) irrational enthusiasm to expand the scope of operationalization of the trading strategy. This asymmetry, resulting (for the time being) only from the behaviour of the function ϕ can be the basis for the enunciation of some conjectures to be the object of empirical tests from the perspective of falsifiability.

- in terms of qualitative changes in propensity, that is, in terms of the propensity 'arrow', things are more complicated. We summarize our position on the issue of genetic mutation as follows:
  the qualitative aspect of propensity is particularly diverse, it is, obviously, the most idiosyncratic part of propensity—as a result, it is the most imponderable part of it;

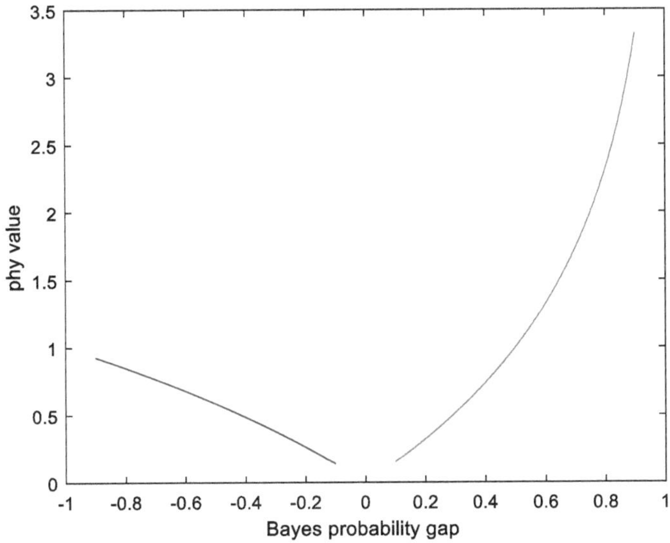

Fig. 5.11 Variable ϕ (an illustrative), with assigned signification thresholds (II). *Source*: Authors

conceptually, what has been called (Samuelson, 1938) revealed preference is generated by precisely this qualitative side of propensity, which does not exhibit the intensity of preference (or the intensity of propensity, as it was called above) but the 'arrow' preference—for example, denotes indications of risk appetite versus risk aversion of the economic operator whose demand (complete, according to Samuelson's weak axiom in the matter) is observed in its concrete manifestation in the market (in our case, in the financial market);[103]

a (relatively empirical) solution would be to establish a list (as far as possible) exhaustive of possible 'arrows' of propensity and then to try an analysis, possibly also based on Bayesian probabilities, to allocate 'numbers' to the items in the list, taking care, of course, that, in dichotomous (probably majority) cases, the assigned numbers contain 'difference up to 1' in relation to the dichotomous alternative in question;[104]

one solution (still empirical although more realistic) would be to sort the positions in the 'arrows' list by a criterion or set of criteria that would provide an ordinal 'map' of those positions; the ordinal calculation is, of course, much more complicated—and, in fact, more uncertain—than the cardinal one (suggested by us above in terms of the propensity intensity), but the distance from the real model of behaviour of the economic agents is smaller;

(g) translation in the preference case (t_c)
- as in the case of other symbolic species and, we repeat, unlike biological species, there is no need for translation in the case of preference mutation.

(h) epigenetic evolution of preference (e_c)
- regarding the epigenetic evolution of preference, it is necessary to examine the possibility that the phenotype of preference (trading strategy) be modified through other channels (causal factors) except the genetic one, which is the one from propensity (preference genotype). Previously, such a possibility was evoked and, in part, discussed in the context of changing the thresholds of significance, respectively of the functional and deliberative components of preference. We summarize, here, the main conclusions already obtained:
  - the deliberative component is modified under the impact of the modification of the functional component;
  - depending on the second-order preference of the economic agent (human agent), there are cases in which the modification of the significance threshold of the deliberative component is replaced by the modification of this very component of the preference;
  - therefore, without any connection to the preference genotype, the preference phenotype is modified (adjusted) under the pressure of the financial market;
  - it is obvious that this change is, on the one hand, of an epigenetic nature and, on the other hand, it also has connotations of the nature of the selection made by the environment of financial market (hence, of the trading strategy), which is the cultural geodesic together with the other contemporary trading strategies;
  - holding, therefore, the possibility of an epigenetic evolution of preference, the above suggestion will be used to discuss the

last issue of preference as a co-species in the financial market—the issue of selection;

Nota bene: one can examine the problem of the ratio (dosage) between genetic evolution and epigenetic evolution in the case of preference, as well as in the case of the other two symbolic co-species discussed in the previous chapter (information, respectively price). Our position in this regard is as follows:

- the evolution of symbolic/cultural species is subject, at the same time, to genetic and epigenetic evolution, precisely by virtue of their cultural character, which gives them a high degree of deliberativeness;[105]
- obviously, the more culture replaces nature in the mental and behavioural structure of the human individual, the more evolution is based on culture (i.e., Lamarckism, as we have seen before) and less on nature (i.e., Darwinism);
- the transition from predominantly Darwinian to predominantly[106] Lamarckian evolution in the case of symbolic (co-) species is gradual, although the speed of transition is increasing as technological, intellectual and spiritual progress transforms society in the teleological direction;[107]
- we believe that the share of the epigenetic evolutionary factor in the total evolutionary causality is increasing in the following order of the symbolic (co-) species discussed in this study: (1) information; (2) the price; (3) preference;[108]

In this context, Fig. 5.12 provides a synoptic picture of the relationship between genetic evolution and epigenetic evolution in the case of the three symbolic (co-) species.[109]

(i) selection of preference (s_c)
  - the process of selecting preference leads us to the very essence of the issue of adaptive preference. Before actually describing the mechanism for selecting the preference, let us mention a few preparatory elements:
    - the selection action is exerted by the environment in which the (co-) species preference evolves,[110] that is, by the cultural geodesic to which are added the other contemporary trading strat-

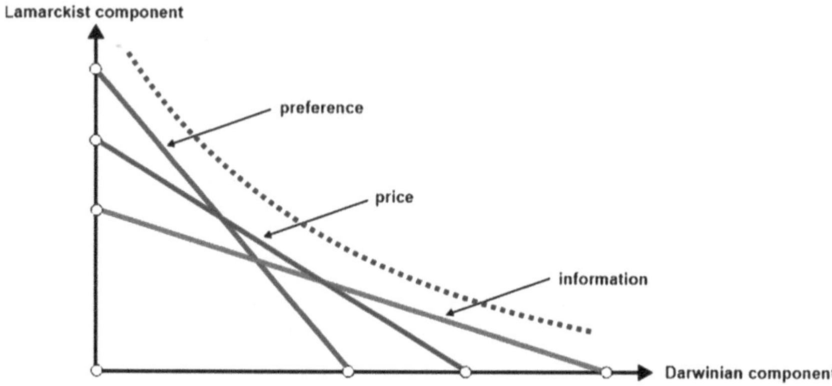

Fig. 5.12 Generic structure of evolutionary factors (components) of symbolic (co-) species. *Source*: Authors

egies—*Nota bene*: we insist on not considering the financial market as the environment of the trading strategy, as it happens, with the necessary differences, both in Fama, in Lo, and Nelson-Winter;

- the object of selection is the trading strategy (i.e., the preference phenotype, as assumed above), generated by the deliberative component of preference;

- to describe the selection of the preference (i.e., more precisely, the trading strategy), we will first make a graphical diagram with the main elements and mechanisms involved in this process (Fig. 5.13).
- based on Fig. 5.13, we can now make our preference selection proposal. The meaning of the notations in Fig. 5.13 is as follows: *Gx*—action/reaction '*x*' of the genetic path of evolution; *Ex*—action/reaction '*x*' of the epigenetic pathway of evolution; *Sx*—action/reaction '*x*' regarding the phenotype selection; *Ax*—action/reaction '*x*' regarding the economic action of the economic agent in the financial market.

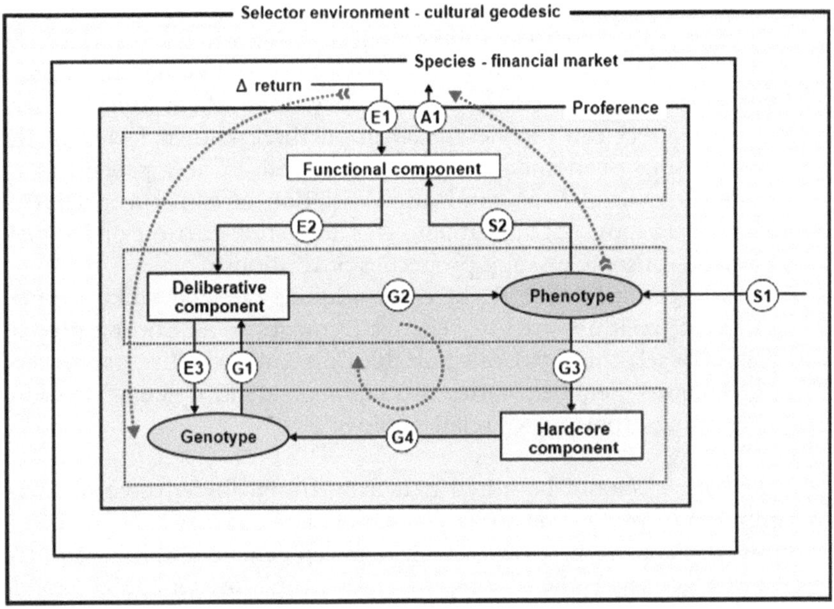

Fig. 5.13 Logical scheme of the generic selection of preference. *Source*: Authors

Short Discussion.

- genetic factor (*G*1) and epigenetic factor (*E*2) combine their impulses to generate a change in phenotype
  - the resultant of this combination is a separate issue; for example, are the two impulses purely additive? Our view is that accepting simple additivity is unrealistic; probably how to get the combined result is a bit more complicated. We make the following assumptions in this regard:

    if one of the impulses is dominant (as a sphere, intensity or even chronology), we think that that impulse will inhibit the other and will generate the modification of the phenotype in the direction and with the meaning that the dominant impulse in question represents;

    therefore, we accept (or rather presume) that, in the matter under discussion, an evolutionary *sui generis* process takes place—the selection of the impulse that will generate the modification of the phenotype is made on competitive criteria;[111]

- another issue related to the combination of the two impulses of change concerns the synergy effect.[112] Therefore, if one of the impulses does not eliminate the other (as suggested above, as a possibility) then a synergy effect may occur. *Nota bene*: the synergy effect can manifest itself in all three known forms of the updating phenomenon: (a) the addition of new properties or relationships;[113] (b) elimination/deletion of some properties or relationships; (c) adjustment—without introduction or elimination—of some existing properties or relations;
- synergy can, therefore, be either positive (generates new properties or relationships) or negative (removes some existing properties or relationships), or adjustable (introduces relatively superficial changes—i.e., below the threshold of identity alteration—into existing properties or relationships);

Nota bene: it should be noted that from the deliberative component two impulses leave: (a) one directly to the trading strategy (phenotype)—as shown in detail above (*G*2), which is the epigenetic impulse—and (b) one to the genotype (hard component or propensity of the economic operator concerned) (*E*3). In fact, this last impulse modifies the genotype which, in turn (through *G*1), transmits the genetic impulse to the phenotype;

- after 'bearing' the resulting change (generated by the genetic factor in combination with the epigenetic one), the phenotype is objectified by the new individual transactions which are inferred from the new profile of the trading strategy (*S*2) and which then act on the market (*A*1), subjecting in this way, the phenomenology of the financial market, so as to allow the (selection) reaction that the financial market environment will exert, that is, the cultural geodesic together with the other contemporary trading strategies;
- on the phenotype, through its hypostatisation in the form of the set of individual transactions, the environment of the financial market exerts its actual selection action (*S*1). The selection action is based on the validation/invalidation of the fitness[114] acquired by the phenotype following the impact (*G*2), with the following possible and exhaustive results:

- validation of the new phenotype profile (e.g., it may present itself to the environment as a trading strategy with a higher risk aversion, in a context where financial market uncertainty has increased, making it more suitable for economic survival);[115]
- invalidation of the new profile of the trading strategy; in this case, the same trading strategy is rejected by the environment as having a lower[116] fitness than the previous one or the one 'required' by that environment.

Notes

1. This is an old problem, which appeared in the field of Newtonian mechanics and for which only particular solutions have been found so far (Euler, Lagrange). In 1912, the Finnish mathematician Sundman proposed a solution (analytical, therefore non-numerical) based on the convergence of a series of powers—direction suggested by Poincaré, as early as 1886, when he showed that the series of powers is divergent), but the series converges so slowly that the analytical solution is practically unusable (Barrow-Green, 2010).
2. Please note that this is not a 'fixed point' concept in the mathematical theory of chaos (nonlinear dynamical systems), generated by the condition $f(x) = x$ and which, in turn, generates either attractors or sources, depending on the values of the derivative of order 1 at the fixed point in question.
3. An even more relevant 'fixed point' could be the natural price or the fair price, but this concept will be examined separately from this book.
4. Obviously, by calculating the possible and viable combinations: $C_3^2 = 3$.
5. It is obvious that the given, fixed preference (the one presumed tacitly or emphatically declared in all the models claimed by neoclassical economic theory) cannot be co-species (and not even species) precisely because of its declared immutability.
6. This inclination is strongly psychological, that is, it contains, along with the rationality supported by the intellect, an a-rational component (maybe even an i-rational one), as well, supported by the subconscious (including the collective subconscious—see Jung's archetype).
7. We remind you that, in the strict sense of the term, in the social field—so, also, in the financial market—there are only singular events (we do not have actual identical repeatability at all).
8. Since the cause is other thing than causation (the first is a contextual instantiation of the principle of causality), the phrase *cause of the cause* does not depart from the logical 'jurisdiction' of causation.

9. This is, in fact, the sense in which we illustrate the phrase cause of the cause, evoked above.
10. But not immutability, as neoclassical economic theory—the (mathematical) *homo œconomicus model*, EMH (Efficient Market Hypothesis)—claims.
11. The uniqueness of social events means that resilience does not behave according to a perfectly reversed trajectory, but manifests what is called hysteresis—a *sui generis memory* of the disorder, which 'acts' even if, in fact, its impact has been exhausted.
12. In the syntagm '*cause of the cause*', the first cause is the propensity and the second cause is the preference—indeed, preference is, in turn, cause of (choosing of) the trading strategy.
13. Therefore, although free will can act without problems on the trading strategy, it is 'forbidden' in its action on the individual transaction. This is a logical cost to be assumed/paid in the context of our theoretical proposal on the evolutionary modelling of the financial market.
14. Relatively recent research—we are referring to behaviourism, which brings to the forefront of behaviour precisely the subconscious, see the two systems of thinking of Kahneman (2012), namely: system 1, i.e., a slow system, and system 2, i.e., a fast system—shows that the subconscious has a much more important role and, especially, as it seems, even a decisive role in the choice. Of course, it is not necessary to go to psychoanalysis, but a-rationality (or even i-rationality) is beginning to be increasingly important features in the decision-making process—the two factors can be subsumed, however, to the concept of emotion, previously used by us. In this context, we consider that we need an economic model of *homo œconomicus*, not a mathematical one, as is the one delivered by neoclassical economic theory.
15. An analytical discussion of inertia, change tension, and its accumulation to a critical threshold can be found in Chap. 17 of the book written by one of the authors (Dinga, 2012).
16. In an analogous (not similar!) way as the factual confrontation of Popper''s prediction—with the difference that, in our case, it is not about the truth, but about performance.
17. This is the methodological reason why the KDF model of the logical structure of preference was presented in the order K - F - D.
18. Recall that the properties of plasticity and elasticity, respectively, were discussed, as a prologue, in detail in FMAB-APH (Dinga et al., 2022).
19. We recall that Lakatos's' proposal, called the research programme, is characterized by the following: (a) involves the coexistence of several research programmes, competing with each other (so way, attracting researchers from one to another), as opposed to the paradigm, which is unique at one point, as Kuhn claimed; (b) factual falsification is no longer a 'no appeal'

criterion of demarcation between science and non-science, as Popper claimed; (c) a research programme contains: (1) a hardcore body that is not affected by factual individual refutations of theoretical consequences; (2) a belt of theorems, lemmas, conjectures that can be refuted empirically but that do not affect the hardcore, so a research programme can continue despite the refutations that occur in the belt part. Of course, as in Kuhn''s paradigm, at some point, the mass of refutations will become critical and the hardcore will also be questioned. All these features have been integrated into our research in the form of significance thresholds.

20. Here, allusion to the Kuhnian concept of normal science.
21. In general, there can be three categories of beliefs: (a) *rational belief*, or deliberative belief—that belief acquired through intellectual reflection, with which the economic agent consciously agrees or elaborates them him/herself, often, programmatically; (b) *faith*, that is belief of i-rational type, or non-deliberative belief—a belief, usually of a religious or strongly metaphysical type; (c) *credence*—a-rational or trustworthy belief—mixed entitlement (in fact, rational, i-rational and a-rational) of some decisional or action behaviours, usually acquired through experience or by observing other economic agents). For example, the last type of belief (*credence*) is invoked by David Lewis (Lewis, 1980) and a few years later by Ned Hall (Hall, 2004).
22. The propensity is not, therefore, apodictic, but has the character of *adumbration* invoked by the phenomenology of Husserlian origin (it suggests without indicating, i.e., it offers possibilities). *Nota bene*: adumbration (suggestion without indication) is also used by Richard Thaler in the development of his *nudge* concept (Thaler & Sunstein, 2009).
23. Hence most of the positions in the literature that associate propensity, almost without exception, to probabilities (see the detailed discussion of the concept of propensity and probability, developed in FMAB-APH (Dinga et al., 2022)).
24. A more appropriate term to describe how propensity (belief, in the last resort) generates the choice of trading strategy, is *nudge*, just mentioned in note 22. About this concept and its characteristics regarding decision and human action, see the work of Richard Thaler and Cass Sunstein, *Nudge. The Book of Niches for Better Decisions Related to Health, Wealth and Happiness* (Penguin Books, 2009).
25. This is about relatively superficial psychological effects (more precisely, gained from experience) while the psychological (subconscious) component of propensity is, somehow, *a priori* (grounded).
26. It is acceptable that the economic operator him/herself has a margin of acceptability of the result in question, within which the significance threshold is not (yet) reached. More precisely, if the significance threshold spe-

cific to the economic agent (which is of an accentuated idiosyncratic nature) is not exceeded, that economic agent does not 'notice' the deviation of the actual result from the expected (or anticipated, as the case may be) one, so, the deviation in question does not generate any feedback.

27. This last relation of order is the consequence of the transitivity (which we postulated) between the three significance thresholds.
28. As the informed reader will immediately notice, this order relation (which, from an algebraic perspective, is a total order relation) is subject to the Condorcet paradox—generalized by Arrow—but this purely logical complication will be ignored here.
29. Conjecturing an equality of the two durations—the one in which the opposition manifested itself, through robustness, to change, and the one in which the process of returning to the previous state is initiated, through resilience—is risky. We consider that such a problem is not theoretical, but empirical, so it is decided only contextually/locally.
30. By 'space' we understand here the issues to which robustness (and resilience as well) must face. Many issues are taken into account, larger `space` is implied.
31. It is easy to notice the paradigmatic behaviour of preference/proference—indeed, analogously to Kuhn-ian paradigm, the anomalies are 'pulled under the carpet' for a while, until they reach a critical (unsustainable) threshold.
32. The idea of this 'attachment' will be taken up again (through the concept of affinity) when discussing the autopoietic model of the financial market.
33. Here we can speak (and the theoretical development can be particularly fruitful, in our opinion, in such a direction) of a second-order preference, or a *preference for preference*. Of course, it is immediately noticeable that this is a paradigmatic behaviour (in Kuhn''s sense): although the significance threshold indicates the need to change the preference component, the economic agent (attached to that component, as the scientific community within a paradigm is attached to that paradigm, respectively to the normal science that operates under that paradigm) ignores that 'alarm signal', by preferring to sweep the anomaly under the mat—the sweep under the mat is done in the form of changing the significance threshold. *Nota bene*: in civil life this phenomenon is frequently encountered: if the alarm is set to the clock, we change the time to ring (later), if we exceed the deadline at which we had to complete a task, we change the deadline and so on.
34. This (very important) issue will be taken up and further examined below.
35. Of course, this shape results from the stylization of the three-dimensional graph (the third dimension being the total utility) from the microeconomic theory of the consumer (the decreasing and convex shape results from the maintenance of the rational decision on the choice).

36. We are of the opinion that these subjective probabilities can only be of the Bayesian (*a priori*) type (as mentioned in FMAB-APH (Dinga et al., 2022)), in the first instance but, obviously, subject to adjustments following the actual activity in the financial market.
37. It is to be mentioned that x cannot ever be null, because the individual always has a terrain of reaction, and the most accessible such a terrain is exactly represented by the significance thresholds.
38. x is considered here as constant, but it could be thought of as a variable, namely as being dependent on θ (*Nota bene*: see the additional comment below in the text).
39. Such an algebraic relation is so common in economic theory and analysis so that, probably, is the result of an intuition on the (deep) preference of the individual's psychology for invariance and invariants. Of course, if yes, then a basis for this assumption is Simon's concept of bounded rationality.
40. As we mentioned before, a return that is too high in relation to expectations must be an alarm signal (assuming that expectations are reasonable, i.e., in accordance with the specifics of the functioning of the financial market and with a minimum of rationality), because, of the many times (as has been shown in practice—see subprime crisis or crisis of financial instruments, such as financial derivatives), such a return signals a hidden Ponzi scheme (whether deliberate or emerging).
41. There is, of course, a natural lower limit of this narrowing (*Nota bene*: such a natural lower limit also exists in the other two components of the preference), namely the need to maintain at least one type of individual transaction, otherwise the trader leaves the financial market—in this sense, the exit of an economic agent from the financial market is equivalent to his decision to 'cancel' the functional component of the preference.
42. This evocation of the concept of probability is justified by the conceptual link between propensity and probability (as it was developed in FMAB-APH (Dinga et al., 2022)). At the same time, we warn the reader that this is a special probability, which concerns the availability of the economic agent, not some intensional property of some financial event outside that agent.
43. The reaction of the preference component to the action of the significance threshold has the size of the marginal substitution rate between the variation of the significance threshold and the variation of the preference component. Thus, if we denote by $r_{\theta/x} = \frac{\Delta x}{\Delta \theta}$, where $r_{\theta/x}$ represents the marginal substitution rate between θ and x (the number of units by which the preference component must be modified when the significance threshold changes by one unit, so that the expected return from the financial market remains invariant), then $\Delta x = \Delta \theta \cdot r_{\theta/x}$.

44. The reader who follows us closely will have no difficulty in replicating the reasoning if the significance threshold widens or if the action is performed by the component of preference and, this time the reaction is expected from the significance threshold (both in the case of narrowing as well as in the case of widening).
45. Indeed, we are not talking about 'individuals', even if it is about individual transactions, but about classes of such individuals. Specifically, one type of individual transaction is a non-singular (i.e., repeatable) individual transaction—the same individual transaction is actually marketed a number of times, depending on the economic interest of the agent (although the case of a single operationalization, in certain particular contexts may be accepted). An individualized transaction actually operationalized on the market is a concrete/particular hypostasis of a type of individual transaction from the 'portfolio' of the functional component of preference/proference. The 'population' generated by the repetition of the operationalization of a fixed individual transaction contains individuals who are fungible with each other—obviously not as such, but as contributors to the formation of that 'population'.
46. So, there is no need for a 'validation' of the number of types of individual transactions by their actual operationalization in the financial market, but only for their acceptability by the agent—so, this is a phenomenon with a strong potential character.
47. Obviously, there are as many financial markets as there are types of financial 'objects' (e.g., types of financial instruments) that are traded (as is the case in the goods market, where there are as many markets for goods as there are such types of goods).
48. Since the 'paradigm' within which we discuss the whole issue of adaptive preference in the financial market is an evolutionary one, we believe that activating one of the trading strategies in the 'portfolio' of the deliberative component (of preference) of the economic agent will be done evolutionarily, that is, by selecting that trading strategy which exhibits the best fitness in the concrete conditions in which the economic agent has to trade in the financial market. Additional details will be provided on this topic in due course.
49. The concept of experience should not be confused with the concept of experiment—in the first case, the economic agent experiences (rather, in the sense of phenomenology—that is, interacts with the specific presence of the financial market), which means s/he is placed within that process, while in the second case, s/he is placed outside the process concerned.
50. In our opinion, the plasticity (sensitivity to change) is higher (and occurs more frequently) in the case of the *intensional* change of the hard component of the preference, than in the case of its *qualitative* change.

51. Please note that this is the strength of conviction, not the strength of justifiability—the strength of justifiability implies a certain reflectivity of the agent, perhaps based on a model of rationality, which is not the case here—propensity can only be called metaphorically as a model of rationality (based on the fact that the trading strategy is 'inferred' from the propensity), but, in fact, it is a model of credence (maybe, even, of a faith), that is, of an *a priori* positioning in front of the world, in this case, in front of the specific process of the financial market.
52. Different beliefs are incommensurable. Here we believe that beliefs/propensities work analogously to paradigms (in the original sense proposed by Kuhn, without the later developments of Lakatos, Feyerabend or Laudan), i.e., no hierarchy/order can be established between two beliefs, nor a point of view (*Nota bene*: of course, it is all the more difficult to establish whether or not one belief has been replaced by another).
53. External observability is inversely 'ordered' in relation to internal observability: from inside, intensional change is less observable than qualitative change while, from the outside, the situation is reversed: qualitative change is less observable than intensional change.
54. Obviously, there is a need to develop a specialized hermeneutics (much more sophisticated than the neoclassical—algebraic—formalization of revealed preferences. At the limit, this hermeneutics can go to a phenomenological approach (in the original sense proposed by Husserl).
55. A significance threshold is qualified as antecedent to another significance threshold if the first is located (from a topological point of view) towards the periphery of preference/proference over the second.
56. However, we will see below that the significance threshold for the hard component of preference is not 'orthodox' (i.e., it is not subject to strict dimensionality, as is the case for the significance thresholds of the other two components).
57. Of course, we must comply with the Kolmogorov conditions on probabilities. In a later phase of the research, however, and under the impact of the results (more or less testable, in fact, in Popperian sense) obtained in the last period of behaviourism and institutionalism/evolutionism, we will examine the problem of supraunit probabilities, respectively of negative probabilities, in connection with the adaptive preference and the trinomial preference—information—price.
58. It is about a volatility that is quite suspicious in the context in which we 'agreed' with the idea that the preference (proference) is relatively rigid.
59. The proposal of this order relation is 'valid', obviously, for the generic case, because idiosyncrasies can establish deviations from it.
60. Here the reasoning is analogous to that developed when (above) the relationship between robustness and resilience regarding the order of rigidity was discussed.

61. The fact that the economic operator would like to change something in a system/mechanism that (successfully) works seems strange and unlikely but, in our opinion, this is not the case: a long period (anyway, above the average 'observed' in the financial market) of above average market gain (or over the most relevant competitor) can be a signal for an imminent catastrophe (see, here, the so-called exuberant behaviour recorded in the preamble of the financial crisis).
62. As we mentioned before, one should not think that the economic agent conscientiously counts the gaps, then makes a very wise reasoning and decides to change this or that component of the preference. Although a certain awareness cannot be ruled out in this matter, the changes in preference (respectively, in its components) occur rather unconsciously (here Samuelson is somewhat right with his concept of revealed preference—only that he could not refrain, like in scorpion's anecdote, to give it a logical and mathematical formalization, exactly in his irrepressible and useless neoclassical style).
63. We point out that we are not talking here about the significance threshold, but about an accumulability (in time or from a dimensional point of view) of the repeated violations regarding the significance thresholds.
64. Somehow, in a quantum way.
65. Here we consider not the moments of the time series of interest for the economic agent (and which counts in the trading decision, more precisely in terms of choosing the individual transaction), but about the moments associated with the manifestation of gaps. Probably, a psychological discount is also valid in this respect (*Nota bene*: can we also talk about a discount in space? Our view is that yes, that is, based on what we mentioned earlier about the proximity effect, so to speak—the last event is more vivid, so more likely to increase the probability associated with it for the decision to change; in fact, behaviourism accepts this conclusion).
66. For example, in the case of consumer (behaviour), this criterion of indifference (between the chosen quantities in a given basket of goods) is the total utility provided by the chosen goods—the substitution between the quantities (respectively, utilities) in question retains the total utility (which is purely algebraically additive) invariant.
67. Of course, return is an objective, interpersonally controllable criterion that can be part of a (however rudimentary) model of rationality. However, it is not only the rational agent who chooses between changing the significance threshold and changing the component of preference involved—more conservative agents will be more likely to change the significance threshold, while more innovative agents will be more likely to change, rather, the very component of the preference itself (*Nota bene*: the term innovative used here has nothing to do with the term innovative agents in the EMH model or other neoclassical models of the financial market).

68. The significance threshold should be understood as an interval (i.e., a one-dimensional number), not as a simple nominal number. The centring of the interval in question is usually done on the nominal number 0).
69. Obviously, if we want to increase (or, in some cases, even decrease) the return, we are talking about another curve of indifference, shifted either to the right or to the left in the bidimensional coordinates: variation of the significance threshold—adjustment of the preference component.
70. As in the case of information and price, we will have to discuss the relationship between emergent and deliberate features in the mutation of preference, which is more complicated and subtle than in the case of the other two evoked symbolic species examined above.
71. That is why, for example, in our opinion, artificial intelligence has nothing to do with information, but only with signals. Although the signal carries the sign, the sign is no longer natural, it requires an interpretation in a symbolic code, which is the cultural code. Of course, artificial intelligence can benefit from a 'dictionary' that tells it what 'information' corresponds to which signal (perhaps by ignoring the intermediate relationship between signal and sign) but all this does not at all make artificial intelligence dealing with information. The reason for this drastic conclusion is psychological: the information is a date (i.e., a sign that has already given a meaning by the holder) that removes uncertainty—it is quite complicated to build a theory of mechanical uncertainty, i.e., artificial intelligence that, presumably, does not have a psyche (e.g., an entity with artificial intelligence will perceive/record a certain wavelength of a photon but will not be able to 'see' the colour associated with that wavelength although, based on an internal dictionary, it will be able to say it is about this or that colour).
72. Although we often say preference instead of adaptive preference, the reader is warned that we always consider adaptive preference in the sense that it was defined and characterized in FMAB-APH (Dinga et al., 2022).
73. No way to assert the inneist character of the preference/belief.
74. This phenomenon has also led to the initiation of a new direction of research in the humanities, namely social psychology, which is different from psychology (individual psychology—either cognitive or behavioural) and sociology.
75. Belief is a propensity, a disposition(ality) of the individual, for any action or position of his/her in the world.
76. We remind you that, in our opinion, the financial market is the species for which the individual called trading strategy stands. In other words, the financial market is nothing more than the interdependent sum (i.e., the logical sum, not just algebraic one) of trading strategies that are operationalized at a given time (or time range) in a given economic space.
77. Which, of course, is not exactly the preference phenotype, although the deliberative component of preference generates the very phenotype of the financial market.

78. The partial nature of the deliberativeness impact is explained by the fact that to a certain extent (less than in the case of the individual transaction, however) there may be a memetic impact on the 'design' and choice of trading strategy (*Nota bene*: this memetic impact is decreasing in the case of the three symbolic species discussed in the paper: namely, in the order of information-price-preference).
79. The emergent (random)/deliberative mix is, in fact, the mark of social evolution (from a conceptual point of view, it can be said that, in social evolution, we have a Darwinist-Lamarckist mix).
80. It is not, of course, the place to develop here too much the idea/concept of substrate but we will say that this concept (derived from phenomenology) can be a starting point for building a *phenomenological evolutionary model—FEM* of the financial market—we consider that our proposal, in the last chapter of this book, and called the *Autopoietic Market Hypothesis*—could be a good start point in this (new) direction of research.
81. The self-generating character of preference (the mechanism of proference) will be (along with other suggestions mentioned throughout the paper) the basis for developing the autopoietic model of the financial market (or the autopoietic hypothesis of the financial market), which will be the second conceptual proposal of our research (along with the hypothesis of adaptive preference of the financial market).
82. It seems that, in the field of financial transactions, we could also talk about flexicurity (a common concept now especially for the labour market, where it expresses a functional mix between job security and job flexibility), i.e., the relationship between financial security (maintaining a 'certain' gain, albeit a modest one) and financial flexibility (uncertain opportunities with high rewards). In our opinion, the concept of flexicurity in the financial market could be a productive direction of research, especially regarding the kinematics of the propensity/belief of the economic agent.
83. Of course, through the variation of the significance threshold of the functional component, respectively by the modification of the functional component itself.
84. Do not confuse the expression *causal complex* with the expression *complex cause*: while the causal complex designates a set—possibly having a unifying internal structure or at least interdependent one—of causal, correlational or conditional factors, while the complex cause designates, in our opinion, a macro-cause in which at least one factor is the free will.
85. To make a connection (somewhat, excessive, but not necessarily inappropriate) with phenomenology and its basic concepts, we can say that the deliberative mutation of the propensity (the genotype of preference) is a simultaneous *agency* and *ownership* effect, while its random mutation is an *ownership*-only effect. *Nota bene*: economic theory has lately been making

interesting and (perhaps) useful excursions for its conceptual reconstruction, in phenomenology, so it is not excluded that such theoretical 'meetings' may be auspicious for financial market theory as well.

86. As we have shown before, rigidity can manifest itself in two forms: (a) *robustness*—a spatial rigidity, so to speak; (b) *resilience*—a temporal rigidity. (*Nota bene*: if we were to make a digression in the sense of Derrida, here, we could say that resilience is the effect of a *differance*—this is the famous concept of differance, as opposed to the concept of difference, proposed by Derrida in terms of language, but not only—that is, of a postponement, timing, or timing of the recovery of robustness, in our case (Derrida, 2016).)
87. Note the (almost explicit) reference that the routine concept makes to the concept of normal science in Kuhn's theory (Kuhn, 1970).
88. It should be noted that the modification of the preference phenotype, unlike the modification of the phenotype in the biological case, is not done by a kind of generational reproduction, but by the direct adjustment of the existing phenotype, adjustment which, depending on the degree of this adjustment, can even lead to the elimination of the phenotype, this time not through the selection made by the environment (cultural geodesic), but as a result of the decision of the economic agent involved.
89. It should be noted that in the biological field (i.e., regarding non-symbolic species), there are objections to considering DNA as an information programme (but we will not develop this issue here further).
90. We repeat that, in the case of symbolic species (or, equivalent, of cultural species), there are no generations arranged chronologically, in the sense of progeny. However, there is a chronological order of the phenotype, in the sense that a phenotype that has undergone a change will function 'later' than one that has not undergone the change in question—the first being the equivalent of the ascendant in biology, and the second—the equivalent of the descendant in biology. As, in the case of symbolic species, we do not have a phenotype building programme (which undergoes a process of individual development), i.e., we do not have an equivalent of the DNA-mRNA pair, so, transcription (and translation) will refer (as in the case of symbolic species previously discussed—information, respectively, price—to the directly takeover, that is, at the level of the existing adult, of the genetic mutation.
91. And, as obviously, the other two symbolic co-species have it—the information, respectively the price.
92. Here we recommend to the interested reader some very interesting nuances (Kahneman, 2012) (interesting if we are sure they are applicable, which we doubt, because the experiments examined seem to favour the confirmation of the pre-accepted hypothesis; more precisely, we consider

that we are no in the situation where the predictive statement has the lowest probability of corroboration, as Popper asks for an authentic empirical test).

93. Although it seems tempting (from the perspective of equilibrium modelling), the idea of a curve of indifference between the change in the propensive 'arrow' and the change in the propensive intensity is obviously wrong, simply because one of the variables is quantitative or may be, easily, endowed with numerical values (the case of propensive intensity), while the other variable is purely qualitative. Of course, the propensive 'arrows' can also be assigned numerical values, but only in a rather artificial way, or, perhaps, a Likert scale can be used for it (which is of an ordinal nature, while the propensive intensity is endowed with a cardinal scale).
94. A possible topological method/technique (if it will be invented for economic, or at least for the financial market, modelling—which is 'endowed' with spatiality and temporality) could use the plasticity property of the hard component of preference/proference to establish topological equivalences. Topological equivalences, as well as algebraic ones—see Noether-type conservation laws (Sato & Ramachandran, 1990)—actually count as invariants.
95. Please note that the Bayes *a posteriori* probability is the Bayes *a priori* probability adjusted on the basis of explicit or implicit data/information (inferred from the observation of other financial market behaviours). Let us make the following notations: be $P(I)$ the previous (*a priori*) probability that hypothesis I is true (or correct); be $P(I|D)$ the subsequent (*a posteriori*) probability of hypothesis I, conditioned by the data D; be $P(D|I)$ the probability of finding the data D if hypothesis I is correct; be $P(D|I_{false})$ the probability of finding the data D if hypothesis I is false; be $P(I_{false}) = 1 - P(I)$. Then the Bayesian rule (theorem) is as follows: $P(I|D) = \frac{P(I) \cdot P(D|I)}{P(I) \cdot P(D|I) + P(I_{false}) \cdot P(D|I_{false})}$.
96. The Bayesian probability may also have the nature of a desire, but the desire is, in our opinion, also based on belief or even on faith.
97. If the deliberative component contains several trading strategies, it can be discussed, of course, how each of them is affected by the genetic mutation but, in principle, being about a qualitative impact, we can consider that the change is the same for all existing trading strategies). Obviously, one could build a list of possible distinct profiles for the various existing trading strategies in the deliberative component and, on this basis, could establish different categories of qualitative impact on them coming from the genetic mutation in question.

98. As in common language, by capacity we effectively mean the nomenclature of compatible (inferable) individual transactions from the trading strategy in question.
99. The constant value of the parameter ϕ is debatable, because, given the impact of the variation of a belief, it is possible that $\phi = \phi(\Delta b_k)$. Next, we will assume this dependence of the parameter ϕ on the argument Δb_k, which turns the parameter ϕ into a function.
100. Please note that there is no need to take the gap between the two probabilities in the module, because the algebraic sign is, of course, important: if the gap is negative, the decrease in probability indicates a reduction in the scope of the deliberative component and vice versa for an increase in probability.
101. We say that $\frac{\partial \phi}{\partial(\Delta b_K)} > 0$.
102. The programme sequence is: x1=[-.9:.001:-.1]; x2=[.1:.001:.9]; y1=log2(1-x1); y2=-log2(1-x2); plot(x1,y1,x2,y2) xlabel ('Bayes probability gap"); ylabel ("phy value"); txt=("Kinematics of phy").
103. We (re) recall that our theoretical 'alternative (response) to the concept of revealed preference is what we called *implicit information*—information inferred by economic agents participating in the financial market from observing the behaviour (decisions, respectively actions subsequent to decisions) of other participants in market transactions.
104. Similar to Kolmogorov"s condition on objective frequential probabilities based on set theory.
105. To the (almost dogmatic) libertarian opinion on the predominance of the invisible hand in social construction (i.e., in the inter-subjective construction of artefacts) we answer that the impersonality of social interaction is based on individual deliberations, that is, based on (individual's) teleology. In fact, from an evolutionary perspective, libertarianism (and perhaps, to a large extent, fundamentalist liberalism) is a kind of social Darwinism.
106. As long as transhumanism (i.e., the technical, not psychological, cybernetization of the human individual) does not exceed a critical limit, Darwinian evolution is maintained, albeit in a downward trend.
107. It should be noted that genetic engineering is a deliberate reduction in the share of genetic evolution in the total evolutionary process.
108. Obviously, the share of the epigenetic factor in the total evolution is directly proportional to the degree of control that the human economic agent has over the (co-) species in question.
109. The lines that describe the composition (possibly, percentage) of the two polar categories of evolution (Darwinist, respectively, Lamarckian), and which can also be curves, decreasing and convex, have, in fact, the role of

indifference curves, for each of the three symbolic (co-) species in part. In an appropriate formalization, these indifference curves may have their relevance in the trinomial preference-information-price (TCIP model of the financial market).

110. The attentive reader has already noticed that we use, here, a certain conceptual license, so to speak: we have shown, throughout the paper, that in order to recover the species in which the trading strategy (i.e., the financial individual) is living, we 'decreed' that this species (remember, lost by Lo, in his AMH proposal) is the financial market. Therefore, what is evolving is the financial market, not the trading strategy (which, like any individual, can instead develop—for example, the modification of the trading strategy, or the deliberative component of the preference/proference that 'hosts' the trading strategy, made under the impact of the change of the functional component, is an element of the development of the trading strategy, not of its evolution). Returning to the conceptual license mentioned above, it is a question of the fact that, for reasons of exposure logic, we substitute the (co-) species financial market with preference. This substitution is not very dangerous, because it is a substitution of the whole preference (i.e., all its three components/layers), not just the substitution between species (financial market) and individual (trading strategy), which is only the deliberative component of preference. Obviously, where necessary, clarifications will be made in the main text or in the notes to help avoid confusion or misunderstanding of the reasoning provided.
111. It seems that, similarly, that is, competitively/evolutionarily, things happen in the realm of reflection (or, to use a language of phenomenology, in the realm of ideation): a thought/idea competes with other thoughts/ideas so, in the end, only one of them 'penetrates' in consciousness and possibly externalizes in a communicable form.
112. As is well known, synergy is the property of a combination (of any kind) of combinable entities, which generates properties or relationships between those entities that, prior to the combination, were not identifiable (i.e., could not be generated) by any of the combined entities as considered separately.
113. It is obvious that the three existing entities in the Universe—things, properties, relations—cannot be talked, after the realization of the combination which, as a rule, takes the form of a supra-system from existing systems, only about properties, respectively relations (not at all about things).
114. We specify that, here, the fitness concept of the trading strategy (of the preference phenotype) has exactly the same meaning as the fitness in biology: the adequacy, from a relevant point of view (in biology: the physical survival of the species through reproduction, in the financial field: the

economic survival of the economic agent by replicating the trading strategy, more precisely the individual transactions logically inferred from the trading strategy in question) of the phenotype to its environment in which the species (in our case, the financial market) functions.

115. The informed reader might ask himself, at this point in the discussion, if there is any conceptual parallel between the validation/invalidation of the new fitness of the trading strategy and the well-known factual falsification of Popper. In other words, is the corroboration (so to speak) of the changed trading strategy equivalent to a positive assessment of the 'truth' of that strategy? Our answer is no: in this case we do not have a problem of truth, but a problem of effectiveness (likewise in the case of biological evolution), so the 'testing' to which the financial market environment (cultural geodesic) subjects the financial individual (trading strategy) is not an epistemic type test, but a pragmatic one, more precisely, a praxiological type test (sometimes, also of a practical type).
116. Obviously, the term 'inferior' is scientifically inappropriate—in the discussed matter there are no value ratings, but only performance ratings—so the correct term is appropriate (or inappropriate).

References

Barrow-Green, J. (2010). *The dramatic episode of Sundman.* Historia Mathematica, 37(2), 164–203.

Derrida, J. (2016). *Of grammatology*, John Hopkins University Press.

Dinga, E. (2012). *Rebuilding Economics. Logical, Methodological and Epistemological Approach.* Lambert Academic Publishing.

Dinga, E., Oprean-Stan, C., Tănăsescu, C.-R., Brătian, V., Ionescu, G.-M., (2022) *Financial Market Analysis and Behaviour. The Adaptive Preference Hypothesis*, Routledge, Francis & Taylor Group.

Hall, N. (2004). Two Mistakes About Credence and Chance. *Australasian Journal of Philosophy*, *82*(1), 93–111.

Kahneman, D. (2012). *Thinking, Fast and Slow*. Penguin.

Kuhn, T. (1970). *The Structure of Scientific Revolutions.* The University of Chicago Press.

Lewis, D. K. (1980). A Subjectivist's Guide to Objective Chance. In R. C. Jeffrey (Ed.), *Studies in Inductive Logic and Probability, Volume II* (pp. 263–293). Berkeley: University of California Press.

Lo, A. (2019). *Adaptive Markets. Financial Evolution at the Speed of Thought.* Princeton University Press.

Nelson, R. R., & Winter, S. G. (1985). *An Evolutionary Theory of Economic Change.* Harvard University Press.

Popper, K. R. (1959). The Propensity Interpretation of Probability. *The British Journal for the Philosophy of Science*, *10*(37), 25–42.

Samuelson, P. A. (1938). *A Note on the Pure Theory of Consumer's Behaviour*. Economica, 5(17), 61–71.

Satchell, S., & Grant, A. (2020). *Momentum: Theory and Practice*. The Wiley Finance Series.

Sato, R., & Ramachandran, R. (Eds.). (1990). *Conservation Laws and Symmetry: Applications to Economics and Finance*. Springer Dordrecht.

Thaler, R., Sunstein, C. (2009). *Nudge. The book of niches for better decisions related to health, wealth and happiness*, Penguin Books.

CHAPTER 6

Trinomial Co-evolution in the Financial Market

Logical Modelling of the Trinomial Preference-Information-Price

Preamble

In the following, we will elaborate on the logical model, based on the previously results, of the trinomial preference-information-price, from the evolutionary perspective. To this end, we will systematize the results obtained with respect to all three symbolic co-species, in an attempt to identify the main lines of interaction that, in the end, will further substantiate the concept of adaptive preference.

A trinomial model (trinomic, triadic) is considerably more complicated than a binomial model (binomic, dyadic) and this, of course, not for a reason related to the degree of complicatedness, that is, from a quantitative perspective, but for qualitative reasons. Let us exemplify some of these reasons.

Firstly, in a trinomial model, we have an augmented structure—three components, compared to two in the binomial model. This leads to an increase in the functionality of the system because, as it is well known, the functionality of a system is given by the interactions between the components of the system in question (i.e., by the interactions carried out inside the 'membrane' of that system). We have three nodes that can generate arcs of interaction with each other (to use terminology from graph

E. Dinga et al., *Co-Evolution of Symbolic Species in the Financial Market*, https://doi.org/10.1007/978-3-031-31698-2_6

theory). If we consider that between two nodes, there are (at the minimum limit) only two arcs (one incident and one excident), together with two loops (arcs in which its incident extremity and the excident one coincide), one for each node, then, in the binomial model, we have at least four arcs. Instead, in the case of the trinomial model, we will have three sets of pairs of arcs, plus the three loops, so at a minimum, we will have nine arcs (a relative increase of 125%). As it is well known, the structure generates the functions of a system, so a larger structure will generate more and (usually) more subtle functions than a smaller structure.

Secondly, in a trinomial model, the phenomenology of reaction norms is much more complicated than in a binomial one. In general, this phenomenology uses as 'vehicle' precisely the arcs mentioned above, but this is only a purely quantitative aspect. The specificity of the reaction norms in a trinomial model lies, in particular, in their qualitative aspects—these aspects will be examined, with a slightly higher degree of detail, below.

Thirdly, in a trinomial model, the synergy acquires very interesting but obviously more complicated valences. If, in the binomial model, the synergy had only one 'source'—the interaction between the two components—in the trinomial one there will be three such 'sources', because we have, *grosso modo* speaking, three different directions of interaction. In addition, the existence of these different synergistic sources leads to an interesting phenomenon of synergy of synergy (or a second-order synergy). Details of the issue of synergy in a trinomial model will also be examined latter.

Reaction Norms in the Trinomial Model

In a system of 'three bodies', the internal interaction (which, we remind, in cybernetic theory is called functionality[1]) is also modellable through the reaction norms. In order to extract the qualitative specificity of the phenomenology of the reaction norms in the trinomial case of the symbolic (co)species in the financial market, we will make some notations, based on which we will extract the main relations of interest:

(a) Notations
- I: co-species information; P: co-species price; C: co-species preference
- $\mathcal{A}_j^x$: the space of fetal acceptability of actions/reactions, in the case of co-species 'x', at the moment[2] 'j' (where: $x \in \{I, P, C\}$)
- $A_j^{x \to y}$: action, at time 'j' from co-species 'x' to co-species 'y' (where: $y \in \{I, P, C\}$); *Nota bene*: if $x = y$, then it is about a loop

- $R_j^{x\to y}$: reaction at time '*j*' from co-species '*x*' to co-species '*y*'
- $\mathbb{A}_j^x$: the set of actions available to co-species '*x*' at time '*j*'
- $\mathbb{R}_j^x$: the set of reactions available to co-species '*x*' at time '*j*'
- L_j^x: significance threshold of the action/reaction associated with co-species '*x*'
- $Q_j^{(\cdot)\to x}$: the amount of action/reaction accumulated in co-species '*x*', up to the time '*j*', of all other two co-species, without any reaction of co-species '*x*'
- $R_j^{x\to(\cdot)}$: the reaction of the co-species '*x*', to either of the other two species[3]

(b) Conditional relationships

$$
\begin{gathered}
A_j^{x\to y} \in \mathbb{A}_j^x \\
R_j^{x\to y} \in \mathbb{R}_j^x \\
A_j^{x\to y} \in \mathcal{A}_j^y ; R_j^{x\to y} \in \mathcal{A}_j^y \\
A_j^{x\to y} \in \left(\mathbb{A}_j^x \cap \mathcal{A}_j^y\right); R_j^{x\to y} \in \left(\mathbb{R}_j^x \cap \mathcal{A}_j^y\right) \qquad (6.1) \\
Q_j^{(\cdot)\to x} = \sum_{\tau=1}^{j} A / R_\tau^{(\cdot)\to x} \\
R_j^{x\to(\cdot)} / \left(Q_j^{(\cdot)\to x} \geq L_j^x\right)
\end{gathered}
$$

Short Discussion

(i) the 'order' in which the actions/reactions between the three co-species occur must be clarified, taking into account the logic of the functioning of the financial market, as outlined so far. It seems that the facts in this matter are as follows:
   - the first action is exerted by information (whether it is information *qua* information—formal information or bound information, in the terminology of the information structure in this research—or it is implicit information, the latter being, in our opinion, the most massive and the most dynamic source of information in the financial market).[4] The justification for this 'priority' of information activism/agency in relation to the other two co-species is based on a hierarchy of symbolic co-species consid-

ered, from the perspective of their inertia. In our opinion, the descending order of the inertia of the three symbolic co-species is as follows: preference-price-information;

- the destination of the first action (i.e., of the information action, or of the informational action) is, in our opinion, the price, identifiable as such also on the basis of its inertial positioning in the context of the three symbolic co-species.

Nota bene: one could, of course, formulate here under the benefit of inventory, that is, under the condition of the resumption and analytical substantiation of the idea, later in the economics of the study, a 'law' of the interaction of symbolic co-species in the financial market, thus: *the action/reaction of a co-species always chooses as a target the co-species against which its negative inertial gradient is minimal, or against which its positive inertial gradient is maximum*. By inertial gradient, we mean the (algebraic) difference between the measures of inertia of the two co-species compared from this perspective. Indeed, based on the order of inertia mentioned above, the inertiality gradient (denoted $G^{x/y} = \mathcal{I}^x - \mathcal{I}^y$, where $\mathcal{I}^x$ denotes the inertial property of co-species '*x*'), may be characterized as follows (*Nota bene*:) it is necessary, however, to make an additional assumption, which is based solely on intuition: we will assume that the property of inertiality is distributed so that the absolute inertial gap information and price is less than absolute gap price-preference: $|G^{I/P}| < |G^{P/C}|$:

(1) information action/reaction cannot 'jump' (over price) to preference; this is the condition of 'forcing' the action/reaction of the information to target exclusively the price:

$$\left(G^{I/P} < 0\right) \wedge \left(\left|G^{I/P}\right| < \left|G^{I/C}\right|\right) \tag{6.2}$$

(2) price action/reaction cannot 'jump' (over preference) to information; this is the condition of 'forcing' the price action/reaction to target exclusively the preference:

$$\left(G^{P/C} < 0\right) \wedge \left(\left|G^{P/C}\right| < \left|G^{I/C}\right|\right) \tag{6.3}$$

(3) price action/reaction can target both belief and information (see above):

$$\left(G^{P/I} > 0\right) \wedge \left(\left|G^{I/P}\right| < \left|G^{I/C}\right|\right) \tag{6.4}$$

(4) preference action/reaction 'jumps' over the price, targeting the information:

$$\left(G^{C/I} > 0\right) \wedge \left(\left|G^{I/P}\right| < \left|G^{I/C}\right|\right) \tag{6.5}$$

(5) price action/reaction 'jumps' over the preference, targeting the information:

$$\left(G^{C/P} > 0\right) \wedge \left(\left|G^{P/C}\right| < \left|G^{I/C}\right|\right) \tag{6.6}$$

Important Remarks:

- information never goes directly to preference, but to price; it (possibly) reaches preference only through price (i.e., in fact, through the return of the financial market);
- the price can go both ways, both to the information and to the preference;
- preference never goes directly to price, but to information; it (possibly) reaches the price only through information;
- *Nota bene 1*: these 'blockages' in the action/reaction circuits in the trinomial preference-information-price are particularly useful because they allow a logical (and, subsequently, quantitative) modelling of the realistic functioning of the financial market.
- *Nota bene 2*: unlike the conditionalities imposed on the actions/reactions that take place along the trinomial arches, the loops (self-reactions), which occur at the nodes of the trinomial, are unconditioned. However, they are not anchored in any logical need that can be thought by the outside analyst but are, rather, ad-hoc processes, based mostly on the idiosyncrasy of the economic agent.

- according to the logic described above, the second reaction in the trinomial is exerted by price, and the third, by preference; obviously, the targets of the reactions always and unconditionally respect the 'law' of the interaction of the co-species in the financial market, as it has been succinctly described above. Also, in all cases, the significance threshold must (at least) be reached for the action/reaction to be triggered towards the target indicated (without alternative) by the proposed 'law', which is discussed immediately below;

(ii) does any action cause or trigger a reaction? We consider that here too the condition of exceeding a certain threshold of significance must be set: the action, in addition to having to verify the 'legal' conditionalities mentioned above, must exceed a significance threshold at destination (i.e., the co-species on which that action is exerted);[5]

(iii) both the action and the reaction, from any co-species, must be, on the one hand, in the set of own actions/reactions of the co-species of origin, and, on the other hand, in the sphere of acceptability/fetality of the recipient co-species. The condition of necessity of the fetality of the action or reaction was also examined in FMAB-APH (Dinga et al., 2022), so here we do not insist on its significance, but only wanted to re-specify this condition of double belonging;

(iv) the transmission of actions/reactions, as well as their spatial and temporal concatenation, can be formally described, based on the above, as follows:

$$A_j^{I\to P} \to \left\{ \begin{array}{l} R_{j+1}^{P\to I} \to \left\{ \begin{array}{l} R_{j+2}^{I\to P} \\ R_{j+2}^{I\to I} \end{array} \right. \\ \\ A_{j+1}^{P\to C} \to \left\{ \begin{array}{l} R_{j+3}^{C\to P} \\ R_{j+3}^{C\to I} \\ R_{j+3}^{C\to C} \end{array} \right. \\ \\ \quad R_{j+1}^{P\to P} \end{array} \right. \tag{6.7}$$

(v) the three behavioural possibilities of the price co-species (P) can be simultaneous or time-lagged (however, there is no relevant logical basis for establishing a temporal hierarchy between them, although, from an empirical point of view—not theoretically—from case to case, such a 'prioritization' could be identified).

A graphical picture of the 'law' of the interaction of symbolic co-species in the financial market is provided in Fig. 6.1.

Therefore, there are two categories of feedback (either positive or negative): one category that works at the level of each co-species (loop reactions of type $R_j^{x\to x}$), and another category that works between co-species (reactions of type $R_j^{x\to y}$). The 'forbidden' reactions are cancelled out in red in Fig. 6.1.

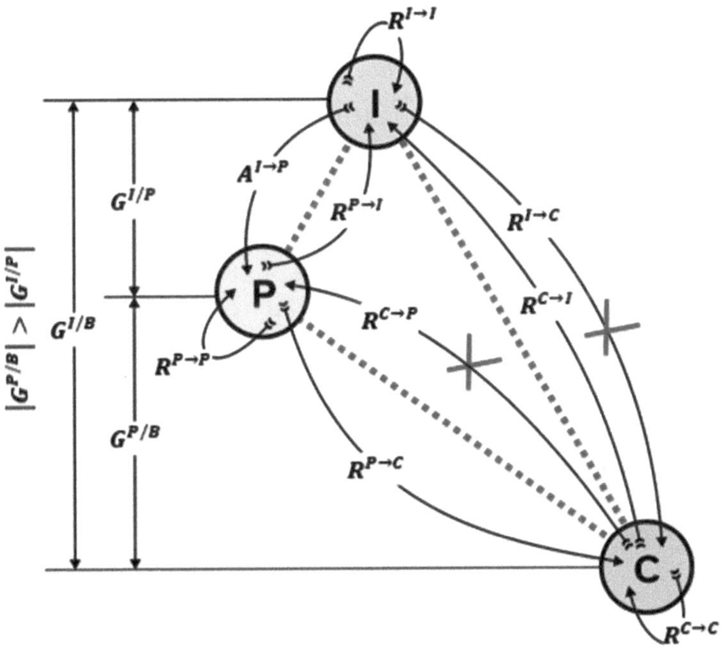

Fig. 6.1 Allowed actions/reactions in the trinomial preference-information-price. *Source*: Authors

Nota bene: the triangle formed by the dotted line in Fig. 6.1 peremptorily suggests the greater 'distance' between information and preference, compared to that between information and price, on the one hand, and between price and preference, on the other hand. This is a direct consequence of the assumed relationships between the inertial properties of the three co-species. Obviously, the concept of 'distance' has, here, a non-dimensional meaning, referring to the inverse proportionality between the probability of an interaction and this 'distance', so to speak.[6]

Synergy in the Trinomial Model

Synergy is one of the great 'surprises' that the structure offers us. This concept was, in general, presented in FMAB-APH (Dinga et al., 2022), but here we will make some developments, because its significance is manifested, mainly, in the trinomial model of the financial market.

Generalities

Reality has three ways of phenomenological manifestation:

(1) *objective reality*: reality is independent on the subject (*Nota bene*: subjects themselves are objects for other subjects—analogous to the phenomenological description of the transcendental 'creation' of the transcendent subject)—Popper's first world (Popper, 1978);
(2) *subjective reality*: reality that is dependent on the subject, that is, the world of feelings, perceptions, and representations that the subject experiences—Popper's second world;
(3) *objectified reality*: reality dependent on the subject (or rather, on the subjective interaction) but opposable to all subjects (objectification of the contents of thinking)—Popper's third world;

Each of the three modes (worlds) of reality is perceptible (hence knowable) under three hypostases, either distinctly or simultaneously, depending on the nature of these modes:

(a) *thing* hypostasis: generic nominal object, defined by quiddity (essence, eidos[7]). *Nota bene*: quiddity is not a property, for it does not distinguish but consecrates the existing; or, as Kant pointed out in connection with the ontological argument (Anselm), existence is not a property;

(b) *property* hypostasis: private nominal object, 'customized', called *hic et nunc* (property involves only the object concerned);
(c) *relationship* hypostasis: connection (of any kind/nature) between objects or between properties or between objects and properties, as the case may be.

Relationships can have three natures:

- *causal* nature: A is the cause of B, which, in turn, is the effect of A, if and only if the exhaustive conjunction is verified: $(A \rightarrow B) \bigwedge \left(\bar{B} \rightarrow \bar{A}\right)$, where the logical constant '$\rightarrow$' means the relation of implication (usually, this is a temporal relationship, so an a-spatial one); *Nota bene*: we have here a syllogistic relation of the *modus tollens* type;
- *structural* nature: A is coexistent with B if and only if the exhaustive conjunction is verified: $\left(A \approx B\right) \wedge \left(\bar{B} \rightarrow \bar{A}\right)$, where the logical constant '$\approx$' means the coexistence (its negations, '$\not\approx$' calls a relationship of non-coexistence); usually it is a spatial, hence a-temporal relationship;
- *functional* nature: A is a function of B, that is, A depends on B in a functional way, if the exhaustive conjunction is verified: $[A = f(B)] \bigwedge [B = f^{-1}(A)]$ (usually, it is both an a-spatial and an a-temporal relationship).[8] *Nota bene*: (1) the introduction of dating, respectively of location, in quantitative equations, refers to a mathematical space and time, not to the corresponding physical concepts; (2) condition $B = f^{-1}(A)$ is not, however, a condition of sufficiency for the existence of the functional relation, since it signifies the bijectivity of the functional relation between A and B (a condition too 'strong', i.e., too particular).

Short discussion

What could we say about the *property-relationship* pair?

- *property is cause for relationship*: a relationship is manifested (comes into existence) causally, conditioned by the existence of a property (or a set of properties) that allows the occurrence of that relationship: if we denote by $\mathcal{R}\left(A,B\right)$ a relation between A and B, respectively with $\mathcal{P}\left(A\right)$ a property of A, and with $\mathcal{P}\left(B\right)$ a property of B, so that $\mathcal{P}\left(A\right)$ and $\mathcal{P}\left(B\right)$ are mutually sensitive (which can be written as $\mathcal{P}\left(A\right)\infty\mathcal{P}\left(B\right)$), then $\mathcal{P}\left(A\right)\infty\mathcal{P}\left(B\right) \rightarrow \mathcal{R}\left(A,B\right)$, where with the logical constant '$\bowtie$' the mutual sensitivity was noted;[9]

- mutual sensitivity means the possibility (or necessity, as the case may be) of generating connections between the objects targeted in the mutual sensitivity analysis;
- there is also the case of unilateral (or unidirectional) sensitivity, in which only one of the objects (A) is sensitive to the other (B); the logical formalization is as follows: $[\left[\mathcal{P}(A)\ltimes\mathcal{P}(B)\right]\rightarrow\mathcal{R}\left(A^{\leftarrow},B^{\rightarrow}\right)$, where the logical constant '$\ltimes$' means 'is sensitive to', and the notations $A^{\leftarrow}$ means 'is impacted by', respectively $A^{\rightarrow}$ means 'impacts'; therefore, a more general case of causing the relationship on the part of the property is that of the existence of a sensitivity of one object to another—the impacting relationship will have the 'meaning' from the insensitive object to the sensitive one; so sensitivity (without predicative) allows (causes) the relationship, while mutual sensitivity allows (causes) the relationship;

- *the relationship is cause for property*: once established, the relationship can generate the updating of the properties
  - on the basis of the above notations, this assertion can be formalized as follows:

$$\mathcal{R}(A,B)\rightarrow\left[\mathcal{P}(A)\right]\vee\left[\mathcal{P}(B)\right]\vee\left[\mathcal{P}(A)\wedge\mathcal{P}(B)\right] \tag{6.8}$$

Nota bene: (1) the two causalities are linked in a circular way (more precisely, in a spiral, because the set of properties, respectively of the relationships, becomes more and more populated, as the process continues); (2) of course, there is an upper limit[10] in the growth of the cardinal of the two sets (of properties, respectively of relationships); (3) moreover, the new properties can inhibit some relationships, just as the new relationships can inhibit some properties—so, it is a question of a net kinematics of the cardinals of the two sets; these issues must be examined within the concept of system.[11]

The Concept of Synergy

(a) *synergy definition*: etymology: (gr.) συνεργία—*sin* (συν): together; ἔργον: operation;
  - (cataphatic definition) synergy is a property generated by relationships;
  - (apophatic definition) synergy is not a relationship generated by property.

Comment:

- any of the three types of relationships are involved (causal, structural, functional);
- synergy is generally observable by intermediation of systems;
- no perception is possible without synergy, in the sense that the fully perceived object already includes the synergy generated by the system resulting from that integration;
- properties are not 'visible' outside of interactions, so outside of relationships;
  - therefore, we do not see the properties as they are, but the properties as they appear generated by relationships;
  - properties are inferred/inferable from relationships[12] and have a necessary character; *Nota bene*: here we have the replication of the *phenomenon-noumen* pair: the phenomenon is the property we observe through 'relationships', and the noumenon is the property itself (*Das Ding an Sich* or, more appropriately: *Eigenschaftan Sich*, here in German, meaning own essence, property in oneself);
- in terms of inferring relationships from properties, we can say the following:
  - it is *necessary* in the case of the purely objective (deterministic) world;
  - it is *contingent*[13] in the case of the purely subjective world or the mixed world (in which subjects and objects coexist).

(b) *Significance of synergy*

- first of all, the synergy violates the qualitative (identity) conservation, through the arising of new properties. *Nota bene*: logically, the disappearance of some properties is equivalent to the appearance of other properties—for example: the property of not (existing) a given property is a new property (so properties receive only apophantic verbal labels[14]);
- secondly, synergy is a genus for the species (better known as a Hegelian dialectical construct) called 'quantitative accumulations cause qualitative leaps' because:
  - quantitative 'dis-accumulations' also cause qualitative leaps;
  - quantitative accumulation (or dis-accumulation) is a relational effect;
  - the relationalization can have additional effects than dimensional variations (i.e., other than quantitative accumulations/dis-accumulations).

Brief discussion on qualitative identity, respectively on its violation through the synergy effect:

- it is generally accepted that the identity of a system is given by its structure;
- as the structure is the cause of the function, it results that the identity of a system is given by its function;
- as the function is a relation, it results that the identity of a system is given by its relational set;
- as the relationship is generated by properties, it results that the identity of a system is given by its set of properties;
- as the properties are 'sensitive' to the synergy effect, it follows that the identity of a system is 'sensitive' to its synergy;
- therefore, this explains the previous statement (presented in the discussion about the significance of synergy) according to which the synergy violates the qualitative conservation, so it alters the qualitative identity.

(c) *modal qualification of synergy*
- in the first Popperian world (purely objective world), the synergy has a *necessary* character;
- in the second and third Popperian worlds (the purely subjective world, respectively the world of objectified inter-subjectivity), the synergy has a *contingent* character; *Nota bene*: the financial market, as we have already shown, is an 'individual' of the third Popperian world;
- an important fact to note: contingency has no degrees, that is, whenever the necessity is not complete (regardless of the degree of incompleteness), we have contingency.

(d) *synergy and evolution*
- synergy is the only engine of evolution 'invented' by nature:[15]
  - *the evolution of non-living objectuality*: the new properties, which 'quantify' the evolution, are effects of the synergistic relationships (see the plasticity of the space-time curve, the generation of new chemical elements in the stellar 'furnaces', etc.);
  - *the evolution of living objectuality*: genetic mutations (random factor—*Nota bene*: not probabilistic, that is, stochastic!—in the process of life evolution in general is a property caused by the relationship, so a synergistic effect);

- *the evolution of subjectuality* (refers only to individuals—and societies of individuals—of the cultural type, i.e., possessing the capacity for representation and, thus, the capacity for reflection and symbolic perception): it is based on a mix between memetic evolution (behaviour ostensibly 'borrowed') (Dawkins, 2016) and semetic evolution (imposed or self-imposed behaviour, of institutional type), and owes its renewal of the properties to the modification of the relationships of memetic type, respectively semetic type, both in space and in time;

Nota bene: it seems that synergy is also the mechanism by which cognitive novelty[16] appears: (1) digital (computer) 'thinking' cannot generate new properties through relational combinations, because these morphological combinations are already contained in the programs introduced into the computer; (2) we could name this type of new properties as *non-emergent properties* (see, in FMAB-APH (Dinga et al., 2022), the discussion about the logical relations between synergy and emergency).

A Taxonomy of Synergy

In order to obtain a typology of synergy, it is necessary, of course, to establish the criteria for its classification. We propose the following set of such criteria: (a) by type of causation; (b) by symmetry; (c) according to the potential; (d) by degree; (e) by mechanism; (f) by sphere; and (g) by impact.

a. classes of synergy according to the type of causality
    - *deterministically caused synergy* (*C/DS*): that synergy that is analytically predictable, based on theoretical and empirical models appropriate to the system in question;[17]
    - *probabilistically caused synergy* (*C/PS*): that synergy that is statistically predictable, based on theoretical and empirical models appropriate to the system in question (based on known probability distributions—either archivistic-objective frequential probabilities, Bayesian-subjective probabilities (allocated based on the principle of insufficient reason of Laplace) or Popperian-propensive probabilities—see the theory of propensity, discussed at length in FMAB-APH) (Dinga et al., 2022);

- *randomly caused synergy* (*C/RS*): that synergy that is unpredictable,[18] because no model of theoretical (i.e., a-contextual) description of the synergistic process in question is possible;

b. synergy classes by symmetry
  - *reversible synergy* (*S/RS*): that synergy that can also move the opposite way, symmetrically with respect to the time variable, and following the same 'trajectory'—if it generated new properties, cancel them, if it cancelled old properties, reactivate them; *Nota bene:* reversibility is considered, regarding this category of synergy, as punctual, the return to the initial state being made 'without rest'[19];
  - *irreversible synergy* (*S/IS*): that synergy that cannot go the other way (it is definitive);
  - *hysterical synergy* (*S/HS*): that synergy that can also move the opposite way, symmetrically with respect to the time variable, but not following the same 'trajectory' (i.e., non-symmetrically with respect to the space variable)—if it generated new properties, we can cancel only some of them, and if it has cancelled old properties, it can reactivate only some of them;[20]

A synoptic representation of these symmetry-based classes is given in Fig. 6.2.

c. synergy classes by potential
  - *escalating synergy* (*P/ES*): characterized by self-catalytic expansion potential—in this case, positive feedback predominates;

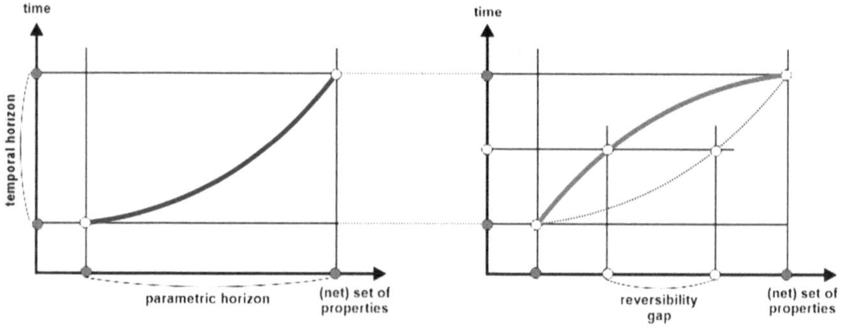

Fig. 6.2 Synergy reversibility working. *Source*: Authors

- *stabilizing synergy* (*P/SS*): characterized by self-stabilizing potential—in this case, negative feedback predominates;
- *oscillating synergy* (*P/OS*): characterized by the potential for non-coincident oscillation[21] (i.e., double hysteresis—both in the escalating phase and in the stabilizing phase); in this case, positive and negative feedback dominance alternates.

d. synergy classes by degree
   - *inertial synergy* (*D/IS*): that synergy which, through the net variation of the set of parameters generated, does not reach the threshold of qualitative (identity) conservation of the system—the variation of the system structure has no impact on the variation of its functions (neither as behaviour nor as functionality);
   - *alternating synergy* (*D/AS*): that synergy which, through the net variation of the set of generated parameters, reaches/exceeds the threshold of qualitative (identity) conservation of the system—the variation of the system structure has an impact on the variation of its functions (either as behaviour or as functionality);

e. synergy classes by mechanism
   - *parametric synergy* (*M/PS*): that synergy that is generated by the relationship (interaction) between the properties of the thing;
   - *relational synergy* (*M/RS*): that synergy that is generated by the relationship (interaction) between relationships;
   - *relametric synergy* (*M/HS*): that synergy that is generated by the relationship (interaction) between the properties of relationships;[22]

f. synergy classes by sphere
   - *static synergy* (*S/SS*): that synergy that is generated by the relationship (interaction) between the properties of things belonging to the target system;
   - *procedural synergy* (*S/PS*): that synergy that is generated by the relationship (interaction) between the properties that appeared as a result of the formation of a supersystem; *Nota bene*: this is the origin of the non-reductionist formulation (based on the Aristotelian suggestion) of synergy: the appearance of properties at the system (or super-system) level that did not exist at the level of components (or systems) before the formation of the system (or super-system).

g. synergy classes by impact
- *primary synergy* (*I/PS*): that synergy that generates additional properties of things;
- *secondary synergy* (*I/SS*): that synergy that generates additional properties of the relationships between things;
- *tertiary synergy* (*I/TS*): that synergy that generates additional properties of the relationships between relationships.

An example of how the synergy works according to the impact criterion is given in Fig. 6.3.

The Structure of Synergic Mechanism
In our opinion, the synergistic mechanism has four components:

- (I) *cause*: the occurring[23] of relationships (new relationships) compared to the previous situation
  - emblematic cases:

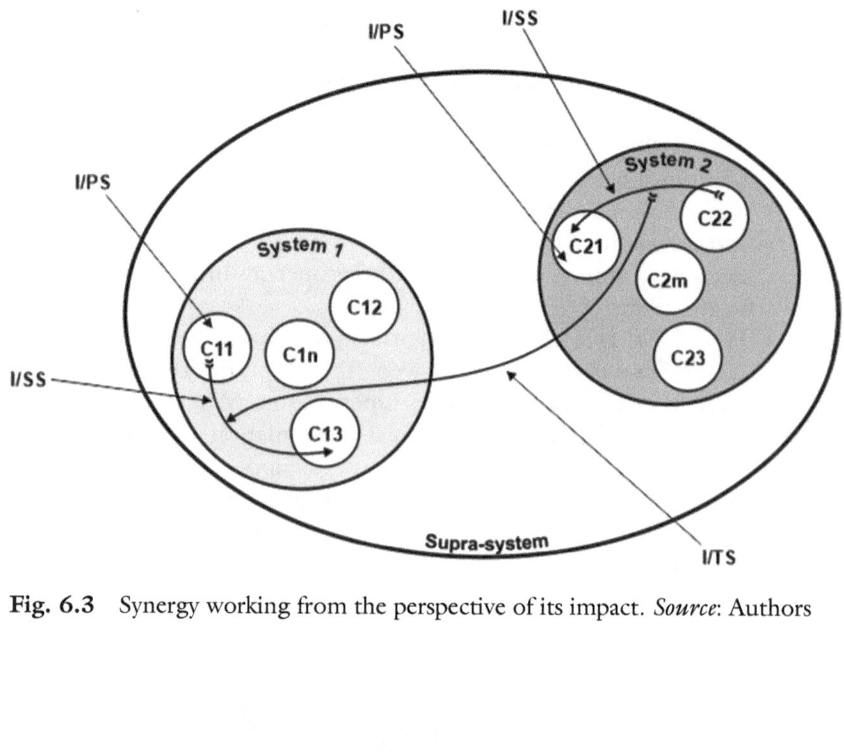

Fig. 6.3 Synergy working from the perspective of its impact. *Source*: Authors

(1) the formation of a supra-system (generates additional relationships that, according to those shown above, will generate new properties or a positive net variation of new properties);
(2) the splitting of a supra-system into component systems (as symmetrically with the formation of a supra-system, it will generate a positive net variation of new properties);
(3) random variations in the set of relationships of a system, that preserves its qualitative identity, will generate net positive variations in the set of properties;

- (II) *effect*: variation of the set of properties (of things or relationships)
- (III) *channel*: relationships between things (or relationships between properties) lead to (net) new properties of things (or relationships between things or relationships between relationships)
- (IV) *stabilizer*: acting on the basis of four categories of thresholds:
  - (P0) thresholds of variation of the set of properties of things (for variation of the set of things)
  - (P1) thresholds of variation of the set of properties of things (for variation of the set of relationships)
  - (P2) thresholds of variation of relationships set (for variation of the set of properties)
  - (P3) thresholds of variation of the set of properties of the relationships (for the variation of the set of relationships)

Figure 6.4 suggests the 'topology' of the generic mechanism of synergy functioning.

Some Developments Around the Concept of Synergy.
Synergy has conceptual and of mechanism connections with two other processes specific to the arising/evolution of systems (as is the case of the financial market): (a) emergence; (b) stigmergy.[24]

(a) synergy and emergence

Emergence (see also the paragraph dedicated, in FMAB-APH (Dinga et al., 2022) to the relationship between synergy and emergence) means an unnecessary and non-deliberate appearance of properties or relationships. The consequences of the emergence can be systematized as follows:

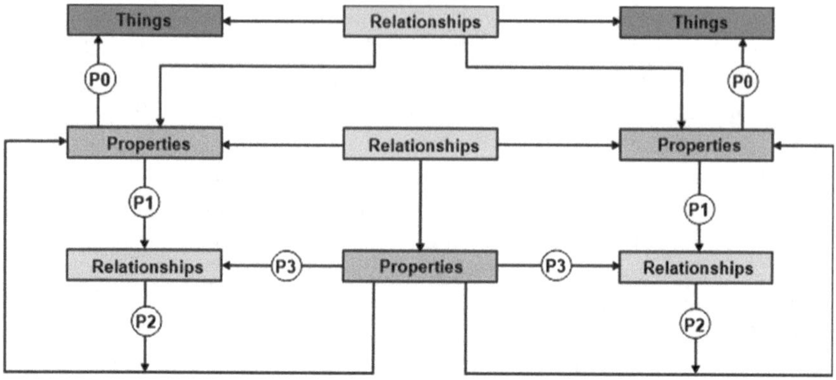

Fig. 6.4 Generic mechanism of synergy functioning. *Source*: Authors

- *in the reality of non-living objectuality* ($R0$): emergence is not possible—we have no non-necessity (more precisely, we have no contingency, that is, possible non-necessary);
- *in the reality of non-cultural living objectuality* (without human beings) ($R1$): emergence is 'maximum' possible (at least at the current level of knowledge)—here we can have contingency (possible non-necessary) and we have non-deliberativeness (i.e., there is no free will);
- *in the reality of living cultural objectuality* ($R2$): emergence is possible, but to a very small extent—social deliberation dominates, which greatly reduces the emergent space. *Nota bene*: however, structuralism poses some problems here (see below);
- *in the reality of subjectuality* ($R3$): emergence is not possible—everything is deliberate. *Nota bene*: however, psychoanalysis poses some problems here (see below).

Short Discussion

(i) structuralism
- framework: (1) structuralism eliminates deliberative decision from social action; (2) structuralism states the existence of certain structural patterns of society that allow the filtering of social action, which thus becomes non-deliberative; (3) the problem is that, in this way, social action also becomes necessary (see, here,

Marx—the historical laws, *Althusser*—the structural Marxism, *Xenopol*—the historical series);
- conclusion: structuralism blocks, in principle, the emergence, from the perspective of infringing of the condition of non-necessity (contingency);

(ii) psychoanalysis
- framework: subconscious causes individual action, but the causation is 'masked' by the justification provided by consciousness, which elaborates a justifying story (see, here, *Kahneman*—the two decision-making systems—fast thinking and slow thinking, respectively);
- conclusion: psychoanalysis blocks, in principle, the emergence, also from the perspective of infringing of the condition of non-necessity (contingency);[25]

Figure 6.5 shows the variation of the sphere of emergence, 'expressed' as a share in the real range [0,1], in the four possible realities (worlds) above mentioned, and Fig. 6.6 shows a Karnaugh type diagram showing the places of the two phenomena (synergy and emergence, respectively) in a logical perspective.

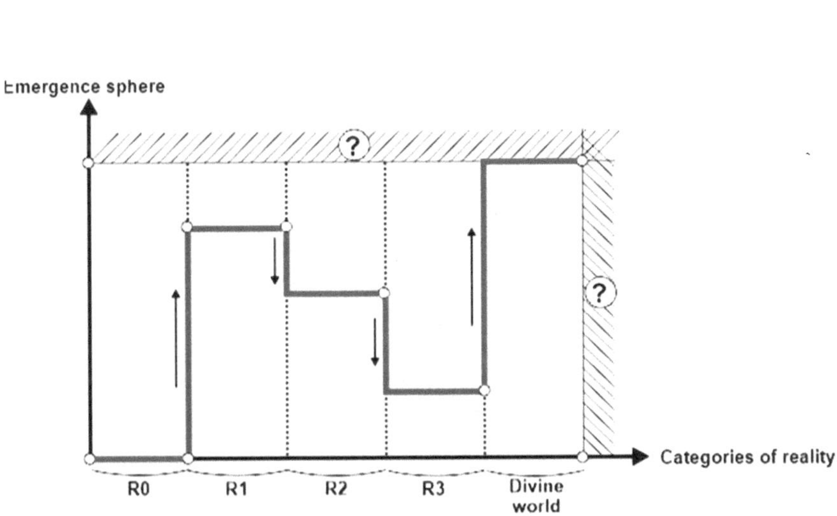

Fig. 6.5 Emergence sphere. *Source*: Authors

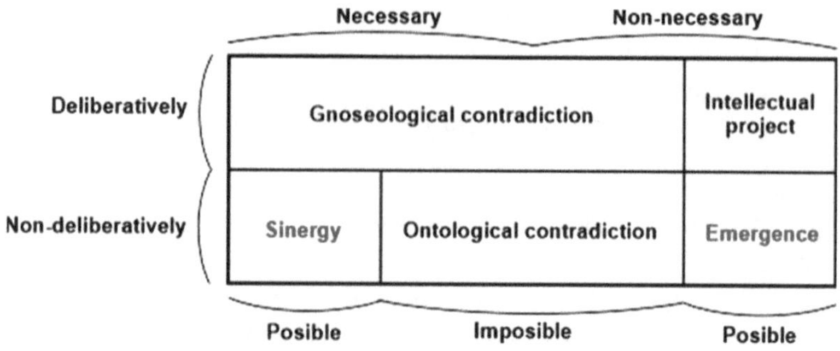

Fig. 6.6 Modal logical positioning of synergy and emergence. *Source*: Authors

(b) Stigmergy and emergence

The etymology of the concept of stigmergy[26] is as follows: (gr.) Στιγμα (stigma)—*sign*, mark and (gr.) Εργον (ergon)—*action*, work

- the <u>function</u> of stigmergy: it denotes a collective action, coordinated by signs (marks) left by other individuals (contemporary or not)—see, here, the concept of memetic behaviour, respectively the process of generating implicit information,[27] widely used in this research;[28]
- the relationships between stigmergy and synergy:
  - while synergy generates properties through relationships, stigmergy generates relationships (e.g., cooperative relationships—contemporary or not) through properties, so we have, this turn, a reversal of the 'arrow' of causality;
  - the 'standard' emblem of synergy is the transgression of the system, while the 'standard' emblem of stigmergy is the non-transgression of the system;
  - given the reversal of the 'arrow' of causality in stigmergy compared to synergy, it can be assumed that there is a circular (or reciprocal, spiral) causality between the two: stigmergy generates synergy (through properties) which, in turn, generates stigmergy (through relationships).

Based on the above, we propose that, from a terminological point of view, for the financial market case,[29] the term (and, obviously, the related concept) of *semergy* be used. From the etymological point of view, semergy comes from (gr.) Σᾶμᾰ (sáma, sema)—sign—and εργον (ergon)—action, work. The rationale for our proposal is as follows: the concept of stigma is restricted to natural signs only but, in the case of the financial market, the cultural sign must be included (seme includes both stigma and cultural institutions as macro-signs, called semes. *Nota bene*: the semes are complementary, on the one hand, to the genes and, on the other hand, to the memes):

- *gene*: the natural (non-cultural) vehicle of biological replication of the individual
- *meme*: non-formal (cultural) social vehicle for behavioural replication
- *seme*: the formal (cultural) social vehicle of behavioural replication

Figure 6.7 shows a three-dimensional picture of the relationship between synergy and stigmergy (if a four-dimensional representation was possible, our concept of semergy could also have been represented).

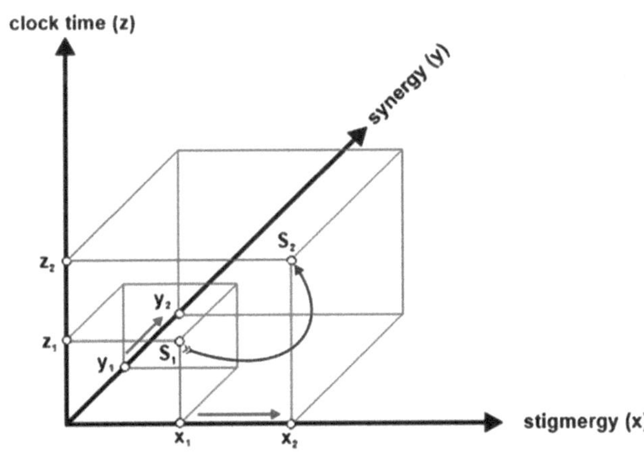

Fig. 6.7 Synergy and stigmergy. *Source*: Authors

A General Evolutionist Picture of the (Co-) Species Preference-Information-Price

The trinomial co-evolution of the financial market aggregates, in a unique model, the evolutionary characteristics of preference, information and price, as they were previously developed. As suggested above, this aggregation is accompanied by 'novelties' (more precisely, it generates these 'novelties') regarding the reaction norms, respectively of synergy/stigmergy/semergy, so that the trinomial model of the (financial) market is summarized.[30]

In this paragraph, it is useful to resume/systematize, in a common picture, the results obtained regarding the three symbolic co-species that form the trinomial model of the financial market.[31] To this end, we construct Table 6.1.

The Logical Model of the Trinomial Preference-Information-Price

In our opinion, the adaptive nature of the preference in the financial market can be logically inferred from the common 'game' of the reaction norms and synergy (including in its variants of stigmergy, respectively, semergy). In this context, we will develop some considerations regarding the impact of the two factors on the configuration of adaptive preference, which will allow us to develop further the evolutionary logical model of the trinomial preference-information-price.

Table 6.1 Overview of the evolutionary characteristics of financial market symbolic co-species

	Information		*Price*		*Preference*	
	Name	*Symbol*	*Name*	*Symbol*	*Name*	*Symbol*
Phenotype	Accessed informational mix	p_i	Expected price (value)	p_p	Trading strategy	p_c
Genotype	Implicit information	g_i	Expected-actual price gap	g_p	Propensity	g_c
Mutation	–	m_i	–	m_p	–	m_c

Source: Authors

Elements of Modelling

(a) preamble
- there does not appear to be a logical and/or chronological order of impulse initiation (i.e., action, in the terminology used here), between the three components of the trinomial model (*Nota bene*: we will note this model from now on with CIP—preference (C), information (I), price (P));[32]
- we therefore assume an indifference between the three components of the trinomial regarding the initiation of the impact. However, precisely from the perspective of this indifference, there can be, from a theoretical point of view, three types of triggering of the process of functioning of the model:
  i. *functional* initiation: if the action starts from the information, that is, from the mutation produced in the implicit information: Δm_i;
  ii. *decisional* initiation: if the action starts from the price, that is, from the mutation produced in the gap between the value[33] (expected price) and the actual price: Δm_p;
  iii. *credential* initiation: if the action starts from preference (belief, credential), that is, from the mutation produced in propensity: Δm_c;
- remember that two classes of reaction norms (respectively of action norms, as the case may be) are forbidden: (a) for the case of functional initiation—action/reaction from information (i.e., from Δm_i) to preference (i.e., to Δm_c); (b) for the case of credential initiation—action/reaction from preference (i.e., from Δm_c) to price (i.e., to Δm_p);
- there are, therefore, middle[34] terms[35] in the logical mechanism of the CIP trinomial, namely:
  i. in the circuit I - C: the middle term is P;
  ii. in the circuit P - I: the middle term is C;
  iii. in the C - P circuit: the middle term is I;

(b) short helpful discussion
- we have assumed that any of the nodes (C, I, P) of the CIP model can be the initiator of some impulses in the trinomial mechanism. Obviously, the initiation of an impulse refers only to action, not to reaction. However, the CIP trinomial, at any time of its observation, is already in a process of transmitting (accord-

ing to the 'rules' stipulated in Fig. 6.1) the reactions (configured according to the reaction norms) between these nodes. The vast majority of cases of observation of the CIP trinomial will only highlight the reactions and only by chance will an action be observed. So, the question is: how can an action be triggered by the CIP mechanism? In this regard, we make the following considerations:

- the first action—more precisely, the primordial action—(regardless of the three types of initiation of the CIP mechanism) is, in principle, unobservable—it could be (if the interests of research or action so require) inferred by deduction but this is extremely difficult, if not impossible, because in the economic field we do not have trajectories, but processes;[36]
- we can, therefore, hope at most to identify/observe an action that is by no means the first trigger (the first 'flick') of the trinomial process, but represents the initiation of a new circuit of reactions between nodes. This action is not a primordial action, but an ordinary one. An ordinary action occurs under the following logical conditions:

  the impulse received by a node through the last received reaction is extinguished, so it can no longer react;[37] such depletion of reaction capacity can be caused by three distinct situations: either by synergistic neutralization (see below), by reaching rigidity thresholds for the affected node,[38] or by the non-fetality of the reaction norm in question;

  synergistic neutralization occurs when receiving a new reaction is the opposite of the immediately preceding reaction (e.g., if implicit information—that is, inferred from observing the behaviour of other financial market players—indicates a current upward price trend, then the following implicit information indicates a downward trend in the current price,[39] the expected node *P* will not send any reaction to node *C*; the same effect occurs if information on the current upward price trend is followed (or accompanied) by information on the (stronger) upward trend relative to risk rather than the price upward trend);

with regard to the threshold below which a reaction received by a node no longer generates a subsequent reaction of that node, the reason is similar to that regarding any significance threshold (aspect discussed at length, previously, regarding other phenomena in the financial market);

the non-fetality of the reaction norm has the same effect as the non-existence (non-production) of that reaction norm. As shown above, here we are dealing with a bright cone—the node involved does not 'see' the reaction norm if it is not in its own bright cone, that is, in its fetality sphere;

- the visibility (and, therefore, the reactivity) of a node in the CIP trinomial to a received reaction is filtered by three eligibility instances. In our opinion, the order of strength of the three filters is the following: (a) *fetality* (F_f)—which is a filter of selective type (acceptance vs rejection); (b) ***neutralization*** (F_n)—which is a filter of qualitative type (successive reaction norms have different 'signs'[40]) (*Nota bene*: the result of mutual neutralization must, however, be below the significance threshold); (c) *reaching the significance threshold* (F_p)—which is a filter of *quantitative* type (quantity that becomes equal to the significance threshold[41]). Figure 6.8 provides a synoptic picture of the functioning of the three filters.

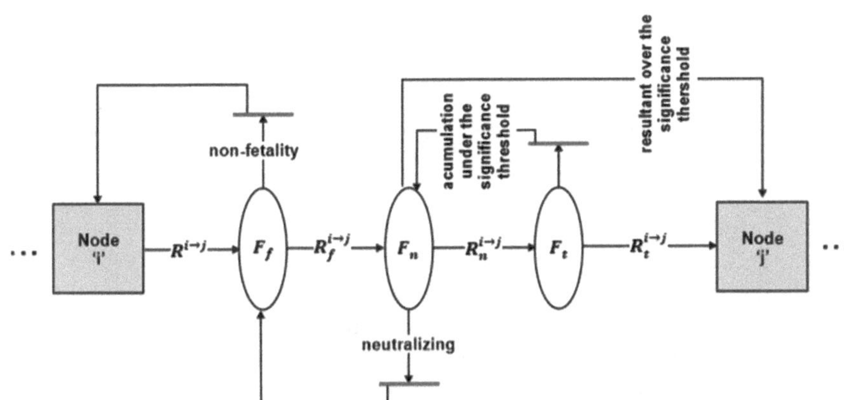

Fig. 6.8 Functioning of the three filters in the generation of the reaction norm in the CIP model. *Source*: Authors

A Sketch of the Model

An evolutionary trinomial logical model of the financial market must be able to answer at least the following basic questions:

a. how mutations occur in co-species involved in the CIP model?
b. how intra-(co-) species mutations are transmitted?[42]
c. how inter-(co-) species mutations are transmitted?[43]
d. how fitness should be defined at the level of the (co-) symbolic species C, I and P, and how it is validated, both by the proximate environment of the (co-) species in question and by the extended environment (cultural geodesic) of the trinomial?[44]

We offer our opinion on the answer to these questions.

(a) the occurring of mutations

The mutation in the genotype of the information occurs, therefore (see Table 4.1) at the level of the implicit information deduced/inferred by the economic agent from the observation of the behaviours exhibited by the other agents in the financial market. The idea that the information mutation appears only at the level of implicit information requires an additional argument: in fact, the implicit information, once modified by the 'financial scene' observed by the economic agent, generates a specific halo, also modified, regarding both formal and bound information, so that, in fact, the mutation in the implicit information (i.e., in the genotype of the (co-) species called information) generates the phenotype of this (co-) species (i.e., the accessed informational mix) through this process of haloing[45]—in fact, this process is responsible for updating the informational phenotype.

(b) intra-(co-) species transmission of mutations

The process of haloing of the accessed informational mix consists of two phenomena that occur under the impulse/impact of the genetic mutation of the (co-) species in question: (1) modification of the content of formal information (usually legal, imperative information) related to the action which is possible, specific to the economic operator concerned; (2) the modification of the content of the bound information which is compatible, necessary, useful in the new configuration of the content of the implicit information just acquired (i.e., as a result of the genetic mutation produced). In short, the intra (co-) species transmission of the genetic mutation accurately describes the actualization of the phenotype (co-) species in question. Updating the phenotype should not be understood as a completely rational/rationalized process—it is, in fact, a mixture of rationality (understood as a logical necessity, in inferential form) and contingency (the latter component includes both elements of i-rationality, as well as elements of a-rationality, such as the change of intentionality simply under the action of free will).

(c) inter-(co-) species transmission of mutations

Strictly speaking, a transmission of the inter-(co-) species genetic mutation is not possible as such. At the biological level, a scheme of such transmission could be constructed through phenotype-level interaction (hence, an indirect transmission). However, we believe that, as far as symbolic (co-) species are concerned, such a 'lateral' transmission of genetic mutations can occur directly. We provide the following arguments:

- in the case of symbolic (co-) species (i.e., in the case of the logically living entities), there are no differences in nature between their genes, as is the case in the field of biological living entities. Ultimately, all three genotypes (implicit information, price gap, propensity) can be reduced to explicit information,[46] which allows, in principle, the inter-(co-) species transmission of the mutation;
- before analysing the case of each (co-) symbolic species in terms of inter-(co-) species transmission of mutations, it should be remembered that, unlike the biological living case, this transmission uses the reaction norm vehicle, and not phenotype (physical) reproduction vehicle. Unlike the biological living case, the symbolic genome is not a 'program'[47] for configuring the phenotype (including as a result of the mutation suffered by that genome)—so, the phenotype is updated directly, usually at a 1:1 scale, by the genetic mutation, it incorporates 'on the go'.;
- a particularly important issue that needs to be clarified at this point is this: is the genetic mutation in one (co-) species transmitted 'laterally' (to another (co-) species) at the genotype or at the phenotype level? The issue is relevant both from a theoretical[48] and a pragmatic perspective (of the actual behaviour of the economic agent in the financial market). We make the following considerations in this matter:

- the inter-(co-) species genetic mutation is transmitted laterally to the genotype level. The explanation for this positioning lies in the fact that mutational transmission must respect a principle that we could call *the principle of interaction at the level of the minimum entropic gradient* or, in short, the principle of the minimum entropical. Such a principle (even if the literature has not yet given it a name) works in any known interaction;[49]
- the inter-(co-) species epigenetic mutation is transmitted laterally, also at the level of the genotype.[50] Lateral transmission at the genotype level of the inter-(co-) species epigenetic mutation has no alternative—it could not be transmitted directly at the phenotype level, because the latter only 'recognizes' its own epigenetic mutation. The idea of an *identity mark of the epigenetic mutation*—which results from the last assertion—presents some difficulties of acceptance, so we will present two additional considerations in support of the idea in question:

  although epigenetic, an 'internal' mutation (i.e., occurring within a given (co-) species) is compatible with the phenotype of that (co-) species. We can speak, in this case, of a self-induced internal fetality or of a *necessary* internal fetality, which is not true with the reaction norms, which have (or do not have, as the case may be) a *contingent* fetality; the necessary internal fetality of the epigenetic mutation is of the same nature as the necessary internal fetality of the genetic mutation.[51] As a result, the internal epigenetic mutation is transmitted vertically directly to the phenotype, as is the internal genetic mutation;[52]

  as an effect of the action of the identity mark of the epigenetic mutation, we cannot accept an epigenetic mutation transmitted laterally (i.e., inter-(co-) species) directly to the external phenotype (i.e., of the other (co-) species) even if the mutation in question verifies the criterion of fetality of the reaction norm, that is, verifies a contingent external fetality, as in the case of lateral transmission of the genetic mutation.

A graphical picture of these considerations is given in Fig. 6.9.

- regarding the symbolic (co-) species *information*: as suggested in Fig. 6.1 and shown in Fig. 6.9, the variation of the implicit information (Δm_i) is transmitted, by the reaction norm $R_g^{I \to P}$, to the price

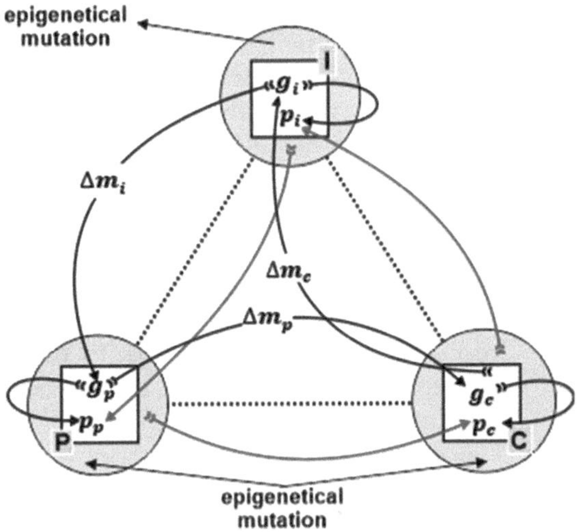

Fig. 6.9 Genetic and epigenetic mutation in CIP model.
Source: Authors

genotype, which is the medium term to preference. Instead, the epigenetic mutation is transmitted, through the reaction norm $R_e^{I \to P}$, directly to the price phenotype (*Nota bene*: the lower indexes ' g ', respectively ' e ' mean the genetic mutation, respectively the epigenetic mutation). The epigenetic mutation in the information can be located as follows:

- changes in the normative framework governing the organization and functioning of the financial market,[53] that is, the change in the current stock of legal information in force;
- changes in the stock of bound information (which verifies the accessibility criteria from the perspective of the economic operator concerned);
- financial or economic crises, as well as other economic or non-economic[54] shocks, internal or external, which affect, in one way or another, the dimensional, structural or kinematic functioning of the financial market;

- regarding the symbolic (co-) species *price*: the variation of the price gap (Δm_p) is transmitted, by the reaction norm $R_g^{P \to C}$, to the genotype of preference, that is, to propensity, which is the medium term to information. Instead, the epigenetic mutation is transmitted, through the reaction norm $R_e^{P \to C}$, directly to the preference phenotype, that is, to the trading strategy. The epigenetic mutation in the case of price can be located as follows:

  - the intervention of administrative prices, therefore linked to the normative functioning of the 'sector' prices in the financial market, which modifies (in this case, by stiffening) the actual price;[55]
  - the imposition of the actual price by a very strong player in the financial market (e.g., a monopoly—either natural or institutional);
- regarding the symbolic (co-) species *preference*: the variation of the propensity (Δm_c) is transmitted, by the reaction norm $R_g^{C \to I}$, to the genotype of the information, that is, the implicit information,[56] which is the medium term to the price. Instead, the epigenetic mutation is transmitted, through the reaction norm $R_e^{C \to I}$, directly to the information phenotype, that is, to the accessed informational mix. The epigenetic mutation in the case of preference can be located as follows:
  - a relevant share of the imitation[57] of the behaviours observed in the financial market (*Nota bene*: note that this is not about extracting implicit information from the observation and interpretation of financial market behaviours, as is the case with the genetic mutation of the (co-) species information—this time there is no interpretation of those behaviours, so no implicit production of information, but only an external imitation, so to speak, that is, without the involvement of the change in propensity);
  - integration of the economic agent in a supra-system, which means a behaviour convergent and consistent with the behaviour of the supra-system—again, we do not have a variation of the propensity, since the change of preference, as a result of the impact of integration in the supra-system, is of epigenetic nature;[58]

(d) (co-) species fitness and its validation

Regarding the fitness and its validation, we will have to discuss, separately, two aspects: (d1) fitness and validation at the level of each (co-) symbolic species; (d2) fitness and its validation at the level of the CIP trinomial. (*Nota bene*: can we talk about a fitness—of course, also of a symbolic nature—at the level of the CIP trinomial? Can we talk, so to speak, about a CIP phenotype, or rather, about CIP a macro-phenotype?)

(d1) fitness (co-) of symbolic species

Fitness, that is, the degree of adequacy of an individual (or species, as the case may be) to its environment inside which that individual is functioning,[59] exactly implies to define this environment. As assumed in this study, the environment of the CIP trinomial (more precisely, of the financial species called financial transaction) is the cultural geodesic, that is, the set of norms (formal or informal), along with habits, traditions, memetizations (so to speak) and others like them, as well as all the other contemporary trading strategies that operate in the financial market. By abuse of language (as we have warned several times before), we will consider the trinomial CIP as a species, although, in reality, the 'true' species of the financial market is, as we just (re-)mentioned, the financial transaction.[60] In this conceptual context, each of the components of the CIP trinomial has its own environment, which will be examined and defined in the following.

- regarding the symbolic (co-) species *information*: the environment (which is also the selector of individuals of this (co-) species) consists of three components that are inter-conditioned both structurally and causally: (i) the other two (co-) species of the CIP trinomial—see Fig. 6.9—that is, of the binomial preference—price; (ii) the financial market—which validates, in the first instance, the information as a component of the trinomial; and (iii) cultural geodesic—which ultimately validates information as a component of the financial transaction;
- regarding the symbolic (co-) species *price*: the environment (which is also the selector of the individuals of these (co-) species) consists of three components that are inter-conditioned both structurally and causally: (i) the other two (co-) species of the CIP trinomial—see Fig. 6.9—that is, the binomial preference-information; (ii) the financial market—which validates, in the first instance, the price as a component of the trinomial; (iii) cultural geodesic—which ultimately validates the price as a component of the financial transaction;
- regarding the symbolic (co-) species *preference*: the environment (which is also the selector of individuals this (co-) species) consists of three components that are inter-conditioned both structurally and causally: (i) the other two (co-) species of the trinomial CIP—see Fig. 6.9—that is, the binomial information—price; (ii) the financial market—which validates, in the first instance, the preference/propensity as a component of the trinomial; (iii) cultural geodesic—which ultimately validates the preference/propensity as a component of the financial transaction.

We are of the opinion that an order of 'priority' should be given in the selection of fitness acquired by a certain component of the CIP trinomial as follows:[61] (1) the first selection is made by the first circle of the selector environment (described as point (i)) if the previous result is positive (i.e., the examined fitness has been accepted/validated), then the second circle of the selector environment is applied (the one described in point (ii)); (3) if this last result is also positive, then the third circle of the selector environment (the one described in point (iii)) applies.

Figure 6.10 provides a synoptic picture of the fitness mechanism (or rather, of the selection—positive/affirmative, respectively negative/

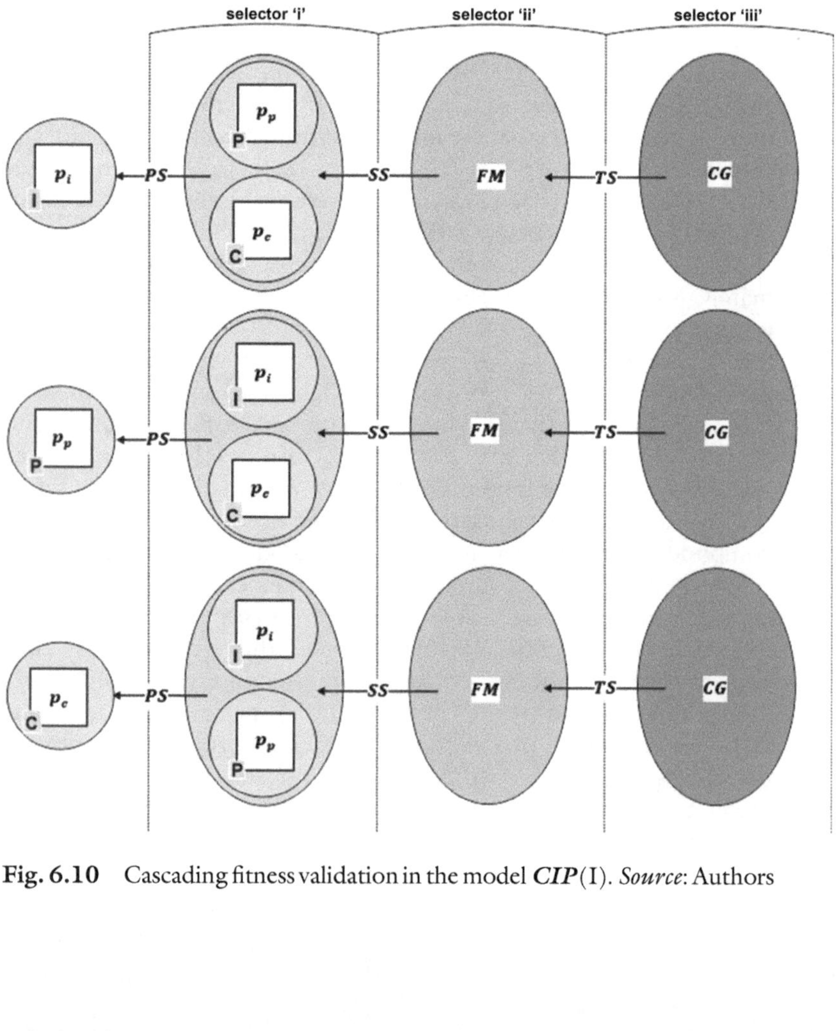

Fig. 6.10 Cascading fitness validation in the model *CIP*(I). *Source*: Authors

refutative it operates). The new notations are as follows: *FM*: financial market; *CG*: cultural geodesic; *PS*: primary selection; *SS*: secondary selection; *TS*: tertiary/definitive selection.

(d2) *CIP* fitness

Regardless of the answer we reach in our research on this topic, the question is justified and even, in our opinion, mandatory. We develop, in this matter, the following considerations:

- ultimately, the CIP configuration will give the financial individual—that is, in the terminology of this study, the trading strategy,[62] which justifies the need to examine the issue of CIP fitness;
- according to Fig. 6.10, the third selector (called cultural geodesic), which is the very environment in which the species called financial market evolves, gives the final verdict on CIP fitness; this means that, in fact, CIP fitness is the result of selecting (in cascading way[63]) each of the phenotypes of CIP model components;
- in this context, in fact, the mechanism shown in Fig. 6.10 should be adjusted in such a way that the second and third selectors, respectively, do not target each of the three components of the CIP model separately, but their synergistic combination. In this sense, the validation of fitness at CIP level will be done according to the suggestion provided by Fig. 6.11.

Some Polemical Issues in the Trinomial Preference-Information-Price

In the above, several conjectures/assumptions have been made regarding the different behaviours of the generic economic agent in the financial market. Also, some 'adjudications' of positions were made purely declaratory, by 'decree', so as not to complicate the reasoning required at that time and place. In this paragraph, we will present some arguments in defence of those positions or, as the case may be, we will highlight some vulnerabilities, weaknesses or contradictions (if any) associated with those positions. Specifically, we will examine the following four issues that seem controversial in the CIP trinomial model: (a) the issue of the identity mark of the epigenetic mutation; (b) the problem of orders and composition of synergies/stigmergies/semergies; (c) the issue of (co-) species, financial individuals, financial species and the selector environment; and (d) the problem of entropy.

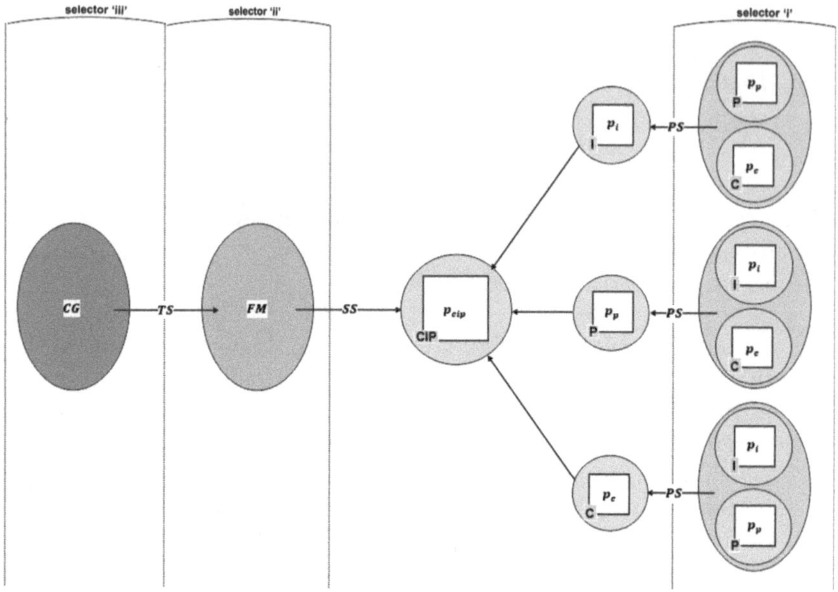

Fig. 6.11 Cascading fitness validation in the model ***CIP*** (II). *Source*: Authors

(a) the identity mark of the epigenetic mutation

The ('decreed') impossibility of the lateral transmission (to another (co-) species) of the epigenetic mutation directly to the external phenotype has been conjectured as anchored by the concept of the identity mark of this type of mutation—that is, by the existence of an exclusive compatibility with the internal phenotype, which is the phenotype in which it was 'born'. This conceptual prohibition has, on the one hand, an obvious vulnerability and, on the other hand, an equally obvious advantage:

- *the vulnerability*: The symbolic (co-) species considered—preference, information, price—have a relatively high degree of functional and behavioural compatibility,[64] sufficient for those (co-) species to be part of the CIP model. This compatibility obviously applies to both the genotypes and the phenotypes involved—which means that, in general, the target genotype of the epigenetic mutation cannot differ radically (beyond the convergence, consistency or coherence threshold) from the phenotype in which that epigenetic mutation was occurred;

- *the advantage*: The prohibition of the lateral transmission of the epigenetic mutation directly to the genotype of the external/foreign phenotype allows the distinction made in FMAB-APH (Dinga et al., 2022) to be maintained—namely, the distinction between adaptation and evolution: in this sense, we will note, from the evolutionist perspective, the transmission (either vertical or lateral) of the genetic mutation, and from the perspective of adaptation, we will retain the lateral transmission of the epigenetic mutation.[65]

(b) synergies of different orders and their composition

We have seen before that there can be positive synergies (generating new properties) as well as negative synergies (removing some properties).[66] Of course, the result of the simultaneous action of the two categories of synergies will be either a net positive or a net negative synergy. In this regard, we can note the following:

- the composition of synergies of the same order[67] within the CIP implies a typology of synergy according to its order; in this matter we make the following proposal:
  - *first-order synergy*: synergy that generates new properties (including, of course, in the negative sense discussed above);[68]
  - *second-order synergy*: synergy that generates new relationships between properties (also in an ambivalent sense—either positive or negative) or new properties of relationships;[69]
- based on the above typology, together with the previous typology (positive synergy vs negative synergy) and with the distinction between proper synergy (predictable synergy) and improper synergy, which is also called emergence (unpredictable synergy), we can formulate an 'algorithm' of composing synergies in a supra-system such as that of CIP (Fig. 6.12 puts in a conceptual logic diagram—Karnaugh diagram—the three dichotomies of synergy, and Fig. 6.13 suggests a way of composing synergies according to their orders).

(c) individual, (co-) species, species, selector environment

This is, perhaps, the most delicate issue of our proposal, so we will develop more extensive considerations in this area.

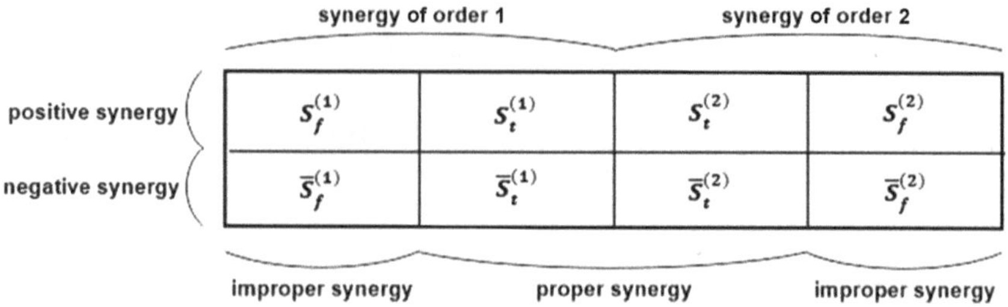

Fig. 6.12 Significant conceptual distinctions of synergy in the model ***CIP***. *Source*: Authors

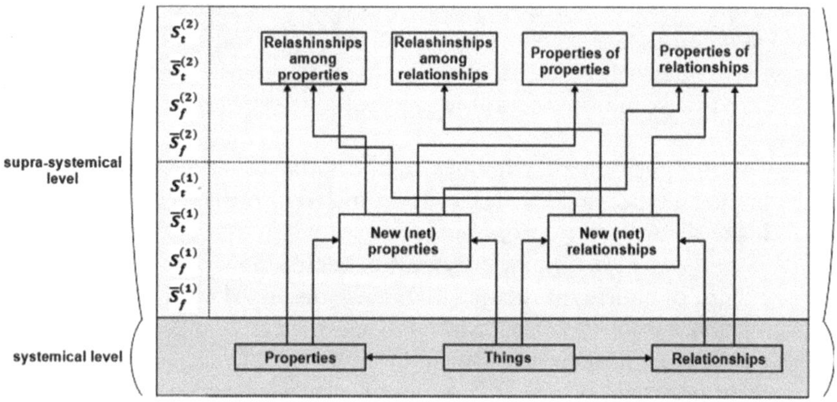

Fig. 6.13 General operating of synergy orders in the model ***CIP***. *Source*: Authors

(c1) setting the issue

- according to the evolutionary-master model (the one in biology, i.e., referring to living physical and natural species), there must be: individual, species, selector environment;
- according also to the model mentioned above, the individual is 'endowed' with a *necessary* device called genotype (the initiator,[70] usually contingent,[71] of evolution) and with a *contingent* device called epigenotype (which generates evolutionary initiations also of contingent type);

- at the level of the individual (which represents the phenotype), developments take place, while the evolution process is 'reserved' for the species;
- both development and evolution take place through the selector filter of the environment;[72] the environment performs the selection process, which, unlike the case of mutation (either genotypic or epigenotypic) which is random, has a directional but, of course, non-deliberative character—the direction or finality is conferred by the fitness criterion (more specifically, the possibility of intergenerational reproduction facilitated by a certain degree of fitness adaptation to the involved environment);

(c2) our proposal

- in the present study, the evolutionary-master model in biology is only a benchmark, it is not taken over *tale quale*; we briefly mention its main coordinates:
  - it is about symbolic species or (co-) species (as in the case of the information-price binomial, respectively of the preference-information-price trinomial), not physical ones; in other words, we are talking about living species in a logical sense; of course, the individual of the species is also defined in this sense of logically living;
  - the financial individual (financial phenotype) is represented by the trading strategy; the financial individual is 'born' directly as an adult, so, in the matter of symbolic species, the development of the individual disappears;
  - the hypostatization of the individual, in order to expose himself to the selector environment, is done through the individual transaction, inferred (either intuitively, or rationally, or, most often, through an intuition-rationality mix) from the trading strategy;
  - the financial individual is the result of the interaction between three symbolic (co-) species: preference, information, price; metaphorically, it can be said that the pro-creation (reproduction) of the financial individual needs three parents—preference, information, price. Here we need to introduce a more detailed 'defence': it is obvious that a curious idea appears here, namely that the individual is generated by species (even if it is conceptually wrapped in the trinomial preference-information-price), instead of the

causal/conditional relation having the directional arrow inversely positioned—from the individual to the species (as the biological case);

this doubling of the generative process of the individual, respectively of the species, is an effect (relatively necessary) of the hypothesis of the symbolic species, on the basis of which our whole model of the trinomial CIP is built; the dilemma will be resolved, that is, a solution/interpretation will be proposed at point (c3);

- the financial species is exactly the financial market.[73] Questions may also arise here:

first of all, such an assertion implies a very important consequence: in the financial field there is only one species, namely the financial market. As a result, the evolutionary aspect in the financial field will refer to the financial market only;

secondly, the selector environment is 'taken out' of the financial framework of society—this selector environment (cultural geodesic, respectively the situational context, in the terminology we prefer)—but this is exactly what we want to do: if we had adopted the suggestion (Lo, 2019) according to which the selector environment is the financial market itself, that drives to the disappearing, as we have already shown, of the financial species itself in the model in question, it would have meant that a financial phenomenon, for example, the trading strategy, to be validated (from the perspective of fitness) also by a financial phenomenon, namely the financial market. However, the fitness of the financial individual (i.e., of the trading strategy) refers not only to the optimization (maximization or minimization) of some financial criteria but also to (and perhaps especially to) the adequacy of that individual to the normative structure of the society, to the (formal or informal) rules that must be respected, including those concerning ethics, deontology and morals.[74] This broad, multidimensional fitness can only be examined and validated (or invalidated, as appropriate) by an environment that exceeds the financial process itself[75]—in our opinion, cultural geodesic and the situational context of society are much more appropriate and productive in this purpose;

- the selector environment is the cultural geodesic (generated by the situational context of the society in question). We have presented above some arguments in favour of considering the cultural geodesic (respectively the situational context) as the environment in which financial individuals (trading strategies) operate in their particular situations (individual transactions), and by rejecting the proposal that the financial market itself constitutes the selector environment of the financial individual. Here we bring one more argument in favour of this choice: it is a commonplace that any economic event is the effect of an economic action, that is, it is an artefact. But an artefact is designed and made by human individuals, in a given axiological and normative framework (namely, cultural geodesic)—it is obvious that the fitness of the trading strategy must be compatible or highly compatible (depending on the desired degree of financial performance) with this cultural geodesic, therefore, the selector environment cannot be the financial market itself.

Nota bene: The artefact quality of any economic event, including any financial event, brings into question the fact that, in the social field, evolutionism is strictly related to institutionalism. In fact, in the opinion of one of the authors of the present study (Dinga, 2021), institutionalism is a species of evolutionism, so, theoretically, it should be included in evolutionism—there are, however, authors who deal with institutionalism itself, but from an evolutionary perspective (Fürstenberg, 2016). However, the weight of institutionalism—as a general framework of human action—in substantiating the decision and in executing the action in the financial field is so important and significant so that the selector environment of the financial species (financial market) can only be the cultural geodesic.

(c3) our positioning

- we propose that this relationship from the (co-) species as aggregated in the CIP model to the financial individual be considered, by analogy with the biological evolutionary model, as representing the stage of 'development' of the financial individual; in this new context, the parallelism between the generative process (co-) species—individual and that of the individual—species becomes intelligible and theoretically acceptable;

- the development of the financial individual (of the trading strategy) also requires a duration, as in the biological case, but a much shorter one. As we mentioned, naming the stage of choosing the trading strategy through the CIP model, as being the stage of development of the financial individual, is metaphorical in nature, because once the CIP model decided on the profile (structure, configuration, etc.) of the trading strategy, it is 'born' directly into adulthood;
- it follows that the name of the (co-) species assigned to the three components of the CIP model (preference, information, price,) is somehow forced. It serves mainly to keep the reader's attention to the idea that the mechanism of (co-) species is, in fact, applied;[76]

(d) financial market entropy and entropy gradient

The problem of entropy in relation to the financial market (considered to be the species of the financial world) seems to offer some interesting suggestions for logical and, at the limit, quantitative modelling, including in terms of factual predictions, so in terms of falsificationist testing. Whereas the issue of entropy in relation to the financial market will be taken up extensively (and in depth) when we examine the autopoietic model of the financial market (which, in addition to entropy, will also include anti-fragility, all, of course, from an evolutionary perspective), namely in our book *Economic and Financial Behaviour: The Autopoietic Market Hypothesis* (Palgrave Macmillan, 2023), here are just a few general considerations:

- financial market entropy must refer to the presence and accessibility of the behaviours that operate the trading strategies (in this case the individual transactions inferred from those trading strategies)—the higher this presence and accessibility, the lower the financial market entropy and vice versa;[77] more elaborate suggestions in this regard are provided in scientific articles published by the authors (Dinga et al., 2021);
- it is, perhaps, possible to introduce here the idea of a sensitivity of the economic agent in his/her action (either passive or active) to observe other behaviours in the financial market (more precisely, the operation of other trading strategies) from which to obtain the implicit information useful for designing or adjusting one's own trading strategy or only individual transactions within the sphere of the held/preferred trading strategy. So, this sensitivity could be

called the *entropic gradient*—the functioning of the entropic gradient will be examined later (both relative to the autopoietic functioning of the financial market and to its functioning generated by the attraction of natural values). In any case, we can already say that the potential success of the economic agent (more precisely, of the trading strategy operated by him/her) is directly proportional to the entropic gradient. The latter, in turn, is directly proportional to the 'reserve' of different trading strategies that are functional in the financial market and liable to be 'copied' by the economic operator concerned in order to increase the own financial gain. It is obviously to be expected that, as economic agents homogenize, according to the rule of the invisible hand, the trading strategies used, the entropic gradient will decrease and, consequently, the entropy of the financial market will increase. A graphical picture of this financial market entropy phenomenology can be shown in Fig. 6.14.

Quantitative Formalization in the Trinomial Preference-Information-Price

Preamble

The main objective of this section is to identify, based on previous qualitative assessments, the possibilities of quantitative formalization of the trinomial preference-information-price. This approach has, in addition to its

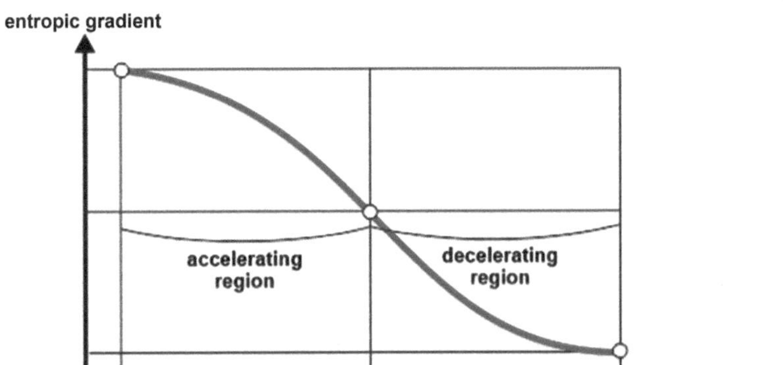

Fig. 6.14 Relationship entropic gradient—entropy in the financial market. *Source*: Authors

intrinsic utility (complementing the previous qualitative and logical analysis) an epistemological utility as well: it provides a basis for formulating predictions and, as direct consequence, for empirical/factual testing of hypotheses/conjectures issued in connection with the trinomially functioning of the financial market.

The approach of the formal-quantitative aspect will be made within the following basic *methodological coordinates*:

- the choice of those variables that are recorded (or, at the limit, recordable) in relation to the functioning of the financial market;
- the use of Bayesian subjective probabilities (a priori and a posteriori, respectively) as the most realistic probabilities usable in the financial market, given that real economic agents are far from the radical axioms of the *homo œconomicus* mathematical model;
- considering of the *implicit information* as the basic information taken into account by the economic agents in the design and implementation of their own trading strategies;
- the use of *thresholds*, both for the co-evolutionary process of the CIP trinomial and for the phenomenological 'switches' in the financial market;[78]
- the acceptance of the *bounded rationality* hypothesis, on the one hand, and of the (a-rational) intuition, on the other hand, as structurally constitutive for the real behaviour of the economic agents in the financial market;
- maintaining *propensity* as the hardcore of preference (as theorized above), including as the primary source of a priori Bayes probability distributions;
- ignoring the decisions regarding the extensive variation of the significance thresholds regarding the preference components[79] (functional, deliberative, hard) and considering only the actual modification of the three components themselves, according to the previously assumed 'priority' order;[80]
- the formalization of the CIP model does not involve time series (i.e., statistical modelling), but follows the strict analytical formalization[81]—therefore, the probabilities used are not the frequential ones,[82] but the subjective Bayesian probabilities.

Two directions of quantitative formalization will be developed: (a) the formation of the trading strategy (i.e., the financial market phenotype); and (b) the synergy-feedback-evolution interaction in the CIP trinomial.

Forming/Choosing/Adjusting of the Trading Strategy
We have seen that the trading strategy (i.e., the financial individual 'born' directly as an adult) is a result of the operation of the CIP trinomial. In this section, we will try to translate this result into a quantitative formalization.

Notations

- ST_0: the initial trading strategy of a given economic operator (*Nota bene*: in general, we will have ST_t as the trading strategy of the given economic agent at time '*t*');
- r_0: the initial return of a given economic operator applying the transaction strategy ST_0 (*Nota bene*: in general, we will have r_t as the return of the given economic agent at time '*t*');
- r_t^e: expected/anticipated return at time '*t*';
- r_t^a: current (effective) return at time '*t*';
- $\tilde{r}_t$: inflection point (of the function *r*) in the kinematics of the financial market return;
- g_t^r: the gap between the expected/anticipated return and the current/actual one, at the moment '*t*';
- $g_t^{r(I)}$: the gap between the expected/anticipated return and the average market return at time '*t*';
- $g_t^{r(II)}$: the gap between the expected/anticipated return and the best return in the market, at time '*t*';
- σ_t^g: the significance threshold of the return gap at time '*t*';
- $\sigma_t^{g(I)}$: the significance threshold of the return gap at time '*t*', for the case of the average return of the financial market;
- $\sigma_t^{g(II)}$: the significance threshold of the return gap at time '*t*', in the case of the return of the most competitive economic operator in the financial market;
- $\left(ST_0, r_0^e, g_0^r\right)$: the vector of the initial state of the given economic agent (*Nota bene*: in general, for the moment '*t*', we have $\left(ST_t, r_t^e, g_t^r\right)$);
- $\overline{r}_t^a$: the average effective return of the financial market;
- $\overline{\overline{r}}_t^a$: the effective return of the most competitive economic operator in the financial market;
- φ_t: the fitness of the economic agent (trading strategy) compared to the fitness 'allowed' by the normative framework (formal and informal) of the society;

- $\overline{\varphi}_t$: the fitness of the economic agent/trading strategy compared to the average return of the financial market;
- $\overline{\overline{\varphi}}_t$: the fitness of the most competitive economic agent (the most competitive trading strategy) in the financial market compared to the economic agent considered (the considered trading strategy);
- $\tilde{\varphi}_t$: the competitive region of the financial market (the fitness of the most competitive economic agent in the financial market compared to the average return of the financial market);[83]
- $\Delta\varphi_t$: the variation of the fitness of the economic agent (trading strategy) compared to one's own existing fitness;
- $\Delta\overline{\varphi}_t$: the variation of the fitness of the economic agent (trading strategy) compared to the fitness that 'delivers' the average return of the financial market;
- $\Delta\overline{\overline{\varphi}}_t$: the variation of the fitness of the most competitive/performing economic agent (trading strategy) compared to the fitness of the economic agent (of the given trading strategy);
- λ_t^s: the rate of selectability/eligibility of the economic agent compared to the average return of the financial market;
- Δg_i^t: variation of the implicit information (of the genotype of the information (co)species), at time 't';
- c_t: the cost required to infer additional implicit information (the cost of observing financial behaviour on the market plus the cost of inferring/interpreting the observed behaviour);[84]
- θ_t^I: the significance threshold of the variation of the informational genotype (g_i: the implicit information) that causes changes in the informational phenotype (p_i: the accessed informational mix);
- θ_t^P: the significance threshold of the price genotype variation ($g_p \equiv g_i^r$: the gap between the expected and the current/actual return) which causes changes in the price phenotype (p_p: the expected price or value);
- θ_t^C: the significance threshold of the variation of the preference genotype (g_c: the propensity of the economic agent) that causes changes in the phenotype of the preference (p_c: trading strategy);
- $\overline{\Delta g_i^t}$: the final variation of the informational genotype as it is affected by the synergy effect of the nominal/initial variation of Δg_i^t;

- $\bar{\Delta} g_p^t$: the final variation of the price genotype as it is affected by the synergy effect of the nominal/initial variation of Δg_p^t;
- $\bar{\Delta} g_c^t$: the final variation of the preference genotype as it is affected by the synergy effect of the nominal/initial variation of Δg_c^t;
- s_i^t: the coefficient of the synergy effect of the nominal/initial variation of the informational genotype (implicit information);
- s_p^t: coefficient of the synergy effect of the nominal/initial variation of the price genotype (return gap);
- s_c^t: coefficient of the synergy effect of the nominal/initial variation of the preference genotype (propensity);
- $\bar{s}_i^t$: the coefficient of the synergy effect of the nominal/initial variation of the informational epigenotype;
- $\bar{s}_p^t$: the coefficient of the synergy effect of the nominal/initial variation of the price epigenotype;
- $\bar{s}_c^t$: the coefficient of the synergy effect of the nominal/initial variation of the epigenotype of preference (propensity);
- ρ_i^t: coefficient (supraunit, subunit or equal to unity) of transcribing the variation of the informational genotype into the informational phenotype;
- ρ_p^t: coefficient (supraunit, subunit or equal to unity) of transcribing the variation of the price genotype into the price phenotype;
- ρ_c^t: coefficient (supraunit, subunit or equal to unity) of transcribing the variation of the preference genotype into the preference phenotype;
- $\rho_{i/p}^t$: coefficient (supraunit, subunit or equal to unity) of transcribing the variation of the informational genotype in the price genotype, provided $\left(\rho_{i/p}^t \geq 1\right) \vee \left(\rho_{i/p}^t < 1\right)$;
- $\rho_{p/c}^t$: coefficient (supraunit, subunit or equal to unity) of transcribing the variation of the price genotype into the genotype of preference (i.e., in the change of propensity), provided $\left(\rho_{p/c}^t \geq 1\right) \vee \left(\rho_{p/c}^t < 1\right)$;
- $\rho_{c/i}^t$: coefficient (supraunit, subunit or equal to unity) of transcribing the variation of the genotype of preference (propensity) into the informational genotype,[85] provided $\left(\rho_{c/i}^t \geq 1\right) \vee \left(\rho_{c/i}^t < 1\right)$.

Relations of Definition, Calculus and Decision

$$\begin{aligned} g_t^r &= r_t^e - r_t^a \\ \overline{\varphi}_t &= r_t^e - \overline{r}_t^a \\ \overline{\overline{\varphi}}_t &= \overline{\overline{r}}_t^a - r_t^e \\ \tilde{\varphi}_t &= \overline{\varphi}_t + \overline{\overline{\varphi}}_t = \overline{\overline{r}}_t^a - \overline{r}_t^a \end{aligned} \tag{6.9}$$

$$\lambda_t^s = \frac{\overline{\varphi}_t}{\overline{r}_t^e} = \frac{r_t^e}{\overline{r}_t^a} - 1 : (\text{a}) \text{ for } \left(\lambda_t^s \geq 0\right) \rightarrow \left(r_t^e \geq \overline{r}_t^a\right)$$

so, the trading strategy[86] is selectable; (b) for $\left(\lambda_t^s < 0\right) \rightarrow \left(r_t^e < \overline{r}_t^a\right)$, so, the trading strategy is non-selectable. *Nota bene*: of course, we will have to accept degrees of selectability/eligibility, depending on the numerical value of λ_t^s (the name of *rate* suggests exactly this), which leads to a hierarchy of trading strategies (again, not of the economic agents involved!) which are operated in the financial market, from the perspective of this selectability/eligibility;

$$\begin{aligned} r_{t+1}^a &= r_t^a - c_t \\ \overline{\Delta}g_i^t &= s_i^t \cdot \Delta g_i^t \\ \overline{\Delta}g_p^t &= s_p^t \cdot \Delta g_p^t \\ \overline{\Delta}g_c^t &= s_c^t \cdot \Delta g_c^t \\ \Delta p_i^t &= \rho_i^t \cdot \overline{\Delta}g_i^t \\ \Delta p_p^t &= \rho_i^t \cdot \overline{\Delta}g_p^t \\ \Delta p_c^t &= \rho_c^t \cdot \overline{\Delta}g_c^t \\ \overline{\Delta}p_i^t &= \overline{s}_i^t \cdot \Delta p_i^t \\ \overline{\Delta}p_p^t &= \overline{s}_p^t \cdot \Delta p_p^t \\ \overline{\Delta}p_c^t &= \overline{s}_c^t \cdot \Delta p_c^t \\ \Delta\varphi_t &= \varphi_{t-1} + \overline{\Delta}p_i^t \\ \Delta\overline{\varphi}_t &= \overline{\varphi}_{t-1} + \overline{\Delta}p_i^t \\ \Delta\overline{\overline{\varphi}}_t &= \overline{\overline{\varphi}}_{t-1} + \overline{\Delta}p_i^t \\ g_t^{r(I)} &= r_t^e - \overline{r}_t^a \\ g_t^{r(II)} &= \overline{\overline{r}}_t^a - r_t^e \end{aligned} \tag{6.10}$$

From a qualitative point of view, the kinematics of the selectability rate is suggested in Fig. 6.15.

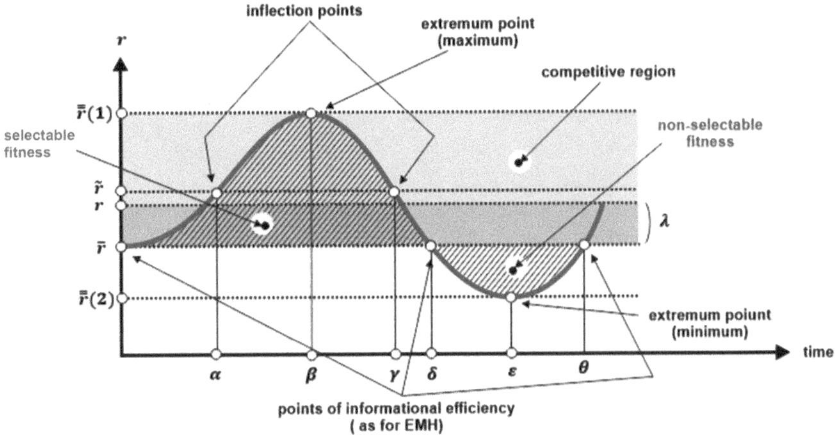

Fig. 6.15 The general (presumptive) form of the selectability rate in the financial market. *Source*: Authors

We suggest that the analytic form of the variable r be a polynomial of order 3 (allowing, proximally,[87] inflection points):

$$r = a + b \cdot x + c \cdot x^2 + d \cdot x^3 \tag{6.11}$$

Short qualitative analysis:

$$\begin{aligned} & x = 0 \rightarrow \bar{r} = a \text{ or } \bar{r} = a + b\delta + c\delta^2 + d\delta^3 \text{ or} \\ & \quad \bar{r} = a + b\theta + c\theta^2 + d\theta^3 \\ & \frac{\partial r}{\partial x} = b + 2cx + 3dx^2, so: \bar{\bar{r}}(1) = b + 2c\beta + 3d\beta^2; \bar{\bar{r}}(2) \\ & \quad = b + 2c\varepsilon + 3d\varepsilon^2 \\ & \frac{\partial^2 r}{\partial x^2} = 2c + 6dx, \text{so}: \tilde{r} = 2c + 6d\alpha \text{ or } \tilde{r} = 2c + 6d\gamma \end{aligned} \tag{6.12}$$

The diagram of the quantitative model of CIP is provided in Fig. 6.16.

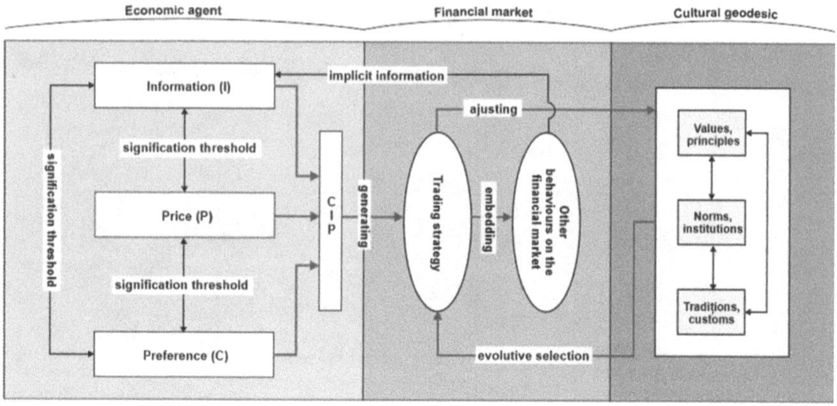

Fig. 6.16 Graphic scheme of the quantitative model of the trinomial ***CIP***. *Source*: Authors

The Quantitative Model

- let us consider an initial trading strategy of a given economic operator (ST_0).[88] The economic operator concerned applies his/her strategy ST_0 and obtains a return from the financial market (e.g., an actual price) r_0;
- obtaining the actual return causes the economic operator to assess the situation: for example, s/he compares the obtained return with the expected return (thus, the actual price obtained—either as a seller or as a buyer—will be compared with the price expected or the anticipated value[89]); the operation performed is of the nature of determining the gap: $g_i^r = r_i^e - r_i^a$;
- if the gap (calculated in this order of terms) is negative, the economic agent will decide to change the trading strategy; if the gap is positive, s/he will maintain the trading strategy;
- however, the difference from zero of the above gap (i.e., considering that difference nominally, regardless of its absolute value) is not sufficient to make a decision, either active or passive, so we need to introduce a significance threshold[90] here: σ_i^g. Moreover, it is important (because it is particularly relevant to the economic operator) to consider the direction in which the gap occurs, so there can be two alternative decisions: (a) $g_i^r \geq \sigma_i^g$ involves maintaining the trading

strategy;[91] (b) $g_i^r < \sigma_i^g$ involves updating (i.e., modifying/adjusting, removing/replacing) the own trading strategy;

- we will not discuss case (a) ($g_i^r \geq \sigma_i^g$) because it involves maintaining of the *statu quo* regarding the trading strategy: the economic agent does not change the winner strategy, based on the rule of thumb that the *better is the good's killer*;
- we will therefore be interested in case (b) ($g_i^r < \sigma_i^g$), in which the actual return is lower than expected/anticipated one ($r_i^e - r_i^a$). The first action taken by the economic operator will be to examine the possible causes of the situation of the return gap below the significance threshold (note that we have agreed, to simplify the reasoning, that all the significance thresholds of the given economic agent remain invariant). The first of these possible causes is, of course, the change in the structure of the behaviour of other economic agents in the financial market—which is (logically) equivalent to the change in the structure of trading strategies operated in the financial market. Therefore, an observation of these changes (we assume, of course, that the economic operator is competent, at least on average, to make such observations) leads to a change in the implicit information (i.e., the genotype of the information (co-) species: g_i—see Table 4.1) inferred from these observations, which in turn leads to a change in the accessed informational mix (i.e., the phenotype of the information (co-) species: p_i—see Table 4.1) of the economic agent concerned. Consequently, there will be pressure to update the trading strategy in question.[92] The following formalities could be retained here:
- at the level of (co-) species *information*:

$$\begin{gathered}
g_t^r < \sigma_t^g \rightarrow \Delta g_i^t \\
\Delta g_i^t \rightarrow \overline{\Delta} g_i^t = s_i^t \cdot \Delta g_i^t,\ \text{where} \left(s_x^t \geq 1\right) \vee \left(s_x^t < 1\right)^{93}, \\
\text{with}\ x \in \{i,p,c\} \\
\overline{\Delta} g_i^t > \theta_t^I \rightarrow \Delta p_i^t = \rho_t^i \cdot \overline{\Delta} g_i^t \\
\overline{\Delta} p_i^t = \overline{s}_i^t \cdot \Delta p_i^t = \overline{s}_i^t \cdot \rho_t^i \cdot \overline{\Delta} g_i^t = \overline{s}_i^t \cdot \rho_i^t \cdot s_i^t \cdot \Delta g_i^t, \\
\text{where} \left(\overline{s}_x^t \geq 1\right) \vee \left(\overline{s}_x^t < 1\right), \\
\text{with}\ x \in \{i,p,c\}
\end{gathered} \tag{6.13}$$

– at the level of (co-) species *price*:

$$
\begin{aligned}
\Delta g_p^t &= \rho_{i/p}^t \cdot \overline{\Delta} g_i^t \\
\overline{\Delta} g_p^t &= s_p^t \cdot \Delta g_p^t = s_p^t \cdot \rho_{i/p}^t \cdot \overline{\Delta} g_i^t = s_p^t \cdot \rho_{i/p}^t \cdot s_i^t \cdot \Delta g_i^t \\
\overline{\Delta} g_p^t > \theta_t^P &\rightarrow \Delta p_p^t = \rho_t^p \cdot \overline{\Delta} g_p^t = \rho_t^p \cdot s_p^t \cdot \rho_{i/p}^t \cdot s_i^t \cdot \Delta g_i^t \\
\overline{\Delta} p_p^t &= \overline{s}_p^t \cdot \Delta p_p^t = \overline{s}_i^t \cdot \rho_t^p \cdot s_p^t \cdot \rho_{i/p}^t \cdot s_i^t \cdot \Delta g_i^t
\end{aligned}
\tag{6.14}
$$

– at the level of (co-) species *preference*:

$$
\begin{aligned}
\Delta g_c^t &= \rho_{p/c}^t \cdot \overline{\Delta} g_p^t \\
\overline{\Delta} g_c^t &= s_c^t \cdot \Delta g_c^t = s_c^t \cdot \rho_{p/c}^t \cdot s_p^t \cdot \rho_{i/p}^t \cdot s_i^t \cdot \Delta g_i^t \\
\overline{\Delta} g_c^t > \theta_t^C &\rightarrow \Delta p_c^t = \rho_t^c \cdot \overline{\Delta} g_c^t = \rho_t^c \cdot s_c^t \cdot \rho_{p/c}^t \cdot s_p^t \cdot \rho_{i/p}^t \cdot s_i^t \cdot \Delta g_i^t \\
\overline{\Delta} p_c^t &= \overline{s}_c^t \cdot \Delta p_c^t = \overline{s}_i^t \cdot \rho_t^c \cdot s_c^t \cdot \rho_{p/c}^t \cdot s_p^t \cdot \rho_{i/p}^t \cdot s_i^t \cdot \Delta g_i^t
\end{aligned}
\tag{6.15}
$$

closing of the *CIP* circuit:

$$
\begin{aligned}
\Delta g_i^{t+1} &= \rho_{c/i}^{t+1} \cdot \overline{\Delta} g_c^t \\
\overline{\Delta} g_i^{t+1} &= s_i^{t+1} \cdot \Delta g_i^{t+1} = s_i^{t+1} \cdot \rho_{c/i}^{t+1} \cdot s_c^t \cdot \rho_{p/c}^t \cdot s_p^t \cdot \rho_{i/p}^t \cdot s_i^t \cdot \Delta g_i^t \\
\overline{\Delta} g_i^{t+1} > \theta_{t+1}^I &\rightarrow \Delta p_i^{t+1} = \rho_{t+1}^i \cdot \overline{\Delta} g_i^{t+1} = \rho_{t+1}^i \cdot s_i^{t+1} \cdot \rho_{c/i}^{t+1} \cdot s_c^t \cdot \rho_{p/c}^t \cdot s_p^t \cdot \rho_{i/p}^t \cdot s_i^t \cdot \Delta g_i^t \\
\overline{\Delta} p_i^{t+1} &= \overline{s}_i^{t+1} \cdot \Delta p_i^{t+1} = \overline{s}_i^{t+1} \cdot \rho_{t+1}^i \cdot s_i^{t+1} \cdot \rho_{c/i}^{t+1} \cdot s_c^t \cdot \rho_{p/c}^t \cdot s_p^t \cdot \rho_{i/p}^t \cdot s_i^t \cdot \Delta g_i^t \\
\Delta g_i^{t+1} &= \rho_{c/i}^{t+1} \cdot s_c^t \cdot \rho_{p/c}^t \cdot s_p^t \cdot \rho_{i/p}^t \cdot s_i^t \cdot \Delta g_i^t
\end{aligned}
\tag{6.16}
$$

$\frac{\Delta g_i^{t+1}}{\Delta g_i^t} = \rho_{c/i}^{t+1} \cdot s_c^t \cdot \rho_{p/c}^t \cdot s_p^t \cdot \rho_{i/p}^t \cdot s_i^t$ which represents the marginal kinematics of the variation of the informational genotype[93] in the trinomial model *CIP*

– at the level of *CIP*:
  the result that interests us at the CIP level is, in fact, the resulting phenotype, that is, the trading strategy; in the above notation, the trading strategy generated by the model at time '*t*' is given, in fact, in the form of the variation of the trading strategy operated at time '*t*' that will operate at time '*t* + 1' (both as an effect

of genotypic variation as well as the epigenotypic variation of the CIP model), that is, $\overline{\Delta} p_i^{t+1}$:

$$\overline{\Delta} p_i^{t+1} = \overline{s}_i^{t+1} \cdot \rho_{t+1}^{i} \cdot s_i^{t+1} \cdot \rho_{c/i}^{t+1} \cdot s_c^t \cdot \rho_{p/c}^{t} \cdot s_p^t \cdot \rho_{i/p}^{t} \cdot s_i^t \cdot \Delta g_i^t \tag{6.17}$$

Therefore, the trading strategy that would be operated at the time of 't + 1' is:

$$p_i^{t+1} = p_i^t + \overline{\Delta} p_i^{t+1} \tag{6.18}$$

- at the level of cultural geodesic (selector environment)
  at the level of cultural geodesic, the selection of the trading strategy is made.[94] As we have shown above, the selection is not made by the financial market (Lo, 2019), which we consider to be the financial species of the financial 'world'. The selection criterion is the fitness of the trading strategy in question. The following considerations describe the selection process performed by cultural geodesic:
  - the fitness of a given trading strategy (more precisely, the fitness generated by the update indicated by the 'quantity' $\overline{\Delta} p_i^{t+1}$) is examined by two courts: (a) the normative geodesic court (GC_t^N); (b) the operational geodesic court (GC_t^O);
  - the normative geodesic court is represented by the formal and informal normative framework regarding the functioning of the financial market, as well as by the 'stock' of traditions, customs and so forth which characterizes the society in question; the operational geodesic court is represented by the totality of the trading strategies (and, obviously, by the totality of the individual transactions associated with these strategies) which, at the moment when the respective selection is operated, are active in the financial market;
  - the selection of the trading strategy is done in two stages, although we would be tempted to say that the distinction (both logical and chronological) of these stages is quite difficult to achieve: (I) stage of type selection α (when operating GC_t^N); (II) β type selection stage (when operating GC_t^O);
  - the selection of type α verifies the acceptability of $\overline{\Delta} p_i^{t+1}$ from the perspective of the norms in force: this selection is of

dichotomous type (acceptance vs rejection) and is carried out as follows: the changes brought by $\overline{\Delta} p_i^{t+1}$ that violate GC_t^N are sanctioned (by the 'visible hand') by a specific cost (of a legal nature) that decreases[95] the actual return of the economic agent regarding that trading strategy concerned. So, in fact, it is the economic agent who, under the pressure of GC_t^N, maintains or abandons the trading strategy in question;[96] it should be noted that, in principle, this selection is made without lags (although, as mentioned, the cost-benefit analysis may introduce lags in the decision to abandon or adjust the trading strategy in question);

- the β type selection verifies the acceptability of $\overline{\Delta} p_i^{t+1}$ from the perspective of the financial market *statu quo*, that is, from the perspective of the other trading strategies operated by the other economic agents: the changes brought by $\overline{\Delta} p_i^{t+1}$ that violate GC_t^O are simply sanctioned by the 'invisible hand'[97] of the financial market, namely by the lower return than the average of the market or than other competitors; it should be noted that this selection is (almost) always made with lags—the economic agent subject to this sanction may resist for a while (for various reasons, some of which are belong to preference, in fact) until s/he makes the necessary decision due to pressure, exercised by GC_t^O;

- from a formal-quantitative point of view, we can write the following relations regarding the selection of the trading strategy:
  (a) $\left(\Delta\varphi_t \in GC_t^N\right) \rightarrow \alpha$ acceptability (in principle) of the trading strategy $\left(TS_{t+1}, r_{t+1}^e, g_{t+1}^r\right)$;
  (b) $\left(\Delta\varphi_t \notin GC_t^N\right) \rightarrow \alpha$ rejectability[98] (in principle) of the trading strategy $\left(TS_{t+1}, r_{t+1}^e, g_{t+1}^r\right)$.

Nota bene: logically, case (b) is blocked,[99] so we will continue to examine only case (a) on the two theoretically possible sub-cases:

- (a1) in the case of the average return 'delivered' by the financial market:
  - (a1.1) $\left(g_t^{r(I)} < \sigma_t^{g(I)}\right) \rightarrow$ the β rejectability (in principle) of the trading strategy from this perspective;
  - (a1.2) $\left(g_t^{r(I)} \geq \sigma_t^{g(I)}\right) \rightarrow$ the β acceptability (in principle) of the trading strategy from this perspective;

Nota bene: logically, case (a1.1) is blocked, so we will only examine case (a1.2), with reference to the benchmark of the best competitor in the financial market:

- (a2) sub-case of return of the best competitor in the financial market:
  - $\left(g_t^{r(II)} \leq \sigma_t^{g(II)}\right) \wedge \left(g_t^{r(I)} \geq \sigma_t^{g(I)}\right) \rightarrow$ the β acceptability (in principle) of the trading strategy in this perspective;[100]
  - $\left(g_t^{r(II)} > \sigma_t^{g(II)}\right) \wedge \left(g_t^{r(I)} \geq \sigma_t^{g(I)}\right) \rightarrow$ the β rejectability (in principle) of the trading strategy in this perspective.

Figure 6.17 shows the logical reasoning made by the economic agent regarding the selection process of the trading strategy operated by the cultural geodesic.

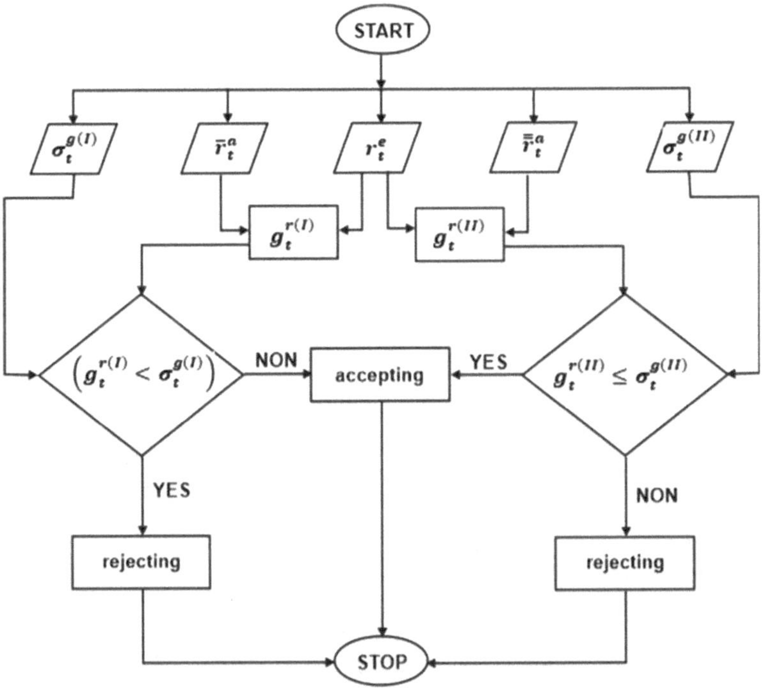

Fig. 6.17 The logical scheme of the trading strategy selection in the model *CIP*. *Source*: Authors

Notes

1. We recall that the external interaction of a system, that is, the interaction between the components of the system and the environment of that system, is called behaviour.
2. It is obvious that the space of fetal acceptability of reactions from other co-species changes over time, so its validity must be dated (in our case, dating at time ' *j* '). This change is either caused from inside or occurs precisely as a result of reactions received from outside. In fact, the discussion of the concept of adaptive preference outside of dating is obviously inconceivable.
3. But, obviously, in some circumstances, it may even be a loop reaction (i.e., a negative internal feedback). In the following, this eventuality will be subsumed to the concept of phenomenology and mechanism of autopoiesis of the financial market (in this case, of the three symbolic co-species), in order to initiate the hypothesis of the autopoietic market.
4. Which led us, as the attentive reader will already notice, to the conjecture that in the financial market (real, not imaginary, as latter is in the EMH model), behaviour takes primacy over information (Dinga et al., 2022).
5. The same reasoning applies, of course, to the case of the reaction, especially since, apart from the initial moment of triggering the operation of the mechanism in question, we only have reactions to reactions.
6. To pull the metaphor to the end, it is about the inequality of the triangle in Euclidean geometry. However, we do not advise the enthusiasts of analogy to start writing various algebraic relations in the field, although a topological approach would probably not be completely uninteresting in this matter.
7. The redefinition of the concept of *eidos* (taken from ancient Greek philosophy) is made by Edmund Husserl, in the new science of knowledge which he called *Phenomenology* and means pure essence, built by the intentionality of consciousness through the perception developed in *epoché* conditions (suspension of natural attitude in the process of perception).
8. Property verified, for example, by what is called pure science (such as mathematics or logic).
9. Of course, it is necessary to define what is meant by sensitivity between properties. For example, in microbiology the term *affinity* is used (introduced by biologist Monod), but it is also used in psychology. In economics, such a sensitivity can be defined starting from the *quid pro quo* situation (e.g., the relationship between supply and demand is based on this *quid pro quo*).
10. Which, in a punctually dedicated discussion of this issue, must be identified, either theoretically or under certain empirical conditions.

11. A system, $\mathcal{S}$, is a collection of elements that are indistinguishable from each other by at least one property and are distinguishable from each other by at least one property, as follows: (1) the property of indiscernibility allows the formation of the system *qua* system; (2) the property of discernibility allows the formation of the cardinal of the system; (3) the formalization of any system can be the following: $\mathcal{S} = \{e_1, e_2, \ldots, e_n\}$, where e_i are the elements of the system, and n is its cardinal. If we denote by p_i the set of properties of element e_i, such that: $p_i = \{\alpha_i^1, \alpha_i^2, \ldots, \alpha_i^{k_i}\}$, then, by a convenient renumbering, $\bigcap_i (p_i) = \{\alpha_i^1, \alpha_i^2, \ldots, \alpha_i^{k_w}\}$, where $1 \le k_w \le \min_i(k_i)$, and $\min_i(k_i) < \max_i(k_i) - 1$.
12. Here we find, once again, the basic idea of the concept of revealed preferences.
13. Recall that contingent means the possible non-necessary (for example, the financial market is a contingency).
14. Although we consider that, for our readers, the probability of a confusion (of a phonological nature) between the terms apophatic and apophantic is very small, we do, however, mention this risk.
15. Philosophically (perhaps not even metaphysically), it must be considered that nature only invents, while humans either discover or invent (*Nota bene*: it is relatively common to find that some technological inventions already existed in nature but had not been discovered).
16. The issue of novelty through synergy involves, however, the nuance of the *novelty* attribute.
17. By analytical we mean *identically applicable to any 'individual' in a population* (here, applicable to any synergistic episode in that class of interest). We remind you that, regarding the concept/term of analytic, it has two distinct meanings from the one used by us above: (a) the meaning of Descartes—the component elements (simple and clear) of a cognitive aggregate; (b) the meaning of Kant—the analytical sentence is that sentence in which the predicate (more precisely, the predicative qualification) is contained, logically, in the subject of the sentence—*Nota bene*: in this last sense, the analytical sentence is, obviously, a pure tautology).
18. In our opinion, the only case of ontological unpredictability is the case of the presence of free will (the other cases in which we speak of randomness are gnoseological cases, not ontological ones—*Nota bene*: a more nuanced discussion must, however, be taken in the case of quantum mechanics, where the subject-object interference is not yet positively solved).
19. This means to ignore the hysteresis effect.
20. Or, some and others, in different degrees from '1'.
21. Do not confuse oscillating synergy (from the perspective of potential) with reversible synergy (from the perspective of symmetry).
22. Of course, a broader discussion (but which could not bring significant added value to the present research) could also refer to the properties of properties.

23. As previously established, appearance also means disappearance (disappearance is an 'appearance' of an absence).
24. Stigmergy (as will be shown below) is a concept that aspires to capture collective action (convergent or not, deliberate or not) in the processuality of a system. In fact, stigmergy is inherent in the financial market more than synergy is.
25. We can consider that psychoanalysis implies a sui generis structuralism at the level of the subject, or, equivalently, that structuralism implies a psychoanalysis at the level of society (this aspect is approached in the literature—see, here, the Freudo-Marxist current).
26. The concept of stigmergy was introduced in 1959 by French biologist Pierre-Paul Grassé on the behaviour of termites.
27. To be noticed that our concept of implicit information is not else than a stigmergistic effect (*Nota bene*: the same about Samuelson's concept of revealed preference).
28. It is impossible not to notice the direct relationship of stigmergy (as well as implicit information) with semiotics and hermeneutics.
29. In fact, for the case of any field of human action, that is, of any social field that involves practice and praxeology.
30. As we will try to show below, the trinomial co-evolutionary model can be considered a much more stable macro-predictor of the financial market than the individual predictor of the three co-species taken separately, precisely as a result of interdependence, on the one hand, of the three co-species, and, on the other hand, of the 'pair' reaction norms—synergy/stigmergy/semergy—*Nota bene*: in the following, in order to facilitate reasoning, we will integrate the three concepts (synergy/stigmergie/semergie) in a unique concept for which we propose the term *SSSergie*. The justification for this conceptual and terminological unification is that, in reality, all three phenomena act simultaneously and interdependently.
31. For information and price, we have taken over the results obtained previously.
32. The use of the abbreviation '*C*' for preference is derived from the quasi-equivalence between preference, propensity, belief (so '*C*' comes from *credence*), on the one hand, and from the need to distinguish between the '*P*' of the price and the '*P*' of preference, on the other hand.
33. Obviously, the expected price of a given economic agent does not need to coincide *objectively* with the value (although this coincidence is not prohibited), because, from that economic agent's perspective, the expected price is, *subjectively*, always equal to the value. And all that matters in the decision and the behaviour of the economic agent is, of course, his subjective representation regarding the expected price/value.
34. The term middle has, approximately, the meaning of the middle term in a syllogism.

35. By middle term in the CIP trinomial we mean that component of the trinomial that cannot be bypassed (ignored, circumvented) in a circuit (usually open) from a first component to a last component, whatever would be the order of the components among them. *Nota bene*: we call circuit a complete path of the chain (or nodes)—the circuit can be closed, when the initial node receives the last impulse or open, when the last impulse stops at the final node (which does not coincide with the initial one).
36. A *trajectory* is characterized by the fact that in the equation/law of 'motion' it is sufficient to replace the variable time (t) with ($-t$) to deduce the effect from cause. The *process*, unlike the trajectory, does not allow such a mechanical reversibility 'without rest', it, even if it is reversible, holds a reversibility of hysteresis type, which no longer finds the origin (cause). Here, as we will show in the following studies, the mathematics of intervals can be useful in quantitative modelling of the financial market functioning.
37. The suggestion of *energetic depletion* or *entropic blocking* is irresistible here and, in our opinion, such a suggestion can be very productive in developing the modelling of the financial market functioning within the CIP trinomial model, a model that could replace (or complete, as appropriate) both modelling based on fractals (quite unrealistic, given the presence of free will) and modelling based on chaos theory (which presupposes an excessive sensitivity, just as unrealistic, to the initial conditions—in reality, there is a wide margin of tolerance of the change in the initial conditions, that is, in other words, there are quite high thresholds for initiating the claimed sensitivity to the initial conditions). However, both fractal and chaotic modelling can serve as tools or ways to empirically test the hypotheses/conjectures issued regarding the functioning of the financial market (Brătian et al., 2021).
38. The stiffness threshold is the threshold for the quantitative accumulation of the impulse (reaction) below which the node does not perceive that impulse, so it does not react (we can call the time to reach the response threshold as *dead time*, and the size of the threshold as *dead zone*).
39. Of course, the size of the variation must be the same (and of an opposite sign). However, in order to complicate things, it is obvious that, from a psychological point of view (and maybe even from the calculation!), an increase with a value/size does not have the same meaning as a decrease of the same value/size (not to mention that the order in which the two opposing variations occur may influence the assessment in question). These different perceptions (and evaluations) regarding the increase, respectively the decrease, are well highlighted by the behaviourist researches, including also other perspectives: past versus future, gain versus loss and so forth.

40. Here the term 'sign' obviously meaning (which is idiosyncratic) for the economic agent involved.
41. Assuming, of course, the additionality of the successive reaction norms, that is, their qualitative identity—otherwise we return to F_n filter.
42. Conceptually, by transmitting the intra-(co-) species mutation we mean the updating of the phenotype starting from the genotypic mutation.
43. The problem of transmitting the mutation of one co-species to another co-species (or of the inter-special mutation) is a difficult one and not yet scientifically resolved, not even in the field of biological living. For example, in the literature, there is talk of the so-called *oblique* mutational influence (which means a mutational influence that is also intra-special but avoids parents) (Russo, 1987). However, we appreciate that, in the field of symbolic (co-) species (or, as we prefer to say, of logical (co-) species), the problem of transmitting the inter-(co-) special mutation is considerably simpler and easier to instrumentalize.
44. The concepts of near environment and extended environment will be defined at the right time.
45. The relatively barbaric term '*haloness*' refers to the modification of the content of formal, respectively bound information, considered appropriate (consistent, convergent) with the new configuration of the implicit information just formed.
46. With greater care for propensity, however, which cannot be directly converted into explicit information but this is only indirectly possible—for example, we can use the phenomenon of revealed preference originarily discussed by Samuelson (1938).
47. There are also opinions (which we have addressed above) that reject the conceptual image of the genome (DNA) as a 'program' for configuring the phenotype, like a computer program—see, here, the concept of automaton (Wolfram, 2002). However, the process of developing the phenotype (*Nota bene*: not of evolution!) cannot be completely detached from the connotation of the program—especially in the case of remaking some organs or parts of organs of the phenotype (adult individual), see here also the famous stem cells.
48. For example, in the case of biological living, oblique hereditary transmission (the conceptual equivalent of what we have called here lateral transmission of the genetic mutation) is also done at the genotype level.
49. Not only in the world of biological living, but also in other worlds, equally: the non-living world, respectively the cultural world (economy, society). For example, carnivorous animals interact with herbivorous animals, with respect to their minimum entropic gradient, compared to their entropic gradient with respect to grass. Or, students interact with the teacher, not directly with scientists and so forth.

50. Of course, the assertion that the epigenetic impact is transmitted at the genotype level is, prima facie, a *contradictio in terminis*, but in the absence of more appropriate terms, and based on the following explanations, we propose to the reader not to reject it.
51. In fact, this is the 'justification' for the combination of epigenetics and genetics in the present discussion: the necessary nature of the internal fetality of the epigenetic mutation.
52. The use of the predicate 'internal' is required by the fact that, in the matter of the interaction of (co-) species, we have internal mutations (genetic, respectively epigenetic) (transmitted directly, i.e., without any transport vehicle, to own phenotype) and external mutations (genetic or epigenetics), which requires a transport vehicle that we have called the reaction norm. In the internal case, we have a necessary, non-problematic fetality, while in the external case we have a contingent, questionable fetality.
53. It should be noted that deregulation is a kind of regulation (just as economic decline is a kind of economic growth). In fact, the financial market (like any free economic market, by the way) must be regulated only to the point where it is capable of self-regulation. When regulation exceeds this threshold, due deregulation must be carried out (*Nota bene*: of course, setting the threshold at which regulation/de-regulation triggers self-regulation is an empirical issue, that is, contextual, not theoretical).
54. For example, the persistent (at the time of this study) pandemic shock of COVID-19 or, more recently, the war (in the form of an armed invasion) launched by the Russian Federation against Ukraine.
55. Of course, such an eventuality also has an impact on the genetic mutation at the price level (i.e., in terms of the price gap), but we consider that, coming from outside the CIP system, this disturbance has, first of all, epigenetic significance.
56. The implicit nature of the information generated by the variation of the propensity (belief) of the economic agent is not without problems. Our opinion is that, being generated by belief, the information in question cannot be explicit, because belief itself is not (entirely) rationalized and, therefore, not even (entirely) conscious. As such, the information (more precisely, the variation of information) generated by the variation of propensity is vague, rather impressionistic, which is also implicit information inferred by the economic agent from observing and interpreting the behaviour of other contemporary economic agents operating in the financial market.
57. It is a memetic behaviour, taken, without changing the propensity, from the dominant behaviour (or more insinuating than others) manifested in the financial market. In a separate article by the authors, such behaviour was called *take-make behaviour*.

58. A conclusive example for such an epigenetic variation of preference is that of the process of accession of some states—such as Romania—to the European Union, the latter behaving like a supra-system: thus, the Member State will develop a convergent and consistent behaviour with the Treaties of the Union (TEU and TFEU, respectively), as well as with common strategies and programmes, even if that State's propensity is not affected. Continuing this example, from a purely economic point of view, Romania may lose as a result of the economic sanctions imposed by the European Union on the Russian Federation as a result of the Russian's war against Ukraine, but these sanctions must be respected due to our country's membership to the European bloc. There is a cost of membership, as there is a benefit of membership (for example, by abolishing customs duties as a result of the functioning of the single market between Member States).
59. The use of the term 'functions' instead of 'lives', 'carries out its activity' and so forth is justified by its generality (the origin of the use of this term can be traced, for the social and therefore economic field, to the classic sociological functionalism of Talcott Parsons).
60. This can obviously raise an interesting (and important) question from the perspective of the goal of constructing an evolutionary theory of the financial market, as our study aspires: is the species called *financial market* 'endowed' with a single individual (of course, seen from the perspective of the class, as in the case of the biological living entities), namely the trading strategy? Our answer to this presumptive question is affirmative (we are referring, of course, to a given product /financial instrument, because for each such product/financial instrument traded, the human individual has his own trading strategy), that is, we do not consider other individuals (more precisely, classes of individuals) to form the financial market species (*Nota bene*: we repeat, this is about the particular financial market). Of course (but we will not develop our research in this direction, at least not until the critics force us to do so, from a scientific point of view) it could be considered that the very components of the CIP trinomial could be individuals of the species called trading strategy, in which case the financial market would be the environment of this species, as, for example, proposes Lo—obviously, in this presumptive case, the whole conceptual construction developed so far by us must, structurally and logically, be revised.
61. We propose, in fact, a cascading selection: a certain selection can only be exerted if the immediately preceding selection is positive—that is, the fitness in question has been validated (*Nota bene*: the informed reader immediately notices that here we have what is called verificationism, not falsificationism and even less confirmabilism). The problem of the possibility of falsificationism, respectively of confirmabilism (we refer to the social

field, because it seems that, in the field of biological living, only verificationism is possible) is not superfluous, but at least at this stage of research, it will not be examined.

62. We remind you that, in turn, the trading strategy (the financial individual who is part of the species called financial market) is objectified by concrete, particular situations, which we have called individual transactions—the latter represent a kind of 'individuals' of the financial individual, although it would be correct to call particular hypostatizations of the financial individual (*Nota bene*: it is not necessary to insist that both the financial individual and the financial species, as defined in this study, are ideal entities, the only real entity being the individual transaction).
63. To say again that Andrew Lo's proposal (Lo, 2019), which accepts that the financial individual (in our terminology) is the trading strategy, 'jumps' over the species, considering that the financial market (which we consider the species of which the trading strategy is its financial individual) is, in fact, the environment of the financial individual, who therefore selects it from the perspective of fitness. One of two: either we accept that the species and the selector environment coincide (being the financial market), or we accept that the financial individual (trading strategy) and its species coincide. In our opinion, any of these conceptual 'short circuits' are problematic (i.e., it raises questions rather than answers), which is why we proposed our solution: the trading strategy is the financial individual, the financial market is the financial species, and cultural geodesic ('immersed' in the situational context of the society in question) is the environment, that is, the selector of the financial individual (the latter as hypostasized through in particular individual transactions).
64. We recall the difference between the functionality and behaviour of a system: functionality refers to the interactions between the components of the system (i.e., inside its 'membrane'), while the behaviour refers to the interactions between the components of the system and its environment (i.e., interactions involving crossing the membrane of the system).
65. The vertical transmission of the epigenetic mutation (i.e., within the same (co-) species) is located in the 'territory' of evolution.
66. The temptation to introduce, logically, a third type of synergy—neutral synergy, which leaves the nomenclature of properties of the supra-system unchanged—is also forbidden by the very logic: first, neutral synergy is self-contradictory, because, by definition, it is creative/constructive (the destruction of properties that existed before the emergence of the supra-system is also a creative action, just as destruction is, logically, also a creation. *Nota bene*: just as economic decline it is also an economic growth, i.e., a negative growth), and secondly, the invariance of the nomenclature of properties of the supra-system may be a result of perfectly symmetric

actions (quite unlikely, but not with zero probability) of both positive and negative synergy—one destroys exactly what the other builds.

67. By synergies of the same order we mean the synergies that intervene over existing synergies of the same order. Although the definition seems circular, it is not, because: synergies of an (any) given order have the same effect on the nomenclature of properties of the supra-system—in this sense, the identification of the existence of the same order of synergies acting at a given time on a system can be inferred from the (empirical) finding of the generation of the same type of properties (either positively or negatively)—here we have another example of the type of revealed preference, which could be called *revealed synergy*, to paraphrase Samuelson.
68. Obviously, this is the standard acceptance (currently accepted by the scientific community) of the concept of synergy (although there are many cases where negative synergy is ignored—the one that 'destroys' properties—here there is the phrase *creative destruction* alleged to have been formulated by Joseph Schumpeter, although in reality the phrase (perhaps not exactly as a formulation, but exactly as a meaning) is first encountered at Werner Sombart and, in a somewhat more ideologized way, at Karl Marx.
69. One can, of course, develop the discussion by asking the question: are properties primitive in relation to relationships, or are the latter primitive in relation to properties? The question is not superfluous at all, as it can generate new foundations for economic (and social, by generalization) behaviour—perhaps a co-evolution of property and relationship would not be without scientific interest, as a paradigm of economic behaviour. In our opinion, relationships are more primitive (i.e., more fundamental) than properties—which, obviously, requires the introduction of the concept of *simpliciter* relationship (i.e., relationship without properties, a particularly difficult concept). Here we have a new mermaid song to examine the possibility of a phenomenological theory of the financial market (perhaps based on *trope theory*, relatively recently developed in phenomenological research). From another perspective, the problem of synergy could be raised, which triggers other synergies—in which case we would be dealing with a *synergistic hypercycle* (perfectly analogous to Manfred Eigen's self-catalytic hypercycle). It can be added to the aforementioned that Maturana and Varela had in mind (even if they did not produce a logical-philosophical justification for this) exactly this priority of relationships in relation to properties when they built their concept so general (hence indistinguishable) of *cognition*.
70. The term 'usually' is justified by the fact that, relatively recently, the issue of deliberate (so non-random, although contingent, still) intervention has been raised in the genome of living beings (including in the case of humans—see so-called transhumanism).

71. Our expression (necessary device but which is a contingent initiator of evolution) seems self-contradictory, so we will provide, here, the necessary explanations. The necessity for the genotypic device is given by its structural character (some would say, programmatically character, more precisely by DNA programming), but its contingency is given by the random character of the mutations that can occur at the level of genes/alleles. From a logical point of view, therefore, we must accept an intra-contingent necessity, respectively an intra-necessary contingency. *Intra-contingent necessity* refers exactly to the functioning of genetically caused evolution: mutation is contingent but, once it occurs, its impact on the individual (and, implicitly, on the species) is necessary (i.e., mandatory) (*Nota bene*: an example from everyday life: the decision to boiling water for tea making is contingent—it can be taken or not—but once taken, the water will necessarily boil at about 100 °C). *Intra-necessity contingency* mirrors intra-contingent necessity: intergenerational transmission of mutation is necessary, but accidents can occur during this process—for example, the individual preparing to reproduce itself is killed, which is an intra-necessity contingency. (*Nota bene*: in the example with tea, after the water in the kettle starts to heat up, I change my mind and interrupt this heating which is necessary according to the laws of thermodynamics—so I intervene contingently in a necessary process.) The full picture of the correlation between necessity and contingency could therefore be as follows: (a) intra-necessity necessity (NN); (b) intra-contingency necessity (CN); (c) intra-contingency contingency (CC); (d) intra-necessity contingency (NC).
72. We specify that evolution implies development (*Nota bene*: logically, the absence of development in the case of the symbolic/logical phenotype can be replaced by a zero duration of development), because the intergenerational transmission of mutations can be done only by the adult individual. The selector environment also acts on the adult individual (phenotype), which means that the intergenerational transmission of the mutation (i.e., the generation of evolution) can be blocked at any time (*Nota bene*: this blockage is, obviously, contingent) in relation to the environment) at the level of development.
73. We no longer develop here the idea, presented several times before, that the most elaborate attempt to develop an evolutionary model of the financial market (not of the economic process, where there are older and somewhat more articulate attempts) has 'lost', on the way, the species, jumping from the individual (trading strategy, as in the case of our proposal) directly to the environment (financial market). The suggestion (implicit, because it was not made *expressis verbis*) is that the selection made by the environment is exercised directly on the species seems unacceptable (Lo, 2019).

74. We have explained elsewhere the conceptual distinctions between ethics, deontology and morality—they are not substitutable for each other.
75. We advise the reader to take into account, at this point in the discussion, the following clarifications: (1) the problem of an environment that differs from the species on which it will exert its selection action does not arise in the biological field, where one of the components of the environment is represented by the other individuals of the same species, respectively the other contemporary species; (2) the separation, from the point of view of nature, between the species and the selector environment is mainly in the field of symbolic species. (*Nota bene*: we recall that Niklas Luhmann is the main supporter, taking a position diametrically opposed to that of Andrew Lo—not very convincing, however, in our opinion—of this separation: he considers that the selector environment of the social individual that he calls communication is the psychism, essentially from the social mark.) In fact, our current position is provisional, following that, in further research in this book, we will compose a mixed financial market environment, namely consisting of two components: (a) cultural geodesic—different in nature from the trading strategy (the individual financial market), respectively from the financial market (financial species); (b) the other contemporary trading strategies in the financial market—which, obviously, have the same nature as the financial market. These other trading strategies, contemporary in the financial market with the examined trading strategy, we will call, a little further, *operational geodesic*.
76. It does not seem to us that (for the time being) be too productive the possibility of replacing the term (co-) species with another term that completely eliminates the risk of confusion—such a term could be, for example, that of *proto-individual*: *proto-individual information*, *proto-individual price*, respectively *proto-individual preference*, so that the financial individual (trading strategy) is generated, causally/conditionally by the *proto-individual CIP model.*
77. The analogy with the increase in thermodynamic homogeneity as an indication (and measure) of the increase in entropy in a closed system is obvious. Given the existence of a single financial species (the financial market itself as such), we can consider that the financial market is a closed system (*Nota bene*: as, in fact, both Niklas Luhmann and Andrew Lo, considered, each on their own issues of scientific interest).
78. In this respect, the continuous, 'smooth' quantitative modelling (overwhelming in the known models of the financial market), is as unrealistic as the fundamentalist hypotheses of the *homo œconomicus* mathematical model.
79. This methodological disregard does not affect the reasoning of the quantitative model, because we can assume, quite simply (which is logically equivalent), that there is a dead zone where are 'prepared' the variation of

the component in question of the preference as long as the adjustment is made only up to the significance threshold of that component.

80. Of course, considering also the variation of the significance threshold range could be a provocative suggestion for future researches.
81. Obviously, analytical formalization excludes (or makes useless, rather, redundant) strictly numerical formalization in solving the proposed equations.
82. As is well known, frequential probabilities require archives of results (either experimental or experiential), the probabilities in question being simple average behavioural extrapolations (i.e., at the average level of the population or sample in question), under the assumption (completely unrealistic!) of invariance of conditions and the law of motion—we repeat that, in the social/economic field, neither the initial conditions nor the law of motion (i.e., the principles of behaviour) are invariant, although, obviously, the principles of behaviour (see our discussion on symbolic utility) have extremely high persistence/inertia. Instead, Bayesian probabilities are specific to the singular, unrepeatable (objective) event, as is the case with any economic event (*Nota bene*: and this is perfectly compatible with the concept of propensity).
83. We have previously shown that an economic agent can have as a benchmark the average return of the financial market (as does, e.g., EMH) or the return of the best competitor in the financial market (according to the Grossman-Stiglitz thesis, there will always be a such a competitor, although this logical necessity has not been demonstrated by the two authors—nor has subsequent literature done so yet—the existence in question being presumed or 'decreed'). The economic operator concerned may set as its own objective either one or the other of the two benchmarks, taking into account that the strict maintaining at the level of the average return of the financial market means informational efficiency of the market, so it means a zero profit.
84. This cost will reduce the future return.
85. As we will see below, this is the event (moment, praxiological occasion) by which the variation of the propensity, converted into the variation of the Bayesian probabilities, leads from the a priori Bayes probability to the a posteriori Bayes probability (of course, from an analytical point of view, the Bayes theorem of transition from a priori probability to a posteriori probability has to be used here).
86. Not the economic agent involved!
87. Given that the abscissa of the inflection point is given by the real solution of the second-order derivative of the function, the first (proximal) polynomial order that allows this is the third order one. According to Ockham's razor, (reformulated, by the way, by Leibniz, as a principle of sufficient reason), if the third order satisfies the condition we need, we should avoid

choosing a higher order polynomial. *Nota bene*: the satisfaction condition we are talking about here is analogous to the one we are talking about in the phenomenology of perception—another argument for the direction of phenomenological research in economics, including financial market theory (or financial theory).

88. We note that an economic agent operating in the financial market always has an initial trading strategy, no matter how 'rudimentary' is it—usually it is designed exclusively on its own propensity, but it can also be conditioned by a superficial evaluation, at prima facie (i.e., based on available implicit information) of market observed behaviours. Therefore, in our opinion, it is not necessary to discuss separately the formation of this initial trading strategy.
89. The attentive reader remembers the clear distinction we made earlier between expectation and anticipation—however, from the perspective of the economic agent's interpretation of the return obtained and, therefore, of the decision s/he will take in regarding of the modification of the trading strategy, this conceptual distinction is not relevant.
90. Empirical testing of the significance threshold (which is, of course, idiosyncratic) is no more difficult or less decisive than extracting the revealed preference.
91. The particular case $g_i^r = \sigma_i^g$ is interesting because, although indifferent to the economic agent from a logical perspective, it may not be indifferent from a psychological perspective. For simplicity, we can consider that this case will be solved by the economic agent concerned on the basis of the implicit information obtained as a result of observing the other behaviours in the financial market, so memetically (e.g., as herd effect).
92. An economic operator has its own nomenclature/portfolio of trading strategies—each of which is tracked individually (or sometimes directly at the level of the so-called optimal portfolio—see Markowitz, Sharpe or other aggregate models)—because each of them is associated own return gap, so, at the financial market level, we have a set of sets of trading strategies. All identifiable financial market trading strategies represent financial individuals of a single financial species: the financial market itself.
93. Of course, such circuit closures in the CIP model can be also made starting from (co-) species price, respectively from (co-) species preference, as was done here starting from (co-) species information.
94. We remind the reader that, in the social field (i.e., where there is deliberation and purpose), selection, although directed—especially through the formal/codified normative framework—is no longer cumulative (or no longer exclusively cumulative). In our opinion, the selection in this field is, overwhelmingly, of the jumping type (Gould, 2007). Note: The idea of punctuated equilibrium has been developed by Gould, along with Niles

Eldredge (Gould & Eldredge, 1977). However, as this study itself shows, the fitness of a trading strategy is up-to-date (so adjusted) by permanent (albeit discrete) changes in previous fitness, that is, there is an element of cumulativeness—what we want to argue is that this element of cumulativeness is no longer decisive, as in the biological realm.

95. The extent to which the sanction in question reduces (or should reduce) the actual return is a multidimensional issue involving both psychology, anthropology, systems theory, and, in particular, tax theory (an example for the latter, although with a relatively low relevance, is the Laffer curve, another example is the internalization of negative externalities in the case of trading strategies that pollute the environment).
96. At the level of the economic agent, a cost-benefit analysis intervenes here: if the monetary value of the sanction is covered by the monetary value of the gain brought by the maintenance of the penalized (and penalizable further) trading strategy, then the economic agent will continue to operate that trading strategy (if moral or ethical commandments does not prevent him/her from doing so, of course). The interested reader may find relevant analyses in this area (albeit in the unrealistic framework of neoclassical economic theory) in Gary Becker (Becker, 2009).
97. It should not be understood, therefore, that the financial market is the one that applies the sanction, although the sanction is applied within the functioning of the financial market—the sanction is applied by the component GC_t^O of the cultural geodesic.
98. Both the acceptability and the rejectability of the trading strategy are only 'indications' or 'indices' that GC_t^N gives to the economic agent, therefore the effective acceptance, respectively the effective rejection of the targeted trading strategy remains at the discretion of the economic agent (human individual), who may also have non-economic (non-monetary) reasons in making the decision.
99. This case may be subject to further updates/adjustments, either on a genotypic or epigenotypic basis (of course, with the predominance of the deliberative component of these updates/adjustments).
100. The fact that, in general, $\sigma_t^{g(I)} \neq \sigma_t^{g(II)}$, seems quite obvious, because the benchmark of the best competitor in the financial market is a *first best* benchmark, while the benchmark of the average market return is of the *second best* type or, most of the time, of the *survival best* type. However, here we have a certain relativism: the performance of the best competitor is, of course, a second best solution for that competitor, but it is a solution (which appears as) *first best* for the economic agent who takes as benchmark the solution of the best competitor.

References

Becker, G. S. (2009). *Human Capital: A Theoretical and Empirical Analysis, with Special Reference to Education*. University of Chicago Press.

Brătian, V., Acu, A.-M., Oprean-Stan, C., Dinga, E., & Ionescu, G.-M. (2021). *Efficient or Fractal Market Hypothesis? A Stock Indexes Modelling Using Geometric Brownian Motion and Geometric Fractional Brownian Motion*. Mathematics, 9(22), 1–20.

Dawkins, R. (2016). *The Selfish Gene*. Oxford University Press.

Dinga, E. (2021). Institutionalism As A Species Of Evolutionism. *Management of Sustainable Development, 13*(1), 49–54. https://ideas.repec.org/a/blg/msudev/v13y2021i1p49-54n9.html

Dinga, E., Oprean-Stan, C., Tănăsescu, C.-R., Brătian, V., & Ionescu, G.-M. (2021). *Entropy-Based Behavioural Efficiency of the Financial Market*. Entropy, 23(11), 1396.

Dinga, E., Oprean-Stan, C., Tanasescu, C.-R., Brătian, V., & Ionescu, G.-M. (2022). *Financial Market Analysis and Behaviour: The Adaptive Preference Hypothesis* - Taylor and Francis Ltd.—Routledge.

Fürstenberg, K. (2016). Evolutionary Institutionalism: New Perspectives. *Politics and the Life Sciences, 35*, 48–60.

Gould, S. J. (2007). *Punctuated Equilibrium*. Belknap Press of Harvard University.

Gould, S. J., & Eldredge, N. (1977). Punctuated equilibria: The tempo and mode of evolution reconsidered. *Paleobiology, 3*(2), 115–151.

Lo, A. (2019). *Adaptive Markets. Financial Evolution at the Speed of Thought*. Princeton University Press.

Popper, K. (1978). *Three Worlds*. The Tanner Lecture on Human Value.

Russo, T. (1987). *Parental and oblique transmission and interaction between traits in the evolution of non-genetic traits: suggestions for a cultural ecology*. Coenoses, *2*(2), 85–95. https://www.jstor.org/stable/43460951

Samuelson, P. A. (1938). A Note on the Pure Theory of Consumer's Behaviour. *Economica, 5*(17), 61–71.

Wolfram, S. (2002). *A New Kind of Science*. Wolfram Media.

CHAPTER 7

Co-evolution of Symbolic Species and Decision-Making in the Financial Market

Preliminaries

Our book is, par excellence, a theoretical one, namely a logical and conceptual approach to the financial market, from an evolutionary perspective, more exactly, from the perspective of the evolution of symbolic species—namely of preference, information, and price. The basic objective of the book is to provide, the scientific community, with a new vision of the ways in which the financial market (seems) to work, in the light of the new theoretical and experimental acquisitions, like, especially, institutionalism and behaviourism (both considered by authors as species of the genus called evolutionism). Since human beings are crucial in emerging and functioning of the symbolic species (as artefacts of different nature), and, in addition, human beings are (still) massively conditioned by their biology, that is, by their intrinsic evolutionism, the ground assumption of the book is that all the symbolic species are governed, more or less obvious, by a deep 'current' of evolutionism. Of course, the symbolic species, as living in the cultural environment (under the cultural geodesic, as coined else by one of the authors), their evolving path suffers many adaptations as comparative with the biological species or with the artificial species generated by the artificial intelligence (AI). By the way, we did not call the species discussed in the book (preference, information, price) as artificial species, although they are artefacts like the 'standard' artificial species, because the species of interest bear a strong and inalienable

E. Dinga et al., *Co-Evolution of Symbolic Species in the Financial Market*, https://doi.org/10.1007/978-3-031-31698-2_7

symbolism—not in the semiotic sense, but in a praxiological one. It is important to mention here that the praxiological paradigm of sustainability—which is both the effect of the optimality paradigm and the logical and social negation of it—is not only completely consistent with the evolutionary model of the symbolic species presented in the book but, more than that, a sustainable path and an evolutionist path of the symbolic species almost cannot be logically distinguished.

A question arises here, namely whether our proposal can sustain a grounding of decision-making in the financial market, and, if yes, which would be the main components or coordinates of such a sustaining. In this chapter, some opinions on this matter will be delivered, without any claims to constitute action recipes either for traders in the financial market or for governmental institutions, authorities, or organizations (by contrast with many other approaches of the financial market phenomenology—Efficient Market Hypothesis, Fractal Market Hypothesis, to take only two well-known examples—or of some techniques in that field, including those awarded with Nobel Prize, as Black-Scholes tool). This positioning is not a false modesty (*Nota bene*: the modesty is that quality of one who has nothing else than that quality) but is, rather, an honesty with which the authors present their proposal in order to be (critically) discussed in its findings, arguments, and (if we are lucky), in its openness to new scientific horizons aimed at better understanding this crucial region of the nominal economy, called financial market.

In what follows, we examine, with caution, although with (enough) imagination, the general features of the decision-making process in the financial market which could base on our proposal. We will discuss all these from four perspectives or, the same, for four (generic) economic actors as presumed to operate actions (either acts or abstentions) in a (generic) financial market: (1) the individual trader/investor; (2) the government; (3) the analyst (like, say, the authors of this book or our colleagues in the scientific community around the financial market topic); (4) the general public. As the title of the book announces, this analysis will address only the general framework but, being general, such a framework is the best basis for particular analyses and decisions which aspires to enter the evolutionary model of the financial market. This book is the second one of the authors' endeavours to contribute to edifying an evolutionary paradigm of the financial market (and of the economy as a whole), the first proposing the adaptive preference hypothesis[1] and it will be followed by a third one, dedicated to an autopoietic market hypothesis.[2]

What Should be Expected from a General Framework of Co-evolutionary Financial Market

From a general framework of a theoretical model of the financial market (as our evolutionary binomial or trinomial models in this book), the justified expectations regarding the decision-making process are the following four: (a) the principles of functioning of the model involved; (b) the limits of that functioning; (c) the predictability of outcomes; and (d) the testability of predictions. We will briefly comment on the content of these categorial expectations.

Seven Epistemological Issues

(1) *Principles*

Any logical model delivers, at the most abstract level, principles—principles of cognition/knowing, principles of behaviour, and principles of testing (the truth or, after the case, the convenience). The principles have two crucial roles: (i) to guide the adepts of the model in the case; (ii) to (previously) inform the other participants[3] at the social game about the guiding of those adepts (Nozick, 1993). The basic finality of the principles is, of course, that of providing a *sui generis* intelligibility[4] of the world from the perspective of the field involved (in our case, the financial field). The double guiding role of the principles has its peculiarities in the case of the co-evolutionary model of symbolic species as such a model has been developed in this book.

(i) Internally guiding (inside principles)

One of the most relevant principles of the co-evolution of symbolic species under the two logical models exposed in the book, namely, the binomial information-price—BIP, and the trinomial preference-information-price—TCIP, is that of the *cultural rationality* as a last resort of co-evolution. The dominance of Lamarckism in the co-evolution of symbolic species gives important features regarding the deliberativeness and, so, the rationality of the co-evolution involved. Although may be (and, in reality, is) an adumbration area between the individual interest and the normative framework (which requires the social monitoring and control), it may be said that the principle of cultural rationality is prominent. The cultural rationality has a hybrid nature: it is both a theoretic rationality and a practical one (Mele & Rawling, 2004).

A second principle acting for the adepts of the proposed model is that of *necessary balance* inside the co-evolutionary model. Of course, such a necessity is of social nature, not a natural one. This means that the opposition to that necessity is possible and effective,[5] based on the free will.[6] That necessary balance is guided not anymore by a simple cost-benefit analysis because the cost implied addresses the normative penalties, that have important aspects linked to ethics, self-esteem and so forth. Consequently, the individual involved expects the impersonal species (either in BIP or in TCIP) to control each other so their functionality dynamically harmonizes. Somewhat, the proposed co-evolutionary models internalize the well-known Smith's invisible hand in the internal logic of those models.

A third principle from which the adepts of the co-evolutionary models can benefit is that of the *second-best solution* to be focused on. Indeed, the co-evolutionary models of symbolic species do not any more belong to the optimality praxiological paradigm but to the sustainability praxiological paradigm. In the sustainability paradigm, extremization is not possible both as such and as a target, since the finality belongs rather to surviving than getting the first best solution.[7]

(ii) Externally guiding (outside principles)

The participants in the financial market phenomenology, other than the very adepts of the co-evolutionary models of this market, also get benefits, from the perspective of the principles, generated as follows:

- based on the self-regulation, generally own to the (co)evolutionary models in the financial market, the participants (either players or stakeholders) with trading strategies take into consideration such *self-regulation* (i.e., negative feedback) which will smooth, earlier or later, the unusual gaps between expected returns and the actual ones;
- this expectation, at the principle level, will be objectified in decisions and actions (either as acts or abstentions, after the case) which will be, more or less, harmonized with the own functioning and dynamics of the financial market as the subject of those (co-)evolutionary models. It can be said that *implicit coordination* of decisions and actions are, in fact, the most natural interventions in the financial

market, because exactly their compatibility and consistency (i.e., non-contradictoriness) with the own principled 'philosophy' of such a market;

- for the participants to the financial market functioning, its principles in the (co-)evolutionary models act as non-codified norms, that is, as 'natural laws', which are, in an impersonal way, subject to an implacable logic—the financial market 'targets' the *survival* because and to the extent that the economic agents themselves target the survival;
- the inherent principles of (co-)evolutionary models *avoid* (generally) *catastrophes*;[8] these external principles (as property of internal principles) are close to the first one, namely, self-regulation, but it is important to be separately signalized, since the past, current and further financial catastrophes are direct (and inevitable) effects of neoclassical models of the financial market;
- searching for surviving, not optimizing, gives (co-)evolutionary models of financial market the *permanent fractality*, so impetuously claimed by Edgar Peters (1994). Not only this necessary fractality addresses the horizons of expected returns, but also the fractal distribution in the financial market addresses many other variables and parameters of its functioning and ending;[9]
- the (co-)evolutionary models of the financial market appeal again, and in a pressed way, the fact that economic (including financial) activity is a *game of cooperation*, not a competition. Do not forget that the most known (and still used) models in the economic and financial field are based on the principle of competition (*Nota bene*: however, the game theory—especially the evolutionary game theory manages to escape this fancy). This suggestion already was in animal behaviour (in biological studies), where individuals cooperate to get food and very rarely fight for that.

(2) *Limits*

Of course, any models operate with abstractions, simplifications and reductionisms (ASRs). None of these three logical operations, common enough in scientific research, discredit the modelling in any field but, on the contrary, they are often indispensable. Despite this crucial role of ASRs, in fact, exactly they constitute the origin of the limits that the models in the case bear. Although (very) many unrealistic suppositions of the much too famous neoclassical models of economy and of the financial market are eliminated or, at least, avoid by elaborating (co-)evolutionary models of the financial market, the limits of such last models must be highlighted, from a scientific position of the authors. This demarch is justified since the evolutionary approaches in the economic/financial field are still incipient and, as we know, are not based on a general theory of evolution in the social field (*Nota bene*: a general theory, on the model of Maynard Keynes theory of Macroeconomics, in the matter of social evolution, would be of an incommensurable signification and relevance, but it seems, we have still to wait for such a grandiose elaboration).

(a) the general pattern used in social evolution modelling is that from Biology, that is from biologically living entities. Although, as a point of departure, such a dependence could be fruitful enough, further it surely reduces the relevance of a genuine social evolution. It is quite obvious that the biological changes of human beings have an infinitesimal rhythm compared with the social (i.e., economic or financial) changes[10] or, at least, pressure for changes (Lo, 2019). Consequently, biology could, at most, suggests a way of approaching, but not a 'copy-paste' (or tale quale) overtaking in modelling evolution for symbolic species;
(b) the mutation (as known from the Biological region) is not always working in (co-)evolutionary models of the financial market, so if the last models are too rigid related to it, they reduce their explanation (and, of course, prediction) force;
(c) the symbolic phenotype is born directly as an adult. It does not suffer growth or development processes, although is subject to evolution, so the rhythm of changing it is (could be) very fast;
(d) a crucial peculiarity regarding the symbolic species is that of the location of the genotype: the genotype is located in the psychological device of the human being, not inside the structure of the symbolic phenotype. So, a (co-)evolutionary model of the financial market should accept changes in symbolic species (as well as symbolic individuals) simply as effects of the changes that occurred in that psychology, sometimes without any relationship with the objective path of the financial market in the case;
(e) a very significant limit consists in the inevitable mix between random change pressures on the financial market, which are coming from the impersonal working of that market, and deliberative (even programmatic, as the case could be) change pressure on the finan-

cial market, which could have completely external reasons (e.g., political or ideological) related to the real functioning of the market in the case;

(f) the (co-)evolutionary models of the financial market need a new (logical and quantitative) formalism, inspired rather by fields like entropy, sociology, biophysics and anthropology, together with the already accessed: Economics, Psychology, standard Mathematics (especially Calculus), and Chaos Theory. In our opinion, such formal construction should integrate Topology as well.

(3) *Predictability*

It seems the (co-)evolutionary modelling of the financial market phenomenology is much more natural than the neoclassical modelling. In our opinion, the neoclassical modelling (and, implicitly, neoclassical theorizing) is somewhat externally related to the financial market, acting as an intellectual (deductive) grid that has been thrown on reality, hoping to be found sufficient overlapping between ex-cathedra model and the reality itself. Obviously, no theory does not proceed else, in no field, natural or social or humanistic. But, here, the problem is that the neoclassical model is specially designed to ignore at an incredible scale the anomalies (here, in Kuhn's sense) that the experiments and experiences provided for so long time.

On the contrary, the (co-)evolutionary model of symbolic species, as the authors dare to propose to the attention of the scientific community in the matter, seems to be extracted from the interior of the financial market phenomenology itself, by an abductive method.[11] Based on these characteristics, the predictability[12] that can be associated with the (co-)evolutionary model of the financial market can be featured in the followings:

- the primary source of predictability in the (co-)evolutionary model of the financial market is constituted by the very principles evoked above (both internal and external), since they—to the extent in which are known or correctly intuited—provide a quasi-certainty about the expected behaviour in the market;
- as suggested before, those principles act as genuine predictors for what could decide and what actions could perform the participants in the financial market. Of course, the way in which the economic

agents internalize the principles is completely idiosyncratic and hidden enough related to competitors;

- in fact, the predictability in the models like those two proposed in this book resides in the very 'necessity' of the models in the case: indeed, the constraints of co-evolution (especially regarding the reaction norms so discussed in the previous chapters)—either in BIP or TCIP model—forbid or, at least, strongly dilute the decision/actions too much away from the lines indicated by the co-evolutive principles. Such 'necessity' is not of a natural kind but a mix between social and individual 'necessity': from the social side acts the normative framework, and from the individual side acts the own rationality models (both theoretical and practical) held by individuals' consciousness;
- practically (more exactly, praxiologically), it is expected that the decisions (followed by the corresponding actions) move in a narrow tunnel around the cultural geodesic. So, the predictions should be made inside such a tunnel, taking into account that: (a) the normative framework is transparent for (known by) all individuals and organizations on the financial market, acting as a common macro-predictor; (b) the individual (hidden, so unknown) models of rationality can be, however, approximated, in their main lines, by appealing the co-evolution intrinsic rationality of the financial market;
- it is expected, as well, that decisions in the financial market be predictable from another point of view, namely, the perspective of the natural values (especially regarding the price, so the return). Indeed, since the (co-)evolution is focused on survival, that means sustainability (or indefinite replicability), it can be presupposed that the main economic/financial variable in the financial market takes their natural values (*Nota bene*: by natural value we understand those values having the potential to be maintained, principled, on the long or very long term). Consequently, the predictability is reduced, in such a context, rather to the predictability of natural values than to the predictability of the competitors' behaviour.

(4) *Truth*

The problem of truth in modelling the financial market (and, more extensively, the economic phenomenon) is difficult enough, at least for the following reasons:

a) the financial decisions/actions are 'endowed' with purposes; they do not focus on simple finalities. Consequently, the 'truth' addresses the (semantic) coincidence between the prescriptive statement (before performing the action) and the descriptive statement (after performed action). As known, corroboration (in the falsifiability theory) means the (semantic) coincidence between the predictive statement and the descriptive one—as, in the social case, never exist pure predictive statements but only combinations between predictions and prescriptions—what we can call ***presdictions***, from ***pres***criptions and pre***dictions***—it results that we will not really test the truth in its standard meaning (which presupposes the comparison between predictions and descriptions);
b) since the economic activity (*a fortiori*, the financial activity) is of praxiological category, it seems that pragmatism (in its James-ian sense) has a large camp of manifestation here. As Milton Friedman (cynically) suggested, it does not matter the truth of our hypotheses if the predictions made based on them are corroborated. In such a context, the truth acquires connotations (and even denotations) different enough from the standard view.[13]

To conclude, until one will find a more appropriate denomination for such a truth, we propose to speak about a teleological truth, which contrasts with the cognitive truth. Essentially, the teleological truth (TT) is idiosyncratic enough, being different from the cognitive truth which is commonly shared by all individuals. So, the topic of the truth is not cuttingly different from the perspective of (co-)evolutionary models of the financial market compared with that from the perspective of other models of the financial market (neoclassical, behavioural, institutional, and so on).

(5) *Explanation*

The explanation is a description of causality. As the causality is, rather, a principle (see Chap. 1 in this book) of world functioning or, better said, of the observable world functioning, an explanation must be understood as a description of the cause or causal complex/set associated to an event (*Nota bene*: an event is a particular hypostasis of a phenomenon which, in turn, is a particular hypostasis of a process). In such an epistemological framework, the peculiarities of the (co-)evolutionary models of the financial market regarding the explanation are as follows:

(i) the most numerous causes in the financial market are of motivational/intentional nature (see, above, our considerations on the truth in the social field), so are guided, principally, by free will, although the decisions are anchored in models of rationality;
(ii) consequently, the explanation is, rather, a justification, inside the models of rationality in force. In such a framework, the 'legality'; of an explanation means the consistency of decision (so, of action) with those models of rationality. From a logical point of view, the 'legality' of an explanation consists in the validity of inference of decision from the models of rationality;
(iii) regarding the legitimacy of an explanation, things are much more complicated, because the participation of unconsciousness in the decision-making process (as behaviourism claims). As the models of rationality are sufficiently regional (because they are strongly idiosyncratic), it results that the legitimacy of explanation is even sub-regionalized than its 'legality';
(iv) after all, we should conclude that in (co-)evolutionary models of the financial market, the explanation must be anchored, at least from a theoretical point of view to a very different (relatively) invariant. We believe such an invariant is constituted by the very principles (internal and external) generated by the intrinsic phenomenology of the (co-)evolution of the symbolic species in the financial market.

(6) *Testability*

As in the case of truth and explanation, the testability in the (co-)evolutionary models of the financial market is not too different from the cases of other models (and theories) on this market. The main traits of testability in our context are the following:

- testability in the financial matter (*Nota bene*: but this is valid for the entire social domain) must not be understood anymore as scientific[14] testability but in a different sense in which we offer below some still not too refined suggestions/ideas;
- the corroboration of a 'hypothesis' strengthens that hypothesis, in contrast to the natural domain; also, a rejection of a prediction based on a hypothesis does not mean that hypothesis to be rejected as well. The justification for such assumptions can be found in the fact that

the truth is teleological, so is strongly idiosyncratic—for example, one could target an impossible objective, or at least, an unrealistic one;

- as in the scientific testability, however, the experimental conditions are under discussion both if the prediction is corroborated and is rejected;
- the thesis Duhem-Quine is not anymore valid, since all the hypotheses that ground the hypothesis on which a prediction has been elaborated and then rejected are, in turn, presuppositions linked to the teleological truth, namely purposes;
- the issue of the ad-hoc hypotheses has no more signification since targets are, generally, unique.[15] The reason emerges from the same epistemological root: the hypotheses on which the prediction regarding the target is built up are idiosyncratic and subjectively grounded, so the ad-hoc hypotheses become inoffensive in corroborating or rejecting such a prediction;

To conclude, it must be said that testability is, to some extent, different from the scientific testability commonly known. Consequently, both elaboration of predictions and organizing experiments (or, after the case, doing natural experiments) related to (co-)evolutionary models of the financial markets, must be carefully approached, in order to get the maximum of signification and usefulness in the praxiological actions.

(7) *Probability*

The quasi-certainty discussed above objectifies as a priori distribution of Bayes probability. So, basically, in the (co-)evolutionary models of the financial market, it does not work anymore the frequential (i.e., Kolmogorov) objective probability but the subjective (in fact, Bayesian) probability. The Bayes probability is compatible and consistent both with the realistic way in which the individual thinks and acts and with the fact that the financial market has no memory[16] (*Nota bene*: of course, except the hard memory reserved to propensity, more exact to K component of preference, as shown at the appropriate place).

Bayesian probability is probably, the only type of probability that is apt to capture the realistic way in which the individual thinks and acts. It is based on belief (that is, it activates the propensity) and, in fact, is related to possibility.[17] In addition, Bayesian probability is very strongly correlated with our (coined) concept of implicit information—in fact, implicit information means that information inferred by an individual by observing the revealed/objectified/manifested behaviour of the other participants to the financial market phenomenology. But this implicit information is exactly what in Bayesian theory is called as a posteriori probability.[18]

However, no matter if, in the social field the frequential probability should be replaced by the Bayesian probability, some traits of this probability, in relation to the (co-)evolutionary models of the financial market are of interest, as follows:

- being a non-frequential probability, Bayes probability is, in fact, a probability of a singular event (*Nota bene*: based on this observation, we, besides, have recovered the propensive probability introduced by Popper[19]). So, if the inevitable econometricians will desire to do what they know best, namely econometrics, then they should use Bayesian econometrics;
- transforming the a priori probability into an a posteriori probability means integrating the new information about the event focused, so as to vary (either as an increase or a decrease) the a priori probability—but, as mentioned before, is logically equivalent to establishing new degrees for the possibility involved;
- Bayesian probability implies a learning process (*Nota bene*: it is talking about a different type of learning from that of frequential probability, the last's learning being objectified into the archive of probability in the case);
- although Bayes probability is discussed in the literature as a subjective probability,[20] it seems to be an objective one, namely an objective probability of a singular (i.e., unrepeatable) event. Such a qualification is resulting from the fact that a posteriori probability is not only a subjective effect but also the effect of objective information from the environment surrounding the event of interest.

Decision-Making Framework

In this last section of the chapter, we will examine the main characteristics of the decision-making process as they are allowed or generated by the (co-)evolutionary models of the financial market. As shown above, such topic will be approached from four sides (a kind of quadrilateral impact of the co-evolutionary models of the financial market on the process of decision-making): (1) investor (either as an individual or as an organization); (2) the government; (3) the analyst on the financial market; (4) the (general) public.

(1) *Symbolic species evolution and the investor*

The investor is the depositary of the genotype of any symbolic species (preference, information, price—the last as price variation, as discussed in the previous chapters), which means the symbolic species evolution is filtered by the human individual involved in transactions on the financial market. As the symbolic species is a social artefact,[21] the most relevant and influential factor of the environment for a symbolic species is, as a last resort, the society as a whole. In such a context, we will list the main consequences for the decision-making and action performed by the investor in a financial market functioning under the (co-)evolutionary paradigm.

- the implicit information acquired by observing the behaviour on the financial market as it is exhibited by the other participants/competitors (*Nota bene*: the observation in the case is presumed to be performed under IAR condition—interested, attentive, and reflective investor) is 'coloured' differently, based on the proference of that investor. As a result, the financial market will be (and will maintain) approximately uniformly populated with different behaviours. This state of the financial market is reached in an impersonal way,[22] and signifies a low entropy of the financial market[23] because of the diversity of investors' positioning related to the opportunities that the financial market provides;
- this state of the financial market, based on IAR condition, related to the investor, leads to strongly concerted actions (and, obviously, decisions) on that market. This concertation addresses the behaviour, not information or other parameters. As stated previously, the implicit information does not lead the investor to a copy-past behaviour (although such behaviour is not, logically, excluded), that is, it is not speaking about simple memes but about the furtherly grounding of his/her desired behaviour (based on own proference). In fact, at a much deeper layer, the concertation in the case is fed by the very principles of the (co-)evolutionary paradigm of the financial market;
- in the context of the (co-)evolutionary models of the financial market, the investor does not need any more for a common model of

rationality (externally, so ex-cathedra, elaborated) as in the case of neoclassical economics (e.g., see EMH). However, although each investor has, this time, his/her own model of rationality (as analytically explained in the present book), this model of rationality keeps a common hardcore, namely the (co-)evolutionarily principles of the symbolic species. So, we can say that, for the investor, the (co-)evolutionary models of the financial market provide a general (and, it seems, immutable) pattern of behaviour of the symbolic species involved—that is, of the active, under IAR condition, participants to the financial market working;

- based on the (co-)evolutionary models of the financial market, the investor in the financial market does not anymore (want to) beat either the market or the best competitor in the market but has a general and replicable target, the survival around the floor threshold of the return. This target is established since the (co-)evolutionary models of the financial market have as macro-target, the replicability of the functionality of this market, that is, the extremization of return (as other models claim) is excluded. This behaviour and the associated decisions are the result neither of the modesty of the investor nor of his/her incapacity to extremize the return but are the only way in which the sustainability of the financial market can be ensured and guaranteed. The evolutionary logic penetrates our two models (BIP and TCIP, respectively) and the investor is the active factor to instrumentalize and objectify such logic.

(2) *Symbolic species evolution and the government*

The second actor in the financial market as it is designed and is working as a (co-)evolutionary model is the very Government. The Government interests us from two perspectives (or roles it can play in the financial game): (a) as a regulator for the financial market organizing and functioning; (b) as an economic agent playing directly in the financial market. We are, in this respect, of the opinion that the free market cannot exist without permanent and legitimate[24] normative support based on which to be designed (and to be maintained) as a free market (Biebricher et al., 2022)—that is, we are adepts of the Ordoliberalism (or of the so-called the third way/path).

(a) Government as regulator

The (co-)evolutionary models of the financial market introduce at least the following constraints (or operational principles) for the state (government) as a constitutional regulator of the financial market:

- it must restrain its own interest (e.g., the public revenues to the public budgets) in establishing, imposing, and monitoring the rules for the financial market functioning. To allow the financial market to work in a (co-)evolutionary way, the state must be (or become, if it is not yet so) less greedy, in order to be consistent and compatible with the (co-)evolutionary behaviour of the investors. More exactly, the state must, by its fiscal policies, be compatible with the replication of the financial market structures and behaviours on the long term;
- the rules for the (co-)evolutionary financial market must be established in such a way so that the reaction norms of competitors be allowed in a compatible mode with the (co-)evolutionary principles, as mentioned before. In fact, the set of legal reaction norms on the financial market is generated by the participants themselves to that market, but over the individual and idiosyncratic models of rationality must be publicly imposed those (normative) rules which maintain the operational rules on the (co-)evolutionary path. In other words, by establishing the allowed (legal) reaction norms limits, the state does nothing else than to provide the ground for the free (i.e., co-evolutionary) work of the financial market;
- the state must be, in addition, that public power (of last resort[25]) that offers guarantees on the (co-)evolutionarily work of the financial market. To provide such guarantees means, at least, the followings:
  - (i) to enact imperative norms that unambiguously lead the financial market to its free behaviour inside the (co-)evolutionary models (see Ordoliberalism ideology);[26]
  - (ii) to ensure the minimum necessary and maximum legitimate monitoring actions (as possible, of a passive kind) of participants' compliance to the respective norms;
  - (iii) permanently sending signals (in different forms and ways) to the financial market that any fraud regarding its free functioning will be immediately and severely penalized.

(b) Government as a direct player

In some circumstances, the state must play in the financial market in its own right, as an usual economic agent. These circumstances are of two kinds: (1) to provide the public goods—for example, by purchasing production factors to construct a highway; and (2) to smooth the economic cycle—for example, by the acquisition of private goods when the supply exceeds the demand and selling them when the demand exceeds the supply.[27] It must be clarified that, in both direct interventions of the state in the (financial) market, it rather will not respect the (co-)evolutionary rationality of the financial market,[28] so disturbing that rationality. In such cases, the shock will be absorbed by the financial market, including through some. At least in case (2), the very intention to avoid a disturbing will cause, firstly, a disturbing, but the second disturbing is the price to avoid the first one. The second such disturbing is smaller than the first disturbing since, if the state would not intervene, the private speculators would exploit the chance to gain profits and, so, the disequilibrium may be considerably higher.

(3) *Symbolic species evolution and the analyst*

For analysts, the (co-)evolutionary models of the financial market represent a model of intrinsic rationality of that market, which, in fact, offer them: (i) an intelligibility framework of understanding and (ii) a causality mechanism of explaining and prediction.[29] So, the (co-)evolutionary models of the financial market offer the analyst a structural-functional map, as well as a necessary finality of that market, which allows him/her to identify the most expected (in the sense of Bayesian probability) events, phenomena, and processes in the financial market. To be noticed that no neoclassical model, despite their spectacular formalizations (in fact, at a deeper examination, a simple tale quale taking over from Physics—either Mechanical or Thermodynamical. *Nota bene*: recently, the tireless rescuers of neoclassicism in Economics open their eyes to Quantum Physics, since it is cooler in the pervasive post-modernism around us), provides a realistic framework in which the financial market, as a symbolic genus containing symbolic species (as the book has put into evidence—preference, information, price) is working towards its (perpetual) replicability. However, we think the analysts, although may consider that they already have a general logical model of the (co-)evolutionary rationality and paradigm of the financial market, still have to elaborate an adequate formalism for such a model—and, for that, hard work, a courageous disinhibition face to neoclassical models (so often awarded the Nobel Prize), extensive and interdisciplinary knowledge, and a prosperous imagination are needed further.

(4) *Symbolic species evolution and the public*

Prima facie, it seems that the (general) public is not (or could be not) interested in such discussions regarding the most plausible model of the financial market structure, functioning, and finality. However, this statement is certainly wrong. We bring in support of our position the following arguments:

- the outcomes of the financial market functioning generally affect also the individuals who do not access the financial transactions as investors—many monetary variables in the economy are the results, or are significantly influenced by the results (either actual or expected) of the financial market. A (co-)evolutionary model of that market, once accepted, can model, in turn, the behaviour of the large public in their own economic and financial activities;
- the (general) public is interested that the economic system (especially, the most volatile subsystem of it—the financial subsystem) have own (and free, from the perspective of the state) capacities and principles of self-regulating. As shown in the entire book, sustainability cannot be either thought or modelled outside the (co-)evolutionary model;
- the large public is always interested in a free and democratic society. In this general context (with strong ethical coordinates), a (co-)evolutionary model of the financial market is a significant anchor for the basic structure of the society, taking into account that, in contemporary societies, the nominal economy (within which the financial field is prominent and, maybe, leader) acquires more and more dominance over the real economy;
- the cardinal issue of social justice is, too, supported by a fair structure and functioning of the financial market—in our opinion, there is not a fairer position of this market than its (co-)evolutionary model: this model distributes the returns according to not pure chances or corruption (e.g., purchasing inside information) or Ponzi schemes, since the survival commandments (so specific to the co-evolutionary

models) will forbid or smooth any gap which would threaten the long term replicability in the case. The current consumerism (not only regarding the goods but, unfortunately, more and more, in the pharma field—in the last case-based, also, on cynical, if not criminal, using of persuasion, that is, based on immoral use of the pseudo-science) must be offset by a new framework of the social justice.[30] And, yes, the (co-)evolutionary model—of the financial market and of the economic system as a whole—can, in our vision, play a significant and productive role in such a perspective. It is obvious that the large public is (very) interested in this prophecy.

Notes

1. Dinga, E., Oprean-Stan, C., Tănăsescu, C.-R., Brătian, V., G.-M. Ionescu. (2022). *Financial Market Analysis and Behaviour. The Adaptive Preference Hypothesis*, Routledge—Taylor and Francis Group, ISBN: 978-1-032-25518-7.
2. Dinga, E., Oprean-Stan, C., Tănăsescu, C.-R., Brătian, V., G.-M. Ionescu. (2023—in processing). *Financial Market Behaviour. The Autopoietic Market Hypothesis*, Palgrave—Springer.
3. Such participants not must be adepts, themselves, of the model in the case, of course.
4. There is a conceptual difference between intelligibility and causality, more exactly, there is an asymmetric determination between the two concepts: while intelligibility does not provide causality, instead the causality provides intelligibility. However, for praxiological reasons, intelligibility is sufficed for the economic agents actioning on the financial market (see, here, the famous assumption of Milton Friedman regarding the truth of the hypothesis).
5. As known, the opposition to natural necessity is impossible (i.e., ineffective).
6. The (inevitable) presence of free will in the social field (based on which, besides, the symbolic species emerge) is the logical base for the complexity, which is the very effect of unpredictability. *Nota bene*: many researchers confuse the complexity with the complicatedness (the last is simply a historical difficult to describe an entity/system).
7. As the authors will show elsewhere (Dinga et al., 2021), such an inside principle of the evolutionary approach to the financial market is best illustrated by the autopoietic market hypothesis.

8. The catastrophes occur when and to the extent that the positive feedback of a phenomenon (having either positive or negative signification) dominates the negative feedback.
9. In such a context, it can be said that we do not any more need the Chaos Theory (as Edgar Peters claims) to ground the fractal design of the financial market, since the principles of the (co-evolutionary model is al is sufficient in the matter.
10. In this context, the claims of some researchers for the role of (biological) genes in framing economic/financial behaviour seem to us hazardous enough.
11. We remind the reader that abduction is a logical method to build a (causal) explanation based on the most plausible inductive hypothesis which is, then, integrated into a deductive theory/model, so as to be subject to factual testability (falsifiability).
12. Predictability means a cognitive capacity to anticipate an effect, either this anticipation is based on causality or on correlativeness. More on this cognitive capacity, from the perspective of autopoieticity, will be delivered by the authors elsewhere.
13. From an epistemological point of view, Friedman's position has the following signification: in the social field, not the causality is relevant but the correlativeness only (Nota bene: what the irrepressible econometricians do every day in their empirical articles that are published by the highest positioned scientific publications across the world).
14. The term of scientificity is understood in its meaning generally accepted in the philosophy of (natural) science, namely as factual (empirical) falsifiability. For authors is clear enough that either the meaning of scientificity is relaxed to include the social sciences as well or for the social sciences (and, also, for the humanistic ones) another concept of testability, correlated with the concept of the truth in this domains. The term scientificity is understood in its meaning generally accepted in the philosophy of (natural) science, namely as factual (empirical) falsifiability. For authors is clear enough that either the meaning of scientificity should be relaxed to include the social sciences as well or for the social sciences (and, also, for the humanistic ones) another concept of testability, correlated with the concept of truth in this domains, should be edified. We deliver some rough suggestions in the principal text.
15. Even in the case in which the target is established by an organization, not by an individual, that target keeps the trait of uniqueness. So, repeatability cannot be taken as a basis for rejecting the ad-hoc hypotheses.
16. Here, we agree, partially (but in a fundamental way) with the main assumption of EMH.

17. In a sense, probability is a degree of possibility.
18. The a posteriori Bayes probability is obtained based on the Bayes theorem, to which we do not refer here.
19. The propensity was examined for the first time, by Aristotle, in his Physics (which Galilei showed to be wrong).
20. We remind that a kind of subjective probability is, also, the fuzzy theory/algebra, initiated by Zadeh. Indeed, the value (inside the real interval $[0,1]$) of the belonging function is subjectively established, although it does not allow changes as new information is acquired.
21. Even in the case in which a single individual creates an artefact (e.g., an intellectual artefact as is a scientific theory, let us consider Einstein's Theory of Special Relativity), that creation is basically conditioned by society, which means it is a social artefact.
22. Similar to the finality of the invisible hand in a free market, or with the finality of the fractality of time horizons regarding the return.
23. We speak here about behavioural-based entropy, not about informational-based entropy. The concept of behavioural-based entropy in the financial market (which is close enough to the fractal-based entropy of Edgar Peters—although the mentioned author does not call that entropy as such) is largely exposed and discussed by the authors in the article (Dinga et al., 2021).
24. The legal intervention of the state into society (including the financial market) ist hat intervention which is consistent with the law. Instead, the legitimate intervention of the state is that intervention that is focused on those variables which are not self-regulating. Not any legal intervention is legitimate (regarding the illegal legitimate interventions, things are more complicated and it is not necessary to be developed here).
25. The disputes between the participants in the financial market are desirable to be resolved in an amiable way, without the permanent interventions of the state (usually, such interventions are made by the judiciary power, here is why the state intervention must be done in a last resort only).
26. In fact, the normative framework must not be preoccupated by the functioning of the (co-)evolutionary models of the financial market, since by providing the necessary (and legitimate) norms for a free financial market, that market will automatically function within its natural rationality, that is, within the (co-)evolutionary rationality.
27. To be mentioned that the speculators play the same role, from the perspective of the private sector but, while the state is preoccupated with the elimination of possible crises, the speculators simply exploit those opportunities for their own profit.

28. From a logical point of view, such a possibility to disturb the (co-)evolutionary rationality of the financial market is a necessary effect of the fact that these direct interventions have as a horizon the short term (rarely, the medium one), not the long term—while the (co-)evolutionary phenomenon on the financial market works in/for the long term.
29. From a logical point of view, the explanation is an *ex-post* prediction, and the prediction is an *ex-ante* explanation.
30. See the works of John Rawls, Amartya Sen, Robert Nozick and Martha C. Nussbaum regarding the urgency to rethink the issue of social justice as the (main) base for the sustainability praxiological paradigm of the society, in which the (co-)evolutionary model of the financial market could be a 'brick'.

References

Biebricher, T., Bonefeld, W., Nedergaard, P., eds. (2022). *The Oxford Handbook of Ordoliberalism*, Oxford University Press.

Dinga, E., Oprean-Stan, C., Tănăsescu, C.-R., Brătian, V., Ionescu, G.-M. (2021). *Entropy-Based Behavioural Efficiency of the Financial Market*, Entropy, 23(11).

Lo, A. (2019). *Adaptive Markets. Financial Evolution at the Speed of Thought*, Princeton University Press).

Mele, A.R., Rawling, P. (2004). *The Oxford Handbook of Rationality*, Oxford University Press.

Nozick, R. (1993). *The Nature of Rationality*, Princeton University Press.

Peters, E.E. (1994). *Fractal Market Analysis. Applying Chaos Theory to Investment and Economics*, John Wiley and Sons. Inc.

Glossary

Chapter 1

- *Contingent*: logical concept (as opposite to necessary) meaning possible and non-necessary.
- *Contrariety*: opposition without contradiction.
- *Cultural geodesic*: the set of normative framework (either codified or informal), traditions, habits, ethics, "ways to do", etc. that structurally characterizes a community/society.
- *Eutaxiological causation*: that causation for which are responsible three of the four (Aristotle-ian) causes, namely: material cause, efficient cause, formal cause (*Nota bene*: lacks the final cause—the purpose—which forms, instead, the teleological causation).
- *Hub effect*: auto-catalytic effect (associated, usually, with positive feedback: that feedback that acts in the same direction as the gap between input and output—a self-exacerbating feedback).
- *Implicit information*: that information which involuntarily (or, in some cases, voluntarily) is codified in the behaviour of economic agents and which is deciphered by the investor by observing that behaviour. Implicit information is not a meme (in Dawkins's sense), because it does not generate similar behaviour as that observed but it is its own, strongly idiosyncratic information created by the very observer/player in the financial market.

E. Dinga et al., *Co-Evolution of Symbolic Species in the Financial Market*, https://doi.org/10.1007/978-3-031-31698-2

- *Inertia*: a property of systems to maintain their structure (and, consequently, their functions) against the pressure to change it, exerted by perturbation (either internal or external) which does not exceed a given quantitative threshold, called inertial threshold.
- *Non-contradiction principle*: one of the (four) principles in standard logic, formalized as $\overline{A \wedge \bar{A}}$ and meaning: is false that A and its negation can exist simultaneously and under the same logical rapport (*Nota bene*: A is a property or a relationship).
- *Quaternary sector*: social sector to produce knowledge.
- *Quinary sector*: social sector to produce ideology.

Chapter 2

- *Darwinism*: theory of evolution in which the structure generates function (of a system).
- *Experimentum crucis*: an experiment whose result (usually, as rejection of a hypothesis) has the potential to definitively solve a problem/question (e.g., Michelson-Morley experiment decided that the aether does not exist).
- *Habuistical*: a term coined by authors meaning a behaviour based on the hub effect (see Abbreviations—Chap. 1)
- *Lamarckism*: theory of evolution in which the function generates the structure (of a system)
- *Maxigiven*: a term coined by authors meaning somewhat a middle term between maximization and minimization, more exactly, what happens contingently, what is best among what could happen.
- *Proference*: a composed term (in Herbert Simon's manner), from *pro*pensity and pre*ference*. Proference signifies the preference which is the direct emanation of the deep belief/credence of the individual, being, so, much less plastic (rather strongly elastic/resilient) related to the financial market influence. In a sense, proference is the hardcore (in Lakatos's meaning) of objectified preference.
- *Second-best*: addresses a solution (of a problem, question, etc.) which does not extremize but chooses the best (possible, real, not theoretical) solution. The sustainability praxiological paradigm, for example, has accessibility for second-best solutions only, not for best solutions.
- *Seme*: besides gene (biological vehicle of intergenerational replication) and meme (social informal, either cultural or natural, vehicle of intra-generational and intergenerational replication), the seme is a

cultural vehicle to intra-generational and intergenerational replication). The behaviour conditioned by genes and/or memes can be codified in the normative framework of society, so becoming semes. By contrast with genes and memes, the semes can be removed/cancelled simply by exiting the normative framework in force in the society.

- *Third-best*: addresses a solution which deliberatively is worse than the second-best solution. This choice is based on criteria which stay outside the rationality accessible and associated with the problem/question to be solved. For example, the altruistic solutions seem to be of third-best solutions type.

Chapter 3

- *IAR*: interested, attentive, and reflective—the three conditions to be verified by an individual to see the observables (both informational and behavioural) in the financial market

Chapter 4

- *Adaptar*: the system to which another system adapts, in their interaction.
- *Adaptant*: the system which adapts to another system in their interaction.
- *Black-boxism*: approach which ignores the operator (called black-box) that transforms inputs into outputs in a generic system (*Nota bene*: behaviourism applies, generally, black-boxism), so the inputs (reasons to act/abstain) are inferred from outputs (see Samuelson's concept of revealed preference, as standard case of black-boxism).
- *Bound information*: information on which there is a property right, or is hidden or secret, so that to access this kind of information a cost is necessary to be paid.
- *Prevolution*: a term coined by authors from *pre*meditated e*volution*, aimed at signifying the deliberative impulses for the symbolic species to evolve.
- *Punctuatedness*: (in opposition with graduality) the property of a system to suffer the phenomenon of punctuated equilibrium.

Chapter 6

- *Synergistic hypercycle*: a term coined by the authors, meaning something equivalent with Manfred Eigen's concept of self-catalytic hypercycle.

Index[1]

A

B

[1] Note: Page numbers followed by 'n' refer to notes.

E. Dinga et al., *Co-Evolution of Symbolic Species in the Financial Market*, https://doi.org/10.1007/978-3-031-31698-2

H

I

K

L

R

SPRINGER NATURE

GPSR Compliance

The European Union's (EU) General Product Safety Regulation (GPSR) is a set of rules that requires consumer products to be safe and our obligations to ensure this.

If you have any concerns about our products, you can contact us on ProductSafety@springernature.com

In case Publisher is established outside the EU, the EU authorized representative is:

Springer Nature Customer Service Center GmbH
Europaplatz 3
69115 Heidelberg, Germany

Kolibri 360 GmbH
Ferdinand-Jühlke-Straße 7
99095 Erfurt, Deutschland
produktsicherheit@kolibri360.de